THE LAUSIAC HISTORY

OF PALLADIUS

A CRITICAL DISCUSSION TOGETHER WITH NOTES ON EARLY EGYPTIAN MONACHISM

BY

DOM CUTHBERT BUTLER

BENEDICTINE MONK OF THE ENGLISH CONGREGATION
AND OF DOWNSIDE MONASTERY

CAMBRIDGE
AT THE UNIVERSITY PRESS
1898

Cambridge

PRINTED BY J. & C. F. CLAY,

AT THE UNIVERSITY PRESS.

VIRO · DOCTISSIMO

IOHANNI · PEILE · LITT · D

COLLEGII · CHRISTI · MAGISTRO

HOC · OPVSCVLVM

GRATO · ANIMO · DEDICO

PREFACE.

THE Lausiac History of Palladius is probably the chief document dealing with early Christian monachism in Egypt. Of late years it has been subjected to a searching criticism:—Palladius has been said to have merely plagiarised earlier Greek books; or to have translated Coptic ones; or to have written the work out of his own head, so that it is a mere romance, devoid of all historical worth. No sooner had I set myself to the serious study of the Lausiac History, than the received text fell asunder into two parts; and this resolution of the text into its components, and the consequent restoration of Palladius' work to its genuine form, seemed to afford the answer to a number of the criticisms, both textual and historical, that have been made against the book.

The first seven sections of the following Study are devoted to this re-establishment of the Lausiac History in its primitive form. Sections 8—13 consider the question whether the book is a *bona fide* original work of Palladius, containing his own experiences; or was made up out of earlier materials: the discussion turns mainly on the early versions: the result is that the Lausiac History is accepted as the authentic and original work of Palladius. Its historical character is next considered at some length, and principles are laid down for judging books of the same class; these principles are applied not only to the Lausiac History, but also to other documents that deal with the early monks of Egypt; the case of St Anthony, who (it has been said) "never existed," is reconsidered, and an attempt is made to delineate the salient features of primitive Egyptian monachism.

The origins of the monastic system cannot fail to be of interest and importance to the student of ecclesiastical history. In order to clear up the problems that surround the Lausiac History it has been necessary to discuss elaborately a number of minute and technical questions of literary and textual criticism; but it was impossible to determine the historical position of the whole cycle of documents relating to monastic origins in Egypt, before the numerous questions raised concerning the Lausiac History had been considered in detail and definitely answered. If in the course of my work I have had frequently to differ from and to criticise the views of several scholars of great and well-deserved reputation, I may be allowed to plead that, though it was only six years ago that I devoted myself to the special study of the Lausiac History, the literature of early monachism had long been familiar to me.

Before I had advanced far in my labours, I became aware that Dr Preuschen also was at work in the same field. We soon perceived that there was ample room for both of us; and, although we have assisted one another in the supply of what may be called the raw materials, we have otherwise worked quite independently—there has been no interchange of views or discussion of theories. On the main lines of the case we are in entire agreement; but on a number of lesser points, some of no small importance, we differ, as will often appear from the following pages. When Dr Preuschen's *Palladius und Rufinus* was published in last November, Part I of my book (pp. 1—172) was already in type, and §§ 14 and 15 (pp. 173—196) and Appendices I—IV were written. I have been able, however, towards the end of Part I to take account of Dr Preuschen's work, and in Part II I have dealt with it quite freely.

My obligations to various friends are acknowledged in the course of the book. I wish here to thank in a special manner Professor Robinson and Mr F. C. Burkitt, who contributed respectively the section on the Armenian Version and the Note on the Biblical Citations in the Latin Versions: the Rev. Forbes Robinson, Fellow of Christ's College, who has made the translations of the various passages cited from the Coptic Version:

Dr Budge, for placing at my disposal his fine MS. copy of the Syriac *Paradise* of Anan-Isho: and M. Omont, for the assistance he has given me while working in the Bibliothèque Nationale. My thanks are further due to Professor Robinson and to Mr Edmund Bishop, both of whom have read the entire book in MS., and also in proof; there are few pages that do not bear the marks of their criticisms and corrections. Mr Bishop worked with me in the preliminary comparison of the Latin documents and the investigation of their relations, the results of which are embodied in § 4. Professor Robinson, as Editor of the Series, has thrown himself into the work as if it were his own. In the difficult section on the Coptic Version his help amounted to full collaboration.

As the title indicates, this volume is only of the nature of Prolegomena: it is my intention to proceed at once to the preparation of a second volume in which the Greek text will be edited from the MSS.

CUTHBERT BUTLER.

CHRIST'S COLLEGE, CAMBRIDGE.
24 *May*, 1898.

ERRATA.

p. 47, note 4, line 1, *read* ὑπήκουον.
p. 65, line 9, *read* Benjamin.

CONTENTS.

APPENDICES.

THE HISTORIA LAUSIACA OF PALLADIUS.

§ 1. INTRODUCTORY.

THE origins of Christian monachism and the sources of its early history are fields of enquiry to which continental scholars have of late years been devoting considerable attention. Much has been written about various ascetics of the first three centuries; but so meagre is the original information, and so dense the obscurity in which the whole subject is involved, that to find a safe basis for investigating the beginnings of historical Christian monachism, it is necessary to start from the literature of the close of the fourth century and of the early years of the fifth, which portrays the manner of life and the teaching of the multitude of hermits and cenobites who at that time peopled the Egyptian deserts. Again, the early history of divine worship in the Christian Church is a subject which is attracting still more attention ; and any one who has read recent works dealing with the development of the Canonical Office, such as those of the Abbé Batiffol[1] or Dom Bäumer[2], will recognise how important a place is held in such investigations by this same literature. For students therefore of monastic or of liturgical origins it is clearly a matter of necessity to know how far the records of this literature are authentic, and what measure of credibility they can rightly claim.

The two scholars who in our day have made the most elaborate study of the sources of Egyptian monastic history, Dr Lucius and M. Amélineau, are agreed that the extant documents are few, and

[1] *Histoire du Bréviaire Romain.* (Paris : Lecoffre, 1893.)
[2] *Geschichte des Breviers.* (Freiburg i. Breisgau : Herder, 1895.)

that the most important of them are the *Historia Lausiaca* of Palladius, and the *Historia Monachorum in Aegypto*, which goes under the name of Rufinus[1]. The former work is beset with certain textual difficulties, with which neither Lucius nor Amélineau has, in my judgment, successfully grappled; yet on the true solution of these problems must depend to a very great extent our estimate of the historical character of both the above named works. My concern is chiefly with the *Historia Lausiaca*; and to make the discussion which follows more easily intelligible I shall here give a brief sketch of its author's career, in so far as it bears on the subject-matter of his book.

Palladius was born in Galatia in the year 367 : about 387 he embraced the monastic life, and perhaps spent some time in Cappadocia and Palestine, before going to Egypt. In 388 he came to Alexandria, and after some two years passed under eminent masters of the ascetic life in the neighbourhood of that city he withdrew into the desert of Nitria. A year later (390—1) he retired into the still more remote desert, which from the number of hermitages with which it was studded was called "the Cells." Here he lived for about nine years, at first with Abbot Macarius of Alexandria, and then with Evagrius, who was famous during his life for his austerities and his ascetic lore, but after his death fell under the suspicion of Origenism. During this sojourn Palladius enjoyed the instruction of several of the best known of the solitaries, and met the disciples of many more. At the beginning of 400 he was compelled by ill health to quit the desert and betake himself to Alexandria, whence he returned to Palestine. Later on in the same year he became bishop of Helenopolis in Bithynia. He was consecrated perhaps by St John Chrysostom, whose faithful adherent he henceforth was, and in whose persecutions he shared. In 404 or 405 he travelled to Rome in his master's interests, and whilst there he visited some who were leading an ascetic life in the neighbourhood of the city and in Campania. He subsequently suffered a long exile for his fidelity to St Chrysostom, being banished to Syene, and again to

---

[1] Lucius, *Die Quellen der älteren Geschichte des ägyptischen Mönchtums* (Brieger's *Zeitschrift für Kirchengeschichte*, 1885, p. 163). Amélineau, *De Historia Lausiaca*, p. 3 (Paris: Leroux, 1887).

the Thebaid, where he passed three or four years among the monks of Antinoopolis; he also lived for some time in Palestine among the monks who dwelt on the Mount of Olives. In 417 his troubles came to an end; and in 420 he wrote his *Historia Lausiaca*, a series of biographical sketches of the monks whom he had known, either personally, or through the reports of their disciples. This work he dedicated to one Lausus, a chamberlain at the court of Theodosius II.; and from this circumstance it receives its title[1].

Palladius has won from a master of the old school of historical scholarship and criticism the following high encomium: "On peut dire qu'il y a peu d'histoires qui méritent plus de croyance que celle-la. Car il y paroist partout un grand caractère de simplicité et de sincérité, avec beaucoup d'exactitude, et un grand soin de s'informer de la vérité des choses, sans y rien ajouter pour les rendre plus agréables ou plus merveilleuses. Pallade fait profession dans sa préface de ne dire que ce qu'il a vu luy-mesme, ou appris des auteurs originaux; et il n'y a presque pas de page de son livre qui ne fasse voir qu'il s'est acquitté de cette promesse avec beaucoup de fidélité." So Tillemont[2]. In quite recent times a very different verdict has been pronounced by Dr Weingarten. He declares that the time has come to "lay the axe to the root of the superstitions" handed down as the records of early monachism; and he sets to work to some purpose. Paul the Hermit "never existed." As for St Anthony, the life of him attributed to St Athanasius has no historical value whatever; it is a mere "Tendenzschrift," a romance written for the purpose of propagating an ideal. If such a personage ever lived, he must be placed not in the third century but in the second half of the fourth; for there were no Christian solitaries or monks in Egypt before the year

---

[1] This account, put together by Tillemont (*Mémoires*, xi. 500—523) out of Palladius' own writings, has been adopted by subsequent writers; even Dr Weingarten accepts it in its main outlines. I believe that Dr Lucius stands alone in regarding as fabrications the details given by Palladius about himself. There are a few chronological difficulties; but these are fairly met by the supposition that Palladius, writing at a distance of from 20 to 30 years from the events he narrates, is not always minutely accurate in his notes of time. The question will be dealt with in detail in Part II. of this Study (§ 15).

[2] *Mémoires*, xi. 524.

340. The *Historia Lausiaca* and *Historia Monachorum* are mere
fairy tales, which must not be regarded as in any sense historical
sources, and which deserve no more credit than Gulliver's Travels.
Only one fact can be gleaned from these romances, viz. that the
earliest form of the monastic life was the eremitical[1]. The late
date at which Weingarten set the beginnings of Christian monachism called forth much criticism even on the part of writers of
his own school; but his estimate of the two works in which we
are interested has been accepted in many quarters. Dr Zöckler,
however, an historical critic of tried repute, cannot adopt so
extreme a view of the untrustworthiness of Palladius. In the
first edition of Herzog's *Encyclopädie* he had expressed himself
somewhat favourably as to the historical character of the Lausiac
History, and had thereby brought upon himself a rebuke from
Weingarten. But in the second edition he emphasised his earlier
verdict. He does not question that the biographies have been
highly coloured and enriched with wonders; but in his judgment
it is not conceivable that they are mere fictions and romances;
in the case of most of the holy men portrayed, the details of their
manner of life, their sayings and doings, are given with an
actuality and a precision which do not admit of so extreme a
hypothesis[2].

Dr Lucius' view of the histories of Palladius and Rufinus is
hardly more favourable than Weingarten's. In his eyes Palladius
is a "monkish falsifier of history," and his book is an uncritical
patchwork put together from several different sources. These
elements may at best be a mixture of historical facts and monkish
fables, with perhaps here and there some personal reminiscences.
Lucius altogether rejects the idea that the Lausiac History records
the personal experiences of its author. Palladius, in his view,
systematically substitutes himself for the person of each of the
various writers whose materials he uses: he relates their experiences—or what profess to be such—as his own: the fact that

[1] *Ursprung des Mönchtums* (Brieger's *Zeitschrift für Kirchengeschichte*, 1876,
pp. 1—35, 545—574); reprinted separately (Gotha, 1877). Weingarten defended
his position against his critics in Herzog-Plitt, x. 758 ff., Article *Mönchtum* (1882).

[2] Herzog-Plitt, *Encyclopädie für protestantische Theologie*, xi. 173—5, Article
Palladius (1883). In various later writings that will be mentioned in the course
of this Study, Zöckler enforces the same view.

the work is thrown into the form of a personal narrative is but a device to give it a seeming unity. Lucius refuses to believe that the writer ever was a bishop, and hints that it is more than likely that he never set foot in Egypt, and indeed never left his native Galatia[1].

M. Amélineau has approached the problem of the Lausiac History by another road. He has made a special study of Coptic and Arabic Christian literature, and has devoted much time to the Christian antiquities of Egypt. He has conducted his researches in the chief libraries of Europe, and has further made explorations and investigations in various parts of Egypt itself. It is not too much to say that he has done more than any living scholar to illustrate the history of early Egyptian monachism[2]. His judgment therefore on the question before us should carry a greater weight than those which are reached by the somewhat subjective methods of other writers. So far from thinking that the author never was in Egypt, M. Amélineau bears witness to the accuracy of the descriptions which Palladius gives of special localities and of their natural scenery: he is convinced that he must have visited these spots. A comparison of the Lausiac History with Coptic records leads him to the conclusion that, in general, where Palladius relates what was done or seen or heard by himself, he is worthy of credit; but that information which he derived from Coptic writings, or learned by hearsay, must be received with great caution[3].

Having thus summarised the opinions expressed by the most recent critics of the Lausiac History, we must now address ourselves to our task, which falls into two parts. The First Part is Textual; its object is to call attention to the various redactions in which the *Historia Lausiaca* has come down to us, and to determine which of these forms is to be regarded as the original work, and in what language the materials were first written: this will involve an examination of the several versions. The Second Part is Historical; the results gained in the First Part

---

[1] *Die Quellen der älteren Geschichte des ägyptischen Mönchtums* (Brieger's *Zeitschrift für Kirchengeschichte*, 1885, pp. 192—196).

[2] A list of M. Amélineau's works on the subject will be given in § 12.

[3] *De Historia Lausiaca*, pp. 8, 18, 72, &c.

will form the basis of a discussion of some of the problems which belong to the early history of Christian monachism and the development of the monastic idea in East and West down to St Benedict's time.

PART I. TEXTUAL CRITICISM.

§ 2. REDACTIONS OF THE 'HISTORIA LAUSIACA.'

IN the sixteenth century much uncertainty prevailed as to what precisely was the *Historia Lausiaca.* This uncertainty arose from the fact that three Latin translations, representing three different redactions of the book, were in the field. No Greek text had as yet been printed, when Rosweyd in the first edition of his monumental *Vitae Patrum*[1] faced the problem and decided in favour of the longest of the three redactions. This he placed in the body of his collection : the other two he relegated to the small print of an Appendix. His judgment has not been challenged by

---

[1] Antwerp, 1615 and 1628. Rosweyd was a Jesuit, one of the earliest pioneers of the great seventeenth century historical school, and projector of the *Acta Sanctorum* carried out by the Bollandists. His *Vitae Patrum* is a folio volume of upwards of a thousand pages of texts (Latin only) and erudite notes. It consists of ten Books and an Appendix.

Book I., which occupies nearly half the volume, contains the lives of SS. Paul the Hermit, Anthony and Hilarion, and a number of similar biographies from different hands ;

Book II. is the *Historia Monachorum in Aegypto ;*

Books III., V., VI. and VII., are collections of the *Apophthegmata Patrum*, or short anecdotes and sayings of the chief Fathers of the Desert, often full of shrewdness and deep knowledge of human nature ;

Book IV. is made up of extracts from Cassian and Sulpicius Severus ;

Book VIII. is the Lausiac History of Palladius. (In the edition of 1628 a few alterations have been made to bring the Latin into conformity with the printed Greek texts.)

Books IX. and X. are similar collections of short biographies by Theodoret and John Moschus.

Rosweyd's *Vitae Patrum* is reprinted for the most part in volumes LXXIII. and LXXIV. of Migne's Latin Patrology.

It is well to observe that all the materials essential to the discussion here entered upon may be found in Rosweyd.

the scholars of the present day. It has been accepted without criticism by Weingarten, Lucius, Zöckler and Amélineau in the discussions already referred to. It has been accepted by W. Möller[1], by a number of contributors to the *Dictionary of Christian Biography*[2], and by Dr Grützmacher in a monograph which has quite recently appeared[3]. Bishop Lightfoot[4] and Dr W. Wright[5] have also accepted it, as we may gather from their passing references; for, unlike the scholars named above, they have not had occasion to deal directly with the problems that arise out of the Lausiac History. In fact all recent writers who have dealt with the matter, so far as I know, acquiesce in Rosweyd's verdict; and they further accept as the genuine work of Palladius the Greek text printed in Migne (*P. G.* XXXIV.). They take no serious account of the other redactions—indeed they seem hardly to be aware of their existence[6].

Now no one who reads with attention the *Historia Monachorum* and the *Historia Lausiaca*, as authenticated by Rosweyd, can fail to notice that the former work is contained bodily in the latter. The *Historia Monachorum* purports to be a personal narrative of a round of visits to the most eminent solitaries of Egypt made in the winter of 394—5; and ever since Rosweyd's time the Latin work, the only form hitherto known, has been regarded as coming from the pen of Rufinus[7]. It is singular that the presence of this work in the Lausiac History has not hitherto received at the hands of critics the careful analysis that so curious a phenomenon deserves. Rosweyd offers only the comprehensive suggestion that one of the writers borrowed from the other, or else both borrowed from some unknown common source[8]; and one or other of these alternatives has satisfied the critics of our day. Weingarten

---

[1] Herzog-Plitt. XIII. 100, Article *Rufinus* (1884).

[2] Articles *Palladius, Rufinus, Heracleides*, &c., &c.

[3] *Pachomius und das älteste Klosterleben* (Freiburg, 1896), pp. 1—4.

[4] *Ignatius and Polycarp* (ed. 2, 1889), I. 153—4.

[5] *Catalogue of Syriac Manuscripts*, III. (passim).

[6] I suppose no work could be named more up to date or more scientific than the new edition of Potthast's *Wegweiser* (1896); and there (p. 891) we find a formal restatement of the traditional view.

[7] The *Historia Monachorum* forms Book II. in Rosweyd's *Vitae Patrum*.

[8] *Vitae Patrum*, Prolegomenon IV. § 2 (Migne, *P. L.* LXXIII. 23).

enunciates the idea that Palladius borrowed from Rufinus, and this is the view adopted in Potthast; W. Möller believes in a Greek document, translated into Latin by Rufinus and incorporated in his history by Palladius; Lucius strongly advocates a similar theory, in which he is followed by Grützmacher, and by Zöckler in his most recent pronouncement on the question[1]. Amélineau, on the other hand, holds that both writers made independent translations of a Coptic original.

A study of the Latin texts in Rosweyd had suggested to me a solution of the problem different from any of these, at once simpler and more in accord with the facts of the case. A subsequent examination of the Greek printed texts and manuscripts led to the same result, and confirmed the suspicion that the difficulties of recent writers are due to a failure to examine with adequate care the extant texts. I propose therefore in the first place to indicate the steps by which I arrived at my conclusion.

The three Latin forms of the Lausiac History, printed by Rosweyd, are these:—

I. The version which had been given in the earliest printed editions of the *Vitae Patrum*, copies of three of which may be found in the British Museum, dated hypothetically in the Catalogue between 1470 and 1480: Rosweyd, Appendix, pp. 978—995 (ed. 1615); 984—1001 (ed. 1628).

II. The version first printed by Le Fèvre d'Estaples, Paris, 1504, under the title *Paradisus Heraclidis*: Rosweyd, Appendix, pp. 933—977 (ed. 1615); 939—983 (ed. 1628). (Rosweyd reprints Lipomanus' edition, Venice, 1554, in which some considerable gaps had been filled up by translations from a Greek MS. at Venice.)

III. A translation made from the Greek by Gentian Hervet, and published at Paris in 1555. This is the redaction accepted by Rosweyd as representing the genuine work, and printed as Book VIII. of his *Vitae Patrum* (pp. 704—783 in both editions; in the second edition, however, with some alterations based on Greek MSS.).

---

[1] *Askese und Mönchtum* (Frankfurt a. M., 1897), p. 213; in 1882 he shared Weingarten's view.

Of these three Latin redactions, I. may be at once eliminated. We shall see hereafter that internal evidence shows it to be but a corrupt redaction, at once loaded with interpolated matter and incomplete[1]. No Greek text corresponding to it is known to me ; and the other early versions (Latin, Syriac and Coptic) show that this was not the redaction current when they were made.

The Greek text of II. was printed by Meursius (de Meurs) at Leyden in 1616, from a tenth century manuscript of the Palatine Library, then at Heidelberg, now in the Vatican[2]. It is contained also in an Arundel MS. in the British Museum, in a Vossian MS. in the Leyden University Library, and in several others in the Bibliothèque Nationale at Paris, and elsewhere. These MSS. will be described and classified in the proper place.

A Greek text purporting to be the text of III. was published at Paris by Fronto Ducaeus (Du Duc) in 1624 ; the subsequent editions of the Greek are based upon this, and it is substantially the text now commonly used, and found in vol. XXXIV. of Migne's Greek Patrology. There are three Greek manuscripts of III. at Paris, one of them (incomplete) dating from the tenth century. But Du Duc's Greek text was not based on MSS. of this redaction; but was patched up from copies of II. and of the *Historia Monachorum* so as to correspond in structure with Hervet's Latin translation[3]. A list of the Greek editions of this redaction is given in the footnote[4].

---

[1] Cf. § 9. To adduce but one piece of internal evidence out of several :—the Proëm in this redaction, as in the others, contains a promise to give some account of the solitaries of Lower Egypt, of Syene and Tabennisi, of Mesopotamia, Palestine and Syria, and of Rome and Campania. In the other redactions this promise is fulfilled ; but here the information is all but wholly confined to Lower Egypt. The chapters relating to the monks of St Pachomius in Tabennisi are not to be found, nor is anything said about them beyond the brief account of St Macarius' visit to Tabennisi. Of Asiatic monks only two are noticed, and of Italian none at all. This of itself makes it clear that I. is but an abridged, or, rather, a truncated redaction of the Lausiac History.

[2] *Palladii Episcopi Helenopoleos Historia Lausiaca.* Joannes Meursius primus Graece nunc vulgavit et notas adjecit. Lugduni Batavorum, MDCXVI. (This is not the text printed in Tom. VIII. of Lami's edition of the *Opera Joannis Meursii*, Florence, 1741 &c.)

[3] The genesis of Du Duc's text and of the later editions will be explained in the *Introduction* to the Text.

[4] The editions are :—(i) Du Duc's own edition, Paris, 1624; in Tom. II. of the

We may now return to Rosweyd's Latin redactions II. and III.
A comparison of these brings out the fact that, speaking roughly,
the main difference between them lies not in the text of individual
biographies but in the number of the biographies which they
contain; for III. contains all those in II. and many more. In
nearly all cases the Lives common to both redactions are identical
in substance, being as a matter of fact independent translations
of the same original. We may therefore conveniently speak of
redaction III. as the Long Recension, and of redaction II. as the
Short Recension of the Lausiac History.

§ 3. THE 'HISTORIA MONACHORUM IN AEGYPTO.'

After these preliminary details concerning the work which
forms the chief subject of the ensuing investigation, some account
must be given of another work, very similar in character, which
has been already referred to and will frequently be mentioned in
the course of this Study, the *Historia Monachorum in Aegypto*.
This work describes a series of visits paid in the winter of 394—5
to a number of hermits and monks in the Thebaid and Lower
Egypt by a party of seven persons[1]. The writer represents himself throughout as having been one of the party: and Rosweyd
established the fact once for all that the current Latin text is

Auctarium to La Bigne's *Bibliotheca Veterum Patrum*. There are some lacunae in
the Greek text as compared with Hervet's Latin, and some differences of reading.

(ii) Paris, 1644; and again, 1654; in the *Magna Bibliotheca Veterum Patrum*,
Tom. XIII.; an exact reprint of (i).

(iii) Florence, 1746; in Tom. VIII. of Lami's edition of Meursius' works. The
Greek of the lacunae of (i) and (ii) had been printed by Cotelier from two Paris
MSS. (*Ecclesiae Graecae Monumenta*, III. 158—170), and Lami reproduces Du Duc's
text, printing these fragments, not so as to fill the lacunae, but at the end of the
chapters in which they should stand.

(iv) Paris, 1860; in Migne's Greek Patrology, Tom. XXXIV., cols. 995—1260. The
same text; but Cotelier's fragments are inserted in their places, so that the Greek
text is continuous and the lacunae no longer appear.

[1] The date is thus fixed: (i) The party was with John of Lycopolis shortly
after Theodosius had gained his victory over Eugenius, i.e. towards the middle or
end of September 394. (ii) When they reached Nitria, Macarius of Alexandria was
already dead: he died at the end of 394, or the beginning of 395.

from the hand of Rufinus[1]. But Rufinus himself cannot possibly have been one of the party of seven whose tour is described[2].

[1] *Vitae Patrum*, Prolegomenon IV. § 10 (Migne, *P. L.* LXXIII. 35). The following are the grounds on which this conclusion has been ever since accepted :

(i) St Jerome in his letter to Ctesiphon (*Ep.* 133; Vallarsi, I. 1029 f.), after speaking of Evagrius, continues: "Huius libros per orientem Graecos et interpretante discipulo eius Rufino Latinos plerique in occidente lectitant. qui librum quoque scripsit quasi de monachis, multosque in eo enumerat qui nunquam fuerunt; et quos fuisse describit Origenistas et ab episcopis damnatos esse non dubium est; Ammonium videlicet et Eusebium et Euthymium et ipsum Euagrium, Or quoque et Isidorum et multos alios, quos enumerare taedium est.......ita ille unum Ioannem in ipsius libri posuit principio, quem et catholicum et sanctum fuisse non dubium est." The list of names and the fact of John standing first, show that he is speaking of the *Historia Monachorum*. The 'qui' at the beginning of the second sentence clearly refers to Rufinus, not to Evagrius, who cannot be supposed to have included in his biographical series 'ipsum Euagrium.' Moreover St Jerome goes on to say that this same writer published a translation of a work of Xystus the Pythagorean under the name of Xystus, Pope and Martyr; and one of a work of Eusebius of Caesarea under the name of Pamphilus, both of which accusations he elsewhere brings against Rufinus. St Jerome's testimony is therefore explicit.

(ii) At the end of c. 29 of the *Historia Monachorum* occur the words:—"Sed et multa, ut diximus, alia de operibus sancti Macarii Alexandrini mirabilia feruntur, ex quibus nonnulla in XI. libro Ecclesiasticae Historiae inserta qui requiret inveniet." This refers to the second of the two Books which Rufinus added to his translation of Eusebius; and there (c. 4) additional information about Macarius may be found.

(iii) Many MSS. bear the name of Rufinus, though still more bear St Jerome's; but in face of the letter to Ctesiphon, just cited, the latter attribution is certainly wrong.

(iv) It is worth while to add that the writer represents himself and his companions as monks of the monastery on the Mount of Olives which was founded by Rufinus, who himself lived there.

Lucius does not hesitate to say that the authorship of few works of Christian antiquity is more securely established than that of the *Historia Monachorum* in its Latin form (*l. c.* p. 167).

[2] This has been shown by Tillemont (*Mémoires*, III. 657, 8): among his reasons the following seem conclusive:

(i) The tour was made in 394—5; now Rufinus was in Egypt on two occasions only, viz., for a considerable time about 375, when he visited several of the solitaries; and again at a date prior to 385; but at the end of 394 he appears to have been in the neighbourhood of Jerusalem.

(ii) All the party were laymen, except one who was a deacon (c. 1); but by 394 Rufinus was a priest.

(iii) In the *Historia Monachorum* (cc. 28, 29), the two Macarii are spoken of as not having been seen by the writer; whereas Rufinus declares distinctly that he had seen both of them, and had received their blessing (*Hist. Eccl.* II. 8).

Gennadius in his account of Petronius who became bishop of Bologna, says: "scripsisse putatur uitas patrum monachorum Aegypti[1]." This suggested to Tillemont the theory that Rufinus edited materials supplied to him by Petronius, who may have made the journey[2]. This theory was accepted by Fontanini and others, but it has found scant favour among modern writers. Quite recently however, Zöckler has put it forward again, and defended it as the one plausible conjecture as to the authorship[3]. But indeed it cannot be upheld in face of a fact which has been strangely overlooked by writers on these questions.

The discussion has hitherto been conducted on the assumption that the Latin is the original, or at least that, if it be a translation, the Greek original is no longer extant[4]. And yet, so long ago as 1686, Cotelier described the contents of four Paris MSS. of a *Paradisus*, and printed considerable portions of the text[5]. It is extraordinary that Cotelier did not himself recognise what this *Paradisus* really was[6]. Even before I had an opportunity of examining the manuscripts used by Cotelier, I was satisfied from his own description that the work in question was nothing else than the Greek text of the *Historia Monachorum*. Later on, I found a copy of it in the British Museum, and another in a Leyden manuscript. I also examined Cotelier's four manuscripts, as well as others of the same type, at Paris[7]. All of them I found to contain the Greek of the *Historia Monachorum* and to present

---

[1] *De Scriptoribus Ecclesiasticis*, XLI. (*P. L.* LVIII. 1082).

[2] *Mémoires*, XII. 658.

[3] *Evagrius Ponticus*, p. 100 (*Biblische und kirchenhistorische Studien*, München, 1893, Heft IV.); also *Askese und Mönchtum* (1897), pp. 213—215. In a review of the last named work, Grützmacher declares in favour of the same hypothesis (*Theol. Literaturzeitung*, 1897, No. 9).

[4] Thus Lucius speaks of the possibility of reconstructing the original Greek text by current critical methods (*l. c.* p. 175).

[5] The description is given in his *Ecclesiae Graecae Monumenta*, III. 564—6; the text *ibid.* 171—184. All this matter is reprinted in Migne, *P. G.* LXV. 439 ff., and is therefore easily accessible. Another copy of the work is fully described by Montfaucon in the *Bibliotheca Coisliniana*, pp. 138—140.

[6] He seems to have supposed that it was excerpted from the Lausiac History and translated into Latin by Rufinus; a hypothesis wholly inadmissible, for the Lausiac History was not written until after Rufinus' death (cf. § 4).

[7] These manuscripts are briefly described in Appendix I. Dr Preuschen is preparing a critical edition of the Greek text. [Published Nov. 1897.]

the same text as those portions of the Long Recension of the Lausiac History which correspond with the Latin *Historia Monachorum.* What Cotelier printed was the Prologue and most of the parts of the work which are not found in the long *Historia Lausiaca.* In Appendix I. directions are given whereby anyone may reconstruct for himself out of vols. XXXIV. and LXV. of the Greek Patrology nearly the whole of the Greek text of the *Historia Monachorum.*

An important question now arises: Which of these is the original—the Greek or the Latin text? Here I cannot help thinking that Tillemont's usual penetration has failed him. Relying on St Jerome's formal statement that the book was written by Rufinus ('qui librum quoque scripsit'), and on the fact that he blames Rufinus for what he disapproves of in it, Tillemont concludes that the work was written in Latin[1]. But a study of the Greek manuscripts, which Tillemont evidently had not seen, has led me to the opposite conclusion. The following reasons make it clear, in my judgment, that the Greek is the original.

(1) Though the Latin is certainly by Rufinus, it has been shown that the reminiscences and the highly personal character of the narrative cannot belong to him[2]. That he translated the work of some one else is the obvious explanation of this difficulty.

(2) The Greek text does not contain the reference to Rufinus' own Ecclesiastical History[3]. The explanation is again simple, if the Greek is the original and the Latin a translation by Rufinus.

(3) The Latin (c. 27) speaks of Evagrius as still alive; but he died at the beginning of 400, whereas the Latin was written after that year, for it refers to Rufinus' translation of Eusebius' Ecclesiastical History, the earliest possible date of which is 400 (Tillemont, XII. 656). If the Greek is the original, and if it was written a year or two after the journey recorded, the anachronism disappears.

(4) It will be seen hereafter (§ 8) that Sozomen had the

---

[1] *Mémoires,* XII. 658—9. St Jerome's words are cited above, p. 11, note.
[2] Cf. above, p. 11, note.
[3] Cf. above, p. 11, note.

work before him, and speaks of it as written by a Greek author named Timotheus.

I add one argument based on critical and linguistic considerations.

(5) In the account of Apelles the Latin text tells us that he lived "in uicina regione" (c. 15); the Greek MSS. present a variety of readings:—

$$\dot{\epsilon}\nu\ \tau o\hat{\imath}\varsigma\ \mu\acute{\epsilon}\rho\epsilon\sigma\iota\ \tau\hat{\eta}\varsigma\ \text{'}A\chi\acute{\omega}\rho\epsilon\omega\varsigma$$

„   „   „ $\tau o\hat{\imath}\varsigma\ \dot{\alpha}\chi\omega\rho\epsilon\acute{\iota}o\iota\varsigma$

„   „   „ $\tau\hat{\eta}\varsigma\ \ddot{\alpha}\nu\omega\ \chi\acute{\omega}\rho\alpha\varsigma$

„   „   „ $\tau o\hat{\imath}\varsigma\ \dot{\epsilon}\nu\ \dot{\omega}\rho\alpha\acute{\iota}o\iota\varsigma.$

(The $\tau o\hat{\imath}\varsigma\ \dot{\alpha}\nu\omega\tau\acute{\epsilon}\rho o\iota\varsigma$ of the printed text in c. 60 of the Long Recension is an emendation of Du Duc's.)

The first reading is without doubt the true one. It is found in a greater number of Greek MSS.[1] It is the reading which Sozomen had before him; for he says of Apelles: $\delta\iota\acute{\epsilon}\pi\rho\epsilon\pi\epsilon\ \pi\epsilon\rho\grave{\iota}$ $\text{'}A\chi\omega\rho\iota\nu$[2]. It is the reading of a very early Syriac translation, and occurs in a Syriac MS. written in A.D. 532[3]. Lastly, it is geographically correct: Achoris was a town between Antinoo and Heracleopolis, and it stands in this position in the itinerary in the *Historia Monachorum*; this precise and accurate information cannot be supposed to have been introduced by the conjecture of a later copyist, but must be the account of the author who himself made the journey which he describes. The various Greek forms exhibit successive stages of corruption, all easily to be accounted for on the supposition that $\text{'}A\chi\acute{\omega}\rho\epsilon\omega\varsigma$ was the original reading, but not one of them explicable as representing the Latin 'uicina.' 'Vicina' could not by any process of corruption have grown out of Achoris in a series of Latin MSS.; nor could a Greek translator have turned 'uicina' into $\text{'}A\chi\acute{\omega}\rho\epsilon\omega\varsigma$[4].

As against all this we have St Jerome's testimony ('scripsit'), which Zöckler no less than Tillemont seems to regard as decisive

---

[1] In the Paris MSS., *Ancien fonds grec*, 1596, 1597, 1628, and *Coislin*, 83; and in the British Museum, *Arundel 546*.

[2] *Hist. Eccl.* VI. 28.

[3] British Museum, *Addit.* MS. 17176 (Wright, *Catalogue*, DCCCCXXIV.).

[4] Dr Preuschen suggested to me $\tau o\hat{\imath}\varsigma\ \dot{\epsilon}\gamma\chi\omega\rho\acute{\iota}o\iota\varsigma$ as a stage of corruption which would account for the rendering 'in uicina regione.'

in favour of Rufinus' Latin being the original[1]. St Jerome's statement however is sufficiently accounted for by the fact that Rufinus was the translator of the work: it is clear that he had not met with the Greek book; a far less surprising circumstance than that Weingarten, Lucius, Zöckler, and other scholars of the same standing, should have overlooked not only the many manuscripts entered in the catalogues of the great libraries of Europe, but also Cotelier's notice, even though reprinted in the Greek Patrology.

On a review of the evidence there can be no reasonable doubt that the Greek is the original and the Latin a translation made by Rufinus. In Appendix I. will be found some technical matters connected with the manuscripts, versions and textual history of the *Historia Monachorum*, and a conjecture as to its probable author.

§ 4. RELATIONS BETWEEN THE THREE DOCUMENTS—THE TWO RECENSIONS OF THE 'HISTORIA LAUSIACA' AND THE 'HISTORIA MONACHORUM.'

In dealing with the two recensions of the *Historia Lausiaca* and with the *Historia Monachorum*, it will be convenient in the first instance to use the Latin versions, which are all three at hand in Rosweyd: the Greek texts which underlie them are not easily accessible[2]. The following nomenclature will be used:—

A = the Long Recension of Palladius, printed by Rosweyd as Book VIII., and currently received as the genuine work;

B = the Short Recension, in Rosweyd's Appendix, pp. 933—977 (ed. 1) and 939—983 (ed. 2);

C = the *Historia Monachorum*, Book II. in Rosweyd.

In Migne's Latin Patrology the same materials will be found in three different volumes, the pages of Rosweyd being given in

---

[1] *Evagrius Ponticus*, p. 100.

[2] What is printed as the Greek of the Long Recension is not really what it purports to be, but is a made-up text; Meursius' edition of the Short Recension is not generally accessible; the Greek text of the *Historia Monachorum* has not yet been edited as such, and though the greater part is in print, still it is in so disjointed a state that it would be impossible to use it for our present purpose.

the case of A and of B. A is in *P. L.* LXXIII. 1085 ff.; B in
LXXIV. 243 ff.; C in XXI. 387 ff.[1]   A is also printed opposite the
Greek text in Migne's Greek Patrology, XXXIV. 997 ff.

As the groundwork of the enquiry, a Table is here drawn
out, exhibiting the result of a rough comparison of the three
documents. A, being the most comprehensive, is taken as the
basis of the comparison. The figures are the numbers of the
chapters in Rosweyd, and the Table shows how the three documents
correspond in regard to subject-matter.

TABLE.

A	B	C	A	B	C
1			30	12	
2			31	13	
3	1		32	14	
4			33	15	
5			34	16	
6			35	17	
7			36		
8		30	37	18	
9		2	38		
10	2		39	19	
11			40	20	
12			41		
13			42	21	
14			43	22	
15	3		44		1
16			45		
17	4		46		
18	5		47	22 (end)	
19		28	48		3
20	6	29	49		4
21			50		6
22	7		51		12
23			52		7 and 8
24	8		53		8
25		25	54		9 (part)
26	9		55		
27			56		10
28	10	31	57		
29	11		58		

[1] C here stands among the works of Rufinus, and the pagination is that of
Vallarsi's edition of Rufinus. The text, however, is the same as Rosweyd's.

A	B	C	A	B	C
59		11	106		
60		15	107	37	
61			108		
62			109		
63		16	110	38	
64			111	39	
65			112	40	
66		19	113	32	
67			114	54	
68		20	115	56 (½)	
69		21 and 22	116		
70		23 (½)	117	28, 29 (scraps), 33	
71		17	118	33 and 42 (½)	
72		32	119	49	
73		33	120		
74		13	121		
75		14	122	50	
76		18	123		
77	23		124		
78			125		
79			126		
80			127		
81			128		
82	23 (end)		129	29	
83	24		130		
84			131		
85			132		
86	25	27	133		
87	26		134		
88	27		135	55	
89	34		136	51	
90			137	48	
91	35		138		
92			139		
93			140	56 (½)	
94			141	57	
95	„ and 36		142	42 (½)	
96	45		143		
97	46		144	43	
98			145	44	
99	47		146		
100			147	52	
101	28		148	53	
102	30 (½)		149		
103	31		150 (a) (b)		Epilogue
104	30 (½)		151	58	
105	41				

From this Table two results are obvious at a glance.

I.   The whole of A, with the exception of three portions (78—81, 116 and 150 a), is found either in B or in C[1].

II.   In eight cases only do B and C appear to overlap, *i.e.* to deal with the same subject-matter.

In reference to the first of these results, it is important here to add that the whole of B is represented by the figures of the second column and all but a small remainder of C by the figures of the third column.   That is to say, the whole of B is contained in A, and so is nearly the whole of C.

It will be convenient now to investigate the eight cases in which B and C appear to overlap.   In the following three it is found that A and B are substantially the same, while the accounts in C are completely independent:

Macarius of Egypt (A 19, B 6, C 28);
Chronius (A 25, B 9, C 25);
Evagrius (A 86, B 25, C 27).

In the other five cases, viz. :

Amoun of Nitria (A 8, B 2, C 30);
Or (A 9, B 2, C 2);
Macarius of Alexandria (A 20, B 6, C 29);
Paul the Simple (A 28, B 10, C 31);
John of Lycopolis (A 43—47, B 22, C 1);

the following phenomena are revealed :—

(1)   Comparing A and B, we find that in every case the whole of B is contained substantially in A[2].

(2)   Comparing A and C, we find that in every case a greater or less portion of C is contained substantially in A.

(3)   Comparing B and C, we find them in all cases to be

---

[1]   The absence of 78—81 is only apparent, for the passage is found in the Latin *Harl.* ms. 4719, and others of B (cf. § 9).   It has been stated already that certain lacunae in the early editions of the Latin B were filled up in the later from a Greek ms.; but these passages are found in both Latin and Greek mss. of B. A 116 and 150 a are the only passages found in A but not in B.   On the other hand four short passages of B are not found in A (cf. B 2 circ. fin., 19 circ. fin., 22 circ. init., 29 circ. fin.).

[2]   By "substantially" is here meant that the matter of the accounts is the same, though there may be changes of order, or slight modifications in detail, or at times greater diffuseness or compression.

entirely independent accounts, having nothing whatever in common.

Turning now from the monks of whom lives occur in all three documents, to those whose lives are found only in two of them: a collation of the sections common only to A and B shows that the accounts are substantially the same. This is also the case in the. sections common only to A and C. But there are· no sections common only to B and C.

The facts here adduced were in the first instance gathered from a careful comparison of the Latin versions only. It may be well to state at once that the examination of the Greek texts makes the above results stand out still more clearly.

To sum up, the state of the case may be broadly expressed by the formula $A = B + C$.

The Prologue and certain passages of C are not contained in A, and there are a few other apparent exceptions; but the cases not covered by the formula are much fewer in the Greek texts than in the Latin. And any one who studies the Greek, or even reads with attention what is here to follow, will be satisfied that the residue does not affect the truth embodied in the formula, that in regard of matter the book A is made up of the two books B and C.

We may next consider the hypotheses which have been put forward by recent critics to account for the presence of C in A. One theory which naturally occurs to the mind, and was actually suggested by Rosweyd and Cotelier, must be mentioned, but only to be put aside, viz., that A is the source from which both B and C have been derived[1]. It is certain that the Latin version of C is the handiwork of Rufinus. Now Rufinus died in 410, immediately after the Sack of Rome by Alaric in that year. But the Lausiac History, in both recensions, speaks of this Sack of Rome (A 118, B 42) and of events which are known to have occurred after it, *e.g.* the death of Melania; moreover in the Preface Palladius says it is now the twentieth year of his episcopate, and his consecration took place in 399 or 400. It is therefore impossible that C, written before 410, should have been derived from A, written after that year.

---

[1] *Vitae Patrum*, Prolegomenon xiv.; *Ecclesiae Graecae Monumenta*, III. 566.

The hypotheses put forward in recent times are:—

(1)   That C is an original Latin work of Rufinus, and that Palladius embodied a Greek translation of it in his Lausiac History.   This is the theory defended by Weingarten[1] and formerly held by Zöckler[2]: but it is excluded by the production of the Greek original of C, with which these writers were not acquainted.

(2)   That there was a common Coptic source, of which Rufinus and Palladius made independent selections, translating them, the one into Latin, the other into Greek.   This theory was put forward by Amélineau[3]; but it cannot any longer be even considered. For in the Greek texts the parts common to A and C are identical; and it is impossible to conceive that a translation by Palladius from the Coptic, and another Greek translation, whether from Coptic or Latin, could thus verbally agree.   Nor can it be said that perhaps the Greek of C is not a second translation, but has been excerpted from A; for it contains matter found in Rufinus' Latin, but not in A.   But after all, M. Amélineau merely suggests his thesis tentatively, as being in his judgment a better solution of the problem than any hitherto offered, without producing any direct evidence in its support[4].

(3)   That there was an original Greek work which was translated into Latin by Rufinus and incorporated in his History by Palladius.   This is the theory held by W. Möller[5], and, with certain elaborations, by Lucius[6], whose particular solution of the problem has been adopted by Grützmacher[7], by Zöckler in his

---

[1] "Rosweyd hielt sie sehr mit Unrecht für eine Uebersetzung aus dem Griechischen.   Sie ist eine echte Schrift des Rufinus und in seinem eignen Namen geschrieben." *Der Ursprung des Mönchtums*, p. 25 (note).   It now appears that Rosweyd was right in his surmise, and his modern critic wrong.

[2] Herzog-Plitt, xi. 174; also the monograph *Evagrius Ponticus*, pp. 100, 101.

[3] *De Historia Lausiaca*, pp. 59—72; *L'Égypte chrétienne au iv* et v* siècles*, Tom. i., Fasc. ii., p. 498.

[4] "Nullum ad hanc sententiam confirmandum argumentum afferre possum." (*De Historia Lausiaca*, p. 63.)

[5] Herzog-Plitt, xiii. p. 100.

[6] *Die Quellen, &c.* (*Zeitschrift für Kirchengeschichte*, 1885); the main purpose of the essay is to establish the thesis.

[7] *Pachomius und das älteste Klosterleben*, pp. 1—4; also in *Theol. Literaturzeitung*, 1897, No. 9.

most recent contribution to the discussion[1], and by Batiffol[2]. And at first sight it might seem as if the production of the Greek of C was its verification; for has not a Greek work been found which actually was translated by Rufinus and is also incorporated in the document which passes as Palladius' History?

But when the case is more carefully looked into, it will appear that the production of this Greek original is no less fatal to the characteristic positions of Lucius' theory than to those of Weingarten and Amélineau. For it, too, postulates that it was Palladius himself who introduced the matter of C into the Lausiac History, and it assumes as its basis that the Greek of A—the Long Recension—is the authentic text, the "canonical Palladius" as Zöckler calls it[3].

Against this view it will here be maintained that not A but B must be taken as representing the genuine Lausiac History, and that A is a clumsy fusion by a later redactor of the two pre-existing works B and C. Thus the precise point at issue at this stage of the enquiry is whether it was Palladius himself, or a later redactor, who incorporated ·C in the Lausiac History. On the decision reached depends the place which Palladius' work must take among the historical memorials of the time. For the arguments whereby Lucius seeks to show that it is but a second-hand compilation, practically worthless as an historical source, owing to the impossibility of discriminating the materials out of which it is made and thus sifting fact from fable, are all based upon phenomena peculiar to A. If B, then, prove to be the real Lausiac History, these arguments of Lucius simply fall, and the book may be accepted for what it professes to be, a first-hand authority, the personal memoirs of its writer. After the genuine form of the work has, so far as is possible, been determined, it will remain to subject it to the ordinary tests of veracity and credibility. This will be done in Part II. of this Study, when Weingarten's criticisms will be considered, and an attempt made to form a judgment as to the historical character of the whole of this group of writings.

---

[1] *Askese und Mönchtum*, 213.
[2] *Anciennes Littératures Chrétiennes: La Littérature Grecque* (Paris, 1897), 253, 257.　　　　[3] *Askese und Mönchtum*, 220.

Meantime the question immediately before us may be formulated thus: Is it A, or is it B, that represents the genuine text of the Lausiac History?

§ 5. COMPARISON OF THE GREEK TEXTS OF THE THREE DOCUMENTS IN SELECTED CASES.

(a) John of Lycopolis.

It has already been pointed out that in certain cases our three documents all contain lives of the same person. This is so with the famous John of Lycopolis, the Seer of the Thebaid, in whose prophetic powers Theodosius had such confidence that he sent to consult him as to the conduct of military expeditions[1]. Accounts of John are found in A 43—47, in B 22, and in C 1; and for clearness' sake, let the statement already made (§ 4) be repeated: that here, as elsewhere, B and C offer quite different texts, even when they describe the same facts. As the present is a characteristic example of the mutual relations of the three documents, I shall begin by giving a brief analysis of their respective contents, with references to the readily accessible Latin versions.

(See Table opposite.)

The account in A (Rosweyd, pp. 738—746; *P. L.* LXXIII. 1141—1153) is made up of the matter from B and C as follows:—

c. 43	= B 1, C 2 and B 2, C 3, B 3, B 4, B 6, B 7, B 5, C 4, C 5.
cc. 44, 45, 46 (except the end)	= C 6.
c. 46 (end)	= C 7, C 8.
c. 47	= B 8[2].

---

[1] This is a matter of history apart from these documents. Cf. Gibbon, *Decline and Fall*, c. XXVII.; also *Dict. Christ. Biog.*, III. 403. Tillemont has collected and coordinated all the materials concerning John (*Mémoires*, x. 9—29).

[2] It will be noticed that the section C 1 does not occur in A; this, however, is one of the passages found in Rufinus' Latin of the *Historia Monachorum*, but not in the Greek MSS. C 5 (John's discourse) is much shorter in A than in the Latin C; but here again A agrees with the Greek MSS. of C. These are two of the passages discussed in Appendix I. where Rufinus differs from the extant Greek text. For the present purpose it is only necessary to note that A is made up of the whole of the texts of B and C, as found in the Greek MSS.

B, c 2		Rosweyd†	P. L. lxxiv.	C, c l		Rosweyd	P. L. xxi.
1. John's early life and vocation; description of his cell.		959} 965} col. 1, med.	301 A, B.	1. Description of John's cell and manner of life.		449 col. 1, fin. to 450 col. 1, init.	391 A, B.
2. His prophetic gifts, especially in the case of Theodosius.		959} 965} col. 1, lin.	301 B, C.	2. His prophetic gifts shown in the case of Theodosius.		450 col. 1, med.	391 c.
3. Palladius goes to visit John alone.		959} 965} col. 1, fin. col. 2, init.	301 c, D.	3. Various miracles and prophecies.		450 col. 1, med. to 451 col. 1, med.	392 A, to 394 A.
4. The interview; John's predictions about Palladius' future career.		959} 905} col. 2, med. to 960} 965} col. 1, med.	302 A, B, C, D.	4. Party of seven visit John: their interview.		451 col. 1, med. to 451 col. 2, fin.	394 B, C, D, to 395 A, B.
5. Palladius' return; after two months Evagrius and his other disciples go to visit John.		960} 965} col. 1, med.	303 B.	5. John's discourse.		451 col. 2, fin. to 453 col. 2, fin.	395 B, to 398 D.
6. Sketch of Palladius' after-life, shewing the verification of John's prodictions in his regard.		960} 905} col. 1, fin.	303 B, C.	6. John's anecdotes of many monks who had fallen away.		453 col. 2, fin. to 457 col. 1, med.	398 D, to 404 D.
7. John's manner of life.		960} 905} col. 1, fin. col. 2, init.	303 D.	7. Announcement of Theodosius' victory and speedy death.		457 col. 1, fin.	404 D, 405 A.
8. Story of Poemanin.		960} 965} col. 2, init.	303 D, 304 A.	8. The visitors leave and soon hear the news of John's death.		457 col. 1, fin.	405 A.

† In the first column of references to Rosweyd, the upper number gives the page in the first edition, the lower the page in the second; the pages in the two editions are the same in all respects other than numbering. The difference in pagination begins only at p. 787. The letters A, B, C, D in the columns of references to Migne, are the letters printed in the margin space of the pages in the Patrology, and are here given to facilitate the identification of the passages.

I now propose to print in parallel columns so much of the three Greek texts as will enable the reader, by the help of a few directions, to reconstruct for himself, from vol. XXXIV. of the Greek Patrology, the full texts of the three accounts of John of Lycopolis as found in the Greek originals of our documents. Those passages which throw light upon the nature and mutual relations of A, B and C are given in full.

NOTE.—In the first column (A) of the following texts the portions from B (which, according to my hypothesis, forms the groundwork of A) are printed in ordinary type; passages interwoven from C are in spaced type; additions and such alterations as may be supposed to have been made of set purpose by the Redactor stand out in 'Clarendon type; omissions are indicated by gaps. It is to be understood that, except where references are given to

---

A.

Paris Gr. 1626 (cent. xii): cf. Migne
P.G. XXXIV. 1107.

Γέγονέ τις Ἰωάννης ἐν Λυκῷ τῇ πόλει ὃς ἐκ παιδίου μὲν ἔμαθε τὴν τεκτο- νικήν· ᾧ ἀδελφὸς ὑπῆρχεν βαφεύς. εἰς ὕστερον δὲ γεγονὼς ὡς ἐτῶν εἰκοσιπέντε ἀπετάξατο· καὶ διατρίψας ἐν   μονα- 5 στηρίῳ πέντε ἔτη, ἀνεχώρησεν μόνος εἰς τὸ ὄρος τῆς Λυκῶ, εἰς αὐτὴν τὴν ἀκρωρίαν ποιήσας ἑαυτῷ τρεῖς θόλους· καὶ εἰσελθὼν ᾠκοδόμησεν ἑαυτόν. ἦν οὖν ὁ εἷς θόλος εἰς τὰς χρείας τῆς σαρκὸς, ὁ δὲ εἷς 10 ἔνθα εἰργάζετο, ὁ δὲ ἄλλος ἔνθα προσ- ηύχετο. οὗτος τριάκοντα ἔτη πληρώσας ἐγκεκλεισμένος, καὶ διὰ θυρίδος λαμβάνων παρὰ τοῦ διακονοῦντος αὐτῷ   τὰς χρείας, κατηξιώθη χαρίσματος προφήσεων. ὃς ἐκ 15 τῶν ἔργων ἔκδηλος γέγονεν πᾶσιν

B.

Paris Gr. 1596 (cent. xi): cf. Meurs.
97—102.

Γέγονέ τις Ἰωάννης ὀνόματι ἐν Λυκῷ τῇ πόλει ὃς ἐκ παιδίου ἔμαθε τὴν τεκτο- νικήν· ᾧ ἀδελφὸς ὑπῆρχε βαφεύς. ὃς ὕστερον γενόμενος ἐτῶν εἰκοσιπέντε ἀπε- τάξατο· καὶ διατρίψας ἐν διαφόροις μονα- στηρίοις πέντε ἔτη, ἀνεχώρησε μόνος εἰς τὸ ὄρος τὸ Λύκων, εἰς αὐτὴν τὴν ἀκρωρείαν ποιήσας ἑαυτῷ τρεῖς θόλους· καὶ εἰσελθὼν εἰς αὐτοὺς ἐνοικοδόμησεν ἑαυτόν. ἦν οὖν ὁ εἷς θόλος ἔνθα προσηύχετο· ὁ δεύτερος ἐν ᾧ εἰργάζετο καὶ ἤσθιεν· ὁ ἄλλος εἰς τὰς χρείας τῆς σαρκός. οὗτος τριάκοντα πληρώσας ἔτη ἐγκεκλεισμένος, καὶ διὰ θυρίδος λαμβάνων διὰ τοῦ διακονοῦντος τὰ πρὸς τὴν χρείαν, κατηξιώθη χαρίσματος προρρήσεως. ἐν οἷς καὶ τῷ μακαρίῳ Θεοδοσίῳ τῷ βασιλεῖ

A. Readings of Hervet's ms.
    9 ᾠκοδόμησεν] ἐνῳκοδόμησεν (inaedificavit)

B. Readings of Paris Gr. 1628 and Coislin 282 (= P and C respectively).
    1 ὀνόματι] om. PC   ἐν—πόλει] (xs 1596 ἐκ Λυκῶν τῆς πόλεως)   2 παιδίου] παιδὸς μὲν P; παιδία μὲν C   3 ὃς] εἰς P; om. C   4 ὕστερον] add. δὲ PC   γενό- μενος] add. ὡς P   7 τὸ Λύκων] τῆς Λυκῶ P (sic alii); λεγόμενον Λυκῶ C   Λύκων] add. καὶ P   ἀκρωρείαν] add. καὶ C   8 ποιήσας] ἐποίησεν P   καὶ] om. C   9 εἰς

Migne (*P. G.* xxxiv.), the full texts are printed; so that however great the intervals may be in columns B and C, the texts are always continuous. I have not in any case relied on Migne's text, but always on a ms., indicated at the beginning of each piece. As it is not my purpose here to produce a critical text, a full apparatus is not given. In the columns containing B the readings of the Paris ms. *ancien fonds grec* 1628 (cent. xiv.) are recorded. This manuscript alone, of those known to me (not to mention certain fragments), presents a text differing substantially from that of Meursius and the corresponding parts of Migne; and it will be found useful later to have some samples of the differences between it and the other authorities for the text of the Lausiac History. The proofs of the text of the extracts (but not of the apparatus) have been compared with the mss. by Dom Gabarra, sub-prior of the Paris cell founded from the Benedictine abbey of Ligugé, who has also verified many other points for me.

C.

Paris Gr. 1627 (cent. xiii): cf. Preuschen 4—24.

NOTES.

A. Paris ms 1626 is the best representative known to me of the Long Recension; but the ms used by Hervet was on the whole a better ms; its readings are therefore recorded from the Latin.

B. The kindred Paris mss 1596 and 1597, though not free from certain corruptions of their own, hand down a tradition of the B text independent of the mss used by Meursius and Du Duc; they have therefore been chosen for these Extracts.

Part of the Coislin ms 282 contains a text akin to the otherwise unique Paris ms 1628; as the Life of John of Lycopolis falls in this portion, its readings are recorded in the critical apparatus, as an aid towards controlling the text of 1628.

Ἐθεασάμεθα ἐν τοῖς ὁρίοις Λυκῶ τῆς
Θηβαΐδος τὸν μέγαν καὶ μακάριον Ἰωάννην,
ἄνδρα ἅγιον ὡς ἀληθῶς καὶ ἐνάρετον,   15
(Cf. NOTES on C, p. 27.)

αὐτοὺς] om. PC   ἐνοικοδόμησεν] ἀνῳκοδόμησεν PC (et alii)   οὖν] add. αὐτῷ C
ὁ] (om. ms 1596)   10 ἔνθα προσηύχετο and 11 εἰς—σαρκὸς are transposed in P
and C   ὁ δεύτερος] καὶ ὁ εἷς P ; ὁ δὲ εἷς C   ἐν ᾧ] ἔνθα P   11 ὁ ἄλλος] καὶ ὁ
ἄλλος P ; ὁ δὲ ἄλλος C   14 διὰ] παρὰ PC   διακονοῦντος] add. αὐτῷ PC   τὰ πρὸς]
om. PC   τὴν χρείαν] τὰς χρείας PC (sic alii)   16 καὶ] om. C

C. Readings of Paris Gr. 1600.
13 Ἐθεασάμεθα] ἐθεασάμην οὖν ἐγὼ (Rufinus, *uidimus*)   ὁρίοις] add. τῆς
15, 16 as in A (ὃς ἐκ κ.τ.λ.)

A.

προφητείας χάρισμα κεκτημένος. καὶ
γὰρ πάντα τὰ ἐκ τοῦ θεοῦ ἐρχόμενα
τῷ κόσμῳ τῷ εὐσεβεστάτῳ βασιλεῖ
Θεοδοσίῳ προεμήνυεν, καὶ τὰ ἐκβησόμενα πάλιν προαπήγγελλεν· τήν 5
τε τῶν τυράννων αὐτῷ ἐπανάστασιν,
καὶ τὴν ταχεῖαν αὐτῶν πάλιν ἀναίρεσιν, καὶ τὸν τῶν ἐπιρρεόντων αὐτῷ
ἐθνῶν ἀφανισμόν. ὡς καὶ τινος
στρατηλάτου πρὸς αὐτὸν κ.τ.λ. (P.G. 10
xxxiv. 1108, A.)

παρὰ τοῖς βασιλεῦσιν εὐδόκιμος
ἔσῃ· ὅπερ καὶ γέγονεν, καὶ τὰ συμ-
βάντα τὴν πρόρρησιν ἐβεβαίωσαν.
ἔλεγεν δὲ ὅτι οἰκείῳ θανάτῳ ὁ χρισ- 15
τιανώτατος βασιλεὺς   τελευτήσει. εἶχεν δὲ καί τινα ὑπερβολὴν
ὁ ἀνὴρ προφητείας κ.τ.λ.

The account of John's prophecies and
miracles goes on as in P.G. xxxiv, from 20
1108 A to 1113 B (ηὐχαρίστησε).

Καὶ τί δεῖ λέγειν περὶ τῶν ἄλλων
ἔργων αὐτοῦ, ἀλλὰ ἅπερ αὐτοψὶ
παρειλήφαμεν; ἑπτὰ γὰρ ἀδελφοὶ
ξένοι   ἦμεν ἐν τῇ ἐρήμῳ τῇ τῆς 25
Νιτρίας, ἐγώ τε καὶ οἱ περὶ τὸν μακάριον
Εὐάγριον.
ἐξητοῦμεν δὲ μαθεῖν τὴν ἀκρίβειαν τίς ἡ
ἀρετὴ τοῦ ἀνδρός. λέγει οὖν ὁ μέγας
Εὐάγριος κ.τ.λ.   30

The account of Palladius' visit and
interview with John goes on to 1115 B;
but the passage ἀναχωρήσας οὖν…τούτῳ
τῷ μακαρίῳ 1114 D does not occur
here in the MS, but only at 1115 B, 35
just as in Hervet's Latin, the clumsy
doublet of the printed Greek text being
thus avoided. Then 1115 B.

ἀναχωρήσας οὖν αὐτοῦ, ἦλθον ἐπὶ τὴν
ἔρημον εἰς τὸν τόπον τὸν συνήθη, διηγού- 40

B.

διαφόρους ἀπέστειλε προρρήσεις, περί τε
Μαξίμου τοῦ τυράννου, ὅτι νικήσας αὐτὸν
ὑποστρέψει τῶν Γαλλιῶν. ὁμοίως δὲ καὶ
περὶ Εὐγενίου τοῦ τυράννου εὐηγγελίσατο
τοῦτο αὐτῷ, ὅτι νικήσει μὲν τοῦτον, αὐτὸς
δὲ τὸ πέρας τοῦ βίου ἐκεῖσε πληρώσει,
καὶ τὴν ἐκεῖ βασιλείαν τῷ υἱῷ αὐτοῦ κατα-
λείψει. τούτου ἐξῆλθε φήμη πολλὴ καὶ
μεγάλη ὡς ἐναρέτου ἀνδρός. διὸ καὶ ὁ ἐν
ἁγίοις ἀριθμούμενος βασιλεὺς Θεοδόσιος
προφητικῇ τιμῇ τοῦτον ἐσέβετο.

Ὄντες οὖν ἡμεῖς ἐν τῷ ὄρει τῷ τῆς
Νιτρίας ἐγώ τε καὶ οἱ περὶ τὸν μακάριον
Εὐάγριον καὶ Ἀλβίνιον καὶ Ἀμμώνιον
ἐξητοῦμεν μαθεῖν τὴν ἀκρίβειαν τίς ἡ
ἀρετὴ τοῦ ἀνδρός. λέγει οὖν ὁ μακάριος
Εὐάγριος κ.τ.λ.

As in A; but the passage ἀναχωρήσας
οὖν…τούτῳ τῷ μακαρίῳ occurs as in
1114 D, and not as in 1115 B.

ἀναχωρήσας οὖν αὐτοῦ, ἦλθον ἐπὶ τὴν
ἔρημον ἐπὶ τὸν τόπον τὸν συνήθη, αὐτὰ

A. 25 ξένοι om. H   27 Εὐάγριον] add. καὶ Ἀλβίνιον καὶ Ἀμμώνιον (ego et beatus
Euagrius et Albinius et Ammonius)

B. 1 τε] om. C   3 ὑποστρέψει] ὑποστρέψεις P (et alii) (MS 1596 add. ἐκ)   δὲ]
om. C   4 τοῦ τυράννου] om. P   5 τοῦτο αὐτῷ—7 καταλείψει] om. PC   8 ἐξῆλθε
φήμη πολλή] φ. ἐξ. π. C (et alii)   καὶ μεγάλη] om. PC   9 ἀνδρός] om. P

C.

προφητίας χάρισμα κεκτημένον. καὶ
πάντα τὰ ἐρχόμενα τῷ κόσμῳ
τῷ εὐσεβεστάτῳ βασιλεῖ μηνύων
τά τε ἐκβησόμενα πάλιν ἀπήγγελλεν·
τὴν τῶν τυράννων ἐπανάστασιν, 5
καὶ τὴν ταχεῖαν αὐτῶν πάλιν ἀναίρεσιν.

ὡς καὶ τινος στρατηλάτου πρὸς
αὐτὸν κ.τ.λ., as in A.

εὐδοκιμήσεις παρὰ τοῖς βασιλεῦσιν· ὅπερ
καὶ γέγονεν, οὕτως συμβάντος αὐτῷ. προέφη
δὲ ὅτι καὶ ὁ χριστιανικώτατος βασιλεὺς
Θεοδόσιος οἰκείῳ θανάτῳ τελευτήσει. εἶχεν 15
οὖν ὑπερβολὴν προφητείας ὁ ἀνὴρ
κ.τ.λ.

The account goes on as in A.

Καὶ τί δεῖ λέγειν περὶ τῶν ἄλλων ἔργων
αὐτοῦ, πολλῶν ὄντων, ἃ καὶ διὰ τὸ πλῆθος
παρελίπομεν ; μόνον δὲ περὶ ὧν αὐτοψὶ
παρειλήφαμεν λέξωμεν· παρῆμέν ποτε πρὸς 25
αὐτὸν ἀδελφοὶ ξένοι πάντες.

NOTES.

It will be of use to compare with A the
readings of these two mss.

C. In Appendix I. it is shown that
ms 1627 contains a unique and important
text of portion of the *Hist. Mon.* The
text of this ms is therefore printed, and
its divergences from the normal text are
indicated in the critical notes.

The other Greek mss present a text of
the same type as that which has been incorporated in A. Attention will therefore
be called only to a few points of special
interest. Paris Gr. 1600 (cent. xi) is chosen
as a good representative of the ordinary
Greek mss.

C. 1—3 (p. 25). This introductory
passage is considerably longer in Rufinus'
version, which gives an account, different
from that of Palladius, of John's cell and
manner of life.

C. 22—25. The text of 1627 is partially
attested by Rufinus' version: Sed multa
sunt ejus gesta quae enarrare longum
est. unde omissis his interim quae
auditu comperimus, ad ea quae oculis
nostris inspeximus, ueniamus (Rosweyd
451). The other Greek mss have the same
text as A 22—24.

---

9 διὸ—11 ἐσέβετο] om. PC   10 ἁγίοις] ἀγγέλοις cet.   25 ἐν τῷ ὄρει τῷ] εἰς τὸ ὄρα
τὸ C; ἐν τῇ ἐρήμῳ P (sic cet.)   27 καὶ 'Αλβ. καὶ 'Αμ.] om. P (ms 1596 'Αλβάνιον
39 ἐπὶ τὴν ἔρημον] om. P; ἐπὶ τὸ μοναστήριον C   40 ἐπὶ] εἰς C (sic alii)   τόπον
add. μου C (sic alii)   αὐτὰ] om. C

C. 1—12 as in A   12 ὅπερ καὶ γέγονεν] γέγονέν τε οὕτως   12—18 as in A
23 πολλῶν ὄντων—25 παρειλήφαμεν λέξωμεν] ἀλλ' ἢ περὶ ὧν αὐτοψὶ παρειλήφαμεν (cf. A
24 αὐτοψὶ) (αὐτὸν εἰ sic ms 1627)   25 παρῆμεν—26 πάντες] ἑπτὰ γὰρ ἦμεν ἀδελφι
ξένοι πάντες (cf. p. 29); Rufinus, *Septem fuimus simul comitantes*

A.

μενος ταῦτα πάντα τοῖς μακαρίοις πατράσιν,

οἵτινες μετὰ δύο μῆνας
ἦλθον καὶ συνέτυχον αὐτῷ.

B.

ταῦτα διηγησάμενος τοῖς ἁγίοις πατράσι
τὰ περὶ τοῦ θεσπεσίου καὶ πνευματοφόρου
ἀνδρός. οἵτινες μετὰ δύο μῆνας διαπλεύ-
σαντες ἦλθον καὶ συνέτυχον τούτῳ τῷ
μακαρίῳ. ἐγὼ δὲ ὁ ἄθλιος κ.τ.λ. . . . .
. . εἶδέ τις πώποτε. As in P.G. xxxiv.
1114 D, to 1115 A (fin.).

                      διηγήσαντο
οὖν ὅτι ἐλθόντες πρὸς αὐτὸν ἠσπά· 10
σατο ἡμᾶς, φαιδρῷ τῷ προσώπῳ
ἑκάστῳ προσιλαρευόμενος· ἠξιοῦμεν
δὲ αὐτὸν εὐθὺς εὐχὴν τελέσαι πρῶτον
ὑπὲρ ἡμῶν κ.τ.λ.
The account of the visit, of John's 15
discourse and anecdotes, and his prophecy of Theodosius' death, goes on as
from 1115 B to 1130 D.
δοὺς δὲ ἡμῖν εὐλογίας ἐν εἰρήνῃ
πορευθῆναι προσέταξεν· εἰπὼν ἡμῖν 20
καὶ προφητείαν τινά· ὅτι σήμερον τὰ
ἐπινίκια τοῦ εὐσεβεστάτου Θεοδοσίου
εἰς τὴν Ἀλεξάνδρειαν εἰσεληλύθασιν
τῆς τοῦ τυράννου Εὐγενείου ἀναιρέ-
σεως· καὶ ὅτι δεῖ τὸν βασιλέα οἰκείῳ 25
θανάτῳ τελευτῆσαι· ὅπερ καὶ συνέβη
κατὰ ἀλήθειαν οὕτω γενέσθαι.
Ἦν δὲ ἰδεῖν...δοξάζοντας.   1130 D.
Ὡς δὲ πολλοὺς...αἰῶνας.   Ἀμήν.
                              1131 A. 30
Οὗτος καὶ τῇ δούλῃ...ἐτραυμάτησαν.
1131 A B (c. 47, on Poemenia, from B).
                FINIS.

Οὗτος καὶ τῇ δούλῃ...τραυματίσαντες,
as in A (the account of Poemenia).
                FINIS.

A. 9 διηγήσαντο] iique haec nobis narrarunt

B. 1 διηγησάμενος] διηγούμενος C   ἁγίοις] μακαρίοις PC   πατράσι] add.
περὶ τὸν ἅγιον Εὐάγριον C   2 τὰ περὶ—3 ἀνδρός] om. PC   3 διαπλεύσαντες]
πλεύσαντες P   4 τούτῳ τῷ μακαρίῳ] αὐτῷ PC   5 ὁ ἄθλιος] om. PC

Leaving the reader to draw his own conclusions from the
evidence that has just been laid before him, I pass on to deal
in a similar way with the still more significant triple account of

(b) *Paul the Simple.*

For here B and C give us not merely different accounts of
the same man, but different versions of the same story concerning

C.　　　　　　　　　　　　NOTES.

ὡς δὲ ἠσπάσατο 10
ἡμᾶς φαιδρῷ τῷ προσώπῳ,
　　　ἠξιοῦμεν αὐτὸν εὐθὺς εὐχὴν
τελέσαι πρῶτον ὑπὲρ ἡμῶν κ.τ.λ.

The account goes on as in A; and John's discourse is as in A (1116 A to 15 1121 c), without the additional matter found in Rufinus' Latin.

δοὺς δὲ ἡμῖν εὐλογίας ἐν εἰρήνῃ πορευθῆναι προσέταξεν· εἰπὼν ἡμῖν καὶ προ- 20
φητείαν τινά· ὅτι σήμερον τὰ ἐπινίκια
τοῦ εὐσεβεστάτου βασιλέως Θεοδοσίου
εἰς τὴν Ἀλεξάνδρειαν εἰσεληλύθασιν τῆς
τοῦ τυράννου Εὐγενίου ἀναιρέσεως· [καὶ
ὅτι δεῖ τὸν βασιλέα οἰκείῳ θανάτῳ τελευ- 25
τῆσαι. ἅπερ συνέβη κατὰ ἀλήθειαν οὕτως γενέσθαι.

'Ὡς δὲ πολλοὺς...αἰῶνας. 'Ἀμήν.]
FINIS.

C. 28. The passage ῟Ην δὲ ἰδεῖν...δοξά- ζοντας does not occur here, but in Cap. II, on Abbot Hor, cf. 1028 A, to which it clearly belongs, and where alone it is found in Rufinus' translation. Similarly the pas- sage Οἶδα γὰρ ἐγὼ ἄνθρωπον...ταῦτα ἑωρα- κέναι 1130 B c, is found under Hor in Rufinus, but under John in the Greek manuscripts.

C. 10 πρὸς αὐτὸν ἀπελθόντες. ὡς δὲ κ.τ.λ. Rufinus, qui ad eum uenimus 11 add. ἑκάστῳ προσιλαρευόμενος (cf. A), and so Rufinus, unumquemque nostrum gratifice alloquitur 24 ἀναιρέσεως] MS 1627 here passes without a break to the middle of B's account of John: evidently a page had been lost. The concluding passage is supplied from MS 1600

---

him; and it is in the highest degree interesting and instructive to observe the manner in which the two variations of the one tradition are dovetailed together in A. The chapters in the Latin versions are A 28, B 10, C 31; but Rufinus' account differs materially from the Greek of C.

A.

Paris Gr. 1626 (cent. xii): cf. Migne
P.G. xxxiv. 1076.

Διηγεῖτο δὲ κ.τ.λ....καὶ τοῦτο λιμώττων.
1076 c to 1081 λ.

τούτοις οὖν τοῖς   ῥήμασιν ἀποσοβεῖ
τὸν Παῦλον. καὶ ὡς οὐκ ἠνείχετο αὐτοῦ,
κλείσας δὲ τὴν θύραν ὁ Ἀντώνιος οὐκ 5
ἐξῆλθεν ἐπὶ ἡμέρας τρεῖς δι' αὐτὸν, οὐδὲ
πρὸς τὴν ἰδίαν χρείαν. ὁ δὲ γέρων παρέ-
μενε μὴ ἀναχωρῶν. τῇ δὲ τετάρτῃ ἡμέρᾳ
χρείας αὐτὸν καταλαβούσης ἀνοίξας ἐξῆλθεν,
καὶ ἰδὼν πάλιν τὸν Παῦλον λέγει αὐτῷ· 10
Ἄπελθε ἐντεῦθεν, γέρων, τί με ὑποπιάζεις ;
οὐ δύνασαι ὧδε μεῖναι. λέγει αὐτῷ ὁ
Παῦλος· Ἀδύνατόν ἐστιν ἀλλαχοῦ με
ἀπελθεῖν εἰ μὴ ὧδε. περιβλεψάμενος δὲ
ὁ Ἀντώνιος, καὶ θεασάμενος ὅτι τὰ πρὸς 15
τὴν τροφὴν οὐ βαστάζει, οὐκ ἄρτον, οὐχ
ὕδωρ, οὐχ ἕτερόν τι, καὶ τετάρτην ἡμέραν
ἔχει καρτερήσας νῆστις, ἐλογίσατο

ὅτι μή ποτε καὶ ἀποθάνῃ ἄπειρος ὢν
τοῦ νηστεύειν καὶ κηλιδώσει μου τὴν ψυχήν. 20
εἰσδέχεται οὖν αὐτόν. τότε ἔφη πρὸς
αὐτὸν ὁ Ἀντώνιος· Δύνασαι σωθῆναι
ἐὰν ἔχεις ὑπακοὴν, καὶ ὅπερ ἂν ἀκούσῃς παρ' ἐμοῦ, τοῦτο ποιήσεις. ὁ δὲ
Παῦλος ἀποκριθεὶς εἶπεν· Πάντα 25
ποιήσω ὅσα ἂν προστάξεις. καὶ τοιαύτην ἀνέλαβεν πολιτείαν σκληραγωγίας ἐν
ταῖς ἡμέραις ἐκείναις ὁ Ἀντώνιος οἵαν οὔτε
ὅτε ἦν ἐν ἀρχαῖς τῆς νεότητος. δοκιμάζων
οὖν αὐτοῦ τὴν γνώμην ὁ Ἀντώνιος, 30
εἶπεν πρὸς αὐτόν· Στῆθι καὶ πρόσευξαι ἐν τῷ τόπῳ τούτῳ ἕως εἰσέλθω
καὶ ἐνέγκω σοι ἔργον ὅπερ ἐργάσῃ.

B.

Paris Gr. 1597 (cent. xiii): cf. Meurs.
70—75.

Διηγεῖτο δὲ κ.τ.λ....καὶ τοῦτο λιμώττων.
As in A.

τούτοις καὶ τοῖς τοιούτοις ῥήμασιν ἀπεσόβει
τὸν Παῦλον. καὶ ὡς οὐκ ἠνέσχετο αὐτοῦ,
κλείσας τὴν θύραν ὁ Ἀντώνιος οὐκ ἐξῆλθεν
ἐπὶ ἡμέρας τρεῖς δι' αὐτὸν οὐδὲ πρὸς τὴν
ἰδίαν χρείαν. ὁ δὲ γέρων παρέμενεν
οὐκ ἀναχωρῶν. τῇ οὖν τετάρτῃ ἡμέρᾳ
χρείας αὐτὸν ἀναγκασάσης ἀνοίξας ἐξῆλθε,
καὶ ἰδὼν αὐτὸν πάλιν λέγει τῷ Παύλῳ·
Ἄπελθε ἔνθεν, γέρων, τί με ὑποπιάζεις; οὐ
δύνασαι ὧδε μεῖναι. λέγει αὐτῷ ὁ Παῦλος·
Ἀμήχανόν ἐστιν ἀλλαχοῦ με ἀποθανεῖν
ἢ ὧδε. περιβλεψάμενος οὖν ὁ Ἀντώνιος,
καὶ ἰδὼν ὅτι τὰ πρὸς τροφὴν οὐ βαστάζει,
οὐκ ἄρτον, οὐχ ὕδωρ, οὐχ ἕτερόν τι, καὶ
τετάρτην   ἔχει καρτερήσας νῆστις,
ἐλογίσατο ὁ μέγας Ἀντώνιος, ὅτι μή ποτε
καὶ ἀποθάνῃ ἄπειρος ὢν τοῦ νηστεύειν, καὶ
κηλιδώσω μου τὴν ψυχήν, εἰσδέχεται αὐτὸν
τότε.

καὶ τοιαύτην ἀνέ-
λαβεν ὁ Ἀντώνιος σκληραγωγίαν πολιτείας
ἐν ταῖς ἡμέραις ἐκείναις, οἵαν οὐδέποτε ἐν
ἀρχαῖς τῆς νεότητος.

A. Readings of Hervet's ms.

14 ἀπελθεῖν] so also the other Greek mss of this redaction ; Hervet's *moriar* need
not imply ἀποθανεῖν   28 οὔτε] om. H

B. Readings of Paris Gr. 1628, P (and of Coislin 282, C, but only where it
differs from standard text).

1 λιμώττων] λιμῶν   4 ἠνέσχετο] ἠνήχθετο   6 οὐδὲ] (ms 1597 οὔτε)   7 ἰδίαν]
om. P (ἑαυτοῦ C)   ὁ δὲ γέρων—8 ἀναχωρῶν] ὁ δὲ οὐκ ἀνεχώρησε   8 οὖν] δὲ (ms 1597
τὴν οὖν τετάρτην ἡμέραν)   9 ἀναγκασάσης] ἀναγκαζούσης   10 καὶ ἰδὼν—τῷ Παύλῳ]
καὶ πάλιν λέγει αὐτῷ   13 ἀμήχανον] add. μοί   με] om. P   ἀποθανεῖν] τελευτῆσαι

C.

Paris Gr. 1600 (cent. xi): cf. Preuschen 92—94.

Γέγονε δέ τις Παῦλος ὀνόματι, ἁπλοῦς 15
λεγόμενος. οὗτος τὴν ἑαυτοῦ γαμετὴν ἐπ'
αὐτοφώρῳ καταλαβὼν μοιχευομένην, μηδενὶ
μηδὲν εἰπὼν ἐπὶ τὴν ἔρημον πρὸς Ἀντώνιον
ὥρμησεν· καὶ προσπεσὼν αὐτοῦ τοῖς ποσίν,
παρεκάλει συνεῖναι αὐτῷ σωθῆναι βουλό- 20
μενος. ἔφη δὲ πρὸς αὐτὸν ὁ Ἀντώνιος·
Δυνήσει σωθῆναι ἐὰν ἔχεις ὑπακοήν, καὶ
ὅπερ ἂν παρ' ἐμοῦ ἀκούσῃς τοῦτο ποιεῖς.
ὁ δὲ Παῦλος ἀποκριθεὶς εἶπεν· Πάντα
ποιήσω ὅσαπερ ἂν προστάξεις.   25

                              δοκιμάζων
δὲ αὐτοῦ τὴν γνώμην ὁ Ἀντώνιος λέγει 30
πρὸς αὐτόν· Στῆθι καὶ πρόσευξαι ἐν τῷ
τόπῳ τούτῳ ἕως οὗ εἰσελθὼν ἐξενέγκω
σοι ἔργον ὅπερ ἂν ἐργάσῃ. καὶ εἰσελθὼν

NOTES.

A. The readings of Hervet's Greek ms are again recorded; they bear out the statement that it was a better ms than 1626.

B. The text is printed from Paris Gr. 1597, because the earlier 1596 is imperfect, beginning only at the middle of the Life of Paul the Simple.

Coislin 282 contains in this part a text almost the same as the standard B text only its departures from this text are indicated in the critical notes, under the sign C. It will be observed that it sometimes agrees with A, and in a few cases with the peculiar readings of 1628 (P). Here again it will be of interest to compare the readings of 1628 with those of A.

C. The text is a typical representative of the standard text. The readings of Coislin 83 (cent. x) are recorded as an example of the variations in the mss. The Life of Paul the Simple in 1627 is of redaction A.

— ———

C. It may be useful to have Rufinus' Latin corresponding to C (Rosw. 483):

Fuit quidam inter discipulos sancti Antonii Paulus nomine, cognominatus Simplex. hic initium conuersionis suae hujusmodi habuit. cum uxorem suam oculis suis cum adultero cubantem uidisset, nulli quidquam dicens, egressus est domum, et moestitia animi tactus in eremum semetipsum dedit, ubi cum anxius

---

15 ἰδών] θεασάμενος   16 οὐχ ἕτερόν τι] om. P   17 νῆστις] (many MSS νήστης)
18 ἐλογίσατο—ὅτι] om. P   19 ἀποθάνῃ] add. φησί   ἄπειρος—νηστεύειν] om. P
20 κηλιδώσω] κηλιδώσει (alii κηλιδώσῃ)   21 τότε] om. P   27 σκληραγωγίαν
πολιτείας] om. P (πολιτείαν σκληραγωγίας C et alii)   28 ἐκείναις] add. πολιτείαν
28 ἐν —29 νεότητος] (add. αὐτοῦ C) ἐν νεότητι

C. Readings of Coislin 83 (cent. x).

15 Παῦλος] add. μαθητὴς Ἀντωνίου   19 ποσίν] γόνασι   22 δυνήσει] δύνῃ   ἔχεις]
ἔχῃς   23 ποιεῖς] ποιήσῃς   25 προστάξεις] προστάξῃς   30 λέγει] εἴρηκεν
32 ἕως οὗ] ὅπως   33 ἄν] om.

A.

καὶ εἰσελθὼν εἰς τὸ σπήλαιον προσεῖχεν αὐτῷ διὰ θυρίδος ἀκινήτῳ
μένοντι ἐν τῷ τόπῳ ὅλην τὴν ἑβδομάδα, ὑπὸ τοῦ καύματος φρυγομένῳ.
ἐξελθὼν δὲ μετὰ τὴν ἑβδομάδα, βρέξας 5
θάλλους ἐκ φοινίκων, λέγει αὐτῷ· Δέξαι,
καὶ πλέξον σειρὰν, ὡς βλέπεις με. πλέκει
ὁ γέρων μέχρις ἐνάτης ὀργυίας δεκαπέντε
μόχθῳ πολλῷ. θεασάμενος δὲ ὁ μέγας
Ἀντώνιος   δυσηρεστήθη καὶ   10
λέγει αὐτῷ· Κακῶς ἔπλεξας·
ἀπόπλεξον, καὶ ἄνωθεν πλέξον· νῆστει αὐτῷ
ὄντι ἑβδόμην ἡμέραν ἄγοντι, καὶ ἡλικιώτῃ, τοσαύτην αὐτῷ ἐπήγαγεν σῆψιν, ἵνα
δυσφορήσας ὁ γέρων φύγῃ τὸν Ἀντώνιον καὶ 15
τὸν βίον τῶν μοναχῶν. ὁ δὲ καὶ ἀπέπλεξεν,
καὶ πάλιν ἔπλεξεν τοὺς αὐτοὺς θάλλους πάνυ
δυσχεραίνων διὰ τὸ εἶναι αὐτοὺς ἀπὸ τῆς
πρώτης πλοκῆς ἐρυσιδωμένους. θεασάμενος
οὖν ὁ μέγας Ἀντώνιος ὅτι   οὔτε 20
ἐγόγγυσεν, οὔτε ἐμικροψύχησεν, οὔτε κᾶν
πρὸς βραχὺ ἠγανάκτησεν,
            κατενύγει ἐπ'
αὐτῷ. καὶ δύναντος τοῦ ἡλίου, λέγει αὐτῷ·
     Παπία, θέλεις φάγωμεν ἄρτου 25
κλάσμα: λέγει αὐτῷ ὁ Παῦλος· Ὡς δοκεῖ σοι,
ἀββᾶ. καὶ τοῦτο δὲ πάλιν   κατέκαμψεν
τὸν Ἀντώνιον, τὸ μὴ προσδραμεῖν προθύμως
τῇ τῆς τροφῆς ἀγγελίᾳ ἀλλ' αὐτῷ ἐπιρρῖψαι
τὴν ἐξουσίαν. Θὲς οὖν φησι   30
    τράπεζαν. καὶ ὑπήκουσεν.
φέρει ἄρτους ὁ Ἀντώνιος, καὶ ἐπιτίθησι τῇ
τραπέζῃ παξαμάτας τέσσαρας ἐξ οὐγκιῶν
ἕξ. καὶ ἑαυτῷ μὲν ἔβρεξεν ἕνα, ξηροὶ γὰρ
ἦσαν, ἐκείνῳ δὲ τρεῖς. βάλλει ψαλμὸν ὁ 35
Ἀντώνιος ὃν ᾔδει, καὶ δωδέκατον αὐτὸν
ψάλας, δωδέκατον ηὔξατο, ἵνα καὶ ἐν τούτῳ
δοκιμάσει τὸν Παῦλον· ὁ δὲ γέρων προ-

B.

καὶ βρέξας
θάλλους ἐκ φοινίκων, λέγει αὐτῷ· Δέξαι,
πλέξον σειρὰν, ὡς βλέπεις με. πλέκει
ὁ γέρων ἕως ἐννάτης ὀργυίας δεκαπέντε
μόχθῳ πολλῷ. θεασάμενος δὲ ὁ μέγας
Ἀντώνιος τὸ πλέγμα δυσηρεστήθη καὶ ἐπιφερόμενος λέγει αὐτῷ· Κακῶς ἔπλεξας·
ἀπόπλεξον, καὶ ἄνωθεν πλέξον· νῆστει
αὐτῷ ὄντι τετάρτην ἡμέραν ἄγοντι, καὶ
ἡλικιώτῃ, τοσαύτην ἐπάγων σῆψιν ἵνα
δυσφορήσας ὁ γέρων φύγῃ τὸν Ἀντώνιον καὶ
τὸν βίον τῶν μοναχῶν. ὁ δὲ ἀπέπλεξε, καὶ
πάλιν ἔπλεξεν τοὺς αὐτοὺς θάλλους πάνυ
δυσχερεστέρους διὰ τὸ εἶναι αὐτοὺς ἐκ τῆς
πρώτης πλοκῆς ἐρυσιδωμένους. θεασάμενος
οὖν ὁ μέγας Ἀντώνιος, ὅτι ὁ γέρων οὔτε
ἐγόγγυσεν, οὔτε ἐμικροψύχησεν, οὔτε κᾶν
πρὸς βραχὺ ἠγανάκτησεν, οὐδ' ὅλως τὸ
πρόσωπον αὐτοῦ διέστρεψε, κατενύγει ἐπ'
αὐτῷ. καὶ δύναντος τοῦ ἡλίου, λέγει αὐτῷ
ὁ Ἀντώνιος· Παπία, θέλεις φάγωμεν ἄρτου
κλάσμα; λέγει αὐτῷ ὁ Παῦλος· Ὡς δοκεῖ σοι,
ἀββᾶ. καὶ τοῦτο πάλιν ἐπὶ πλεῖον ἔκαμψε
τὸν Ἀντώνιον, τὸ μὴ προσδραμεῖν προθύμως
τῇ τῆς τροφῆς ἀγγελίᾳ ἀλλ' αὐτῷ ἐπιτρέψαι
τὴν ἐξουσίαν. Θὲς οὖν φησιν ὁ Ἀντώνιος
τῷ γέροντι τὴν τράπεζαν. καὶ ὑπήκουσε.
φέρει ἄρτους ὁ Ἀντώνιος, καὶ ἐπιτίθησι τῇ
τραπέζῃ παξαμάτας τέσσαρας ἔχοντας ὡς
ἀπὸ ἓξ οὐγγιῶν. καὶ ἑαυτῷ μὲν ἔβρεξεν ἕνα,
ξηροὶ γὰρ ἦσαν, ἐκείνῳ δὲ τρεῖς. βάλλει
ψαλμὸν ὁ Ἀντώνιος ὃν ᾔδει, καὶ δωδέκατον
αὐτὸν ψάλας, δωδέκατον ηὔξατο, ἵνα καὶ ἐν
τούτῳ δοκιμάσῃ τὸν Παῦλον. ὁ δὲ γέρων προ-

A.   10 Ἀντώνιος] add. τὸ πλέγμα (id quod contexuerat)   21 ἐμικροψύχησεν] add.
οὐδ' ὅλως—διέστρεψε (neque uultum suum omnino auertisse), cf. B 22; then the clause
οὔτε κᾶν—ἠγανάκτησεν

B.   6 ἐκ φοινίκων] om. P   δέξαι] add. καὶ C (мв 1597 βρέξε)   7 ὡς βλέπεις
με] ὡς κἀγώ   9 μόχθῳ πολλῷ] μοχθήσας PC   δὲ] οὖν   10 τὸ πλέγμα] om. P
ἐπιφερόμενος] om. P   12 νῆστει] νῆστι   13 τετάρτην ἡμέραν ἄγοντι] om. PC
14 τοσαύτην ἐπάγων σῆψιν] ταύτην ἐπαγαγὼν τὴν σῆψιν   15 καὶ—16 μοναχῶν] om. P

C.

εἰς τὸ σπήλαιον προσεῖχεν αὐτῷ διὰ θυρίδος ἀκινήτου μένοντος ἐκ τοῦ τόπου ὅλην τὴν ἑβδομάδα, ὑπὸ καύματος φρυγομένου. ἐξ- 3 ελθὼν δὲ μετὰ τὴν ἑβδομάδα,

NOTES.

(Rufinus' Latin of C.)

oberraret, ad monasterium peruenit Antonii, ibique ex loci admonitione et opportunitate consilium capit. cumque adisset Antonium, ut iter ab eo salutis inquireret, ille intuens hominem simplicis naturae esse, respondit ei ita demum eum posse saluari si his quae a se dicerentur obediret. tunc ille omnia quaecumque sibi praeciperet facturum se esse respondit. ut ergo promissionem ejus probaret Antonius ante fores cellulae stanti, Hic, inquit, expecta me orans donec egrediar. et egrediens Antonius mansit intrinsecus per totum diem et per totam noctem ; per fenestram tamen ex occulto frequentius respiciens uidebat eum indesinenter orantem et nusquam prorsus moueri, sed stare in aestu diei et rore noctis, et ita esse mandati memorem ut ne parum quidem loco moueretur. egressus autem die postero Antonius,

17 τάνυ—19 ἐρυσιδωμένους] εἰ καὶ δυσχερέστερον διὰ τὸ ἐρυτιδῶσθαι   20 οὖν] δέ   μέγας] om. P   ὁ γέρων] om. P   21 κἂν πρὸς βραχὺ] om. PC   22 οὐδ' ὅλως—23 διέστρεψε] om. PC   κατανύγει] κατενύγη   ἐπ' αὐτῷ] om. P   25 ὁ Ἀντώνιος· Παπία] om. P   27 ἐπὶ πλεῖον] om. P   29 ἐπιτρέψαι] ἐπιρρίψαι   30 θὲς—34 οὐγγιῶν] θεὶς οὖν τὴν τράπεζαν φέρει ἄρτους. καὶ θεὶς ὁ Ἀντώνιος τοὺς παξαμάδας ἔχοντας ἀνὰ ἓξ οὐγγιῶν   33 ὡς (om. μs 1597)   34 οὐγγιῶν] (μs 1597 οὐγγίας)   καὶ] om. P   35 ξηροὶ] (μs 1597 ξηρὰ)   τρεῖς] add. καὶ   37 καὶ ἐν τούτῳ] om. P   38 δοκιμάσῃ] (μs 1597 δαμάσῃ)   ὁ δὲ γέρων—1 (p. 34) συνηύξατο] ὁ δὲ πάλιν προθύμως συνηύχετο

C. 3 φρυγόμενος

B. P.   3

A.

θυμώτερον τῷ μεγάλῳ συνηύξατο. ᾐρεῖτο γὰρ μᾶλλον ὡς οἶμαι σκορπίους ποιμᾶναι, ἢ μοιχαλλίδῃ συζῆσαι. μετὰ δὲ τὰς δώδεκα προσευχὰς, λέγει τῷ Παύλῳ ὁ μέγας Ἀντώνιος· 5

κάθισον, φησί, καὶ μὴ φάγεις ἕως ἑσπέρας, ἀλλὰ πρόσεχε μόνον τοῖς ἐδωδίμοις. ἑσπέρας δὲ 10 γενομένης. καὶ τοῦ Παύλου μὴ βεβρωκότος, εἶπεν πρὸς αὐτὸν ὁ Ἀντώνιος· Ἀνάστα, εὖξαι, καὶ κάθευδε. ὁ δὲ καταλιπὼν τὴν τράπεζαν ἐποίησεν οὕτως. μεσούσης δὲ τῆς νυκτὸς 15 ἤγειρεν αὐτὸν εἰς εὐχὴν, καὶ ἄχρις ἐνάτης ὥρας ἡμερινῆς παρέτεινεν τὰς εὐχάς. παραθεὶς δὲ πάλιν τράπεζαν, καὶ πάλιν ψάλας καὶ προσευξάμενος,
ἐκαθέσθησαν τοῦ φαγεῖν 20 ἑσπέραν βαθεῖαν. φαγὼν οὖν ὁ μέγας Ἀντώνιος κ.τ.λ.......ἀπὸ μεσονυκτίου ἕως ἡμέρας. P.G. xxxiv. 1082 B, init. ad fin.
καὶ ἔπεμψεν αὐτὸν εἰς τὴν ἔρημον κ.τ.λ....τὴν κατὰ 25 τῶν δαιμόνων ἐλασίαν. 1082 c and D.

Ὡς οὖν ἴδεν τὸν γέροντα κ.τ.λ....παρὰ πάσῃ τῇ ἀδελφότητι. 1082 D, to 1084 A.

FINIS.

B.

θυμώτερον τῷ μεγάλῳ συνηύξατο. ᾐρεῖτο γὰρ ὡς οἶμαι σκορπίους μᾶλλον ποιμᾶναι, ἢ μοιχαλίδι συζῆσαι. μετὰ δὲ τὰς δώδεκα προσευχάς,

ἐκαθέσθησαν τοῦ φαγεῖν ἑσπέρας οὔσης βαθείας. φαγὼν οὖν ὁ μέγας Ἀντώνιος κ.τ.λ.......ἀπὸ μεσονυκτίου ἕως ἡμέρας. As in A.

Ὡς οὖν εἶδε τὸν γέροντα κ.τ.λ....παρὰ πάσης τῆς ἀδελφότητος. As in A.

FINIS.

B.   2 μᾶλλον] after γὰρ, as in A   3 μοιχαλίδι] add. γυναικί   20 τοῦ] om. PC
21 οὔσης] om. P   μέγας] om. PC   22 ἀπὸ] om. PC

It is hardly necessary to point out that the accounts in B and C, though evidently variants of the same tradition, differ considerably in detail. According to B, Paul is represented as breaking his fast on the evening of the fourth day; and after a night spent in prayer, St Anthony declares him to be a monk; nor was it till after some months that he was sent into the desert to live in solitude. According to C, Paul's fast extends over full eight days, [in Rufinus' Latin only two,] and then, after a slight

C.

εἶπεν πρὸς αὐτόν·
Δεῦρο, μετάλαβε τροφῆς. ὡς δὲ παρέθηκεν
τράπεζαν καὶ τὰ σιτά, Κάθισον, φησί, καὶ
μὴ φάγῃς ἄχρις ἑσπέρας, ἀλλὰ πρόσεχε
μόνον τοῖς ἐδωδίμοις. ἑσπέρας δὲ γενο- 10
μένης, καὶ τοῦ Παύλου μὴ βεβρωκότος,
λέγει πρὸς αὐτὸν ὁ Ἀντώνιος· Ἀνάστα,
εὖξαι, καὶ κάθευδε. ὁ δὲ καταλείπων
τὴν τράπεζαν ἐποίησεν οὕτως. μεσα-
ζούσης δὲ τῆς νυκτὸς ἐγείρας αὐτὸν εἰς 15
προσευχήν, ἄχρις ἐννάτης ὥρας ἡμερινῆς
παρέτεινεν τὰς εὐχάς. παραθεὶς δὲ πάλιν
τράπεζαν, ἐκέλευσεν αὐτὸν μεταλαβεῖν. ὡς
δὲ τρίτον τὸν ἄρτον τῷ στόματι προσενή-
νοχεν, ἀναστῆναι προστάξας αὐτῷ καὶ 20
ὕδατος μὴ ἅπτεσθαι.

ἔπεμπεν
εἰς τὴν ἔρημον κ.τ.λ.......τὴν κατὰ τῶν 25
δαιμόνων ἐλασίαν. As in A.

οὓς γὰρ οὐκ ἠδύνατο ὁ μακάριος Ἀντώνιος
ἐκβαλεῖν δαίμονας, τούτους πρὸς Παῦλον 30
ἀπέστελλεν· καὶ αὐθωρὸν ἐξεβάλλοντο.

FINIS.

C. 8 σιτά] σιτία 9 ἄχρις] ἕως
ἐγείρει 17 παρέτεινεν] παρατείνας
τρίτον after ἄρτον 21 ὕδατος] ὕδωρ

NOTES.

(Rufinus' Latin of C.)

instituere eum et docere coepit de singulis quomodo opere manuum solitudinem solaretur: et digitis quidem corporis opus carnale, cogitatione uero mentis et animi intentione operaretur quae Dei sunt. cibum quoque in uesperam ei sumere praecepit, sed obseruare ne umquam ad saturitatem usque perueniret, et praecipue in potu, confirmans non minus per aquae abundantiam phantasias fieri animi quam per uinum calorem corporis crescere. et ubi plene eum qualiter se in singulis agere deberet instruxit, in uicino ei, hoc est tribus a se millibus, cellulam constituit.

C. 26. One sentence occurs which is not found in A: after πᾶσαν ἡμέραν. (Migne, 1082 D) καὶ διδάξας αὐτὸν σπυρίδας πλέκειν, μεθ' ἡμέρας τινὰς κελεύει πάσας αὐτὸν ἀναλύειν τὰς σπυρίδας. καὶ παραλύσας κ.τ.λ. The passage does not occur in the MSS of A (because the fuller account of B has already been given), but a trace of it is found in Rufinus' translation: contextas sportellas resoluere ac denuo contexere.

12 ἀνάστα] ἀναστάς 15 ἐγείρας]
18 τράπεζαν πάλιν 19 δὲ] add. μόνον

meal, St Anthony sends him to the desert for three days. In A the periods of fasting are added together, so that they become twelve days in all: the two accounts of the other tests imposed on Paul by St Anthony are similarly combined; and Paul is represented as being sent into the desert twice.

(c) *Amoun, the First Monk of Nitria.*

In the Latin versions Amoun is found in A 8, B 2, C 30.

When we turn to the Greek texts, we see that the first half of A's account (*P. G.* xxxiv. 1025) coincides with B. The next two paragraphs (1026: Μόνου οὖν αὐτοῦ......ὁ ἀνὴρ διεπράξατο; in Hervet's Latin: Cum is ergo solus......hic vir fecit, Rosweyd, p. 714) are from C; but as they are incorporated bodily without any adjustments, it would throw no light on the

---

A.

Paris Coisl. 370 (cent. x): cf. Migne
P.G. xxxiv. 1026.

Τοῦτο οὖν τὸ θαῦμα διηγήσατο ὁ μακάριος
Ἀθανάσιος ὁ ἐπίσκοπος Ἀλεξανδρείας,
γράψας εἰς τὸν περὶ Ἀντωνίου βίον, ὅτιπέρ
ποτε μοναχῶν ἀποσταλέντων παρὰ
Ἀντωνίου πρὸς Ἀμοῦν φωνῆσαι αὐτόν· 5
ἦν γὰρ ἐν τῇ ἐσωτέρᾳ ἐρήμῳ ὁ
Ἀντώνιος. ὡς δὲ ἀπίεσαν πρὸς αὐτὸν
οἱ ἀδελφοί, ἀναστὰς ὁ γέρων συνεπορεύετο
αὐτοῖς· καὶ μέλλων παρέρχεσθαι τὸν Λύκον
τὸν ποταμὸν ἅμα Θεοδώρῳ τῷ μαθητῇ 10
αὐτοῦ, εὐλαβεῖτο οὖν ὁ ἅγιος ἀποδύσασθαι,
ἵνα μὴ γυμνὸν ἑαυτόν τις ἴδῃ ποτέ. καὶ ἐν
τῷ αὐτὸν διαλογίζεσθαι περὶ τούτου εἰς τὸ
πέραν εὑρέθη τοῦ ποταμοῦ, ὡς ἐν ἐκστάσει
διαπεράσας διὰ πορθμίου ὑπ' ἀγγέλου 15
μετενεχθείς. οἱ δὲ ἀδελφοὶ κολύμβῳ
διεπόρθμευσαν. ὡς δὲ παρεγένοντο
πρὸς Ἀντώνιον, πρῶτος ὁ Ἀντώνιος
εἶπεν πρὸς αὐτόν· τοῦ θεοῦ ἀποκαλύψαντός μοι πολλὰ περὶ σου, καὶ 20
τὴν μετάθεσίν σου δηλώσαντός μοι,
ἀναγκαίως σε πρὸς ἐμαυτὸν προσεκαλεσάμην, ἵνα ἀλλήλων ἀπολαύσαντες,
ὑπὲρ ἀλλήλων πρεσβεύσωμεν. τάξας
δὲ αὐτὸν ἐν τόπῳ τινὶ κεχωρισμένῳ 25
μακρὰν, μὴ ἀναχωρεῖν ἐκεῖθεν ἄχρι

B.

Paris Gr. 1597 (cent. xiii): cf. Meurs.
23—4.

Τούτου θαῦμα διηγήσατο ὁ μακάριος
Ἀθανάσιος ὁ ἐπίσκοπος Ἀλεξανδρείας,
γράψας εἰς τὸν περὶ Ἀντωνίου βίον, ὅτιπερ

μέλλων παρέρχεσθαι τὸν Λύκον
τὸν ποταμὸν ποτε ἅμα Θεοδώρῳ μαθητῇ
ἑαυτοῦ, εὐλαβεῖτο   ἀποδύσασθαι,
ἵνα μὴ γυμνὸν ἑαυτὸν ἴδοι ποτέ. καὶ ἐν
τῷ   ἀπορεῖν   εἰς τὸ
πέραν εὑρέθη τοῦ ποταμοῦ, ὡς ἐν ἐκστάσει
περάσας δίχα πορθμίου ὑπὸ ἀγγέλου μετενεχθείς.

A.   Readings of Paris Gr. 1626 (p) and of Hervet's ms (H).

1 τοῦτο—θαῦμα] τούτου θαῦμα τοιοῦτον p; *Hoc miraculum* H   5 πρὸς Ἀμ. φωνῆσαι
αὐτόν] πρὸς αὐτὸν καὶ φωνοῦντες αὐτόν p ; H has πρὸς αὐτόν (*ad ipsum*) and omits the
rest   8 οἱ ἀδελφοί] om. pH   9 μέλλων] (Coisl. 370 μέλλοντα)   11 οὖν ὁ ἅγιος]
om. pH   12 τις] om. pH   15 διαπεράσας] περάσας p   διὰ] so p and Coisl.
390, 295, 282; H had the true reading δίχα (*absque*)   22 ἀναγκαίως] (Coisl. 370
ἀναγκαῖος)   26 ἄχρι] μέχρι p

present investigation to print them here. Not so, however, when we come to the conclusion of the Life, where the independent and materially different versions of the same tradition, which are found in B and C, are interwoven into a single narrative in A.

C.

Paris Gr. 1600 (cent. xi): cf. Preuschen 91.

Ηλθον δέ ποτε μοναχοί τινες πρὸς αὐτὸν παρὰ 'Αντωνίου ἀποσταλέντες, καὶ φω- 5 νοῦντες αὐτόν· ἦν γὰρ ἐν τῇ ἐσωτέρᾳ ἐρήμῳ ὁ 'Αντώνιος. ὡς δὲ ἀπῇεσαν πρὸς αὐτόν, διῶρύξ τις τοῦ Νείλου ηὔρετο μέση. οἱ δὲ ἀδελφοὶ ἐξαίφνης ἴδον αὐτὸν μετατεθέντα ἐν τῷ πέρατι, 10

αὐτοὶ κολύμβῳ διαπεράσαντες. ἐπεὶ δὲ πρὸς 'Αντώνιον παρεγένοντο, πρῶτος 'Αντώνιος λέγει πρὸς αὐτόν· Τοῦ θεοῦ μου περί σου πολλά μοι ἀποκαλύψαντος, καὶ τὴν μετάθεσίν σου 20 δηλώσαντος, ἀναγκαῖόν σε πρὸς ἐμαυτὸν μετεκαλεσάμην, ἵνα ἀλλήλων ἀπολαύσαντες, ὑπὲρ ἀλλήλων πρεσβεύσωμεν. τάξας δὲ αὐτὸν ἔν τινι τόπῳ κεχωρισμένῳ μακρὰν, μὴ ἀναχωρεῖν ἐκεῖθεν ἄχρι τῆς μεταθέσεως 25 προετρέψατο. τελειωθέντος δὲ αὐτοῦ κατὰ

NOTES.

A. Coislin 370 has been chosen as it is the oldest ms known to me that contains a portion of redaction A; its text is not as good as that of Paris Gr. 1626, or of Hervet's ms; the readings of these two mss are given in the critical notes. This portion of Coislin 282 is from redaction A; thus this single ms contains in different parts three distinct types of the text.

B 14, 15, and 6—11 on next page. The words in small type have fallen out of 1597, but occur in the ordinary B mss; (cf. Meursius).

C. The following is the Latin of Ruffinus, corresponding to C (Rosw. 483):

Sed et multa alia per eum signa Dominus ostendit. nam et fluuium Nilum cum transire uellet, et exuere se erubesceret, uirtute Dei subito in alteram ripam translatus dicitur. beatus autem Antonius in summa admiratione uitae eius iustitiam atque animi uirtutes habuisse memoratur.

B. Readings of Paris Gr. 1628.

2 (ms 1597 ἀρχιεπίσκοπος) 'Αλεξανδρείας, γράψας] om. P   3 ὅτιπερ] ὅτι   9 μέλλων παρέρχεσθαι] παρερχόμενος   10 τὸν] om.   ποτε] om.   Θεοδώρῳ] add. τῷ   11 ἑαυτοῦ] αὐτοῦ   εὐλαβεῖτο] καὶ εὐλαβούμενος   12 ἑαυτὸν] αὐτὸν   ἴδοι] ἴδῃ (sic alii)   ποτέ—13 ἀπορεῖν] om.   14 τοῦ—15 περάσας] om.   15 ὑπὸ ἀγγέλου after μετενεχθείς

A.

τῆς μεταθέσεως διεκελεύσατο. τελειωθέντος δὲ αὐτοῦ κατὰ μόνας, εἶδεν
αὐτοῦ τὴν ψυχὴν ὁ Ἀντώνιος ἀναλαμβανομένην εἰς τὸν οὐρανὸν ὑπὸ
ἁγίων ἀγγέλων. οὗτός ἐστιν ὁ Ἀμοῦν ὁ 5
οὕτως βιώσας καὶ οὕτως τελευτήσας.

τοῦτον τὸν Λύκον τὸν ποταμὸν μετὰ
δειλίας ἐγὼ πορθμίῳ διεπέρασά ποτε. 10
διῶρυξ γάρ ἐστιν τοῦ μεγάλου Νείλου.

B.

οὗτός ἐστιν ὁ Ἀμοῦν ὁ οὕτως
βιώσας καὶ οὕτως τελευτήσας, ὡς τὸν
μακάριον Ἀντώνιον ἰδεῖν τὴν ψυχὴν αὐτοῦ ὑπὸ
ἀγγέλων ἀναγομένην εἰς τὸν οὐρανόν. τοῦτον
τὸν Λύκον ποταμὸν μετὰ δειλίας ἐγὼ πορθμῷ
παρῆλθόν ποτε. διῶρυξ γάρ ἐστιν τοῦ μεγάλου
Νίλου.

A. 1 διεκελεύσατο] προετρέψατο pH (hortatus est)   5 ἁγίων] om. pH
9 τοῦτον to end om. p, found in the other four authorities   10 διεπέρασα] παρῆλθον
Coisl. 295

A study of these three sets of parallel passages will probably
have sufficed to convince the reader that the Long Recension
of the Lausiac History is not an original work, but a con-
glomerate fashioned out of the Short Recension and the *Historia
Monachorum*. But since A has been in unchallenged possession
for so long a time, and has in our own day been accepted without
suspicion as the genuine work of Palladius, even by prominent
critics who have made a special study of the subject, it seems
desirable that the case against this recension should here once
for all be fully stated, so that one prolific source of misconception
and confusion in the investigation of monastic origins may be
finally removed. In the following section, therefore, it will be
shown that A contains the recognised marks of a text that is not
original, but composite and derived.

§ 6. ORGANIC CORRUPTIONS IN THE LONG RECENSION OF THE 'HISTORIA LAUSIACA.'

By the term *Organic Corruptions* I mean such corruptions as
are not due to the errors of copyists, but are inherent in the very
structure of the text, e.g., anachronisms, contradictions, confusions,
doublets, etc. Striking instances of such anomalies in A are found

C.

μόνας, ἴδεν αὐτοῦ τὴν ψυχὴν ὁ Ἀντώνιος
ἀναλαμβανομένην ὑπὸ ἀγγέλων εἰς τὸν
οὐρανόν.

B 6—11. Cf. Nóte, p. 37.

B. 5 οὗτος—6 βιώσας] οὗτος τοίνυν ὁ Ἀμμοῦν οὕτως ἐβίωσε   6 τελευτήσας]
ἐτελεύθη (sic)   7 ἰδεῖν after αὐτοῦ   8 εἰς τὸν οὐρανόν] om.   9 Λύκον] om.
πορθμῷ] πορθμίῳ   10 ποτε] om.

in the account of Abbot Or, in the Latin A 9, B 2, C 2. The
phenomena presented are quite different from those of the cases
already considered, and it will be enough to print just so much of
the texts as may enable the reader to reconstruct the three
accounts out of *P. G.* xxxiv. 1026—1028.

A.	B.	C.
Ἐν τῷ ὄρει τούτῳ τῆς Νιτρίας γέγονεν ἀνὴρ θαυμάσιος ἀββᾶ Ὤρ ὄνομα αὐτῷ πατὴρ μονὰς ἔχων ἀδελφῶν χιλίων, κ.τ.λ. . . . . ἰδὼν δὲ ἡμᾶς ὁ ἀνὴρ κ.τ.λ. . . . . . . ὡς ἀγγέλων χορούς ὑμνούντων τὸν θεόν. ᾧ πολλὴν προσεμαρτύρει ἀρετὴν πᾶσα μὲν ἡ ἀδελφότης κ.τ.λ. [1028 A] . . . . Ἐγὼ γὰρ αὐτὸν οὐ κατείληφα ζῶντα κ.τ.λ. . . . . ἐλάλησέν τί ποτε.	Ἐν τῷ ὄρει τούτῳ τῆς Νιτρίας γέγονεν ἀνήρ τις θαυμάσιος ἀσκητὴς ὀνόματι Ὤρ· ᾧ πολλὴν προσεμαρτύρει ἀρετὴν πᾶσα μὲν ἡ ἀδελφότης κ.τ.λ. [as A] . . . . ἐγὼ γὰρ αὐτὸν οὐ κατείληφα ζῶντα κ.τ.λ. . . . . . ἐλάλησέν τί ποτε.	Ἐθεάσαμεθα δὲ καὶ ἕτερον ἄνδρα θαυμαστὸν ἐν Θηβαΐδι ἀββᾶ Ὤρ ὄνομα αὐτῷ πατὴρ μοναστηρίων ἀδελφῶν χιλίων κ.τ.λ. . . . : . . . . ἰδὼν δὲ ἡμᾶς ὁ ἀνήρ, κ.τ.λ. . . . . ὡς ἀγγέλων χορούς ὑμνούντων τὸν θεόν. FINIS.
FINIS.	FINIS.	

(A 4 μονὰς ἔχων, so Paris 1626 and Hervet.)

We learn from B that a certain Or had dwelt in Mount Nitria
(near Alexandria), but was dead before Palladius came there; the

account is quite short, and professes to be based on what Palladius learned from Melania, who had visited Nitria at an earlier date and had seen Or. The party of seven whose tour is described in C visited a monk named Hor near Lycopolis in the Thebaid (Upper Egypt). Now Palladius retired to Mount Nitria in 390 or 391 at the latest; whereas the tour described in C has been fixed at the end of 394. Hence it appears that B and C speak of different men with similar names, or perhaps the same name[1], one of whom was dead before 390, the other still alive in 394; one of whom lived in Nitria, the other in the Thebaid. But in A the two accounts are combined and the two men are made into one. Besides the anachronism, a contradiction stands in the Greek text of Migne. For in the part taken from C the personal character of the interview is retained throughout, even the clause: ἰδὼν δὲ ἡμᾶς, "seeing us he rejoiced and embraced us, and washed our feet with his own hands"; while at the end the statement of B is introduced: ἐγὼ αὐτὸν οὐ κατείληφα ζῶντα, "I did not find him alive." I have already stated that Migne's text is not a true text of A but a manufactured text; and in the extant MS. copies of A now at Paris the open contradiction has been removed by the elimination of the clause in B: ἐγὼ κ.τ.λ. But that the original text of A contained the contradiction may be seen from the Latin of Hervet, where the clause of B still stands: ego cum non offendi vivum. A clumsy effort has indeed been made here also to remove the contradiction, by reading αὐτούς and αὐτῶν instead of ἡμᾶς and ἡμῶν in the above cited clause taken from C, thus making Or embrace and wash the feet not of the seven travellers, but of a troop of three thousand monks who came to live with him.

We pass from a case in which two men are turned into one in A, to a case of the converse, where one man is made into two. B 2 and C 23 give independent accounts of Ammonius, one of the famous "Four Tall Brothers." That this is the Ammonius in question in both places seems beyond doubt; for in B, and in the Latin version of C, his three brothers are mentioned by name. The Greek manuscripts of C indeed omit the first half of the Life

[1] The distinction between the two forms of the name, Or and Hor, is not consistently maintained by the authorities for the texts.

as it stands in Rufinus, the part containing this explicit identification. But from what is said in Appendix I. there is ground for believing that the Latin here represents the original text. In any case, it will hardly be questioned that Ammonius the Tall is the one intended. Now B 2 is reproduced in A 12, and the second half of the Latin C 23 in A 70; so that they appear as biographies of different men.

Similarly A contains a double account of the Nitrian monks, one in c. 7 from B 2, the other in c. 69 from C 21 and 22; also a double account of the Tabennisiote monks, one in cc. 38 and 39 from B 19, the other in c. 48 from C 3.

Moreover, whereas each of the recensions B and C has its own Epilogue, perfectly natural and in place; at the end of A we find both these Epilogues, one after the other, so that the work has a double conclusion. C's Epilogue is an enumeration of the dangers encountered by the party of seven on their journey through Egypt from Lycopolis to Alexandria, and is utterly out of place in A, being separated from its context by some seventy chapters, which deal with monks visited by Palladius in Asia Minor, Palestine, and Italy.

An examination of the parallel texts printed in the preceding section shows that the words and clauses found only in A are of the nature of mere connecting links or transitional phrases, such as a Redactor would have to insert in the process of combining two narratives; and that the alterations and omissions also are for the most part manifest devices of the same kind. At times however the Redactor has not been at the pains to make the necessary readjustments. For instance, c. 125 of A begins thus: Ἐν αἷς καὶ Παύλῃ τῇ Ῥωμαίᾳ τῇ μητρὶ Τοξοτίου, γυναικὶ εἰς τὴν πνευματικὴν πολιτείαν ἀστειοτάτῃ. Here the gender of the relative is at fault, for the preceding four chapters are all about men; the datives Παύλῃ, etc., are unexplained; and the sentence has no verb. Restore the passage to its context in B 29, and all is right: Πλείσταις δὲ ἀστείαις εἰς ἀρετὴν συντετύχηκα παρθένοις τε καὶ χήραις· ἐν αἷς καὶ Παύλῃ κ.τ.λ.[1]

And not only have we here bad grammar, but also bad history.

---

[1] The full context in B is: Ἀναγκαῖον δὲ ἡγησάμην κ.τ.λ. (= P.G. xxxiv. 1220 D). ... παρθένοις τε καὶ χήραις· (1225 A) ἐν αἷς καὶ Παύλῃ κ.τ.λ. (1233 c).

For in cc. 117—124 of A, Palladius has been giving an account of
a group of persons who were leading ascetic lives in Rome and its
neighbourhood and whom he had met on the occasion of his visit
to that city (405)—the younger Melania, Pinianus her husband,
Pammachius, Macarius and Constantius. A makes Palladius continue (c. 125): "Among whom was also Paula." This implies
that Paula was living at Rome at the same time as the others,
and that Palladius had met her there—a double anachronism.
She had left Rome and Italy for ever in 385 and had died in 404.

Similarly B supplies the key to another chronological difficulty
presented by A. A 142 begins: "At that time it fell out that we
were travelling together from Jerusalem to Egypt." But there is
nothing in the preceding chapter of A, or indeed for several
chapters back, to afford any chronological note. On turning to
the same passage in B, it is found to form part of an account of
the two Melanias (c. 42), and the passage immediately preceding
the words "At that time," relates their departure from Rome and
the subsequent sack of the city by Alaric. Thus the note of time
becomes quite clear. Moreover we can see how the mistake crept
into A. B treats of the two Melanias in c. 33, in the first half of
42, and in 49. A throws these detached accounts into one narrative (117, 118, 119), and takes up later the second half of B 42
(142, 143), retaining the words "At that time," though they are
now detached from the original context which explained them.

From the Table given at the beginning of § 5 for the analysis
of the accounts of John of Lycopolis in A, B and C, it appears
that B and C each contain a personal account of a visit of the
writer to John; in B the visit is paid by Palladius alone, in C by
a party of seven, none of whom are named. The two distinct
accounts of the two different personal visits in B and C are combined in A thus:—Palladius tells us in B how on his return to
Evagrius and his friends he related to them all he had seen and
heard; and it is added that after two months they also went to
visit John. In A the party of seven (whose tour in the Thebaid
and visit to John is described in C) is identified with Evagrius'
party; and the narrative of the interview of the seven with John
(C 4, 5, 6, 7, 8) is introduced as being what Evagrius and his
friends afterwards related to Palladius: "And they told us the

following,"—a clause not found in B.   But it can be demonstrated that the party in C cannot have been that of Evagrius.   For the statement made in C is preserved in A, that the party had come from Jerusalem; whereas Evagrius and his disciples came from Nitria, where Evagrius had been for upwards of ten years.   Moreover, in the interview described in C, John asked his visitors if there was any cleric among them.   They replied in the negative. Now one member of the party was a deacon, though the circumstance was known to one only of his companions, and out of modesty he like the rest said that he was not a cleric, wishing to conceal his dignity; John, however, disclosed his secret.   Now as it stands in A, this deacon must needs be identified with Evagrius himself.   He was fifty years of age at the time; and it is quite impossible to suppose that the fact of his being a deacon should have been unknown to his own disciples, who are represented both in B and A as being his companions on his visit to John.   Evagrius therefore cannot have been the subject of the incident related by C, and the application in A of the anecdote to him and his disciples evidently betrays the hand of one who was not personally acquainted with him.   Again, the party of seven, whose tour is described in C, paid a visit to Evagrius himself[1] who therefore cannot have been of their number.   And there was a second deacon among those who are said in B to have gone to see John after Palladius' return; for according to the Greek manuscripts of B, and according to the manuscript of A used by Hervet, one of Evagrius' companions on the journey was his disciple Albinius, who is known to have been a deacon[2]; whereas in the party of seven who visited John there was only one cleric.   Lastly, the true text in A reads: "We were *seven* brothers in the desert of Nitria, I and Evagrius and Albinius and Ammonius."   Thus A's attempt to combine the two narratives by identifying the seven unknown travellers of C with Evagrius and his friends, involves no fewer than five contradictions.

It is certainly a matter of surprise that a text thus teeming with palpable corruptions of all kinds, should not only have passed muster up to the present, but should in our day have been defended

---

[1] *Historia Monachorum*, 27.

[2] *Historia Lausiaca*, A 91, B 35.

as genuine even by such critics as Weingarten, Lucius and Zöckler, the latter declaring it to be a "better text" than that of Meursius (B)[1].

I have already said that this Study was commenced on the basis of the Latin translations.   Naturally the evidence did not stand out with the same clearness and force as it now does from the Greek texts.   But yet an independent study of the Latin had satisfied me, before I investigated the labours of others, that A could not be the authentic text of Palladius, but was a fusion by a later Redactor of the two independent works, B and C.   It was not until I had reached this position that I looked to see what others had said upon the subject.   It was no small satisfaction to find that Tillemont had anticipated my results on the main point; his treatment of the question fills only one page, but he decides without hesitation in favour of what is practically the view enunciated above[2].   Unfortunately he complicated it by the hypothesis that the original of C was the Latin of Rufinus, and that the Greek manuscripts of C represented a translation of the Latin. Ceillier[3] (1742) and Fontanini[4] (1745) adopt Tillemont's view; and as late as 1851 Fessler still puts it forward[5].   But this partial recognition has had no practical effect; since A, not B, has invariably been used by historians and theologians as if it were the authentic text.   Nay more; two eminent critics who have set themselves to study the Greek sources of Egyptian monastic history, Dr Weingarten and Dr Lucius, actually face the question, and mention Tillemont's hypothesis only to set it aside as quite untenable[6].   Weingarten's argument—Why have recourse to a

---

[1] *Askese und Mönchtum*, 220.

[2] *Mémoires*, xi. 641 (Note vii.); p. 647 in Venice edition. (The difference is due to the fact that in this volume the numbers 547—552 are repeated with a * in the Paris edition.)

[3] *Auteurs Sacrés*, x. 72.

[4] *Vita Rufini*, Lib. ii. cap. xii. § vi.; cf. *Opera*, ed. Vallarsi (Migne, *P. L.* xxi. 240—243).   Fontanini indulges in a hope that now that the genuine Lausiac History has been pointed out, "nemo amplius cum larvis luctabitur."

[5] *Institutiones Patrologiae*, ii. 214 (note); in bringing this work up to date Jungmann preserves the note indeed, but introduces Amélineau's theory in the text (ii. pars prior, pp. 202, 211, 212).

[6] Weingarten: "An eine Interpolation durch einen Späteren, der etwa das Werk des Rufinus ins Griechische übersetzt und in den Palladius hineingetragen,

theory of interpolation, since Palladius shows himself credulous enough to accept wonders wherever he found them[1]?—need not be discussed in face of the positive evidence that has been adduced in proof of the fact that A is an interpolated text. It is necessary, however, to examine in detail the arguments put forward by Lucius.

Before I proceed to this discussion, I shall earn the thanks of my readers by reprinting in full the Note in which Tillemont discusses the various documents. It will afford a succinct exposition of the whole problem.

Diverses choses ajoutées à la Lausiaque: Du Paradis d'Heraclide.

Nous trouvons presque mot à mot dans Pallade l'histoire que Rufin a faite des solitaires : et cela tient depuis le 43ᵉ chapitre en partie jusqu'au 76. Il y a peu d'apparence que Pallade qui paroist partout avoir eu beaucoup de simplicité et de fidelité, et beaucoup de soin à marquer d'où il avoit appris ce qu'il disoit, ait inseré toute l'histoire de Rufin dans la sienne, sans en avertir en aucun endroit ; surtout y ayant beaucoup de choses personnelles qu'il se seroit attribuées par ce mélange contre la verité et la vraisemblance. Car par exemple, Pallade qui avoit rapporté fort au long la visite qu'il avoit faite à Saint Jean de Lycople, ne peut pas s'attribuer celle que d'autres luy firent ensuite ni dire qu'il estoit avec luy lorsqu'il vit par esprit de prophetie qu'on apportoit à Alexandrie les nouvelles de la victoire de Theodose contre Eugène. Je croy qu'il suffit de lire ce chapitre pour demeurer convaincu que ce n'est point Pallade qui a mélé l'histoire de Rufin avec la sienne ; et qu'on ne peut point dire non plus comme l'a cru Rosweide, que Pallade ayant écrit cette histoire telle que nous l'avons aujourd'hui en grec, Rufin en traduisit une partie en latin ; quand nous ne saurions pas d'ailleurs que Rufin a fait son histoire longtemps avant l'an 420.   Et mesme il est mort dès 410.

La vérité est donc apparemment que les Vies des Pères écrites par Rufin ayant esté traduites en grec : (et on en a encore plusieurs manuscrits sous differens titres et non sous le nom de Rufin ;) il s'est trouvé quelqu'un qui voyant que cet ouvrage estoit sur le mesme sujet que celui de Pallade, en a voulu faire un seul corps ; et peut-estre que d'autres ensuite y ont entremélé d'autres choses comme l'histoire qu'en cite Saint Jean de Damas, et qui ne s'y trouve point que dans un manuscrit dont nous parlerons bientost.   On

braucht man kaum zu denken ; denn aus dem allein, was Palladius von sich selbst berichtet, ergiebt sich ein Charakter, der Wunder hernahm, wo er sie fand." (*Op. cit.* p. 26, note.) Lucius: "Das System Tillemonts ist jedoch nicht haltbar." (*Op. cit.* p. 174, note.)

[1] Cf. preceding note.

pourroit encore sans doute trouver d'autres preuves de cette confusion, comme de ce qu'il y est parlé en deux endroits, des moines de Nitrie et de ceux de Tabenne.

Mais ce qui est bien remarquable, c'est que nous avons une ancienne traduction de Pallade, où toutes ces additions tirées de Rufin ne se trouvent point. Il y a encore quelques autres endroits differens du grec que nous avons, soit pour le sens, soit pour l'ordre. De sorte qu'il est visible qu'elle a esté faite sur d'autres copies, qu'on ne peut douter avoir esté plus correctes en quelques endroits. Mais dans ceux où elles estoient conformes à la nostre, cette traduction suit et exprime fort bien son texte. Je ne sçay d'où vient qu'on luy a donné le nom de Paradis ou de Jardin d'Heraclide. Il est certain qu'on n'a jamais pu pretendre l'attribuer à Heraclide Évesque d'Éphèse, puisqu'on y voit, aussibien que dans le grec que l'auteur estoit Évesque dans la Bithynie. Mais je ne pense pas que personne fasse difficulté de reconnoistre avec Baronius et Rosweide, que cet Heraclide est la mesme chose que Pallade. Il s'en trouve des manuscrits qui portent le nom de Pallade.

Rosweide donne encore une traduction de Pallade d'un auteur inconnu, qu'il croit estre ancien: mais il y manque diverses choses: et on n'y trouve rien des saintes que Socrate nous assure avoir fait une partie considerable de l'ouvrage de Pallade. C'est sans doute cette traduction qu'on dit avoir esté donnée dès le commencement de l'impression, et réimprimée à Cologne en 1547.

Dans la traduction ordinaire de Pallade, qui est de Gentien Hervet, il y a des endroits qu'on n'avoit point eus en grec, jusqu'à ce que Mr. Cotelier les a trouvez dans des manuscrits, et les a fait imprimer en 1686. Il y ajoute mesme quelquefois au latin d'Hervet. Mais rien de tout cela ne se trouve dans Heraclide: de sorte que nous n'avons garde ni de nous assurer nous mesmes, ni d'assurer les autres que ces endroits viennent de Pallade. Il y en a plusieurs qui viennent de Rufin: et je pense qu'on auroit peine à recevoir ce qui y est dit de la mort de S. Amon. Dans l'un des manuscrits de Mr. Cotelier on trouve l'histoire que S. Jean de Damas cite de Pallade: et cela suffit pour justifier la bonne foy de ce Saint, qui a mis ce qu'il a trouvé dans ses livres, mais non pas pour trouver que cet endroit soit de Pallade. Mr. Cotelier mesme ne l'a point donné sous son nom en donnant les autres.

On trouve aussi dans Heraclide quelques endroits qui ne sont point dans le grec: et ils sont marquez dans l'édition de Rosweide. Celui qui regarde Sabinienne, paroist tout à fait venir de Pallade.

§ 7. THE SHORT RECENSION NOT AN ABRIDGMENT OF THE LONG; NOR THE LONG AN AUTHOR'S SECOND EDITION OF THE SHORT.

The discussion of Dr Lucius' position may best be opened by the question: If A is the true Lausiac History, what is B? Dr

Lucius replies: An abridgment of A. We must begin by testing the four arguments on which he bases this theory[1].

(1) He says that B is an arbitrary abridgment of A, made in the interests of later orthodoxy, so that all passages favourable to Origenism are eliminated; and in proof he mentions pp. 941, 962, 971, 972[2].—The Greek text of B refutes this argument; if any such tendency really has been at work in the Latin, it is due to the translator, or to the copyists.

(2) All superfluous matter is cut out and its place is supplied by more interesting notices from other sources[3].—Lucius gives no references to instances of this process; nor am I able to find any.

(3) There is matter common to B and C, e.g. the accounts of Amoun, the Macarii, and Paul the Simple; this shows that B and C are not independent works fused together in A.—This statement is not in accord with the facts. There are indeed in B and C lives of the same person, or of persons of the same name; but they are in all cases perfectly independent accounts.

(4) The account given by Socrates of the Lausiac History shows that his text was identical with A, and already contained the matter of C. Lucius refers in particular to Socrates' statement that in the Lausiac History may be seen how wild beasts were obedient to the solitaries[4]; he says that this can apply only to A 49, 50, 53[5] = C 4, 6, 8.—The anecdotes, however, about an antelope and a hyena in the Life of Macarius of Alexandria (B 6),

---

[1] *Die Quellen*, etc. (*Zeitschrift für Kirchengeschichte*, 1885), p. 174, note.

[2] The pages refer to ed. 1 of Rosweyd.

[3] Lucius' words are "Alles Nebensächliche wird beseitigt, und durch interessantere Notizen aus anderen Quellen ersetzt."

[4] Ὅπως τε αὐτοῖς τὰ θηρία ὑπήκουν (*Hist. Eccl.* IV. 23). This is the only part of Socrates' description of the work adduced in proof by Lucius. But it will be proper to notice here that Rosweyd based his verdict in favour of A on another statement made by Socrates in the same place—that in the Lausiac History "an account is given of women also who undertook the same course of life as the men there recorded." Rosweyd adds: "There is more about women as well as men in Hervet's edition [=A], as very little is said about women in the other editions" (*Vitae Patrum*, Prolegomenon XIV., Migne, *P. L.* LXXIII. 52); and he decides the question on this single consideration. But his premiss is incorrect; for the information given in B concerning the female solitaries is precisely the same as that in A.

[5] Lucius erroneously gives A 59 as corresponding to C 8.

and anecdotes in the Lives of Didymus (B 1) and of Pachon (B 11), seem enough to account for Socrates' words.

While the arguments of Lucius are thus found to be invalid, there exist on the other hand strong positive arguments against the hypothesis that B is an abridgment of A. In the first place, it is evident that "abridgment" is not a correct description of the process to which A would have been subjected; for the process would have been this:—that the operator, having before him the work A and the work C, simply cut out from A all the matter which its author had taken from C. On this theory, to take a single example, in the case of Paul the Simple the removal of matter borrowed from C left behind in B, not the mere mangled remains of A, but another life of different tenor, yet self-consistent and complete, constructed without change of word or clause, and bearing no trace of the dislocation which the text had undergone[1]. It is impossible to conceive that B's Life of Paul the Simple had not a prior independent existence; or that the fact that A is thus divisible into two distinct Lives is not due to its being a fusion of two pre-existing documents. Moreover, B contains matter not found in A; and this not simply in cases that might be accounted for by mere faults in MSS., but in matter that enters into the very organism of B; for instance, the prophecy of John of Lycopolis about Theodosius' victories and death, and St Anthony's vision of Amoun's soul going up to heaven (both printed in § 5). Again, if B is abridged from A, the man who made the abridgment must have been a critic of no ordinary penetration; for he must again and again have detected and silently rectified blunders and confusions of A, and have removed contradictions which seem to have escaped the notice even of the critics of our day. M. Amélineau is quite satisfied with A's identification of the two parties who visited John of Lycopolis[2]; while Dr Lucius twice follows A in confusing together the two abbots Hor[3]. Lastly, the difference of order and grouping in the second portion of the two recensions has already been mentioned (§ 6). The order in B is certainly in these places the right order, for it avoids the two anachronisms

---

[1] See the three parallel texts printed pp. 30—35.
[2] *De Historia Lausiaca*, p. 59.
[3] *Op. cit.* pp. 178, 197.

which are there pointed out as following from A's arrangement. It will hardly be maintained that the wrong order, which involves anachronisms and absurdities, is the author's order, and that the true order is due to the insight of the later writer who merely made an abridgment.

And yet this is the position which Dr Zöckler must be prepared to defend; for in speaking of its relation to the Greek texts, he pronounces the *Paradisus Heraclidis* to be "a miserable secondary source," which has "*transposed* and greatly abridged the matter of Palladius": he declares that "its later origin and inferior historical worth cannot on the whole be doubted," and that "alongside of the canonical Palladius it exhibits an essentially apocryphal character[1]." It must be noted that Zöckler is professing to compare the *Paradisus* not only with Du Duc's text but also with that of Meursius: but it is evident that he cannot have instituted the comparison even in a cursory way; for, as has been pointed out, in subject-matter and structure the *Paradisus Heraclidis* and Meursius are practically identical. And I am at a loss to imagine what can be the signs of the apocryphal character of B, either in its Greek or in its Latin form, as compared with A. For, to repeat what has already been demonstrated, the only difference in regard of subject-matter between A and B is the absence from B of all matter belonging to C.

I conceive that it must be taken as certain that B is not an abridgment of A, nor derived from A by any discoverable process.

The only remaining hypothesis whereby the Palladian authorship of A could be maintained is that B is a first edition, and A a

---

[1] "Die Frage, wie unser griechischer Palladiustext (veröffentlicht zuerst 1616 durch Meursius, dann besser in demselben Jahrhundert durch Ducäus und Cotelier) zu den aus alter Zeit überlieferten Parallelrecensionen, insbesondere zu der unter eines gewissen Heraklides Namen gehenden (die den Namen *Paradisus* führt und das Palladianische Material teils vielfach umstellt, teils stark verkürzt), sich verhalte, ist für unseren Zweck von geringem Interesse. Am jüngeren Ursprung und geringeren Geschichtswert derselben kann im allgemeinen nicht gezweifelt werden; die Heraklides-Relation insbesondere zeigt gegenüber dem kanonischen Palladius wesentlich apokryphen Charakter. Wir überlassen, zumal selbständig bedeutsames Geschichtsmaterial diesen trüben Nebenquellen sich nicht oder kaum abgewinnen lässt, die Lösung des literar-kritischen Problems anderen Händen." (*Askese und Mönchtum*, 220.) This is the most recent critical utterance upon the subject.

second edition, "enlarged and improved," by Palladius himself.
If this hypothesis fails, it only remains to conclude that the
incorporation of C in the Lausiac History was not the handiwork
of Palladius.

The idea that B and A are successive editions of the work,
made by the author himself, has not been hitherto put forward;
but it is a possible one, and must be examined[1]. Let us briefly
consider what is involved in the theory.

It would have to be supposed that in the account of John
of Lycopolis it is Palladius who represents the "great" Evagrius'
own disciples as not knowing that their master was a deacon;
an absurdity which Palladius, the close friend and enthusiastic
admirer of Evagrius, would have felt much more keenly than we
do. It would have to be supposed that Palladius inserted the
second account of Ammonius the Tall, as if it related to some
one else, failing to recognise C's picture of his illustrious friend.
It would have to be supposed that Palladius re-arranged the
latter portion of his work in such a way as to introduce a gross
anachronism and misstatement about one episode in his own life,
and to separate another from an event so striking as the Sack
of Rome, thereby making meaningless the chronological note
which he gives to fix the date. It would have to be supposed
that it was Palladius who disfigured his own work by all the
errors, confusions, doublets and solecisms which have been pointed
out in these pages as existing in A but not in B.

That these errors exist in A is certain; but of all men
Palladius is the least likely to have made them. And seeing
that B, taken by itself, and C, taken by itself, are straightforward
and consistent narratives, the conclusion seems inevitable that

---

[1] Tillemont, indeed, is disposed to believe that Palladius "retouched" his work
some time after its publication in 420 (*Mémoires*, xi. 640 [ed. Paris], 646 [ed.
Venice]). His reason for so thinking is that in the Greek of A, in the body of the
life of Philoromus (A 113, B 32), and of that of a monk of Ancyra (A 115, B 56),
these persons are spoken of as still alive; whereas at the end of the two accounts
they seem to be spoken of as already dead; and he points out that in the Latin
version of B these discrepancies are avoided. Whatever may be the explanation
of the discrepancies, they lend no countenance to the theory that B is the first
edition and A the second; for the Greek text of B, both in Meursius' edition and in
the mss., agrees in these places with A.

the errors of A are due, not to the author, but to a later and blundering Redactor, who fused together pre-existing works relating to matters concerning which he had no personal experience or knowledge.

And, after all, this recension A is but one, and the most ingenious, out of upwards of half-a-dozen different attempts to fuse the same two works, to be found among the Greek MSS. at Paris alone.

§ 8. Sozomen and the 'Historia Lausiaca.'

So far we have been occupied in removing long standing sources of confusion in regard of the *Historia Lausiaca*; we come now to one that has originated in our own day. It has generally been recognised that the accounts of the Egyptian monks found in the Latin *Historia Monachorum*, in the Lausiac History, and in Sozomen are closely related; and hitherto it had been accepted by critics old and new that Sozomen's notices were directly derived from these two Histories. Dr Lucius, however, in his article so often referred to, started a new theory, viz. that Sozomen had not before him either the *Historia Monachorum* or the *Historia Lausiaca*; but that all three writers made independent use of a common Greek source no longer extant. It must be remembered that Lucius laboured under the disadvantage of not knowing of the existence of the Greek MSS. of either B or C, although one of the former had been printed by Meursius in 1616, and four of the latter described and in part printed by Cotelier in 1686. He assumes, moreover, that A is the authentic Lausiac History, and that it was Palladius himself who in writing it introduced the matter which is found also in C, and which, so Lucius maintains, was taken alike by him and Rufinus from the hypothetical common source. Lucius' theory has quite recently been endorsed by Grützmacher[1] and Zöckler[2]; the former of whom, however, so far modifies it, in

---

[1] *Pachomius und das älteste Klosterleben* (pp. 1—4).

[2] In 1893 Zöckler argued vigorously against Lucius' theory (*Evagrius Ponticus*, 99—103); but by 1897 he was converted to it (*Askese und Mönchtum*, 213, 220).

deference to Amélineau's publications, as to believe that the lost Greek work was itself but a translation of Coptic materials. As a corollary of the theory, Grützmacher leaves on one side as of no value the notices of St Pachomius and his monasteries found in Palladius and Sozomen. Basset, too, in the Introduction to his translation of the Ethiopic Rules of St Pachomius, accepts the Lucius-Amélineau hypothesis as an ascertained fact, and draws from it the same practical conclusions as Grützmacher in regard to Palladius and Sozomen[1]. Thus Lucius' speculations are a living influence, and (as I believe) a source of error and misconception in the investigation of early monastic history; and this fact is an additional reason why it is necessary to examine carefully and in some detail the whole position. Moreover, the solution of an important problem in the textual criticism of the Lausiac History depends upon the question in hand.

Dr Lucius maintains, then: (1) that there existed a Greek book, now lost, containing the matter of the *Historia Monachorum*, the bulk of that of the *Historia Lausiaca*, and an indefinite quantity of additional matter, including probably information about monks of Asia Minor, Palestine, and the East; (2) that Rufinus translated into Latin a section of this book; (3) that Palladius made up his Lausiac History out of the same section and other portions of the same book (together with a small amount of matter from a second lost hypothetical source, and from various lost writings of Evagrius[2]); (4) that Sozomen's chapters on the monks were also based upon this same lost book.

A detailed examination of the minute discrepancies adduced by Lucius, as showing that Sozomen's account is not derived from the *Historia Monachorum* or the *Historia Lausiaca*, is made in Appendix II. Here it is enough to state the general result: viz. that by the establishment of B as the true Lausiac History, and the production of the Greek MSS. of C, nearly all the alleged discrepancies vanish. Of the difficulties that remain, no one is of any serious weight; nor taken together do they raise even a cumulative presumption that the portions of Sozomen containing

---

[1] *Les Apocryphes Éthiopiens*, VIII. *Les Règles attribuées à saint Pakhôme.* (Paris, 1896.)

[2] Lucius, pp. 193—195.

abridgments of matter found in B and C were derived from any other source than these two documents.

On the other hand, when we examine the text of Sozomen, Book VI. cc. 28, 29, 30, and the first half of 31, and compare it with B and C, we find positive reasons for holding that he derived his information directly from these two works[1]. In order to make what follows more easily intelligible a Table is drawn out, comparing Sozomen's order and grouping of the names first with B and C, and then with A.

Cap.	SOZOMEN (Book VI.).	B or C		A
28.	John of Lycopolis	C	1	43
	Or		2	9
	Ammoun the Tabennesiot		3	48
	Be		4	49
	Theonas		6	50
	Copres		9	54
	Helles		11	59
	Elias		12	51
	Apelles		15	60
	Isidore		17	71
	Serapion		18	76
	Dioscorus		20	68
	Eulogius		14	75
29.	Apollos		7	52
	Dorotheus	B	2	2
	Piammon	C	32	72
	John of Diolcos		33	73
	Benjamine	B	14	13
	Marcus		21	21
	Macarius (the Homicide)		17	17
	Apollonius (the Merchant)		15	14
	Moses (the Robber)		22	22
	Paul in Ferme		23	23
	Pachon		27	29
	Stephen		28	30
	Moses (the Libyan)		46	88
	Pior		45 & 46	87 & 88

[1] This is the section of Sozomen which best illustrates the point under discussion; but he used B and C also in I. 13 and 14, III. 14, and elsewhere. In Appendix II. a list is given of the various sources of the monastic portions of his *Ecclesiastical History*. Sozomen's account of Pachomius (III. 14) will be examined separately in that appendix.

Cap.	SOZOMEN (Book VI.).	B or C		A
30.	Origenes	C	26	
	Didymus		24	
	Chronius		25	
	Arsisius, Putubastes, Arsion, Serapion ...	B	7	7
	Ammonius the Tall (and his brothers) ...		13	12
	Evagrius	C	27 & B 45	86
31.	Nitria and Cellia (general sketch)	C	21 & 22	69

NOTE.—The numbers of the chapters in B are given not from the Latin translation but from Meursius' Greek text, in which the work is broken up into chapters agreeing almost entirely with those in A, so that the comparison is more accurate. In the case of C, I have given the numbers from the Latin version by Rufinus as found in Rosweyd, and not from the Greek mss.; for the copies used by Rufinus and Sozomen agreed in a number of clearly marked characteristics, which differentiate them from the extant Greek texts (cf. Appendix I.).

I shall begin the investigation in hand by showing that whatever source Sozomen may have used, certainly it was not A. For :—

(1) There is matter in Sozomen which is found in C in its independent state, but not as incorporated in A. Instances are :

(i) The brief accounts of Origenes, Didymus and Chronius, which occur together in C, just as in Sozomen, but do not occur in A.

(ii) The parallel descriptions of the Nitrian desert and Cellia which are found in Rufinus' translation of C 21, 22, in A 69 (the same here as the extant Greek mss. of C), and in Sozomen (vi. 31), show that the latter account contains a number of details to be found in Rufinus but not in the parallel passage of A; so that A cannot have been Sozomen's source, since both he and A give us in this part independent abridgments of the original Greek text of C (the three passages are printed in parallel columns in Appendix I.).

(iii) The opening sentence of Sozomen's sketch of Evagrius seems evidently inspired by words of C not incorporated in A[1].

(2) The fact that Sozomen begins this section of his history of the monks with John of Lycopolis and Or shows that he is following C and not A; for John and Or (or Hor) without any doubt stood first and second in C, whereas in A they are 43 and 9 respectively; moreover Sozomen rightly places this Or

---

[1] *Hist. Mon.* (cf. *P. G.* lxv. 448).   Sozomen vi. 30.

Ἴδομεν Εὐάγριον ἄνδρα σοφὸν καὶ λό-   Εὐάγριος σοφός, ἐλλόγιμος ἀνήρ, ...
γιον, ὃς τῶν λογισμῶν ἱκανὴν εἶχεν διά-   καὶ ἐπίβολος διακρῖναι τοὺς . . . . λογισμούς,
κρισιν.   καὶ ἱκανὸς ὑποθέσθαι κ.τ.λ.

in the Thebaid and not in Nitria, thus again following C against A, and avoiding the latter's confusion of the two men.

(3) Lastly, looking back at the Table, we see that the column comparing A with Sozomen seems to defy all attempts at explanation on any rational principle; a writer abridging a single work can hardly be imagined to have gone up and down, backwards and forwards, in so purely arbitrary a manner.

After thus demonstrating that Sozomen did not use A, I proceed to show that it was from the two books B and C that he derived his materials in this portion of his History.

The Table just printed enables us to give the following analysis of the contents of these chapters of Sozomen:

CHAPTER 28.

(a) A brief account of thirteen monks of the Thebaid. These monks all occur in C, and (allowing for omissions) in the same order (except Eulogius). Moreover Sozomen says nothing about them which is not found in C.

CHAPTER 29.

(β) The first monk named is Apollos, the account being again abridged from C; where, however, he comes seventh.

(γ) Sozomen then passes on to speak of monks who dwelt in the neighbourhood of Alexandria, and begins with Dorotheus, of whom he gives an account substantially the same as that of B 2.

(δ) A brief notice of two ascetics, John of Diolcos and Piammon, who also dwelt near Alexandria by the sea-shore; an abridgment of the last two chapters of C[1].

(ε) The rest of the chapter describes ten more monks, all inhabiting the contiguous deserts of Nitria and Scete, the matter being abridged from B, with a few unimportant changes of order.

CHAPTER 30.

(ζ) This chapter and the first half of the succeeding one are devoted to an account of Nitria and its monks. First are named Origen, Didymus and Chronius, with just enough detail to show that this part is based upon C.

(η) Next, four others are merely named without any details at all; they are similarly named, and in the same order, in the general description of Nitria given in B 7.

(θ) (B 8—12 deal with monks of an earlier generation.) B 13 just alludes to the Tall Brothers, and gives a detailed account of Ammonius the

---

[1] Sozomen's account of John of Diolcos follows the Greek mss. (and A), not the Latin; Rufinus probably here took liberties with his text.

Tall; and similarly in Sozomen we have a passing reference to the Tall Brothers and a fuller account of Ammonius, the matter being taken from B.

(ι)   B's account of Ammonius ends with a saying of Evagrius, testifying to his holiness; this circumstance presumably leads up to Sozomen's notice of Evagrius, the first sentence of which is inspired by the Greek of C (not incorporated in A), and the body of the notice is taken from B.

CHAPTER 31.

(κ)   In the first half of this chapter Sozomen gives a general description of Nitria and Cellia, founded upon the recension of C translated by Rufinus.

(λ)   At this point he leaves both B and C, and introduces what he has to say of the monks of Rhinocorura in Egypt by words calculated to make us suppose that he had more direct, nay, even personal sources of information,— ἐπυθόμην, ἔγνων[1].

(μ)   The chapters that immediately follow in Sozomen (32—34) treat of the monks of Syria, Palestine, Asia Minor and the East, and are not based on Palladius' work.

I submit that the natural conclusion to which this analysis points, is that these chapters (VI. 28, 29, 30 and half of 31) are founded upon the two works B and C, used alternately: not slavishly indeed, but with the freedom natural to a writer compiling a history out of two or more sources. On the other hand, on Lucius' theory, it would have to be supposed that Palladius and the author of the *Historia Monachorum*, in making independent use of a common source, so chanced to select their matter from it as to take alternate passages, without ever trespassing in the least on each other's ground, even when dealing with the same Life.

Furthermore, if we look back to the analysis of cc. 28 and 29, we see that Sozomen has taken a group of sixteen lives from C (α, β, δ), and then a group of eleven lives from B (γ, ε), the two groups just overlapping, inasmuch as one life from the very beginning of B (γ) comes before the last two lives of C (δ). And a reason can be given for the overlapping. After the account of Apollos (β), Sozomen refers his readers for further information to a book on the monks by one Timotheus, whom he identifies (wrongly) with Timotheus Patriarch of Alexandria

---

[1] Cf. Zöckler (*Evagrius Ponticus*, p. 98), where it is pointed out that Sozomen must have known numerous oral traditions concerning the monks of Palestine also.

(cf. Appendix I.). This mention of Alexandria suggests to his mind the monks who dwelt there, and he singles out from the beginning of B Dorotheus (γ)—of whom there is no account in C—who dwelt in the environs of the city, and whom he calls "the most famous" of them. Continuing at Alexandria, he then returns to the last two chapters of C, and speaks of two ascetics who lived by the sea-shore near the city (δ). After this he gives from B the group in Nitria and Scete, also near Alexandria (ϵ). Chapter 30 gives further information on Nitria, taken from both B and C.

To sum up: the substance of the notices in Sozomen VI. 28 tallies perfectly with that of the lives in C; and the same may be said of the order and grouping[1]. The first notice in c. 29, on Apollos, is also from C; and immediately after it comes a reference for further details about him to Timotheus, "who wrote lives of him and of many whom I have mentioned, and of other illustrious monks." Thus at the very point where for the first time he leaves the monks contained in C, and is about to pass to those in B, Sozomen refers for further information to a Greek work containing a set of the Lives of the solitaries, and describes it in words altogether applicable to C. In face of this, it would be mere fastidiousness, now that the original Greek text of C has been produced, to doubt that it was the work which Sozomen had in his hands. And this affords ground no less strong for the belief that the other portions of these chapters are taken from the other work B, to which the residue of Sozomen's matter similarly corresponds.

Thus Dr Lucius' position is shown to be untenable: the

---

[1] Eulogius, as has been pointed out (p. 55), is out of place; but his position is explained when we look at the context: Sozomen has just recorded the care taken by Dioscorus in admitting his monks to the Sacraments, and this makes him go back to Eulogius, who he says was still more strict. I can offer no explanation why Apollos is out of place, or why this second account of him is introduced; for another, also based on this same chapter of C, has already been given in Book III. 14. In that place, however, he is named Apollonius, as in Rufinus' Latin translation and in the Syriac versions; whereas in VI. 29 his name is given as Apollos, with the extant Greek MSS. This phenomenon suggests the idea that Sozomen may have had a second copy, at least of this Life, and on coming across it in the *Historia Monachorum*, failed to recognise it as already used in his History.

hypothetical work which he postulates as the common source of
Rufinus, Palladius, and Sozomen, is not pointed to by the facts
of the case; indeed the evidence tells all the other way.

§ 9.   The Latin Versions of the 'Historia Lausiaca.'

The general result of the discussions of the preceding eight
sections is that of all printed forms of the *Historia Lausiaca*, that
which is found in Meursius' Greek text and in the Latin *Paradisus
Heraclidis* can alone claim to represent the authentic work of
Palladius.   The question now arises, whether this form of the
work has faithfully and in all respects preserved the original
type.   The evidence at our disposal for answering this question
is threefold: the Greek MSS., the Testimonia or citations and
allusions of later writers, and the early versions.   The evidence
however of the Greek MSS. and the Testimonia (as dealing for
the most part with points strictly textual) will be reserved for the
Introduction to the Greek text which I hope to edit in a future
number of this series.   The versions will be dealt with here; for
they throw light upon certain larger and more fundamental questions that have been raised in regard to the origin and nature of
the Lausiac History: they are indeed also our earliest witnesses
to the text.

It is natural to begin with the Latin versions.

Three Latin translations of the Lausiac History are printed in
Rosweyd's *Vitae Patrum*. Of these, that of the Long Recension (A),
which stands as Book VIII., need not detain us here; for it is
merely a translation made by Hervet in the sixteenth century
from a MS. of a type represented by existing Greek MSS.   One
point, however, in regard to this translation must be noted.   It
first appeared in 1555, and it was reprinted without alteration in
various editions and collections before 1600, and in Rosweyd's first
edition (1615).   In 1624 Du Duc[1] published for the first time a
Greek text purporting to be that of A; facing it he printed Hervet's
Latin, but he made some changes so as to bring it into conformity

---

[1] *Auctarium* to La Bigne's *Bibliotheca*, Tom. ii.

with the Greek MSS. which he used: instances of such changes are to be found at the beginning of c. 10 and at the end of c. 85. In his second edition (1628) Rosweyd adopted these changes; and this altered text is the one printed as Hervet's in all subsequent editions of the Latin,—in the Paris *Magna Bibliotheca Veterum Patrum*, XIII. (1644 and 1654), in Lamy's edition of Meursius' works, VIII. (1746), and in Migne's Patrology (*P. L.* LXXIII. and *P. G.* XXXIV.).

There remain two Latin versions properly so called.

Latin Version I.

This is the document printed as Appendix I. in Rosweyd, under the title *Paradisus Heraclidis* (cf. *P. L.* LXXIV. 243 ff.). It was first printed by Le Fèvre d'Estaples (Paris, 1504); but there are certain lacunae in that edition, and when Aloysius Lipomanus came to edit the book in Tom. III. of his *De Vitis Sanctorum* (Venice, 1554), he had the missing passages, with two exceptions, translated from a Greek MS. of the Bessarion Collection, now Cod. 338 of the Library of St Mark's, Venice. It is Lipomanus' edition, in which the lacunae are thus filled up, that is printed by Rosweyd and by Migne. The following is a list of the lacunae occurring in Le Fèvre's edition:

(a) The *Letter to Lausus* beginning Μακαρίζω σου τὴν προαίρεσιν (*P. G.* XXXIV. 1001).

(β) A passage hostile to St Jerome in c. 23, on Posidonius. After the words: 'Hujus viri etiam praenuntiationem aliquando cognovi' (Rosweyd, 967[1]) should occur the passage: Ἱερώνυμος γὰρ......καὶ Συμεῶνα θαυμασίους ἄνδρας (*P. G.* 1180; A 78—82). This passage is not filled up from the Venice MS. in Lipomanus' edition.

(γ) A similar passage hostile to St Jerome in c. 29, on Paula of Rome (p. 971), corresponding to the Greek: ἧς ἐμπόδιον......πρὸς τὸν αὐτοῦ σκοπόν (*P. G.* 1233; A 125).

(δ) The first few lines in c. 37, on Elpidius (p. 975): Ἰδοὺ δὲ καὶ ἕτερον ......τὸ ὄρος τοῦ Λουκᾶ (*P. G.* 1211 B; A 106). Not inserted in Lipomanus' ed.

(ε) The concluding lines of the whole book (p. 983): ἀλλὰ τοῦτον κατήσχυνεν κ.τ.λ. to the end (*P. G.* 1259).

---

[1] I give the pagination of ed. 2, indicated in Migne: for ed. 1 it is merely necessary to subtract 6.

The MSS. of this version are very numerous; I have been able to examine, or procure adequate information concerning the following. I am indebted to Mr Havelock Ramsay for the information concerning the Roman and Cassinese MSS.

(i)   **British Museum** *Cott. Faust.* A xi.
(ii)   „   „   *Royal* 5. F. v.
(iii)   **Paris** *Fonds la t.* 5314.
(iv)   **Cambridge** Trinity Coll. B. 2. 30.
(v)   „   King's Coll. 4.
(vi)   **Dublin** Trinity Coll. C. 2. 9.
(vii)   **Vatican** *Regin.* 432.
(viii) **British Museum** *Harl.* 4719.
(ix)   **Vatican** *Urbin.* 396.
(x)   „   *Lat.* 1199[1].
(xi)   **Paris** *Fonds lat.* 5386.
(xii)   **Vatican** *Regin.* 589.
(xiii) **Paris** *Fonds lat.* 3588.
(xiv)   „   „   „   5623.
(xv)   „   „   „   12277.
(xvi)   **Biblioteca Vittore Emanuele** *S. Croce* 73.

(Bernard in his *Catalogi Librorum MSS. Angliae*, etc., Oxford, 1697, mentions two copies at Oxford, two at Hereford, and one at Durham. Besides copies of the full work, several sets of selectious are to be found: I may mention the Paris MSS. 17568 and N. A. 1491 and 1492, 'Excerpta ex Libro Paschasii diaconi' (cf. *infra* on nos. xii—xv.); Paris 5406 and 5407, the *Sanctorale Guidonis*, a collection of Lives, etc., one section purporting to be taken from the *Paradisus*, but in reality containing also matter from the second Latin version and the *Hist. Mon.*)

Of these MSS., i—vii. present the same general phenomena and the same lacunae as Le Fèvre's text. In viii—xi., however, the two anti-Jerome passages (β, γ) are preserved; the three MSS. viii., ix., x. are closely related, as appears from the fact that they all contain in passage β the corruption *puella* for *Paula*, and that the book ends at the word *fecerunt*, a sentence earlier than in the other copies. In xii—xv. the passage β is altogether omitted, but γ stands in the text; these MSS. are akin to Rosweyd's *Moretus* MS. (*Prolegomena* pp. lxxii and lxxvi), for

---

[1] Floss (*P. G.* xxxiv. 14, note) refers to the Vatican MSS. 499 and 1312 *et seq.*, as containing copies of the *Paradisus*; Mr Ramsay ascertained that the numbers should be 1199, 1212 and 1213, and that the *Paradisus* contained in the two latter is quite a different work.

they attribute the work to Paschasius the Deacon, and have prefixed his Letter to Eugypius the Presbyter. No. xvi. is an abridgment of the book, with some changes of order; at the end are appended a few extracts from Socrates IV. 23 in a Latin translation. These sixteen MSS. all represent the same text as the printed editions of the *Paradisus*. Certain corruptions run through these MSS. In the chapter on Pambo (A 10) there are four notices of a monk named Origen; in the Latin he is named only on the first occasion; on the second the name is altogether omitted, and on the third and fourth it is turned into Paul. Also the Pachon, who appears in A 29, is in the Latin turned into Pachomius, except in the three Paris 'Excerpta ex libro Paschasii diaconi' (see Note appended to list of MSS. p. 60), in which the true form of the name occurs.

The following four MSS. form a group quite by themselves:

(xvii)   **Monte Cassino** *Cod.* 50.
(xviii)   „   „   *Cod.* 348.
(xix)   **Biblioteca Vittore Emanuele** *S. Croce* 41.
(xx)   **Monte Cassino** *Cod.* 143.

In the *Bibl. Casinensis* II. 40—42 a full list is given of the chapters in xvii., and in Tabella I. a facsimile of the writing; but no extracts are printed in the *Florilegium*. Dom Amelli, the Claustral Prior of Monte Cassino, informs me that in the forth-coming part of the *Bibliotheca* considerable extracts will be printed from the other MS. (xviii.). Mr Ramsay has very kindly sent me several extracts from, and notes upon this group of MSS. The first point to be noticed is that the three MSS. xvii., xviii., xix. are clearly derived from a common ancestor, from which the leaf containing the passage in cc. 2 and 3 (= A 12—14): 'Esca vero ejus...necessarium exhibebat' (Rosweyd, 947-8; cf. *P. G.* XXXIV. 1034 B—1035 C), had been torn out; for the text in all three MSS. runs on continuously: 'semper ulceribus. uideres' etc. It is clear, too, that xvii. was copied directly from xviii.[1] The three MSS. are all written in a Lombard hand. Floss attributes xix. to the beginning of the ninth century[2]; but Reifferscheid (*Die römisch. Bibl.*, Sitz. Akad. Wien. L. 772) assigns it to the tenth. Dom

[1] A blank occurs in xvii., exactly corresponding to an erasure in xviii.
[2] *P. G.* XXXIV. 14.

Amelli places xvii. and xviii. in the eleventh century. No. xx. contains a large miscellaneous collection of *Apophthegmata,* extracts from the *Hist. Laus.* (both versions) and the *Hist. Mon.* and from other Lives. This MS. also is in Lombard writing of the eleventh century; its contents are enumerated in the *Bibl. Casinensis* (III. 271—281), and extracts are printed in the *Florilegium* attached to the volume. Dom Amelli tells me that the text of the passages from the *Paradisus* agrees with that of xvii. and xviii. We thus have the means of comparing the text of these MSS. with that found in the others. I give a list of the passages printed in the *Florilegium:*

Florilegium.		*cf. Rosweyd, ed. 2.*
p. 290	anecdote from A 20 . .	p. 951
p. 299	A 15 and 16	p. 948
p. 305	A 35	p. 961
p. 306	A 83—85	p. 967
p. 313	A 86	p. 968
p. 314	A 6	p. 944

(The account of Pachon, A 29, printed from the end of this MS. on p. 332 of the *Florilegium,* is not taken from either of the Latin versions.)

The text is fundamentally the same as that of MSS. i—xvi. and the printed editions; but there are numerous differences throughout, and sometimes these are very considerable. Dom Amelli has entered the following note in the Monte Cassino Catalogue: "Quae autem hos inter codices et editionem (Migne) discrepantia intercedit, collationem cum Graeco textu et novam ex parte translationis recensionem innuere nobis videtur." After a careful study of the problem, Mr Ramsay writes: "The investigation has left me with very little doubt that the text of MSS. Cass. is the older and Rosweyd's the revision." This judgment is based mainly on a review of the Scripture citations, whereof Mr Ramsay sent me a full conspectus, comparing the readings of both texts with the various Latin Versions. Mr Ramsay writes:

"The point which seems to me to give a safe basis of decision is the *increase of formality* in the Rosweyd text.

"(1) The MSS. Cass. give an independent translation of the Greek, with very little flavour of Latin Versions of any sort, while the Rosweyd text inclines much more to the language of Latin Versions.

"(2) When the MSS. Cass. give only the sense of a passage, Rosweyd gives a real quotation from Scripture.

"(3) When the MSS. Cass. give part of a verse or sentence, Rosweyd has the whole.

"(4) Notice also that in several places where the MSS. Cass. give only one quotation from Scripture, the Rosweyd text reinforces with a second.

"Is not progression in matters of this sort more likely than retrogression?"

An examination of the conspectus sent me by Mr Ramsay leads me to agree in his interpretation of the phenomena; and a comparison of the passages printed in the *Bibl. Casinensis* with the corresponding parts of Rosweyd's text confirms the view that the latter text is a revision of the former, made, as Dom Amelli suggests, by the aid of a Greek MS. And in regard to the Scripture citations, it is of importance to point out that the differences (2), (3) and (4) mentioned by Mr Ramsay, are due to the process of bringing the Latin more into conformity with the standard Greek text of the Lausiac History.

I think, therefore, it may be taken as established that the authentic text of this Latin version has been best preserved in the Cassinese MSS. 50 and 348 and the *S. Croce* MS. 41; and that the text found in the other MSS. is a revision in which (1) the Latin was made to approximate more nearly to the Greek text as found in the generality of extant MSS., (2) certain roughnesses of style, due to excessive literalness, were smoothed over, and (3) the Scripture citations were to a great extent revised by recognised Latin Versions.

It appeared that the Biblical citations were likely to afford the best ground for a judgment as to the age of the version. Mr Burkitt has kindly made a careful study of them for me from Mr Ramsay's conspectus; and his study will be found in the Note appended to this section. His general conclusions are that the original translator did not definitely use any Latin version of the Bible but made his own translation of the Scripture texts occurring in the Lausiac History; his choice of renderings nowhere seems to be coloured by the Vulgate, but in places it does seem to be coloured by Old Latin, and especially by late African readings. Mr Burkitt thinks that on the whole the evidence points to the hypothesis that the version was made in Africa

and before the end of the fifth century.   The revision is quite
under Vulgate influence, and therefore the Biblical citations afford
no clue to the time at which it was made.

Thus this Latin version in its pure form, as preserved in
the Cassinese and *S. Croce* MSS., is seen to be of great value.
The Greek text which it represents is in some respects different
from any of the types of text that have come down to us; but
the discussion of all such matters of detail must be reserved until
the general question of the Greek MSS. comes to be treated in
the *Introduction* to the Text.   In the *S. Croce* MS. 41 the work is
attributed to Palladius; so that the introduction of Heraclides'
name in connection with the authorship is probably due to the
Greek MS. used for the revision[1].

[The Hereford MSS. (O i 3 and P ii 5) are of the same type as i—vii. in the
list: cf. p. 60.   I have seen them since the above was written.]

Latin Version II.

This is the document which appears as Appendix II. in
Rosweyd (cf. *P. L.* LXXIV. 343 ff.).   It was the version printed in
the earliest editions of the *Vitae Patrum*, copies of which, attributed conjecturally to the decade 1470—1480, are to be found in
the British Museum.   It is corrupt in various ways.   In the first
place it is very incomplete, in fact hardly more than a fragment
of the work.   Only a few lines of the Introductory matter have
survived; and the body of the work may be said roughly to consist
of the first thirty chapters of ·A, along with those on Evagrius and
Innocent, and the story of the Lector who was calumniated[2].
Thus it contains only about a third of the matter of the Short
Recension.   On the other hand a considerable amount of additional
matter is found in the printed text.   Some of these additions may
at once be set aside as later interpolations: such are three passages

---

[1] The threefold corruption in the chapter on Pambo, noted above as occurring
in all copies of the revision, does not occur in the original form of the version,
which in this respect agrees with the printed Greek texts.   Pachon's name, too, is
rightly given.   Lacunae (a) and (c) occur in the original version.

[2] The book is made up of the following chapters of A :—1, 2, 3, 29, 4, 5, 12, 9,
10, 13, 14, 18, 19, 20, 21 (next come two chapters not found in any other
redaction; then) 6, 22, 86, 25, 26, 27, 30, 103, 141.

in cc. 9 and 10 on the two Macarii, introduced verbally from cc. 28 and 29 of Rufinus' translation of the *Historia Monachorum*[1]; and the whole of c. 20 (pp. 999—1001), which consists of nineteen *Apophthegmata*, some of which are from the version found in Books III. and VII. of Rosweyd. Other additions, which cannot perhaps be so summarily disposed of, are:

(a) Pp. 986, 987[2], c. 4, on Ammonius the Tall (A 12), in the first paragraph and the last three.

(β) P. 988, c. 6, on Benjamine (A 13), two apophthegmata are added; found also in a shorter form in Cotelier's Collection (*P. G.* LXV. 144, nos. 2 and 3).

(γ) Pp. 990, 991, c. 9, on Macarius of Egypt (A 19), two sermons are added, which I have not met with elsewhere; but the first is based upon apophthegma 23 of Macarius in Cotelier's Collection (*P. G.* LXV. 272, or XXXIV. 249).

(δ, ε) P. 994, cc. 11 and 12, on John Colob and Marcianus; these are not found in any other copy of the Lausiac History, but the second seems to be based upon a chapter of Theodoret's *Philotheus* (Rosweyd, p. 806).

(ζ) P. 995, c. 14, on Moses the Robber (A 22), a passage describing the circumstances of his conversion.

The following MSS. of this Version are known to me:

(i) **British Museum** *Addit.* MS. 22562.
(ii) **Paris** *Fonds lat.* 10841.
(iii) **Vatican** *Urbin.* 48.
(iv) **British Museum** *Addit.* MS. 33518.

(Selections are to be found in the *Sanctorale Guidonis* (*Paris* MSS. 5406 and 5407); and in the *Monte Cassino Codd.* 143 and 324. The latter are of interest inasmuch as the extracts printed in the *Florilegium* attached to the *Bibl. Casinensis* are the only specimens of the version that have been edited from MSS. since the first edition. Cod. 143 contains cc. 10 (part), 14 and 16 of the printed text (=A 20—22, 25—27); printed in Tom. III., pp. 294—299. Cod. 324 contains cc. 9, 10 and 4 (=A 19, 20, 12); printed in Tom. V., pp. 325—332:—I have to thank Dom Amelli for sending me an advance proof of this piece.)

Nos. i. and ii. differ only in unimportant points from the printed text[3]; no. iii. is a copy of the same text, but still more

---

[1] The interpolated pieces are: 'Alia quoque puella...infirmitatis obstaculo' (989, 990); 'dicebant enim aliquando venisse......turbaverunt' (990); 'reversus ergo......non posset' (992).

[2] The pages, as before, refer to the second edition of Rosweyd.

[3] In i. the first and second of the pieces mentioned in Note [1] as interpolated

corrupt,—cc. 9—13 are wanting, and there are additional interpolations from the *Historia Monachorum* and the *Apophthegmata*; the addition β, however, is not found in this MS. No. iv. (*Addit. MS. 33518*), on the other hand, is of considerable interest. Its date is late twelfth century, but it preserves a purer and earlier type of the text of this version than the other known copies. This appears from the following phenomena presented by it:

(*a*) In the printed text the Prologue consists only of some twenty lines, taken, in a slightly abridged form, from the beginning of the Διήγησις, Πολλῶν πολλὰ to ἐν τῇ πρὸς θεὸν ἐλπίδι (*P. G.* XXXIV. 1001); in this MS., while there are certain further compressions, the text comes down somewhat further, to ἀλλ᾽ ἵνα τοὺς τυγχάνοντας ὠφελήσωσιν (*ibid.* 1003). Moreover, prefixed to the Διήγησις are a few lines representing the opening sentence of the Epistle to Lausus: Μακαρίζω down to διδάσκεσθαι θέλεις (*ibid.* 1001).

(*b*) The story contained in A 6 comes in its proper place in this MS., and not after the Macarii, as in the printed text (c. 13).

(*c*) Of the additional matter found in the printed text, only the passages marked (*a*) and (ζ) above occur in the MS.[1] There are, however, throughout the MS. a great number of other interpolations from the *Historia Monachorum*, and one (in c. 10) from the *Historia Ecclesiastica* of Rufinus (II. 4). It does not seem necessary to give a list of these manifest interpolations.

It is clear that all these copies of the version are descended from a single and very incomplete archetype, the main characteristics of which may be determined by a comparison of *Addit. MS.* 33518 with the printed text (Appendix II. in Rosweyd). In the archetype the Prologue (attributed in MS. 33518 to "Heraclius episcopus") consisted merely of fragments from the beginning of the Epistle to Lausus and the Διήγησις, the Prooemium, Ἐν ταύτῃ τῇ βίβλῳ, being omitted. The body of the work contained only those chapters of the Lausiac History found in the printed text[2]. The chapter on Pasco (= Pachon, A 29) had already been transferred to the second place (c. 2) in the archetype. The following

---

from Rufinus, do not occur; and c. 11 (on John Colob) is inserted between cc. 9 and 10 (on the Macarii). In ii. c. 11 (addition δ) does not occur at all.

[1] The first of the three passages indicated in the note on p. 65 as introduced verbally in c. 9 from Rufinus' *Historia Monachorum*, does indeed occur, but in a different place, at the end of the chapter.

[2] c. 19 (= A 141) is wanting in MS. 33518. It is noteworthy that in collections of extracts the collectors always turned to Version I. for the portions not found in our redaction of Version II., thus showing that it was imperfect from an early date.

are the only notable additions common to MS. 33518 and the printed text, and therefore derived from the archetype, but not found in any other redaction of the Lausiac History :

(*a*) The first paragraph of the chapter on Ammonius the Tall and his Brothers and Sisters (c. 4 = A 12) 'Beatus Ammonius' (Rosweyd, 986) is much fuller than the corresponding part of any other known text.

(*b*) The conclusion of the same Life is quite different, the two paragraphs 'Quodam uero tempore' and 'Quodam tempore adueniens' taking the place of *P. G.* XXXIV. 1034 B, C: Παλαιὰν δὲ καὶ καινὴν Γραφὴν ἀπεστήθησεν to the end.

[The final paragraph of this chapter, however, as found in the printed text, 'Dicebat sanctus abbas Dioscorus,' does not occur in MS. 33518, and therefore is known to be an interpolation not belonging to the archetype whence our copies have been derived.]

(*c*) In the Life of Moses the Robber (c. 14 = A 22) there is a paragraph, 'Quodam tempore a quodam uiro religioso' (Rosweyd, 995), describing the circumstances of Moses' conversion, which is proper to this Latin version.

We must try to form some judgment on the nature of these additions. I shall begin with the two passages at the end of the account of Ammonius. It is necessary to print the first of these paragraphs, and I shall give the text as found in *Addit.* MS. 33518 (f. 108):

Quodam uero tempore in heremo edificanti ei cellam superuenit quidam frater et dixit ei: Cur in tali ardore estus affligis teipsum abba? Respondensque beatus Ammonius, ait: Crede mihi, frater, quia donante gratia Dei sanctas Scripturas memoriae commendaui. *Nam uetus et nouum Testamentum ab ineunte etate ad plenum didici, necnon etiam et sanctorum antiquorum patrum orthodoxorum sacerdotum Domini sexcentas myriadas expositionum in lege diuina conscriptas perlegi—sic testabantur ei de hoc et pene omnes in heremo patres*—et si uno die satiatus fuero pane et minime in opere me exercuero, stolidus sensus meus[1] uelut irrationabilium animalium efficitur.

The portion printed in italics is derived from the Greek text:

Παλαιὰν δὲ καὶ καινὴν Γραφὴν ἀπεστήθισεν· καὶ ἐν συγγράμμασιν ἀνδρῶν λογάδων Ὠριγένους καὶ Διδύμου καὶ Πιερίου καὶ Στεφάνου διῆλθεν μυριάδας ἑξακοσίας. ταῦτα δὲ μαρτυροῦσιν αὐτῷ καὶ οἱ μεγάλοι τῆς ἐρήμου πατέρες.

[1] Printed text: extollitur sensus meus et.

The Latin would be much improved by the omission of the part taken from the Greek, and it is perfectly evident that it has been made up out of the text of Palladius and an anecdote or apophthegm which I have not as yet been able to trace. Whether the corruption already existed in the Greek copy from which the version was made, or arose in the Latin, it is impossible to say: but it certainly cannot be looked upon as preserving a more authentic form of the text.

The next paragraph, 'Quodam tempore adueniens sanctus Euagrius' etc. (cf. Rosweyd, p. 987), is but a longer form of an anecdote given by Socrates (*Hist. Eccl.* IV. 23 ad fin.); it may be an expansion of Socrates' story. Its position, appended to a piece evidently spurious, forbids us to even contemplate the possibility of its being authentic.

The additional passage in the chapter on Moses the Robber which purports to describe the circumstances of his conversion and repentance, is just the sort of commonplace which anyone wishing to improve the occasion might have written; it may safely be attributed to a scribe.

There remains only the opening passage in the account of Ammonius. Here the fresh information is really new and quite precise:—Ammonius' elder brother Dioscorus had been elected bishop; they had three sisters (not two); the elder sister was mighty in the Scriptures, and spent the night in reading and contemplation; three other women lived with the sisters, and three very erudite and eloquent men with the brothers; the brothers saw no other women, and the sisters no other men (Rosweyd, 986). I am unable to offer any suggestions that throw light upon the origin or source of this passage; but after seeing that all the other additional passages found in this version have turned out to be interpolations, we can hardly be disposed to look upon this as more authentic than its fellows[1].

---

[1] The copy found in the *Sanctorale Guidonis* (Paris ms. 5406 f. 238, or 5407 f. 257) might at first sight seem to afford a proof that this passage also had been subjected to interpolation; for it there approximates very nearly to the normal Greek form. But on inspection it is clear that the text of the *Sanctorale* had been reduced to that form by the aid of the *Paradisus*, and that in this place it is an amalgamation of the two Latin versions.

Mr Burkitt's examination of the Scripture citations leads him to the conclusion that the version is not later than the seventh century and may be much earlier, but there is no clue to the locality where it was made.

In § 12 it will be pointed out that there are clear affinities between the Greek text from which this Latin version was made and that which (as will there be shown) underlies the Coptic version. This type of the text was an early one; and the Latin version, after due allowance for corruptions has been made, bears witness to the fact that it differed in many of its readings from our extant Greek texts. Whence it appears that Tillemont's unfavourable estimate of Version II.—"généralement cette traduction est peu assurée" (*Mémoires* VIII. 812),—must be revised, in view of the fresh information now available.

To sum up the results of the investigation into the Latin versions :—

(1)   Latin Version I. in its primitive state must rank among the earliest and most important of the authorities for the text.

(2)   Latin Version II., although we are not able to arrive at equally definite conclusions regarding it, is of considerable antiquity and value.

(3)   Both versions represent lost Greek MSS. which contained types of the text at once early and in some respects unique.

NOTE.

The Biblical Text represented by the Rosweyd Recension and by the Monte Cassino MSS. of the Latin Version I.
(By F. C. BURKITT, M.A.)

R denotes the Rosweyd text, C that of the MSS. *S. Croce* 41, *Monte Cass.* 50 and 348. (The references are to ed. 2 of Rosweyd, reprinted in Migne *P. L.* LXXIV.; for ed. 1 of Rosweyd, subtract 6 in each reference.)

A careful comparison of C and R amply verifies the correctness of Mr Ramsay's general proposition. As far as the Biblical passages are concerned we may regard C as faithfully preserving the original translation, while R represents a revised text. It is also clear that R has been assimilated to the standard Greek text of the Lausiac History. But I doubt whether the reviser had anything but his memory to help him in correcting and translating the Greek, and I think it is improbable that he was accustomed to use any Latin Biblical text beyond the ordinary Vulgate.

We must think of the author of the Rosweyd text as sitting with a MS. of the ordinary Greek text of the 'History' before him, from which he from time to time corrects a Latin MS. akin to those of Monte Cassino. The resultant readings (R) of his MS. will thus be either (1) *literal translations of the ordinary Greek*, or (2) *the readings of C unchanged*, or (3) *a mixture of the peculiarities of C with corrections derived from the Greek.* The only readings of R that can tell us anything about the Biblical texts known to the reviser are those which differ from C. Out of these, only those which are not a literal rendering of the Greek or which strikingly coincide with some well marked Latin text have any significance.

Judged by this standard, the only reading of R which seems to shew the influence of the Old Latin is that of Isai lxvi 2 (**956**). The quotation is omitted in the MSS. of C, but is found in the Greek. Here the words that correspond in R to ἐπὶ τίνα ἐπιβλέψω are *supra quem requiescit spiritus meus.* This is not the reading of any Greek MS. or of S. Cyprian, but it is found in several of the later Latin Fathers together with Novatian[1]. It may possibly have been known to the reviser from Cassian, who quotes it together with the Vulgate text of the same passage. But a still more probable hypothesis is that the text of C has been abbreviated at this point. C does not present a rival variant to R, but simply leaves out the second quotation. Possibly, therefore, the fuller text of R is here that of the original translation, as in the parallel case of the quotation from Mc ix 35 (Mt xxiii 11) in R 964.

On the other hand there are abundant signs of the reviser's familiarity with the Vulgate. In four passages of the Psalms (xxiii 3, 4; xlix 16; xc 10; ciii 19—21) he alters C to agree verbally with the Greek, using the exact words of the ordinary Vulgate. In the long adaptation of Rom i 21—28 he sticks closely to the Vulgate renderings, and in the list of the Fruits of the Spirit (Gal v 22, 23) his alterations of C are all in the direction of the purer Vulgate text[2]. At the same time, most of his Biblical passages contain some slight verbal deviations from the Vulgate, generally quite unsupported elsewhere. Thus in Ecclus vii 40 R gives us *in perpetuum* for *in aeternum*, and in Jn v 14 *noli amplius peccare* for *iam noli peccare*[3]. But these are just the sort of variations which characterise quotations made from memory; they do not go to prove the use of any special exemplar.

One variation between C and R seems to be due to palaeographical error. In Prov xxiv 27 (42) ἑτοίμαζε εἰς τὴν ἔξοδον τὰ ἔργα σου καὶ παρασκευάζου εἰς τὸν ἀγρόν is rendered in C *praepara ad perfectionem opera tua et esto ad agrum paratus*, but for the last three words R has *in agro operator*, which is quite different both from the Vulgate and from the Old Latin[4]. It looks as if we had here a corruption of *in agro paratus*, which if written *inagropat'* might easily be expanded into in agro operator[5].

When we turn from the peculiarities of the Rosweyd text to the general character of the Latin translation in its original form, i.e. the text of C, we find ourselves in quite another atmosphere. In C, as in R, the translator is mainly following the Greek of the Lausiac History; but while the Biblical vocabulary of R is largely that of the Vulgate, there is no sign that the Vulgate was used in producing the text of C. On the whole, the choice of renderings in C seems to me to indicate an African source.

But it is obvious that there could have been no intention of assimilating the quotations to any form of the Latin Bible. Even where the quotation is fairly exact the renderings are often those of no Latin text, and in many

---

[1] The authorities are Novatian, S. Augustine, S. Fulgentius, Cassian, Cassiodorus, and S. Gregory.

[2] The true order according to *am*, *fuld*, S. Augustine's *Speculum*, etc., is :— charitas, gaudium, pax, longanimitas, bonitas, benignitas, fides, modestia, continentia.

[3] The confusion in R 964 between Mc ix 35 and Mt xxiii 11 arises from the Greek text of the 'History,' which has μέγας for πρῶτος and δοῦλος for ἔσχατος.

[4] *Speculum* 655: 'praeparare in agro.'

[5] See Thompson's *Palaeography*, p. 102.

cases we find variants and corruptions which are scarcely characteristic of the Latin Bibles of the 4th and 5th centuries. A few examples will make this clear. In the list of the nine 'Fruits of the Spirit' (Gal v 22, 23) no less than four, *viz.* 'laetitia,' 'beneuolentia,' 'abstinentia,' 'simplicitas,' are found in no other Latin text. In 1 Cor vii 16 'maritum' for 'uirum' is unbiblical; so also are 'pro uanitate' for 'in uano' in Ps xxiii 4 ($=\epsilon\pi i\ \mu\alpha\tau\alpha i\varphi$), 'relatio' for 'narratio' in Ecclus viii 11, 'iam *desiste* peccare' for 'iam *noli* peccare' in Jn v 14, and many others[1]. Other peculiarities of C can best be explained from the Greek of the Lausiac History. Thus *nullum in terris uocetis magistrum* is a literal translation of the Greek $\mu\dot{\eta}\ \kappa\alpha\lambda\acute{\epsilon}\sigma\alpha\tau\epsilon\ \delta\iota\delta\acute{\alpha}\sigma\kappa\alpha\lambda\text{o}\nu\ \acute{\epsilon}\pi\dot{\iota}\ \tau\hat{\eta}s\ \gamma\hat{\eta}s$ of the 'History,' (c. 32 of Migne's text,) a remarkable variant of Mt xxiii 8 also attested by Origen (*Delarue* iii 182). Again, in Ecclus xix 27 the wording of C 942 is different from the Old Latin, but all the peculiarities of the text are reproduced in the printed Greek of Palladius. The variations in this verse are important, because they are supported by S. Clement of Alexandria, whose deviation here from the text of all our mss. of the Septuagint is thus shewn not to be the result of accident or carelessness[2].

With these examples before us we may go a step further, and charge the ordinary Greek text of the Lausiac History with occasional assimilation to the standard texts of the Bible. Thus there is a paraphrase of Mt ix 12 in both C and R 965, and in C 941 there is a paraphrase of Rom xiv 23; but the Greek gives us in each case an ordinary quotation from Scripture. But since in the passages previously mentioned the Latin paraphrastic quotation turned out to be a literal translation of the paraphrastic quotation of the Greek of the Lausiac History, we have definite grounds for supposing that in these other passages the Greek has suffered, and that an original allusion has become a strict quotation in the standard text[3].

In at least one instance the Latin Palladius has a reading which certainly implies a different underlying Greek in the Biblical text from which the quotation was originally made. In C 950 we find *nec uerbera appropinquabunt corpori tuo* where the Greek of Ps xc 10 and the ordinary text of the Lausiac History have $\kappa\alpha\dot{\iota}\ \mu\acute{\alpha}\sigma\tau\iota\xi\ o\dot{\nu}\kappa\ \acute{\epsilon}\gamma\gamma\iota\epsilon\hat{\iota}\ \tau\hat{\varphi}\ \sigma\kappa\eta\nu\acute{\omega}\mu\alpha\tau i\ \sigma\text{o}\nu$. Evidently therefore, as Mr Ramsay points out, the text of C implies a variant $\sigma\acute{\omega}\mu\alpha\tau\iota$ for $\sigma\kappa\eta\nu\acute{\omega}\mu\alpha\tau\iota$. But this variant is no more supported in Latin than in Greek, so that there is not the slightest reason for taking *corpori* as the reading of Ps xc 10 familiar to the translator. With greater probability

---

[1] E.g. the allusions to Sap iv 13, Esai xl 12, 1 Cor ix 25.

[2] Similarly the wording of the allusion to Phil i 23 in C 940 comes nearer to the $\dot{\alpha}\gamma\alpha\theta\dot{\eta}\nu\ \dot{\epsilon}\pi\iota\theta\upsilon\mu i\alpha\nu$ of Palladius than to any Biblical text, and in Gal i 18 *ascendi* corresponds to $\dot{\alpha}\nu\acute{\epsilon}\beta\eta\nu$, the word in the N.T. being $\dot{\alpha}\nu\hat{\eta}\lambda\theta\text{o}\nu$ or $\dot{\alpha}\pi\hat{\eta}\lambda\theta\text{o}\nu$. The allusion to Ecclus xxxiv 2 in Palladius includes the phrase $\dot{\alpha}\nu\acute{\epsilon}\mu\text{o}\upsilon s\ \pi\text{o}\iota\mu\alpha i\nu\omega\nu$ (cf. Prov ix 12 LXX, x 4 Vg); this is the origin of *pastor uentorum* in C 978.

[3] Another instance is afforded by the references to Rom i 21—28 and 2 Cor xii 7 in C 975.

we may here suppose that he here blindly followed his Greek copy of Palladius[1].

More than two-thirds of the quotations in the older Latin version of the Lausiac History are thus seen to contain no element which throws light on the question of the Latin Bible known to the translator. We have learnt to believe that he faithfully rendered the Greek before him, and that this Greek was to some extent unlike that printed in Migne. We cannot therefore expect to find in the remaining quotations anything like accurate extracts from any Old Latin text. But the choice of renderings, especially in such parts of the Bible as the Psalms, may be considered here and there to afford some indication of the text familiar to the translator. Yet even so, the quotation of Ps cxlv 5 (C R 944) in the form *Dominus sapientes caecos facit* should make us especially cautious. This represents the Greek σοφοί, while according to S. Augustine and S. Jerome the specifically Latin reading was (as it still is) *Dominus illuminat caecos*[2].

The significant quotations and allusions are as follows:

Gen iii 1 (C 975)

Serpens autem *sapientissimus* ferarum omnium in terris erat.

> *sapientissimus* Latin MSS. known to Aug
> *sapientior* Lucif Amb Aug ¹/₃ Hier ¹/₂
> *prudentissimus* Aug ²/₃ Hier ¹/₂

The Greek is φρονιμώτατος. 'sapiens' for φρόνιμος is a well-established O.L. rendering, e.g. 1 Regn ii 10 v, Sap vi 24 (26), Mt vii 24 (*not* in x 16). In this verse *ferarum* for *bestiarum* is unsupported elsewhere.

Ps xlix 16 (C 975)

Quam ob rem *tu* iustitias *exponis* meas,
et cur testamentum meum ex tuo ore procedit?

> *exponis* Tert Cypr Opt Aug ¹/₄
> *enarras* Hil Amb Aug ³/₄ Hier (and the Latin Psalters)

Except Tert, the authorities which have *exponis* also omit *tu*. Tert Cypr Aug ²/₄ have *iustificationes* for *iustitias*.

In this verse *quam ob rem, cur*, and *ex tuo ore procedit* are unsupported elsewhere.

---

[1] The use of σκήνωμα (like σκῆνος) for the 'earthly tabernacle' of the body would facilitate the change to a Greek, but σκήνωμα is never rendered by *corpus* in any form of the Latin Bible (exc. in 2 Pet i 14, 15, where there is also a Greek variant).

[2] No argument can be drawn from Job xl 8 (975) or Prov xxiv 27 (940). They differ so much from the extant O. Latin (*Spec* 436, *Priscillian* 12; *Spec* 655) that there can be little doubt that they are mere independent renderings of the Greek of the Lausiac History.

Ps ciii 20 (C **959**)

Posuisti tenebras et facta est nox,
in ipsa discurrent omnes *siluarum* ferae.

> *siluarum* Hier $^1/_2$ (and the Latin Psalters)
> *siluae* Aug Hier $^1/_2$

The Greek is τοῦ δρυμοῦ so that *siluarum* may be a reminiscence of the
Latin Bible.   But as the other Latin version of Palladius also has *siluarum*,
the underlying Greek may have been a plural[1].   *Discurrent* and *ferae* are here
unbiblical.

Mt iv 9 C (**983**)

Omnia tibi ista donabo, si me *pronus* uolueris adorare.

> *prostratus* k Aug
> *procidens* a b c f g Hil Amb
> *cadens* d Vg

Here C comes somewhat nearer the 'African' *prostratus* than the 'European' *procidens*, but *donabo* for *dabo* is not found elsewhere in this passage
(cf. Mt xviii 32 *ff*[1]).

Mt vii 16 (C **941**)

Ex fructibus eorum agnoscimus eos

> *ex fr.* k c ff[1] Lucif Op. Impf
> *a fr.* a b f g q'Vg Hil Amb Aug

Here *ex* is 'African,' but the coincidence may be accidental.   *Agnoscimus*
for *cognoscetis* is here unbiblical.

Mc ii 18 ; Lc v 30 (C **941**)

Magister uester cum publicanis et peccatoribus *epulatur* ac potat.

The MSS. of the Gospels have *manducat et bibit*, but '*epulatur*' may have
been suggested by '*epulum*,' the word used by the predominantly African MSS.
c and *e* in Lc v 29 instead of '*cenam*' or '*conuiuium*.'

Lc ix 62 (C **966**)

Nemo super aratrum manum suam *posuit* et retro *aspiciens* aptus fuit
regno *caelorum*

Aug. *Ioh* 122 and *Serm* 100 and *c. Faust* 22 has :—*Nemo ponens* ('imponens'
c. Faust) *manum super aratrum et respiciens retro aptus est regno caelorum*.
In this verse 'aspiciens' for 'respiciens' or 'adtendens' is only found elsewhere in MSS. of the Vulgate.

---

[1] [This conjecture is confirmed by the fact that *Cod. Cass.* 143 (cent. xi) contains
a version of this single chapter on Pachon (in which the text occurs), which
is quite different from either Version I. or Version II. ; and in it the text stands:
"in ipsa pertransibunt omnes bestiae *siluarum*" (*Bibl. Casin. III, Florilegium*
332).   E.C.B.]

The resemblance of C to S. Augustine is all the more striking, as the true Old Latin version had a text which transposed the clause, so that the verse ran : '*No man looking back and putting his hand to the plough is fit for the kingdom of God.*' This reading is found in D *a b c e q* Cyp (Hil), as well as Clem. Alex.

On the other hand the reading of C 966 and Aug seems to be supported by S. Optatus, a 4th cent. African.

We must not however base too much on this verse. The occurrence of *aspiciens* in C 966 shews that the translator is not blindly following the Old Latin, and if (as is quite possible) the original Greek of the Lausiac History had τῶν οὐρανῶν for τοῦ θεοῦ the significant coincidences of C with Aug dwindle into the choice of *ponens* instead of *mittens* to render (ἐπι)βαλών. The verse was naturally much used in monastic circles at this period, and may well have been current in a non-biblical form with 'Kingdom of Heaven' for 'Kingdom of God'; as for instance when Marcus the Egyptian monk thus quotes it as the peroration of his book *De Lege Spirituali.* Palladius gives the verse in the conversation of John of Lycopolis, as conveyed to him through the interpreter, so that it hardly makes a claim to be considered as an exact quotation.

1 Cor iii 18 (C 964)

Si quis ex uobis *putat se* esse *sapientem* in hoc mundo, sit stultus ut sapiens fiat.

> *putat sapientem se esse* Cypr $^2/_2$
> *uidetur sapiens* d, Vg Amb Ambst Zeno

The Greek is δοκεῖ σοφὸς εἶναι. The use of 'putare se' in C seems to suggest that the translator was influenced by the African text, but the position of *ex uobis* is not otherwise attested, nor the use of *ex* for *in*.

Slight as these indications are in comparison with the evidence which shews the translator's general independence of all Biblical texts, they all point in one direction, namely to Africa. In the absence therefore of anything to suggest another locality we may legitimately assume as a working hypothesis that the first Latin translation of the Lausiac History was made in Africa, some time before the end of the 5th century. Where the Rosweyd form of the translation was manufactured there is no evidence to shew, at least so far as the Biblical quotations are concerned.

Note on Latin Version II.

The few quotations in this version seem, like those in Version I, to have been made from the Greek without any marked assimilation to the Latin Bible. Thus in Ps xvii 38 (996) *quiescam* for ἀποστραφήσομαι is quite unbiblical. In Ps ciii 20 (985) we find the O. Latin readings *posuit* for *posuisti* and *siluarum* for *siluae*. Yet it seems more simple to take *siluarum* here as a literal translation of the original Greek, which must have once had a plural, as we have seen from Version I. In the Prophets a reference to Isai xl 12 (987) contains the Vulgate word *molem*.

From the New Testament there are only five passages alluded to or quoted, and of these only three are significant. It is evident that no certain conclusions can be built upon so small a foundation. At the same time we may notice *mansueti* for *mites* in Mt v 4 (985); *iniusti* and *hereditabunt* for *iniqui* and *possidebunt* in 1 Cor vi 9 (995). In Mt v 7 (997) the phrase *ipsi misericordiam consequentur* is used as in the Vulgate. Of these renderings, the variants in 1 Cor vi 9 are both of them in *r* Aug and Iren[lat]. The reference in S. Augustine is to the 4th book of *De Doctrina Christiana*, published in 426 AD, so that this form of the text was still current after the first quarter of the 5th century. *Mansueti* for *mites* in Mt v 4 is a late non-African rendering which did not get taken up into the Vulgate; it is found in *f g h q* and Hilary, but not in the earlier European texts. The only one of the O. Latin authorities which has it and also has the Vulgate reading in Mt v 7 is Cod. Brixianus (*f*), usually supposed to represent a North Italian text.

Version II. thus seems to be earlier than the general victory of the Vulgate in the 7th century and may be much earlier, but the evidence is not sufficient for us to guess at the locality from the quotations alone. Moreover the renderings are chiefly attested by documents concerning the text of which more light is sadly needed by investigators of the history of the Bible in Latin.

F. C. B.

§ 10. THE SYRIAC VERSIONS.

Anan-Isho's "Paradise of the Fathers."

If it is possible to make here a more careful study than has hitherto been made of the Lausiac History in Syriac, and to clear up some confusions and misconceptions, this will be mainly due to the kindness of Dr Budge, Keeper of the Egyptian and Assyrian Antiquities in the British Museum, who placed at my disposal his fine codex of the *Paradise* of Anan-Isho, described in his edition of Thomas of Marga's *Book of the Governors*[1].

This Thomas (who flourished about 840) relates that Anan-Isho, a monk of the great Nestorian monastery of Beth Abhe in Mesopotamia in the middle of the seventh century, made a collection of the current Syriac *Apophthegmata*, or Sayings and Anecdotes of the leading Egyptian monks, and incorporated this compilation in a larger collection, described by Thomas of Marga in these words: "He arranged the whole work in two volumes; in the first part were the histories of the holy Fathers composed by Palladius and Jerome, and in the second part were the Questions and Narratives of the Fathers which he himself had brought together. And he called this book 'Paradise'[2]."

[1] *The Book of the Governors: The Historia Monastica of Thomas of Marga* (2 Vols. 1893). II. 192—206. The contents of the *Paradise* are there given: a number of extracts are printed from it as illustrations in various parts of the work.

[This section was in print before the appearance of Père Bedjan's edition of the Paradise: *Acta Martyrum et Sanctorum*, Tomus VII., vel *Paradisus Patrum*. Edidit Paulus Bedjan, Paris, 1897.]

[2] *Book of the Governors*, Book II. c. xv. The above translation is from Vol. II. of Dr Budge's edition, p. 191 ; a Latin translation is given by Assemani, *Bibl. Orient.* III. i. p. 146.

Besides Dr Budge's copy of the *Paradise* there is one in the Vatican Library (*Codex Syriacus* CXXVI.), whereof a table of contents is given by J. S. Assemani in the *Bibliotheca Orientalis*, and a much fuller account, with *initia* etc. of all the chapters, in the *Bibliothecae Apostolicae Vaticanae Catalogus* of S. E. and J. S. Assemani[1]. I have not seen the Vatican MS.; but from the information supplied by the Assemanis, it is possible to determine how far it agrees in its contents with Dr Budge's copy, and how far it differs from it,—at any rate sufficiently for our present purpose[2].

Thomas of Marga says the *Paradise* was divided into two volumes or parts; in both MSS. however it is divided into four books. But this discrepancy causes no difficulty; for in the MSS. Book I. is the Lausiac History, Book II. is a similar collection of lives also attributed to Palladius, and Book III. is the *Historia Monachorum in Aegypto* attributed, as is usual in the Syriac copies, to St Jerome; thus these three Books make up the first volume spoken of by Thomas of Marga as containing the Histories of Palladius and Jerome. Book IV. of the MSS. is Anan-Isho's own collection of *Apophthegmata*, and corresponds to the second volume in Thomas' description of the *Paradise*.

The character of Book III. and Book IV. is sufficiently evident from what has just been said, and they will be further discussed, Book III. in Appendix I., and Book IV. later on in the present section. But before we turn to Book I., the Lausiac History, it will be well to ascertain the real nature of Book II., which also claims to be by Palladius. In the first place it is necessary to remark that whereas the other three Books are substantially the same in the two MSS., Book II. shows considerable differences. In the following comparison the Vatican MS. will be spoken of as *v*, Dr Budge's as *b*; it will usually be most convenient to cite the

---

[1] *Bibl. Orient.* I. 608—9; *Bibl. Apost. Vat. Catal.* III. 156—171. *Codd. Syriaci* CCCLXXIII.—CCCLXXIV. contain a modern copy of *Cod.* CXXVI. (Mai, *Scriptorum veterum nova Collectio*, v. *45).

[2] [There is also a copy at Paris (*Fonds syriaque* 317), which Bedjan used as the basis of Books I., II. (in part) and III. of his edition. It is not included in Zotenberg's Catalogue, being no doubt a recent acquisition. Bedjan does not tell us the date of the MS.; but says that the redaction is identical with that of Dr Budge's copy. Book IV. is wanting (*Avant-propos*, ix).]

Long Recension (A) of Palladius. I proceed to compare Book II. in *v* and *b*.

v.	*b.*
c. 1. Blessed Mark the Ascete (from A 20, 21).	c. 1. =*v* 1.
c. 2. Eulogius and the Paralytic (A 25, 26).	c. 2. Jerome's *Vita Pauli* (Eulogius occurs in I. 65).
cc. 3—8. Stories not from Lausiac History.	
cc. 9—12. Lausiac History (A 104, 22, 87, 88).	cc. 3—13. =*v* 3—13.
cc. 13—42. Chapters partly to be recognised as taken from the Greek collections of *Apophthegmata*, partly matter which I cannot identify.	c. 14. Evagrius (A 86). (Not in *v* at all.)
	c. 15. Jerome's *Vita Malchi.*
	cc. 16—20. =*v* 21, 22, 41, 42.
	cc. 21—40. The Ἀσκητικόν or History of Pachomius, found as an independent work in Syriac MSS. at the British Museum, and printed by Bedjan (*Acta*, v. 122—176); it is a translation of the Greek work printed by the Bollandists under the title *Paralipomena de S. Packomio* (*Acta SS.* Maii, Tom. III. App. 51*—62*). (Not in *v*.)
	c. 41. "Of Palladius the Writer," in reality A 151, "Of the Brother who lived with me," down to the Epilogue proper. (In *v* in its right place at end of Book I.)[1]

A Syriac MS. at Paris contains extracts from Book II. of the *Paradise*[2]: cc. 1—6 = *v* 14—19; 7 = *v* 25 (apparently); 8 and 9 differ from all in either *v* or *b*; 10—14 are from Book III. Thus the Paris MS. lends some support to the shape of Book II. as found in *v*. But, whatever be its true shape,—a point for the determination of which sufficient evidence is not yet forthcoming,—it is clear that the title ascribing the collection to Palladius cannot be

---

[1] [Bedjan's Bk II. is a mixture of *b* and *v*: he omits from *b* the *Vita Pauli* and *Asceticon Pachomii* (both printed already in vol. v. of his series), but retains all the other matter found in *b* or in *v*. Thus his Bk II. contains 47 chapters.]

[2] Zotenberg, *Fonds syriaque*, Cod. 195.

correct, and that in neither v nor b can more than a few chapters
of Book II. really be his.   The following are the true Palladian
sections of Book II. in the two MSS. :—

v		b	
1	=	1	Marcus (from A 20 and 21—τοῦτο τὸ παράδοξον...εἰ καί τις ἄλλος, P. G. XXXIV. 1065 B).
2	=	(I. 65)	Eulogius and the Paralytic (A 25, 26).
9	=	9	Adolius of Tarsus (A 104), called Aurelius.
10	=	10	Moses the Aethiopian (A 22).
11	=	11	Pior (A 87).
12	=	12	Moses the Libyan (A 88).
—		14	Evagrius (A 86).
(I. 65)	=	41	The Brother (A 151).

We come now to the Lausiac History as it stands in Book I. of
Anan-Isho's *Paradise*.   I shall compare it with the Short Recension (B), which, for convenience sake, will be referred to in its
Latin translation, as printed in Rosweyd (p. 939 ff.).   An examination of the work chapter by chapter yields the following results:

Changes of Order—

In the first half of the work, to the end of the account of Pachomius
and the Monks and Nuns of Tabennisi (B 21, A 42), the order of the Greek
has been substantially preserved: three chapters from the end of the book
(B 41, 56ᵇ, 57=A 105, 140, 141) have been put forward into the earlier
portion, among a group of chapters with which they agree in subject-matter.
But from the point indicated above, the Syriac order is altogether different
from the Greek, though the minor grouping of the chapters is sometimes
preserved.   The Epilogue (Ἐμοὶ δὲ τοῦτο κ.τ.λ. P. G. XXXIV. 1258) has been
transferred to the middle of the book, after the account of Pachomius and
his monks : the Epilogue ends at the same point as in Latin Version I, ἐὰν
πεσὼν προσκυνήσῃς μοι.   The apology on "Those who fell away" (ἀναγκαῖον,
1091 A) is placed before instead of after the story of Valens (A 31).

Omissions in the Syriac—

The following sections had evidently fallen out of the copy used by
Anan-Isho, or out of one of its ancestors :

B 7, 8, 9 = A 22—27.
B 24—27 = A 83—88.
B 29, 30, 32 = A 125—134, 102 and 104, 113.

But all except the chapters on Paul of Pherme, Paula and the holy women, Julian and Philoromus (B 8, 29, 30ª, 32 = A 23 and 24, 125—134, 102, 113) are found either at the very end of Book I. or in Book II.; Evagrius (B 25 = A 86) is found in Book II. in *b*, but not in *v*. B 45 = A 96 is wanting in *b*, but found in *r* 51; and B 56ᵇ = A 140 is wanting in *v*, but found in *b* 28. These are the only lacunae in Book I. of the *Paradise* which seem worthy of mention.

Additions in the Syriac—

The third Introductory piece in *b*, entitled "Counsels to Lausus," being the Greek Διήγησις, Πολλῶν πολλά (and in *v* forming one with the preceding piece, the Προοίμιον), has some lines prefixed which I have not met with elsewhere.

In the Life of Ephraim Syrus (B 28, A 101), ten or twelve lines are added at the beginning, and about half as many at the end, from one of the Greek Lives of Ephraim, not by Palladius[1]. (Printed by Tullberg, p. 9 ff.)

At the end of the account of Macarius Junior (B 4, A 17) is a short passage not found in the Greek, printed in part by Budge (II. 198).

At the end of Macarius of Alexandria is a note by the Collector[2].

In the Epilogue (cf. above) is a short addition on "Those who fell away."

"The blessed woman Tehesia" (*b* 30, *v* 27); the well known and beautiful story of "St Thais the Harlot" (Rosweyd, 374).

"Of a Virgin of Caesarea" (*b* 27, not found in *v*); this I have not been able to identify. [Not printed by Bedjan.]

This is the sum total of additions made in the Syriac *Paradise* to the Greek of the Short Recension[3].

In one part of the Syriac copies it might be difficult to identify the chapters from their titles; I therefore give the following table:

b	*v*	B		A
26	25	16		34
27	—	—	(?)	—
28	—	56ᵇ		140
29	26	57		141
30	27	— (Thais)		—

[1] Cf. *Opera Ephraem*, ed. Assemani, I. xxix.; a Latin translation by Gerard Vossius may be found in Rosweyd (167), and a Syriac, but in a much expanded form, in *Bibl. Orient.* I. 26. (Cf. *Apophthegmata* 2 and 1, *P. G.* LXV. 168.)

[2] Assemani, *Bibl. Apost. Vat.* III. 160; Budge, II. 52. [Bedjan, 80.]

[3] Assemani's statement (*Bibl. Apost. Vat.* III. 161) that the sections on Abraham the Egyptian (*b* 25, *v* 24) and on a Virgin (*b* 29, *r* 26) are Syriac additions, is incorrect; they occur in the Greek texts, A 105 and 141 respectively. Similarly the Preface on "Those who fell away" (properly end of A 31) and Epilogue.

(The chapters of *v* are numbered as in the *Bibl. Orient.*; the numbers differ slightly in the *Bibl. Apost. Vat.*) Timiroun (*b* 37) is Taor (A 138); and Heronion (*b* 46) is Severian (A 114), by a confusion of ഩ and ഛ. The other titles will present no difficulty.

A mere comparison of the lists of contents given by Assemani and Budge[1] suffices to show that, in spite of differences sometimes considerable, *v* and *b* contain the same work. It has been said above that Assemani (*Bibl. Apost. Vat.* III.) gives the *initia* of all the chapters of *v*: and as Dr Budge has printed a number of extracts from *b*, it is to some extent possible to bring the two texts together, sufficiently at any rate to see that they are substantially the same. Moreover, Professor Tullberg of Upsala, in collaboration with his pupil Lagerström, edited a few chapters of the Syriac *Paradise* from various British Museum and Vatican MSS.[2]: and it is clear that the readings there recorded under the sign V are those of the Vatican MS. which we are calling *v*. Thus a fuller opportunity of comparing the two texts is afforded. Fortunately the account of Paul the Simple is printed by both Tullberg and Budge[3]: so that any one may satisfy himself that, making allowance for variants of the usual kind, the two MSS. preserve the same text. M. Rubens Duval, after a critical comparison of the texts in the section thus made generally accessible, pronounces on the whole in favour of *v*: "La copie de M. Budge ne paraît pas valoir le manuscrit du Vatican, qui devra servir de base à l'édition à venir": he indicates, however, cases in which *b* gives "la bonne leçon[4]." The general phenomena of the two MSS. seem to bear out Duval's verdict: for though their common corruptions prove them to be closely related, *b* has certain corruptions of its own not found in *v*:—*e.g.* the *Vita Antonii* is prefixed to the whole collection, the extra chapter I. 27 is introduced, and the form of Book II. as found in *v* seems to be the more primitive, and is supported by the Paris MS. 195 already mentioned. It remains a matter of doubt how far the archetype of *v* and *b* faith-

---

[1] *Bibl. Orient.* I. 608—9; *Book of the Governors*, II. 197—206.

[2] *Libri qui inscribitur Paradisus Patrum partes selectae*, Upsalae, 1851.

[3] Tullberg, 21; Budge, II. 32. Also a few lines from "The Virgin who received Athanasius" (Budge, II. 199; Tullberg, 34).

[4] *Journal Asiatique* (Jan.—Juin, 1894, p. 373 ff.).

fully represents Anan-Isho's collection; for our MSS. are all late.
We learn from Assemani that *v* dates from the thirteenth century;
Dr Budge tells me that the Mosul MS. from which *b* was copied,
belongs in his judgment to the fourteenth or fifteenth century;
and Zotenberg gives 1470 as the date of the Paris fragment. Thus
these MSS. do not bring us within six centuries of the original[1].

But whatever minor corruptions may have crept in, this much
may be safely gathered from the two MSS., that Anan-Isho's copy
of the Lausiac History was in substance the same work as that
which has here been called the Short Recension. It is made up
of:—The 3 *Introd.* pieces; then A 1—21, 28—33, 105, 34, 140,
141, 35, 36, 38—42, 151[b] (*Epil.*), 117 (*init.*), 136, 37; 137—139, 148,
149, 117, 118, 142, 143, 119—124, 144—147, 114, 135, 115, 43
(less C), 47, 77—82, 89—101, 103, 106—112, 83—85, and 151[a]
(in *v*) *or* 25, 26 (in *b*)[2].

NOTE. Two of the chapters in Book II. of the Vatican copy of Anan-Isho's
Paradise seem to call for a special mention, in view of questions as to the
integrity of our text of the Lausiac History. In A 95 (= B 35, on Paphnutius) we read: Ἐμνήσθημεν δὲ καὶ τὰ κατὰ Στέφανον τὸν ἐκπεσόντα εἰς
αἰσχρὰν ἀσωτίαν· καὶ Εὐκάρπιον, καὶ τὰ κατὰ Ἥρωνα τὸν Ἀλεξανδρέα, καὶ τὰ
κατὰ Οὐάλην τὸν Παλαιστῖνον, καὶ τὰ κατὰ τὸν Πτολεμαῖον τὸν ἐν τῇ Σκήτει
Αἰγύπτιον (P. G. xxxiv. 1196 D).

The stories of Hero, Valens, and Ptolemy are told in A 31—33; but of
Stephen and Eucarpius not a word has been said—the Stephen spoken of in
A 30 is another man. This circumstance may raise a doubt as to whether
a portion of the original work has not fallen out of the extant Greek texts.
It is therefore interesting to find in Book II. of the Vatican copy of the
Paradise, though not in Dr Budge's copy, chapters on Stephen and Eucarpius. I am not in a position to supplement Assemani's brief notes (*Bibl.
Apost. Vat.* III. 165). The title of c. 27 of Book II. is thus translated by
Assemani: "Narrationes de iis qui ex rectis operibus exciderunt propter
superbiam et ambitionem. Et primum de Stephano, qui in turpem in-
temperantiam lapsus est." The *initium* is given in Syriac: "There was a
man in Scete named Stephen." Similarly c. 28, "de Eucarpo": "There was
also in the desert a certain man named Eucarpus." Can it be that here the
Syriac has preserved a portion of the original work which has been lost in the
Greek? [Printed by Bedjan, 292—299.]

[1] In Assemani's *Bibl. Mediceae Laurent. et Palat. Cat.* mention is made of an
Arabic copy of the *Paradise*, in which Bk. I. is the *Hist. Laus.* (cod. LIX.). This may
be an earlier type. [I do not know the date of the Paris MS. 317, used by Bedjan.]

[2] [There are several errors in Dr Preuschen's list (*op. cit.* 220).]

Anan-Isho did not make a fresh translation of the Lausiac History, but incorporated in his *Paradise* one already widely current. This version I shall call

Syriac Version I.

All the MSS. used by Tullberg contain this version, but he has given us no means of identifying them. The following is a list of the MSS. at the British Museum which preserve portions of it; I trust the list may claim to be practically complete, for I have gone through all the MSS. referred to by Wright under any heading at all likely to include Palladian matter.

(i.) *Additional* MS. 12173 (Wright, DCCCCXXIII. 2). The title of the work is: "Histories of the Egyptian Fathers composed by Palladius, bishop of Helenopolis, the disciple of Evagrius, at the request of Lausus, the Chamberlain of the Emperor Theodosius." It is not a complete copy: it occupies ff. 118—137 of the MS.: then comes, as if part of the same work, "The sayings of the holy Fathers concerning Humility," and the rest of the MS., to f. 180, is a collection of *Apophthegmata*. The MS. is assigned by Wright to the sixth or seventh century. Contents: The letter to Lausus (Μακαρίζω), and then the sections corresponding to A 43 (less the matter of C), 47, 77—82, 89—101, 103, 110, 111, 106—108, 117 (*init.*), 136, 138, 139, 117, 118, 142, 143, 148, 149, 151ª, 37, 31—33, 105, 34, 140, 141, 35, 36. (This grouping corresponds, to some extent, with that found in Book I. of the *Paradise*.)

ff. 111—117 the Lives of the two Macarii (A 19—21, less Marcus) from the same version, attached without any new title to a set of *Apophthegmata*.

(ii.) *Addit.* MS. 17177 (Wright, DCCCCXXV. 2). Date: Century VI. Part II. of this MS. (ff. 61—118) contains a set of Lives described by Wright as "Another work of Palladius or rather of Hieronymus": as a matter of fact, the greater number are from the Lausiac History. Contents: the sections corresponding to A 1, 2, 6, 9 (less the matter of C), 10, 13—16, 18, the short passage from 20 and 21 on Marcus (indicated above under Book II. of the *Paradise*), 28 (less the matter of C), 29, 41, 42, 83—85, 25, 26 [a few Lives from C; and Jerome's *Vita Pauli*].

(iii.) *Addit.* MS. 17173 (Wright, DCCLXII. 3). Date: Century VII. Contents (ff. 43—79): A 43 (less the matter of C), 47, 77—82, 89—95, 97—99, 101, 103, 110, 111, 106—108, 35, 36, [ff. 56—75 *Apophthegmata*] A 28, [ff. 77—79 *Apophthegmata*].

(iv.) *Addit.* MS. 14648 (Wright, DCCCCXLIII. 1). Date: Century VI. Contents: ff. 116—124 = A 19—21 (less Marcus), attached to same *Apophthegmata* as in i.

(v.) *Addit.* MS. 14650 (Wright, DCCCCXLIX. 3, 6). Date: A.D. 875.

Contents (ff. 9—25): A 31—33, 105, 140 [*Apophthegmata*; Jerome's *Vita Pauli*]; A 86. (f. 69) A. 139.

(vi.) *Addit.* MS. 14577 (Wright, DCCXCIII. 17). Date: Century IX. Contents: among a series of *Apophthegmata*, f. 69 = A 111 and 105.

(vii.) *Addit.* MS. 14649 (Wright, DCCCCL. 11, 14, 15, 22). Date: Century IX. Contents: f. 102 = A 117 (*init.*), 136, f. 107 = A 141, f. 108 = A 37, f. 141 = A 139.

(viii.) *Addit.* MS. 17172 (Wright, DCCLXXX. 4 a, 6 a). Date: Century IX. Contents: f. 120 = A 28 (abridged), f. 164 = A 43 (less matter of C), 47.

(ix.) *Addit.* MS. 17183 (Wright, DCCCXII. 22). Date: Century X. Contents: f. 186 = A 31, 32.

(x.) *Addit.* MS. 12174 (Wright, DCCCCLX. 6, 10, 23, 77). Date: A.D. 1197. Contents: f. 87 = A 20, 21 (less Marcus), f. 124 = A 28, f. 184 = A 25, 26, f. 448 = A 141.

(xi.) *Addit.* MS. 14732 (Wright, DCCCCLXIII. 4, 9, 12, 13). Date: Century XIII. Contents: f. 52 = A 28 (abridged as in viii.), f. 129 = A 20, 21 (less Marcus:—stated to be by St Jerome), f. 157 = A 43 (less matter of C), 47, f. 166 = A 86 (cf. hereafter p. 88).

(xii.) *Addit.* MS. 17262 (Wright, DCCCXXXVII. 4). Date: Century XII. Contents: f. 40 = A 8 (abridged).

This appears to have been the Syriac Version most widely current, and it is the one which Anan-Isho incorporated in his *Paradise*; fully half is extant only in the *Paradise*.

A study of these MSS. makes it clear that most of the special features of the Syriac *Historia Lausiaca* as found in Book I. of the *Paradise*, are not to be imputed to Anan-Isho or to later scribes, but existed in the MSS. of Version I. from the earliest times.

The peculiar grouping of the chapters in Book I. of the *Paradise* is clearly discernible in MSS. i. and iii., both of century VI. or VII. (cf. pp. 83, 84).

The brief section on Mark (the 11 lines from A 20 and 21, *P. G.* XXXIV. 1065 B, cf. p. 80) has been cut out of the chapter on Macarius of Alexandria, not only in the *Paradise*, but also in the copies found in MSS. i. and iv. (cent. VI.) and x. and xi.; and it is found as an independent piece, not only in Book II. c. 1 of the *Paradise*, but also in MS. ii. (cent. VI.). Also the passage on "Those who fell away" (A 31 *fin.*) stands in i. as in the *Paradise* (cf. p. 80).

The lacunae found in Anan-Isho's first book existed also in the copy of the Syriac Lausiac History from which MSS. i. and iii. were derived: in both these MSS. there is a gap from A 82 to A 89; A 102, 104, 113, and 125—134 are altogether wanting; the context of A 22—27 does not occur. But it is remarkable to note that five of the missing sections—A 83—85 and 25, 26—those dealing with Serapion and Eulogius, occur together in MS. ii., at the end of a small selection of Lives from this Version: while in Dr Budge's copy of the *Paradise* this same series of chapters forms the conclusion of the Lausiac History (*b* Book I. 64 "of Serapion," 65 "the Triumph of Eulogius"): (in *v* Eulogius is the second chapter of Book II.). It is therefore clear that in some copies of the Syriac, one of which was used by Anan-Isho, these sections had been restored to the Lausiac History and placed at the end.

Regarded as a translation, the Syriac may on the whole be pronounced a fairly faithful rendering of the Greek; at times however it is little better than a paraphrase, and often there are curtailments or embellishments. Its relation to the Greek MSS. and its bearing on the criticism of the Greek text will have to be considered in the *Introduction* to the Text. Here it may be stated in general that this Syriac version has clearly marked affinities with the Greek text contained in the Paris MS. 1628, as appears from a number of minor coincidences, and also from the fact that in these two alone the Preface to the Holy Women (Ἀναγκαῖον δὲ ἡγησάμην, P. G. xxxiv. 1220 D) introduces neither Melania (as in A), nor Paula (as in B), but the story of the 'Virgin who received Athanasius' (A 136). (Cf. Tullberg, p. 33.)

Syriac Version II.

A second and quite independent Syriac Version existed of no less antiquity than the first. The following MSS. contain portions of it.

(i.) **British Museum** *Addit.* MS. 12175 (Wright, DCCXXVII. 3 g). Date: A.D. 534. Contents (ff. 183—188): A 1—5, 17, 18, 23, 24, 104, 30, 22, 87, 88.

(ii.) **Vatican** *Cod. Syr.* CXXIII. (Assemani, *Bibl. Apost. Vat.* 143). Date: Century VIII. (Assemani). Contents (ff. 257—295): A 1—35.

(iii.) **Vatican** *Cod. Syr.* CCCLXXI. 5 (Mai, *Script. vet. nova Coll.* V. *45). A modern transcript of ii.

(iv.) **British Museum** *Addit.* MS. 17172 (Wright, DCCLXXX. 4 d). Date: Century IX. Contents: f. 125=A 18 (Nathaniel).

I have not seen the Vatican MS., the most important one of this version; but Mr McLean, Fellow of Christ's College, kindly examined it for me; and, though the text is continuous and not broken up into chapters at all, he satisfied himself that, as Assemani states, the MS. contains matter corresponding to the first thirty-five chapters of A. Assemani prints only the first few words. Accordingly, to make quite sure that the version is the same as that contained in the British Museum MS. i., I asked Dom Weickert, of the Collegio Anselmiano at Rome, to transcribe for me the opening passage. His transcription makes it clear that the two MSS. contain the same version, though a number of variants exist. As far as I can judge from the passage before me, the Vatican MS. seems to preserve the more correct text; in the Brit. Mus. MS. the words: "In the second consulate of Theodosius the great king, who is now among the angels because of his faith which is in Christ" (cf. *P. G.* xxxiv. 1009 A), are wanting; also πόλις after Alexandria, and ξενοδόκος. Thus this MS., though written so early as 534, presents a text which seems to be already "worn," as compared with that preserved in the much later Vatican MS. This phenomenon justifies us in presuming that the version probably dates from about the third quarter of the fifth century, some fifty years after the book was first written.

It has been said that Version I. was that which Anan-Isho used for Book I. of his *Paradise*; but it can be shown that he had before him also a portion at any rate of Version II. For the "Compiler of the Book," *i.e.* Anan-Isho himself, speaks of "another codex" in his possession by means of which he supplements his main source. At Bk. I. 15 (= A 17) "of Macarius the Child of the Cross," after giving the account that is found in the Greek, Anan-Isho adds that "in another codex" he found appended an account of how this Macarius used to pray with his arms extended, and he inserts it from this second codex[1]: Dr Budge prints a portion of it (II. 198), and it agrees verbally with an addition found in MS. i. of Version II. (f. 185). It has already been pointed out that from a very early date, already in the beginning of the sixth century, certain Lives had dropped out of the copies of Version I. A set of four of these chapters, missing in Bk. I. of the *Paradise* and in our MSS. of Version I. of the Lausiac History, stands in Bk. II. both in *b* and in *v*. These four Lives are:

9 Adolius (here called Aurelius)	.	.	A 104
10 Moses the Robber (the Ethiopian)		.	A 22
11 Pior the Egyptian	.	.	.	A 87
12 Moses the Libyan	.	.	.	A 88

[1] Assemani, *Bibl. Apost. Vat.* iii. 159 [Bedjan, 55].

If the reader turns back to MS. i. of Version II., he will there see the same series of chapters—A 104, (30), 22, 87, 88; and in that MS. also Adolius is called Aurelius. A comparison of the texts shows that they are the same. Anan-Isho therefore took this suite of Lives from a MS. of Version II. closely akin to our MS. i.; and such a MS. is the one which he speaks of as his "other codex," and which he used in order to partially fill up the gaps of the current copies of Version I.

The following MSS. in other collections may possibly contain further extracts from the Syriac *Historia Lausiaca*: Library of St Catharine's, Mount Sinai, MS. 31 (cf. additional note on p. 130 of Mrs Smith Lewis' *Catalogue*); Royal Library, Berlin, MSS. 109 and 161 (Sachau's *Verzeichnis*). Zotenberg's Catalogue of the Paris *Fonds syriaque* mentions no collection of lives under Palladius' name; but no doubt both there and at the Vatican many single lives from the Syriac versions might be found: (cf. the Paris MSS. 234, 235, 236).

Lives of Evagrius.

The copies of the Life of Evagrius (A 86) require separate treatment. There are eight copies in the British Museum collection, but they do not stand as part of the Lausiac History: they are prefixed to collections of the writings of Evagrius, or are included among Lives of Saints. The following Table gives all the needful technical details.

Manuscript	Reference	No. in Wright	Century	Remarks
i. Add. 12175	ff. 122—123	DCCXXVII.	A.D. 534 (?)	Attributed to St Basil
ii. Add. 14581	ff. 27—29	DCCXXXIV.	VI.	
iii. Add. 14612	ff. 137—139	DCCLIII.	VI or VII.	[Bedjan gives the variants of this copy (p. 1011).]
iv. Add. 14650	ff. 23—25	DCCCCXLIX.	A.D. 875	Not mentioned in Wright's *Index* among the Lives of Evagrius
v. Add. 14578	ff. 1—2	DLXVII.	VI or VII.	Begins at Constantinople episode (*P. G.* XXXIV. 1188 D)
vi. Add. 14635	f. 5	DLXVIII.	VI.	Ends with Constantinople episode (*ibid.* 1193 C)
vii. Add. 14732	ff. 166—168	DCCCCLXIII.	XIII.	
viii. Add. 17166	f. 1	DCCXXXVII.	VI.	Begins at interview with three heretical demons (*ibid.* 1194 B)

Of these Lives of Evagrius, Nos. i-v. are the same translation as that in Dr Budge's copy of the *Paradise* (Bk. II. c. 14)[1]: all these six copies of this translation break off at the words: "He was compelled to partake of things cooked by fire" (*P. G.* XXXIV. 1194 *b*): v. has a few additional lines after this point, but they are not of Palladius. Nos. vi. and vii. present another translation, and No. viii. yet a third; and these contain the conclusion of the Life, which is wanting in i-v. All three translations represent the extant Greek text, there being no trace of any of the additional matter found in the Coptic; but that contained in vi. and vii. (as also apparently that in viii., which is but a fragment) is on the whole a closer rendering of the Greek than that in i-v. It is worth noting here that this last-named translation agrees with some of the authorities for the Greek text in stating that St Gregory Nazianzen ordained Evagrius deacon, while that found in vi. and vii. agrees with others in saying that he was ordained by St Gregory of Nyssa; whence it appears that both readings existed in the Greek MSS. already in the sixth century.

I do not think that there is sufficient evidence for forming an opinion as to whether any of these translations of the Life of Evagrius belonged to either Syriac version of the Lausiac History. None of the known copies comes into direct contact with Palladian matter:—in the Brit. Mus. MS. 14650 (Syr. Version I. No. v.) it is separated by several *Apophthegmata* and the *Vita Pauli*. I think it probably was not in Anan-Isho's copy of Version I.; and I doubt if it stood originally in Book II. of the *Paradise*, as it is found only in *b*, and not in *v*. It is quite possible that all three Syriac translations of the Life were made from Greek copies already detached from the Lausiac History, and prefixed to Evagrius' writings or included among Saints' Lives.

Syriac Redactions of the Lausiac History.

The investigation of the Syriac versions so far pursued naturally leads up to a discussion of the statement made by Dr Wright and repeated by Dr Budge, that "the Syriac copies

---

[1] [Printed by Bedjan, 231.]

of the work of Palladius differ as much from one another as the Greek[1]." It is evident that the point here raised has a most important bearing on the general problem the solution of which has been sought in this Study,—the determination of the authentic form of the *Historia Lausiaca*. It seems clear that Dr Wright's opinion must have been based mainly on the British Museum MSS. which came under his inspection, for but few Palladian Syriac MSS. appear to exist in other libraries. It therefore becomes necessary to make an analysis of the several Syriac works connected with Palladius' name in Wright's *Catalogue* (chiefly vol. III. 1070—1080).

These MSS. form the series numbered DCCCCXXIII. to DCCCCXXXII. by Wright; and the following notes are the result of a personal examination of all of them.

No. DCCCCXXIII. (*Addit.* MS. 12173, Century VI. or VII.). (A fuller account than Wright's of the contents of this MS. is given by Dietrich, *Codicum Syriacorum Specimina* (Marburg, 1855).) Contents:

(1) *Histories of the Solitary Brethren of the Egyptian Desert*, in two Parts, attributed to Palladius, though neither part is really his.

(ff. 2—58) Part I.: a collection of *Apophthegmata* (cf. p. 94).

(ff. 58—73) Part II.: the *Historia Monachorum in Aegypto* of Timotheus, but attributed in the colophon, as is usual in the Syriac copies, to St Jerome, in spite of the fact that Palladius is named in the title as author of the whole work. The first half is very incomplete.

(ff. 73—111) more *Apophthegmata*.

(ff. 111—117) the two Macarii (A 19—21, less Marcus).

(2) *Histories of the Egyptian Fathers composed by Palladius...at the request of Lausus.*

(ff. 118—137) this imperfect copy of the Lausiac History has already been noticed (p. 84).

(ff. 137—180) a series of *Apophthegmata* entitled "The Sayings of the Holy Fathers on Humility" (not by Palladius).

(ff. 180—181) a note on John of Lycopolis.

No. DCCCCXXIV. (*Addit.* MS. 17176, A.D. 532). Contents:

The same as DCCCCXXIII. (1), except that the order of the two Parts is reversed, the *Historia Monachorum* (ff. 2—57) coming before the set of *Apophthegmata* (ff. 58—97).

Stated by Wright, but not by the MS., to be by Palladius. The translation is the same in these two MSS., and is the one incorporated by Anan-Isho in his *Paradise* (Book III.); other translations of the *Historia Monachorum* are to

---

[1] *Catalogue*, 1071; *Book of the Governors*, II. 193.

be found among the British Museum MSS. (cf. Appendix I.); and Wright elsewhere speaks of it as being by Palladius, and being from the Lausiac History[1], misled no doubt by the universal acceptance of the Long Recension of that work. Dr Budge similarly prints a short extract from the Syriac *Historia Monachorum* on "Paphnutius and the Merchant" (Rufinus c. 16, cf. A 65) as being by Palladius[2].

No. DCCCCXXV. (*Addit.* MS. 17177, Century VI.). Contents:

(1) "The Histories of the Egyptian Solitaries by Palladius" (ff. 1—61). The Syriac title is *Narratives of the Monks*, and the book is a collection of *Apophthegmata*, and therefore not a true work of Palladius.

(2) A collection of eighteen Lives called by Wright "another work of Palladius, or rather, of Hieronymus" (ff. 61—118). This collection has been described above (p. 84); it is for the most part a selection of Lives from the Lausiac History, taken from the same translation as DCCCCXXIII. (2).

No. DCCCCXXVI. (*Addit.* MS. 14676, Century XIII., ff. 43—86).

This MS. is mutilated beyond recognition, only narrow strips of the inner margins remaining; its identification with any book is but a guess, and all that Wright says is that "it appears to have contained" the work of Palladius.

No. DCCCCXXVII. (*Addit.* MS. 17215, Century VIII., ff. 46, 47).

A mere fragment, not from the Lausiac History, and not attributed to Palladius in the MS. A dialogue between an Elder and a Disciple.

No. DCCCCXXVIII. (*Addit.* MS. 17174, A.D. 929, ff. 1—184).

The work of Palladius on the Profitable Counsels of the Holy Fathers. Relying on Thomas of Marga's description of the collection or rearrangement of *Apophthegmata* made by Anan-Isho[3], Wright recognises the book before us as that collection,—"It would appear to be the work of the monk Anan-Isho." Moreover, Thomas tells us that Anan-Isho incorporated his collection in his *Paradise*, where it formed the last part. Now a comparison of the titles of the chapters or sections of Book IV. of the *Paradise*, as given by Assemani and Budge[4], with those given by Wright from this MS. shows them to have been the same work. The fact that in the copy before us the work is divided into two Parts is a mere accident; in other copies it is not so divided. Of course it is evident that this work is in no sense at all a redaction of the Lausiac History; it has nothing in common with any of the Greek shapes in which the Lausiac History is found. Nor can it be regarded as being by Palladius, even though both copies of the *Paradise* assert at the beginning of Book IV. that he was the compiler. The Syrian tradition, indeed, regarded Palladius as the one who formed the first great collection of

---

[1] *Catalogue*, 650, 1086, 1088, 1127.

[2] *Book of the Governors*, II. 471.

[3] *Book of the Governors*, Book II., chapters 14 and 15.

[4] *Bibl. Orient.* I. 609; *Book of the Governors*, II. 204—6. [Printed in full by Bedjan 442—992.]

Apophthegmata; an anecdote related by Thomas of Marga contains an explicit statement that it was Palladius who "gathered together the Questions and their Answers from the collections of the books of the Fathers[1]"; but there is no evidence whatever, nor any reason for supposing, that he made any such collection; and it will be shown in § 16 that the great Greek collections were not formed for some time after his death. The Syrian tradition on the point cannot be regarded as authentic. To sum up :—the work before us is Anan-Isho's rearrangement of the *Apophthegmata*, almost in its original form, standing by itself and not as Book IV. of the *Paradise*; it has no connection whatever with the Lausiac History ; it is not a work of Palladius[2].

[1] *Book of the Governors*, II. 547. "Questions and Answers of the holy Fathers" was a common Syriac title for *Apophthegmata*, e.g. *Addit*. Ms. 17177, f. 61; cf. Dietrich, *Codicum Syriacorum Specimina* 6.

[2] I have not hesitated to accept Dr Wright's identification of No. DCCCCXXVIII. with Anan-Isho's collection of the "Questions and Narratives of the Fathers," even though Dr Budge adopts (with Hoffmann) a textual emendation in Thomas of Marga's description which, if the true reading, would make this identification erroneous. I observe:

(1) That the proposed emendation makes Thomas of Marga describe a book such as is not known to exist (six hundred chapters, divided into fifteen books of forty sections each, *Book of the Governors*, II. 190); whereas the actual Syriac text, whatever its obscurities, describes (as translated by Assemani, *Bibl. Orient*. III. i. 146) a work clearly identical with DCCCCXXVIII. (2) Thomas of Marga further tells us that this collection of Anan-Isho's formed the last part of the *Paradise*; and in both our copies of the *Paradise*, Book IV. is in the main identical with DCCCCXXVIII. (3) As there can therefore be no reasonable doubt that this MS. DCCCCXXVIII. preserves Anan-Isho's collection of "Questions and Narratives," and almost in its original form, it follows that the obscurities of Thomas of Marga's text must be cleared up in such a way as to make the description harmonise with the thing described. (4) Hence it is manifest that the Syriac word "Head," translated "Capitulum" by Assemani, and "Chapter" by Budge, here means "Apophthegma"; for what Anan-Isho did was to rearrange the "Conversations of the Elders" (Budge, II. 189), *i.e.* the Syriac collections of apophthegmata, which are called in Latin also "Verba Seniorum" (Rosweyd Book V.); and, as a matter of fact, Anan-Isho's work is a collection of apophthegmata, most of the extracts from it printed by Dr Budge being literal translations of apophthegmata found in the Greek and Latin collections. (5) The difficult passage wherein Thomas of Marga, after saying that the first portion of the work was divided into six hundred and fifteen "heads" (*i.e.* "apophthegmata"), contained in fourteen canons and distinctions, adds that "quodlibet capitulum [apophthegma] convenientem proprio argumento quaestionem subjunctam contineat" (Assemani), can only be interpreted as meaning that all the apophthegmata in each of the fourteen canons or sections had to do with the subject-matter announced in the title of the section, e.g. "On fleeing from men," "On fasting and abstinence," etc. It must be recollected that among the Syrians "Questions and Answers" was one of the regular titles for collections of apophthegmata.

No. DCCCCXXIX. (*Addit.* MS. 14583, Century XI., ff. 1—151).

The same work as the preceding (incomplete).

No. DCCCCXXX. (*Addit.* MS. 17264, Century XIII., ff. 1—65).

Illustrations of the Book of the Paradise. This work is based upon the *Paradise* and is thrown into the form of a dialogue between a teacher and his disciples; it is divided into four Parts, each being a commentary on one of the four Books of the *Paradise*: Part IV. is very incomplete. Part I. is based on the Lausiac History, but it cannot be described as a redaction of it. In the *Catalogue* (1078) Wright speaks of the *Illustrations* as another work of Anan-Isho's; but in his *Syriac Literature* he corrects this statement[1].

No. DCCCCXXXI. (*Addit.* MS. 17263, Century XIII., ff. 1—230).

Part IV. of the *Illustrations*, commenting on Bk. IV. of the *Paradise*: imperfect at the beginning, but along with the preceding MS. it gives the full work. Another copy is entered also in the manuscript catalogue of recent accessions (*Oriental* MS. 2311).

No. DCCCCXXXII. (*Addit.* MS. 17175, Century X., ff. 1—66).

An abridgment of the *Illustrations*.

This exhausts the consecutive series of Syriac works brought together under Palladius's name in Wright's *Catalogue*, III. 1070 —1080; but in the Index, under the heading *Palladius and Hieronymus* are upwards of a hundred references, and there are further references under other rubrics. I have looked out all these references, and I am able to give, for the first time, an analytic Index of the contents of this whole group of the British Museum Syriac Collection. I give Wright's notation only.

I. *The Historia Lausiaca.* (Cf. preceding Lists.)

DCCXXVII. 1 d, 3 g; DCCLXII. 3; DCCLXXX. 4 a, d, 6 a; DCCXCIII. 17; DCCCXII. 22; DCCCCXXIII. 1, 2; DCCCCXXV. 2; DCCCCXLIII. 1; DCCCCXLIX. 3, 6; DCCCCL. 11, 14, 15, 22; DCCCCLX. 6, 10, 23, 77; DCCCCLXIII. 4, 9, 12ᵃ, 13.

Single Lives :—Amoun DCCCXXXVII. 4; Nathaniel DCCCXXVI. 10 (hardly legible); Evagrius DLXVII. 1; DLXVIII. 1; DCCXXXIV. 5; DCCXXXVII. 1 a; DCCLIII. 19.

II. *The Historia Monachorum.* (Cf. Appendix I.)

DCCXXVII. 3 p; DCCXXX. 5; DCCCVIII. 6 (ff. 148—165); DCCCCXXIII. 1, Part II.; DCCCCXXIV. Part I.; DCCCCXXV. 2 (f. 86); DCCCCXXXVII. 2; DCCCCXLI. 6; DCCCCXLIII. 1 (f. 48); DCCCCXLIX. 4; DCCCCLX. 28, 29, 30, 31; DCCCCLXIII. 12ᵇ.

Anyone who has examined the multitudinous Syriac redactions of the apophthegmata in the British Museum collection, will appreciate the utility of Anan-Isho's undertaking.

[1] P. 176 (a reprint from the *Encyclopaedia Britannica*, ed. 9).

III.   *Collections of Apophthegmata.*

a.   *Anan-Isho's Collection* (*Bk. IV. of the Paradise*), DCCCXXXIV. 1, 3, 4;
DCCCXXXVII. 21; DCCCCXXVIII.; DCCCCXXIX. 1.   [Bedjan.]

b.   *Great Collection entitled "Histories of the Egyptian Monks."*   DCCCVIII.
6 (f. 81); DCCCCXXIII. 1 (f. 2); DCCCCXXIV. (f. 58); DCCCCXLIII. 1 (f. 1) (cf.
Dietrich, *Codicum Syriacorum Specimina*).

c.   *Miscellaneous Collections.*

R. F. XLIX. 70.

DIX. 1.

DCCXXVII. 3 a—c, e, f, h—o.

XXXVI. 1.

XLI. 3.

XLIV. 3.

LII. 2.

LIII. 9, 28.

LV. 5.

LXII. 3 (ff. 56, 77), 6, 9, 11, 15.

LXX. 10.

LXXII. 5.

LXXIII. 2.

LXXX. 2, 4 c.

LXXXIV. 2.

XCII. 5, 8.

XCIII. 17, 24.

XCVII. 6.

DCCCI. 13.

VI. 19.

VIII. 6 (ff. 111, 165).

X. 1.

DCCCXII. 19, 22.

XVII. 1.

XVIII. 2, 4.

XX. 2 d.

XXIV. 5.

XXVI. 10.

XXVIII. 1, 4, 5.

XXXIV. 8.

XXXVII. 2, 11.

XL. 6.

XLIII. 1, 4.

LVII.   iv. 16, vi. 14, xlir.,
xlv. 1, xlviii. 3.

LXII.

DCCCCXXIII. (ff. 73, 137).

XXV. 1.

XL. 2.

XLIII. 1 (ff. 41, 58).

XLIX. 1, 3 (f. 11), 4 (f. 43).

LIX. 6, 8.

Fly-leaf entries referred to on
pp. 460, 576, 591, 788, 1005 of *Catal.*

IV.   *Miscellaneous Documents.*

DCCCXXX.; DCCCCXXXI.; *Oriental* 2311; DCCCCXXXII. (abridgment).   (Illustrations of the Paradisc.)

DCCXXX. 9; DCCLII. 14; DCCLXXX. 5; DCCCCXXXIX. 1; DCCCCXL. 1; DCCCCXLI.
7; DCCCCLXIII. 10 (Life of Serapion Sindonita stated in DCCCCLXIII. (Cent.
XIII.) to be by Palladius; but is quite different from *Hist. Laus.* A 83—85.
Printed by Bedjan, *Acta* V).

R. F. XLIX. 56 (Extract from Serapion's Life of Macarius of Egypt; *ibid.*).
DCCLXII. 6; DCCLXXXIV. 1; DCCCCXLVI. 1 (Asketicon of Pachomius; *ibid.*).
DCCCCXLVI. 3 (Note on John of Lycopolis). Also in DCCLXII. 6; DCCCCXXIII. 2.
DCCCCXXVI.; DCCCCXXVII. (Unidentified).

DCCCCXLV. 7; DCCCCLX. 26; DCCCCLXXX. (Erroneous references).

I have no doubt that among these *Apophthegmata* might be found further extracts from the Lausiac History. On the other hand, some *Apophthegmata* are explicitly stated to be "from the work of Palladius, bishop of Helenopolis" (cf. DCCLIII. 28, DCCCLVII. iv. 16, xlv. 1, DCCCLXII.); but they are not really his. I have already referred to the erroneous Syrian tradition that the *Apophthegmata* were collected by Palladius; the notes or colophons at beginning and end of Dr Budge's copy speak of the whole *Paradise* as being "written by Palladius for Lausus," and the book is frequently called the "Paradise of Palladius." Thus among the Syrians not only the Lausiac History but also the *Historia Monachorum* and the *Apophthegmata* came to be attributed to Palladius, and the two last named works were often called the Lausiac History. Dr Wright in his *Catalogue* naturally follows the Syrian practice, and habitually speaks of the *Historia Monachorum* and of *Apophthegmata* as being by Palladius, and even from the Lausiac History. And Dr Budge, both in the *Book of the Governors* and in the *Laughable Stories of Bar-Hebraeus*, prints a number of *Apophthegmata* from Book IV. of the *Paradise* under Palladius' name[1].

The fact of the matter is this, that it was the fashion among the Syrians to ascribe to Palladius any work relating to the Egyptian monks. In this way a number of books came to be identified more or less with the Lausiac History; and only in this loose, and indeed quite untrue, sense can it be said that the Syriac copies of the work of Palladius present different redactions. Of all the Syriac works that went under the name of Palladius, the Lausiac History alone is really his; and of the Lausiac History, properly so-called, two translations have occurred among the several MSS. that have come under view, but only one redaction; no reason has been met with for suspecting the existence of any other redaction among the Syrians. And (almost needless to add) that redaction substantially agrees with the one which has in these pages been known as the Short Recension (B). Both Syriac versions carry back this recension in its main features to the early sixth, if not the fifth, century.

---

[1] Similarly Zotenberg (*Catal.* p. 139). Three of the extracts in the *Laughable Stories* are really from Palladius, cf. next page.

A list is appended of the portions of the Syriac Versions which are in print [elsewhere than in Bedjan's volume].

Version I.

Tullberg (*Paradisus Patrum*) :
A 28.   Paul the Simple (p. 21).
A 29.   Pachon (here called Pachomius) (p. 29).
A 35.   Elias (p. 41).
A 43 (less C) and 47.   John of Lycopolis (p. 1).
A 89.   Chronius of Phoenicia (p. 12).
A 90—95.   Jacob the Lame and Paphnutius (p. 13).
A 101.   Ephraim Syrus (p. 9).
A 117 (init.) and 136.   Virgin of Alexandria and Athanasius (p. 33).
A 138.   Taor (p. 36).
A 139.   Virgin and Colluthus (p. 37).
A 141.   Girl who calumniated a Lector (p. 38).

Budge (*Book of the Governors*, II.) :
Epistle to Lausus : Μακαρίζω (p. 195).
Proemium : 'Εν ταύτῃ τῇ βίβλῳ (p. 196).
A 10 and 11.   Pambo and Pior (p. 35).
A 14.   Apollonius the Merchant (p. 470).
A 15 and 16.   Paesius and Isaias—first half (p. 471).
A 28.   Paul the Simple (p. 32).
A 83.   Serapion Sindonita—the first few lines (p. 586).
A 86.   Evagrius—three lines (= *P. G.* XXXIV. 1194 B) (p. 201).
A 136.   Virgin of Alexandria and Athanasius—portions of the first half (p. 199).
A 147.   Juliana—three lines from the first half (p. 200).
        (The piece on Bessarion, printed p. 572, from Book II. c. 16, is not A 116, but Apophthegma 12 under Bessarion's name (*P. G.* LXV. 141).)

Budge (*Laughable Stories of Bar-Hebraeus*):
A 8.   Amoun of Nitria—the first half (p. 53).
A 20.   Macarius of Alexandria—the story of the hyena (out of Book IV.) (p. 49).
A 29.   Pachon (called Pachomius)—the second half (p. 45).

Cureton (*Corpus Ignatianum*):
A 43.   John of Lycopolis—three lines on John's prophecies, the part omitted in A (p. 351).

Version II.

Assemani (*Bibl. Apost. Vat.* III. 143) :
A 1.   Isidore—first four or five lines.
A 35.   Elias—three lines c. *med.* (end of MS.).

Budge (*Book of the Governors*, II.) :
A 17.   Macarius Junior (in the Syriac "the Child of the Cross")—a few lines not in the Greek (p. 198). [Bedjan 55.]
[A 104, 22, 87, 88, Bedjan 218—226.]

§ 11. THE ARMENIAN VERSION.

(By Professor Armitage Robinson.)

Among the *Lives of the Holy Fathers*, edited from Armenian MSS. by the Mechitarists of S. Lazzaro (Venice, 1855, 2 vols.), the following correspond more or less closely with portions of the Lausiac History. They all occur in vol. I.; the latter part of that volume and the whole of vol. II. being taken up with the *Apophthegmata*[1].

p. 82. Paul the Simple = A 28.

Two recensions of the Armenian version. Neither of them follows closely the Greek or the Syriac (Budge, *Book of Governors*, I. 35 f.). They are paraphrases rather than translations. The closing section gives Paul's time as a monk, and his total age (108 years). It also states the month and day of his death, and is therefore probably a recension for liturgical use.

p. 89. Macarius of Alexandria = A 20, 21.

This shows great freedom of reproduction, but is clearly based on the Greek text, and has no resemblance to the Coptic recension. The mirage story and the antelope story are welded into one, the scene being transferred to the saint's cell. A devil in the form of a maiden offers him first water, and then milk which she has milked from an antelope. The Marcus story is not separated from the Life of Macarius, but follows immediately after his temptation to travel[2]. At the close of it the text passes without a

---

[1] Vol. I. also contains portions of the *Historia Monachorum*.

[2] The order of incidents in A 20, 21 (Migne, *P. G.* xxxiv. 1050 ff.) is confused. The true order, and in some points a better text, is printed, *ib.* 184 ff. from Floss. There the Marcus story follows the temptation to travel, as in the Armenian and Latin versions.

break into the Life of John of Lycopolis. Thus the hyena story and some further matter is altogether wanting.

p. 95.   John of Lycopolis = A 43.

Inc. ‘I Macarius[1] and Evagrius and Albinus and Ammonius wished to know the truth about the blessed John’ (= *P. G.* xxxiv. 1113 B). It agrees with the Greek text in Migne in having lost a sentence by *homoeoteleuton* in col. 1113 D between Εὐαγρίου and καὶ ἐν τῷ μεταξὺ κ.τ.λ. Its closing section (p. 97) contains the statements found in col. 1115 A as to his being 40 years in the desert, never seeing a woman, and never being seen when eating or drinking. Then follows (p. 97) the *Life of John of Lycopolis* from the *Historia Monachorum*.

p. 162.   Serapion = A 83—85.

An abbreviation of the Greek, containing each of the anecdotes. In the case of the second (the Athenian philosophers) the Armenian text is very corrupt or is the rendering of corrupted and misunderstood Greek: the story is completely marred.   There is no break before or after the mention of Domninus.   Instead of μαθητῇ Ὠριγένους (*P. G.* xxxiv. col. 1187 A) the Arm. has simply ‘the disciple.’   After the story of the virgin at Rome (A 85), follows the story of the selling of the little Gospel, and the story of the mourning for the lost treasure: neither of these being in the Short Recension (B) of the Lausiac History.   At the close we read that the saint died in Scete in the cell of his disciple Zacharias.

The story of the little Gospel is as follows:

“And when he had returned thence he came to Alexandria; and he had a little Gospel. He saw a man taken for debt, and he sold the Gospel and gave it for the debt, and released him. Now before this he saw a poor man naked, shivering with the cold, and he took his coat and gave it to him. When he saw him, that kept the way of peace [so, literally: it is probably a confusion of ὁ ἐπὶ τῆς εἰρήνης, *P. G.* xxxiv. 1220 B], he saith unto him: Father, who hath stripped thee? And he holding out the Gospel

---

[1] This sentence explains why John of Lycopolis comes in at this point. Macarius is supposed to be the narrator of that saint’s story. This seems to have arisen from a misunderstanding of the Greek, ἐγώ τε καὶ οἱ περὶ τὸν μακάριον Εὐάγριον κ.τ.λ.

saith unto him : This hath stripped me. And afterwards he sold the Gospel. And when he came to his cell, his disciple Zacharias saith unto him : Father, where is thy tunic ? He saith unto him : My son, I have sent it on before, where we have need of it. And he saith unto him : Where is the little Gospel ? Then he saith : That which said unto me, Sell that thou hast and give to the poor, itself have I sold and given, that we may have boldness there."

This story is told in Leontius's Life of John the Almsgiver (c. xxiii. ed. Gelzer, 1893, p. 48) in the Armenian *Apophthegmata* (vol. II. p. 244) and in a brief form among the *Verba Seniorum* (Ruf.) § 70 (Rosweyd, p. 512), in each case being related of Serapion. In Socrates, *H. E.* IV. 23 it is given in the same brief form as told by Evagrius of 'a certain brother' : cf. *Verba Seniorum* (Pelag.) l. 6, c. 5 (Rosw. p. 582).

But in the Long Recension of the Lausiac History it is told of Bessarion (A 116, a section which is one of two which are found in A, but not in B or C). The narrative there is longer than in any of the other sources referred to.

It is to be noted that in the Armenian the incident which follows almost immediately (the weeping for the lost treasure) has a parallel in the *Apophthegmata* (*sub verbo* Bessarion : Cotelier, reprinted in *P. G.* LXV. 144). This also is attributed to Serapion in the Armenian version of the *Apophthegmata* (vol. II. p. 557 f.)[1].

The composite nature of these latter portions makes it doubtful whether the statement as to the saint's death came from the

---

[1] The following summary may be useful :

Little Gospel.

Apophth. Lat. *Ruf.* Rosw. 512 (very short)	SERAPION.
—— Arm. II. 244	"
Leontius's John Eleemos. c. 23	"
Life of Serapion, Arm. I. 164	"
Long Recension of Laus. Hist. (A 116)	BESSARION.
Socrates, *H. E.* IV. 23 } (very short and told	ANON.
Apophthegm. Lat. *Pelag.* Rosw. 582} by Evagrius)	

Lost Treasure.

Apophthegm. Arm. I. 557 f.	SERAPION.
Life of Serapion, Arm. I. 164	"
Apophthegm. Graec. (Cotelier) *P. G.* LXV. 144	BESSARION.

Lausiac History, where the MSS. vary between ἐν Ῥώμῃ and ἐν ἐρήμῳ, and where there is no mention of a disciple at this point[1].

p. 224.   Eulogius and the Cripple = A 26.

The heading of this piece is 'Story of Ligion of Alexandria': but in the text the name is given as 'Liginus.' Except at a few points, where changes are intentionally introduced, the Armenian follows the Greek pretty closely. We may note the principal alterations, which are in part made in the supposed interest of the saint's character.

Migne, *P. G.* XXXIV. 1073 B Ἀκηδιῶν οὖν καθ᾽ ἑαυτὸν, καὶ μήτε εἰς συνοδίαν βουλόμενος εἰσελθεῖν, μήτε δὲ μόνος πληροφορούμενος, εὑρέν τινα κ.τ.λ.

Arm. p. 224. 'And he thought to enter into a monastery: and he was diligent in attending (*lit.* 'was first' or 'beforehand') night and day in the church of God: And as he went at the ninth hour (cf. Acts iii. 1) to the church, he saw a man,' etc.

1074 C καὶ κολακεύσας τὸν λελωβημένον, ἐμβαλὼν αὐτὸν εἰς σκάφος βουκολικὸν, ἐξῆλθεν τῆς πόλεως ἐν νυκτὶ καὶ ἀνήνεγκεν αὐτὸν εἰς τὸ μοναστήριον τοῦ μεγάλου Ἀντωνίου.

Arm. p. 226. 'And he went and began to coax the cripple, that he might be able to take him to the holy Antony. And Liginus saith to the cripple: Wilt thou, my lord, that we go to pray at the monastery of Antony? And the cripple saith: As thou wilt. And they rose up and went and came to the disciples of Antony, and were there one day,' etc.

Lower down the Armenian adds that Antony 'did not see' Liginus, because of the darkness, at the time when he called him by his name.

At 1075 D we read in the Greek that 'within forty days Eulogius died,' and then again 'within three days more' the cripple died: but at 1076 A we learn that Cronius arrives when the monks are keeping the 'forty days mind' (τὰ τεσσαρακοστά) of Eulogius, and the 'three days mind' of the cripple (cf. *Ap. Const.* viii. 42, Lagarde, p. 276, for these terms). The Armenian avoids the difficulty which these statements involve by simply

---

[1] According to a Syriac MS. Life of Serapion in Brit. Mus. (Wright, *Cat.* II. 695) Serapion dies 'at the convent of Pachomius in the desert.'

saying, in the second place, 'keeping the memorial of the blessed Liginus and of the cripple.'

At the close Cronius takes the Gospel to swear to the truth of his narrative; and he then describes how he had acted as interpreter between Eulogius and Antony, as the latter knew no Greek. The Armenian translator has failed to catch the first point, and he has no interest in the second. So he closes the Life thus: 'The holy father took the Gospel and comforted (them) and spake perfect words concerning them that were perfected in Christ Jesus our Lord.'

These examples show the freedom with which these Lives were reproduced for edification. There is no ground at all for supposing that the changes are based on independent sources of information.

The corruption of the name of Eulogius into Liginus raises the question whether we should postulate an intermediate translation into Syriac. The story of Eulogius is mentioned in Wright's *Catalogue*, III. 1127. The name is written ܠܘܓܝ. This seems to offer us no explanation of *Liginus*. Moreover there, in the heading at any rate, the cripple is said to be a leper. So that the Syriac Version I., at any rate, cannot well be the original of the Armenian.

p. 318.   Evagrius = A 86.

In the Venice edition this Life is not printed with those of which we have spoken above; but forms the first item in the second division of vol. I., coming under the heading 'Paralipomena ex secundâ interpretatione.' This apparently means that the version does not belong to the earliest period of Armenian literature.

The first section, beginning 'In many ways, beloved,' etc. is a very free paraphrase of the first ten lines of the Greek. One curious point deserves notice: the words $\pi\hat{\omega}_{S}$ $\tau\epsilon$ $\mathring{\eta}\lambda\theta\epsilon\nu$ $\mathring{\epsilon}\pi\mathring{\iota}$ $\tau\mathring{o}\nu$ $\mu o\nu\acute{\eta}\rho\eta$ $\sigma\kappa o\pi\acute{o}\nu$ are rendered 'how he came to the remote places of Rebon' (ցռւ.եբոնի). The same word recurs later on as a translation of Melania's words, $\mathring{o}\tau\iota$ $\mathring{\epsilon}\chi\eta$ $\tauo\hat{v}$ $\sigma\kappa o\pi o\hat{v}$ $\tauo\acute{v}\tauov$ $\epsilon\mathring{\iota}_{S}$ $\tau\mathring{o}\nu$ $\mu o\nu\acute{\eta}\rho\eta$ $\beta\acute{\iota}o\nu$, where the Armenian has (literally), 'that thou hast the great diligence of toil of the desert of Rebon' (ցռւ.եբոնի).

The word σκοπός has apparently been misunderstood by the
translator, but I do not understand the word which he has
substituted. The Venice editors print it with a capital letter[1].

After the first paragraph the Armenian follows the Greek
rather more closely. We may note that the native town of
Evagrius is said to be 'Iberia'; and that Gregory *Nazianzen* is
said to have ordained him 'chief of the deacons.' When Melania
bade him tell her the real cause of his long illness (εἶπε οὖν μοι
τὰ ἐν τῇ διανοίᾳ σου), we read, in the Greek, ὡμολόγησεν οὖν αὐτῇ
τὸ κατὰ Κωνσταντινόπολιν αὐτῷ συμβάν. This is probably not
the best reading of the Greek. Other readings are τὸ συμβάν
and τὸ συμπᾶν. The Armenian has, 'He confessed to her concerning his thoughts (or, 'his secrets').' This is mainly based on
the former sentence (τὰ ἐν τῇ διανοίᾳ αὐτοῦ), which the Armenian
does not reproduce: but it presents a curious, though quite
accidental, coincidence with the Coptic, 'Then he manifested all
his thoughts to her[2]' (Amél. *Hist. Laus.* p. 111).

In the passage about his books we read: 'He composed three
books divinely-inspired (or, 'sacred') for (or, 'of') solitaries, and
against word-builders (a usual word for 'poets') and against the
cleverness of demons (or, 'demons of cleverness').' This is a
desperate attempt at rendering τρία βιβλία ἱερά, Μοναχόν (or
μοναχῶν), Ἀντιρρητικόν, οὕτω καλούμενα· τὰς πρὸς τοὺς δαίμονας
ὑποθέμενος τέχνας. It throws, I fear, no light on the Greek text.

The story of the visit of the three heretics is given in the
short form: 'Again, there appeared to him in the day-time three
demons in the likeness of clerics, contending with him concerning
the faith. One of them said that he was an Arian, another a
Eunomian, the other an Apollinarian; and he vanquished them by
his wisdom: and having made known (or 'recognised') the temptations, lifting his hands to heaven unto God,—immediately the
demons disappeared from him.' The last clause may be compared
with the additional words in the Latin Version II. at this point

---

[1] [The following suggests itself as a possible conjecture: in the second passage,
and in the first also in some MSS., the Greek is μονήρη βίον. The translator may
have misread it μονη ρηβιον, and then rendered it "the desert of Rebon." E. C. B.]

[2] This however is a mere echo of the words which precede: 'Tell me openly all
thy thoughts.'

(Rosw. p. 997): they only agree however in the statement that the demons disappeared; and this was a not unnatural supplement to the story. There is no ground for thinking that they come from the longer form of the Greek.

After the statement that the demons who contended with him could not be numbered, comes the story of the announcement of his father's death, which in the Greek comes at the very end. Then follows the account of his prophesying. The Greek is then rendered fairly well to the end of the statement that for three years he had not been troubled by the desires of the flesh. The life then closes thus: 'After such suffering and afflictions and intolerable temptations of demons, and after austerities and unceasing prayers, having lived as a monk in good conversation, having kept the faith and having finished his course he came to his rest in the same desert in Jesus Christ our Lord.'

After this formal close of the Life follows a short section which deserves attention from more than one point of view. It is, as the Venice editor points out, a kind of colophon connecting the Life with the works of Evagrius, which followed. The Armenian text is printed in a somewhat more satisfactory form in Dr Dashian's valuable catalogue of the Armenian MSS. in the Mechitarist Library at Vienna (1895, p. 614)[1]:

'This Evagrius having lived in the desert fifty-four years, by the power of the Holy Spirit of Jesus Christ and our Saviour, made light to shine in mighty wise on me the unworthy.

I have written and set out according to my power three books in ordered and easy and convenient discourses:—the first concerning the true faith of the solitaries: the second against disputers and word-builders (perhaps 'orators and poets'): the third concerning spirits of evil—we have made answer from the holy scriptures to the demons which tempt us; that ye reading and profiting, Christ may make you victorious over the spirit of evil.'

1. The last book here referred to is clearly the 'Αντιρρητικόν. The title and first words are given in the same Catalogue, p. 615,

---

[1] Lists of the works of Evagrius which follow the Life in Armenian MSS. will be found in this Catalogue (see Codd. 235 and 276), and also in Father Carekin's *Catal. of Anc. Arm. Translations* (Venice, 1889), pp. 421 ff.

§ 14: 'Of Evagrius: Answer from the holy scriptures to the
demons which tempt us: The intelligent beings under heaven,'
etc. In an Appendix to Zöckler's *Evagrius Ponticus* (Munich,
1893) Dr F. Baethgen has given a translation of the first two
chapters of this work from an imperfect MS. at Berlin (Sachau
302)[1]. The title agrees closely with the Armenian title, and at
the end of each chapter come the words: 'Praised be our Lord
Christ, which hath given us the victory over the thoughts of—,'
according to the evil thoughts in question. Thus we see that the
closing words of the Armenian colophon are derived from the
'Αντιρρητικόν itself.

2. But this colophon requires further investigation. For a
portion of it is verbally identical with a colophon found in an
Armenian codex of the Acts and Epistles in the British Museum
(*Addit.* MS. 19730) and in some other Armenian Bibles, at the
end of the Epistle to Philemon. Let us set the two colophons
side by side, so far as their common material extends:

B. M. *Addit.* 19730.	END OF LIFE OF EVAGRIUS.
Գրեցի և կարգեցի	Գրեցի և կարգեցի
ըստ կարի	ըստ կարի իմում
առքերուն զգիրս	երիս գիրս
Պաւղոսի արաքելոյ	
յարինեալ և դիւրահաս	յարինեալ և դիւրահաս
ընթերցուածովք	և վայելուչ ճառիւք
I have written and set out	I have written and set out
according to (my) power,	according to my power
in lines, the books	three books
of Paul the Apostle	
in ordered and easy	in ordered and easy
lections.	and convenient discourses.

It seems quite clear that either these colophons are from the
same hand, or else one is imitated from the other.

3. But the first, as Mr Conybeare pointed out (*Journ. of
Philology*, vol. XXIII. pp. 241 ff.: see *Euthaliana*, Texts and Studies,
III. 3, pp. 3 and 8), is a translation of the notable colophon of
Codex H of the Pauline Epistles.

---

[1] The complete work is to be found in the British Museum: see Wright's *Cat.*
II. p. 446, no. 4.

. . . . .
ἔγραψα καὶ ἐξεθέμην κα
τὰ δύναμιν στειχηρὸν·
τόδε τὸ τεῦχος παύλου
τοῦ ἀποστόλου· πρὸς ἐγ
γραμμὸν καὶ εὐκατάλημ
πτον ἀνάγνωσιν· τῶν κα
θ' ἡμᾶς ἀδελφῶν· παρ ὧν
ἀπάντων τόλμης· συν
γνώμην αἰτῶ· εὐχὴ τῇ
ὑπὲρ ἐμῶν· τὴν συνπε
ριφορὰν κομιζόμενος·
κ. τ. λ.

Is then the Armenian colophon at the end of the Life of
Evagrius likewise a translation from a Greek colophon, composed
by a Greek editor of the works of Evagrius? Or is it an Armenian
production which imitates a colophon found in Armenian Bibles?
The question is not easy to answer: but I would note in favour of
the Armenian origin of the colophon the following points:

(1) The verbal agreement between the two colophons in
Armenian seems too close to be readily accounted for as due
to independent translations of the same Greek words. This is
especially the case in regard to the words ' in ordered and easy...'
which represent, but do not literally render, the Greek πρὸς
ἐγγραμμὸν καὶ εὐκατάλημπτον....

(2) The writer of the Armenian colophon has made a mistake
in saying that Evagrius 'lived fifty-four years in the desert.'
This was the total duration of his life. The mistake could
scarcely have arisen from a reading of the statement at the
beginning of the Greek Life: ὅπως ἀξίως τοῦ ἐπαγγέλματος
αὐτὸν ἐξασκήσας τελευτᾷ ἐτῶν πεντήκοντα τεσσάρων ἐν τῇ ἐρήμῳ.
I think it might have come more easily from a hasty perusal of
the Armenian version, where the order of the words is somewhat
different. In any case the error shows that it was only by his
writings, and not through personal acquaintance, that Evagrius
' caused light to shine upon' his editor.

(3) The confusion which we have noted in the account of the
three books of Evagrius as given in the Armenian version of the

Life finds a parallel in the colophon. The last of the three is, as we have seen, the Ἀντιρρητικόν. But so too, both in the Life and in the colophon, must the second book be: 'Against word-builders' (Life); 'Against disputers and word-builders' (colophon).

I am not prepared, however, to say that these indications are decisive of the question.

4. The most curious coincidence of all remains to be noted. The colophon of Codex H is also found in Codex Neapolitan. II. A. 7; and there it begins thus:

Εὐάγριος ἔγραψα καὶ ἐξεθέμην....

Dr Ehrhard of Würzburg, who pointed this out (*Centralblatt für Bibliothekswesen*, 1891, VIII. 9, pp. 385 ff.), also observed that, in the almost obliterated line of Codex H which precedes the word ἔγραψα, part of the name of Evagrius is still to be traced[1]. He went on to conjecture that Evagrius Ponticus was the true author of the elaborate apparatus attached to the Acts and Pauline Epistles under the name of Euthalius. I have shown in my *Euthaliana* that this colophon does not proceed from the original compiler of the Euthalian apparatus, but belongs to an *editio minor*, in which that apparatus is much abbreviated, but which quite probably was made in 396, *i.e.* in the lifetime of our Evagrius.

I can offer no further light upon the coincidence by which a colophon at the close of a Life of Evagrius corresponds so closely with a biblical colophon which contains the name of Evagrius. We seem further than ever from an explanation when we note that in the Armenian Bible MSS. the latter colophon does *not* contain the name of Evagrius at all.

It may be worth while to add that in Syriac MSS., although the Life of Evagrius often precedes a collection of his writings, there is no trace to be found of the colophon with which we have been dealing.

J. A. R.

---

[1] I have been inclined to think that ΕΥΑΓΡΙϘ, not ΕΥΑΓΡΙΟC, originally stood in Codex H, and that afterwards ΕΥΘΑΛΙΟC ΕΠΙCΚΟΠ...... was written over it. But the defacement of the line makes it difficult to speak with any certainty.

§ 12. THE COPTIC VERSION.

M. Amélineau has done more than any one else to make accessible and to illustrate the Coptic records of the early monks; so that his works will be prominently before us in this section and in others to follow. They are somewhat scattered; and therefore a list of those which deal with early Coptic monachism is furnished in a footnote[1]. M. Amélineau maintains that the

[1] The most important of the works in question are those contained in the series of Coptic and Arabic Texts, with Translations and Introductions, entitled *Monuments pour servir à l'histoire de l'Égypte chrétienne au iv° et v° siècles*. Three volumes have so far appeared :—

1. Tome I.—(*Mémoires publiés par les membres de la Mission archéologique française au Caire*, Tome 4).

Fascicule I. pp. 1—478 (1888), containing Lives and documents relating to Abba Schnoudi.

2. Tome I.—*Fascicule II*. pp. 479—840 (1895), containing fragments on Pachomius, Theodore, Horsiisi, Schnoudi, and John of Lycopolis.

3. Tome II.—(*Annales du Musée Guimet*, Tome 17; 1889). *Histoire de Saint Pakhôme et de ses Communautés*, containing Bohairic and Arabic Lives and Sahidic fragments.

4. Tome III.—(*Annales du Musée Guimet*, Tome 25; 1894). *Histoire des Monastères de la Basse-Égypte*, containing Lives and documents relating to Paul the Hermit, St Anthony, the Macarii, and others.

Tome IV., to contain the great Coptic collection of *Apophthegmata*, or Sayings of the Fathers, is promised.

5. *De Historia Lausiaca quaenam sit hujus ad Monachorum Aegyptiorum historiam scribendam utilitas. Adjecta sunt quaedam hujus historiae Coptica fragmenta inedita*. (Paris: Leroux, 1887.)

6. *Voyage d'un Moine égyptien dans le désert*. A French translation of a Coptic *Vita Onuphrii*, cf. Rosweyd, 93. (*Recueil de travaux relatifs à la philologie et à l'archéologie égyptienne et assyrienne*, 1883; reprinted, Vienna: Holzhausen, 1883.)

7. *Fragments Coptes pour servir à l'histoire de la conquête de l'Égypte par les Arabes*. (*Journal Asiatique*, Nov.—Dec. 1888; reprinted, Paris: Leroux, 1889.)

The above include original texts; those that follow are more popular in character:

8. *Étude historique sur St Pachôme et le cénobisme primitif dans la Haute-*

Lausiac History and the other Greek and Latin works of the same period describing Egyptian monastic life were in great measure but translations and adaptations of Coptic materials. The reasons which he brings forward in support of this theory in the case of other works are carefully examined in Appendix III.; and it is there, I think, proved in regard to the chief of them—the *Apophthegmata Patrum*, the *Vita Pauli*, and the *Historia Monachorum*—that the Greek or Latin texts are the originals and the Coptic the translations[1]. The reader who has studied this Appendix will approach the consideration of the Coptic fragments of the Lausiac History with a presumption in favour of the ordinary view that it is an original Greek work. And this presumption, I venture to think, will remain unaffected by an examination of the specific arguments brought forward on the opposite side by M. Amélineau in the case of the Lausiac History. He deals with the question

Égypte d'après les monuments Coptes. (Bulletin de l'Institut Égyptien, 1886; reprinted, Cairo, 1887.)

9. *Les Moines Égyptiens : Vie de Schnoudi. (Annales du Musée Guimet, Bibliothèque de Vulgarisation; Paris: Leroux, 1889.)*

10. *Samuel de Qalamoun. (Revue de l'Histoire des Religions, 1894; reprinted, Paris: Leroux, 1894.)*

11. *Le Christianisme chez les anciens Coptes. (Revue de l'Histoire des Religions, 1886—7; reprinted, Paris: Leroux, 1887.)*

12. *Contes et Romans de l'Égypte Chrétienne. (Collection de Contes et Chansons populaires, Tomes 13 et 14; Paris: Leroux, 1888.) (Especially the Introduction.)*

13. *Rôle of the Demon in the ancient Coptic Religion. (The New World, 1893.)*

14. *Essai sur l'évolution historique et philosophique des idées morales dans l'Égypte ancienne. (Bibliothèque de l'École des hautes études:—sciences religieuses, Tome IV.; Paris: Leroux, 1895.)*

15. *Géographie de l'Égypte à l'époque Copte. (Paris: Imprimerie Nat., 1893.)*

[1] In the note appended to § 13 reasons are indicated that have led me to the belief that the Greek, rather than the Coptic, is the original redaction of the *Vita Pachomii*; M. Ladeuze has made a special study of the redactions of this *Vita*, and though he has not yet published his investigations in full, he has made the statement that the conclusion at which he has arrived is that the Greek is the original (*Muséon*, Avril 1897, p. 171). Mr W. E. Crum tells me that he has found Coptic fragments of the *Vita Antonii*, and that he is satisfied they are translations from the Greek *Vita*. And in regard to the Lausiac History itself Dr Preuschen, who has studied the question attentively, holds the Coptic fragments to be translations from the Greek of Palladius. It seems that this seductive theory of Coptic originals demands much more serious study than it has up to this received.

in his brochure *De Historia Lausiaca* (pp. 28, 29), and relies on a twofold argument:—

(1) There is nothing in Palladius which is uncongenial to Egyptian ways of thinking. His accounts of Amoun of Nitria, Moses the Robber and Paul the Simple contain the same incidents as are related of them in the Coptic Synaxarium; and things told by Palladius of other monks find parallels in the Coptic documents.—No significance however can be attached to this circumstance, unless the accounts are not merely similar, but virtually identical. The Lives of Paul the Simple, for example, in the *Historia Lausiaca* and the *Historia Monachorum* are very like one another, but there is no question of plagiarism on either side. That Palladius should have accurately reproduced Coptic modes of thought is sufficiently accounted for by his long abode in Egypt. And it may very well be that he had read Coptic books and derived from them some of his knowledge about those earlier monks whom he had not seen, and based portions of his history upon the recollection of what he had read therein. But this is not the question at issue. The question is whether considerable portions of the Lausiac History are direct translations from Coptic sources.

(2) The second argument meets this issue. There are in the Lausiac History certain constructions which betray their Coptic origin, and were certainly translated from Coptic into Greek. Three specimens of such Coptic idioms found in the Lausiac History are brought forward,—the oft recurring διηγήσατό μοι ἀδελφός τις, and the form of adjuration or request : τῶν ποδῶν σου ἁπτόμεθα (A 15, 16).—I cannot see any reason why such expressions should not have been employed by a Greek writer. The third instance of a Copticism is taken from one of the parts ·interpolated from the *Historia Monachorum*, and cannot therefore be admitted as evidence in the case of the Lausiac History; it is considered in its proper place in Appendix III. It is true that M. Amélineau says that he gives only a few instances out of many ; but it must be supposed that those which he selects are among the most striking.

We may now proceed to an examination of the texts. Of the Coptic Version of the Lausiac History only a few considerable fragments are known to be extant. Zoega prints excerpts from them[1], and Amélineau the full texts[2]; both writers furnish translations.

---

[1] *Catalogus Codicum Copticorum manu scriptorum qui in Museo Borgiano adservantur* (Romae, 1810).

[2] *De Historia Lausiaca* (Fragments 1—4); *Histoire des Monastères de la Basse-Égypte* (Fragment 5).

The following is a list of the Fragments:

(1) The Dedicatory Epistle: Μακαρίζω σου τὴν προαίρεσιν (*P. G.* xxxiv. 1001);

(2) The Preface, or Διήγησις: Πολλῶν πολλὰ καὶ ποικίλα (*P. G.* xxxiv. 1001—1010);

(3) The Life of Pambo or Pamo (A 10, 11).

(4) The Life of Evagrius (imperfect at the end) (A 86).

(5) The Life of Macarius of Alexandria (imperfect at the beginning) (A 20, 21)[1].

These fragments are all in the Bohairic or northern dialect. The MS. containing 1 to 4 dates from the tenth century; that containing 5 was written in 1153[2]. Fragments 3, 4, 5 contain a considerable amount of matter not found in the Greek. Thus two distinct questions arise in connection with the Coptic fragments:—

(I.)   Which is the original, the Coptic or the Greek?

(II.)   If the Greek prove to be the original, is the additional matter of the Coptic later accretion, due to Greek or Coptic scribes; or is the current Greek text, at any rate in certain places, but an abridgment of Palladius' work?

It will be convenient to keep these two questions separate.

I. *The Original Language.*

A discussion must be instituted concerning each of these five pieces:

(1) The Epistle Μακαρίζω (Zoega *Catalogus* 129; Amélineau *De Hist. Laus.* 73—76).

(2) The Διήγησις, Πολλῶν πολλά (Zoega *op. cit.* 129—130; Amélineau *op. cit.* 76—92).

These two pieces may be taken together, for their very nature precludes the idea of the Coptic being the original. They are addressed to Lausus; the words, "To Lausius the Praepositus"

---

[1] The fragments on John of Lycopolis (Tome i. Fasc. ii. of Amélineau's *Monuments*) are from the *Hist. Mon.*; that on Poemenia (*ibid.* 664) is quite different from *Hist. Laus.* (A 47), though apparently referring to the same episode.

[2] Mai, *Scriptorum Veterum Nova Collectio,* v. *159, *165.

stand in the title of each of them in the Coptic just as in the Greek, and he is further mentioned by name in the body of the Διήγησις. It will be shown in the second part of this Study that the minute autobiographical details given in the Greek Διήγησις harmonize perfectly with the known course of Palladius' career; and they stand here in the Coptic exactly as in the Greek[1]. The two pieces are dedicatory writings to the Greek Lausus from the Greek Palladius; and therefore in their case there can be no question at all of the Coptic being the original: both the pieces were certainly written in Greek.

(3) *The Life of Pambo* (Zoega *Catalogus* 130; Amélineau *De Hist. Laus.* 92—104; cf. *P. G.* XXXIV. 1028; A 10—11, B 2). The structure of the Coptic Life is as follows:—

(α) Certain anecdotes not found in the Greek Life of Pambo (pp. 92, 93 in Amélineau).

(β) The body of the Life, agreeing in main outlines with the Greek Life—A 10 (*Fuit igitur*, p. 94—*processissent*, p. 99).

(γ) More anecdotes not found in the Greek Life (pp. 99—103).

(δ) The story of Abba Pior = A 11 (pp. 103, 104).

It must be noted that Fragments 1 to 4 belong to a single MS., now forming part of the Vatican *Cod. Copt.* LXIV. The pagination is preserved in Amélineau's reprint, and the pages succeed one another continuously from 1 to 90[2]. To the first piece is prefixed the rubric: " The fifth Sabbath of Lent"; and to the fourth piece (though Amélineau does not give it) the similar rubric: " The fifth Sunday of Lent" (cf. Zoega 132). This shows that the Coptic MS. was prepared for liturgical use, the two pieces of Introductory matter and the Life of Pambo being selected for reading on the fifth Saturday of Lent, and the Life of Evagrius on the following day. The facts of the case may be thus stated:—

(a) The first two pieces and the body of the third exist in the one Greek work, the Lausiac History.

---

[1] Amélineau *op. cit.* 77, 78 ; Zoega *op. cit.* 130.

[2] The number ΚΗ in the third line of the Life of Evagrius is an obvious misprint for ΛΗ (*De Hist. Laus.* 104).

(b)   In the Coptic MS. they form a single liturgical lection.

(c)   The first two pieces were certainly selected for the purpose from a Coptic translation of the above-mentioned Greek work—(unless, indeed, it be supposed that the Coptic MS. is a translation of a Greek lectionary).

It seems, then, only natural to suppose that the third piece also (at any rate the portion of it that corresponds to the Greek) was taken from the same source.

And this supposition is confirmed by the following fact: the five lines near the beginning of the Coptic Life of Pambo (de cujus virtutibus...nisi necessarium, p. 92) do not occur in the Greek Life; but they do occur in the account of Abba Or, which in the Lausiac History immediately precedes that of Pambo[1]. If the reader will look at the last paragraph of A 9 (which in the genuine redaction constitutes practically the whole account of Or, cf. B 2), he will see the close verbal agreement between the Coptic and the Greek, and also that in the Greek text of the Lausiac History the Coptic Fuit igitur (p. 94) follows immediately after nisi necessarium (p. 92).

These various considerations tending to connect the Coptic Life of Pambo with the actual Greek work of Palladius, make it almost certain that those portions of the Coptic which correspond in matter with the Greek (β and δ in the schedule above) were translated from the Greek.

A comparison of the texts confirms this position, and shows that the Greek is without doubt the original; for instances can be pointed out in which the divergences of the readings are evidently due to the Coptic translator having failed to understand the Greek.   Thus in the Greek we read: $\mu\eta\delta$' ὅλως ἀνανεύσας, ἡ κἂν προσέχων τῷ σκεύει τῆς θήκης (P. G. XXXIV. 1028 D); for which the Coptic has: "But he did not raise his head, while working" (p. 96).   Here the Copt has not attempted to translate the somewhat crabbed Greek clause, but has substituted the statement (already made) that Pambo was at work weaving palm leaves.   Again, after relating the rebuke she re-

---

[1] In the Old Latin they actually form part of the same chapter: see below p. 114.

ceived from Pambo for her desire of praise, Melania continues: οὕτως οὖν ᾠκονόμησεν, φησὶν, ἡ χάρις τοῦ κυρίου ἐν τῷ εἰσελθεῖν με εἰς τὸ ὄρος (ibid.). The Coptic has: "In this way, therefore, did God give me rest, and I went forth from him" (p. 96). Once again, when Pambo was near his end he sent for Melania, and when she came he was weaving a basket, καὶ τοῦ τελευταίου κεντήματος πρὸς ἀπαρτισμὸν ὄντος he gave the basket to Melania (1033 A): instead of this expression, which was difficult to translate, the Coptic has: "When he drew nigh to his last breath" (p. 97)[1].

In the Greek account of Pambo there are four mentions of a disciple of his named Origen, who is twice stated to have been his *oeconomus*; in the corresponding places in the Coptic the names John, Theodore, Macarius are found instead of Origen. Now one of the groups of Greek MSS.[2] and the Latin Version II agree in this respect with the Coptic. A variety of considerations resulting from the investigations I have made into the grouping and inter-relations of the MSS. and versions, has led me to believe that Origen is the true reading: and I see that Dr Preuschen has arrived at the same conclusion. The substitution of the other names is, I believe, due to the desire of getting rid of the very name of Origen,—a phenomenon of which other examples are forthcoming[3]. It is impossible to enter at this place on any

---

[1] M. Amélineau thinks the Coptic text the better in this place, and says that without doubt the reading κεντήματος is due to the error of some scribe (*De Hist. Laus.* 35, note). But κεντήματος is not only the reading of the Greek MSS.: it is attested by both Latin Versions and by Syriac Version I (Budge, II. 36), all of which interpret the clause as meaning " when the basket was finished."

[2] Dr Preuschen does not mention these Greek MSS. in his critical apparatus (pp. 120 ff.): they are the Paris MSS. *ancien fonds grec* 1626, and *Coislin* 282, 295, 390; also the MS. used by Hervet (cf. 1st ed. of Rosweyd).

[3] In Paris MS. 1627 the name Origen is simply omitted in three of the places in Pambo's Life. The original form of Latin Version I agrees with the common Greek text in giving Origen's name; but in the recension as found in the printed editions the name is omitted in one place and changed into Paul in two of the others. In A 84 Domninus is said to have been a disciple of Origen; in the Armenian Version of this the obnoxious name is omitted. In the Latin *Hist. Mon.* is a short chapter (attested by Sozomen and therefore genuine) on a monk named Origen; this chapter is not to be found in any Greek copy of the work that I have seen. Thus there can be no doubt that the tendency mentioned in the text was

discussion of the textual problem; but if Dr Preuschen and I are correct in the result at which we have arrived quite independently: *i.e.* if the readings common to certain Greek MSS., to a Latin version, and to the Coptic, are in truth corruptions: then it is certain that the common error must have arisen in a Greek copy, and have passed thence to the Coptic, which therefore is proved to be a translation.

Besides the agreements in the proper names common to the Coptic and the Latin Version II, and to a group of Greek MSS., there are a number of other agreements between the two versions, which are not shared by any Greek MS. known to me, and which indicate clearly a special affinity between the two versions. In Lat. II (Rosweyd, 987) Or and Pambo form one chapter (c. V.). This appears to have been the case in the Greek Palladius which the Coptic writer used. The chapter probably bore the single title of Pambo. Hence what is said of Or is attributed to Pambo, by the omission of Or's name. Moreover in the Latin there is no mention at this point of Melania's having been a source of information (as is stated in the other authorities for the text): here again we have a point of connection between Lat. II and the the Coptic. Again, in the Coptic Pambo says to Melania: "God who received the two mites of the widow *will receive thy sacrifice also*," and in the Lat. II: "*nec tuam oblationem tradet oblivioni*"; but the italicised words have no equivalent elsewhere. In the account of the burial (1033 A) the Coptic and Lat. II both have the third person, not the first. These coincidences show that the Greek MSS. which stand behind these two versions were closely related; but there appears to be no extant Greek representative of the type.

Indeed M. Amélineau in the case of Pambo modifies his general theory and admits that the actual Coptic before us, in the parts which correspond with the Lausiac History, is a translation from the Greek. But to account for the additional matter found in the Coptic life, he suggests that probably Palladius derived his materials from a Coptic work, which he translated in an abridged form into Greek; and that then a Copt retranslated the Greek

operative; it existed also, but in a lesser degree, in the cases of Didymus and Evagrius.

into Coptic, having before him also the original Coptic work used by Palladius and filling up from it the gaps of Palladius' abridgment[1].

Against this cumbrous hypothesis, which can have nothing to recommend it, save that it is the only way of reconciling the general theory of Coptic originals with the fact that here a great portion is certainly a translation from the Greek, several objections present themselves. For instance, if the Coptic translator had in his hands the presumed original Coptic work, is it likely that he would have retranslated the Greek at all, instead of merely transcribing the original? Again, the circumstance that a large portion of the narrative purports to be a personal relation by Melania to the writer, points to a Greek rather than a Coptic origin: it is altogether unlikely that she should have told all this to a Copt, whereas it is known that she had personal relations with Palladius, and he quotes her in a number of places as the authority for what he relates.

But what is to be brought forward in the second part of the present section, when we come to deal with the additional matter in Pambo, will quite dispose of the theory.

Thus far, then, we see that in the first three Coptic pieces we have certainly translations from the Greek of the Lausiac History. The Coptic additions in the third piece will be considered later.

(4) *The Life of Evagrius* (Zoega *Catalogus*, 132; Amélineau *De Hist. Laus.* 104—124; cf. *P. G.* XXXIV. 1188—1195; A. 86, B 25).

In order to compare the Coptic with the Greek, it will be convenient to divide the Life into sections as follows :—

---

[1] " Mihi quidem libet dicere Palladii opus ab auctore fragmentorum Vaticanorum translatum esse, sed etiam hunc auctorem alio opere usum esse quo ipse antea usus sit Palladius " (*De Hist. Laus.* 39).

		Greek.	Coptic.
(a)	Introductory, down to the text: "Being made perfect in a short time."	1188 B 8 to C 2.	104 to 106—*Multos annos explevit.*
(β)	His origin, ordination, coming to Constantinople and activity there.	1188 C 2 to D 1.	*Hic igitur homo* (106) *to dimicatos esse* (107).
(γ)	Story of how he came to leave Constantinople; his illness at Jerusalem, and arrival at Nitria.	1188 D 1 to 1194 A 7	*Omnisque civitas* (107) *to in Aegypto adivit* (111).
(δ)	His life in Nitria and Cellia, his austerities, &c.	1194 A 8 to B 11	*Ibi duos annos* (111) *to ricinis impleretur* (116).
(ε)	Three anecdotes.	(not in the Greek)	*Paucisque post diebus* (116) *to cognoscant* (121).
(ζ)	Interview with three demons in guise of clerics.	1194 B 11 to B 15	*Rursus* (121) to end (124) [incomplete].
(η)	Prophecies, confessions, death.	1194 B 15 to 1195 A 2.	[MS. incomplete.]

(a)   In this case it is worth while to contrast the texts:

[All the translations from the Coptic have been made for me from Amélineau's texts by the Rev. Forbes Robinson, Fellow of Christ's College, and Editor of the *Coptic Apocryphal Gospels* in this series.]

P. G. XXXIV. 1188.

Τὰ κατὰ Εὐάγριον τὸν ἀοίδιμον διάκονον τοῦ Χριστοῦ,

ἄνδρα βεβιωκότα κατὰ τοὺς ἀποστόλους, οὐ δίκαιον ἡσυχάσαι,

ἀλλὰ ταῦτα γραφῇ παραδοῦναι

εἰς οἰκοδομὴν τῶν ἐντυγχανόντων καὶ δόξαν τῆς ἀγαθότητος τοῦ σωτῆρος ἡμῶν
ἄξιον ἡγησάμενος

Amél. *De Hist. Laus.* (p. 104).

Now I also will begin and I will speak concerning abba Evagrius the deacon of Constantinople, on whom Gregory the bishop laid hands; for also it is seemly that we should tell of his virtues whom all have praised. Now (δέ) he lived in the life of the apostles. For it is not right to hold our peace concerning his celebrated works and his progress; but rather it is seemly that *we should write them for* edification and *profit to those who shall read them, in order that they may give glory to God our Saviour who giveth power to men to do these things.* For also it was he who taught me the life which is in Christ, and he made me know the holy Scripture

ἄνωθεν ἐκτίθεμαι, πῶς τε ἦλθεν ἐπὶ τὸν μονήρη σκοπὸν καὶ ὅπως ἀξίως τοῦ ἐπαγγέλματος αὐτοῦ ἐξασκήσας τελευτᾷ ἐτῶν πεντήκοντα τεσσάρων ἐν τῇ ἐρήμῳ κατὰ τὸ γεγραμμένον· Τελειωθεὶς ἐν ὀλίγῳ ἐπλήρωσε χρόνους μακρούς.

in spiritual wise (πνευματικῶς), and he told me what old wives' fables were (lit. are), as it is written : That sin may be manifested, that it is sinful.—[More of the writer's personal intercourse with Evagrius]— which *I shall write to you for profit to those who shall read them* and those who shall hear them, *that they may give glory to Christ who giveth power to His servants to do that which pleaseth Him.* May I also be worthy[1] to tell you how from his beginning [he lived] until he came to these measures and these great acts of asceticism (ἀσκήσεις), until he fulfilled sixty years and so rested, as it is written : In a short time he fulfilleth many years.

Here the Coptic is fully twice as long as the Greek, mainly owing to the presence of a passage not found in the Greek, professing to bring out the writer's personal indebtedness to Evagrius. The Greek is in a single compact sentence ; the Coptic is in half a dozen. The end of the first sentence and the beginning of the second render twice over the same Greek words οὐ δίκαιον ἡσυχάσαι, and say in effect: "It is right to tell of his virtues, for it would not be right to hold our peace concerning them." After the passage mentioned above as not found in the Greek, the clause εἰς οἰκοδομὴν......τοῦ σωτῆρος ἡμῶν is repeated (see the sentences in italics), so that it is quite clear that the Greek sentence was cut in two at the word ἡγησάμενος, and the fresh matter inserted ; and that then the Redactor went back and repeated the last clause that he had used, in order to pick up again the thread of the Greek. These doublets make it evident that the Coptic cannot here be an original text, nor is it conceivable that the compact and well constructed Greek sentence should have been an abridgment of the seven sentences of the rambling Coptic. Moreover the clause "to tell you how from his beginning [he lived] until he came," is a mistranslation of the Greek: ἄνωθεν ἐκτίθεμαι πῶς τε ἦλθεν.

---

[1] Lit. *that I also may be worthy*

Section (β) supplies two instances in which the differences between the texts are due to mistranslations on the side of the Coptic. After naming the country and birthplace of Evagrius, and saying that his father was a presbyter, the Greek text and the other versions go on to say that he was ordained reader by Basil, "bishop of Caesarea," and many of the authorities add "the one which is near Argus," evidently to make it quite clear which Caesarea was St Basil's see. The Coptic completely alters the meaning; it says nothing at all about Evagrius being ordained reader, and declares instead that Basil, "the bishop of Cappadocia," made Evagrius' father presbyter of the church that is at Argus (*lit.* at Arkeus, *or* among the Arkeans: the word is plural in form). Once again: in the Greek we read that, when St Gregory departed from Constantinople after the Council, he left Evagrius behind him to help the new bishop Nectarius to confute the heretics. The Coptic reads: " And he overcame all the heretics. This Evagrius therefore and Nectarius the bishop [were] holding discussions (*or* disputations) with one another face to face; for he was very vigilant in the Scriptures, and his understanding was ready to convict all the heretics by his wisdom,"—a passage which would seem to imply that Nectarius was a heretic.

In section (γ) the two texts run quite parallel, and it is a simple question of translation on the one side or the other: *i.e.*, though there are trifling additions and omissions on either side, they are not more than such as are to be found in the case of the Coptic fragments (1) and (2), which, as has already been seen, are mere translations from the Greek. I think that anyone who compares the two texts of (γ) will feel that the additions in the Coptic (*e.g.* ' on account of his pride' (107), ' as a child' (108), ' in bright raiment' (108), ' which he changed twice a day' (110)), are not improvements, and have the appearance of glosses; while the omissions spoil the story (*e.g.* the clause describing Evagrius' fear while standing before the judge, and seeing others punished for the same offence as his own). I select the following cases for special notice:—the Coptic *tamquam si illum quaesivissent* (108, line 16) appears to be a mistranslation of the Greek: τῶν ἐπ' αὐτὸν δῆθεν ἐλθόντων (1193, A 4), and *illi cum furibus vincto dixit*

(109, line 4) a contraction of λέγει αὐτῷ δεδεμένῳ μεταξὺ σειρᾶς τεσσαράκοντα καταδίκων (1193, B 3), which is almost certainly the true Greek reading. Again ταριχεύσας αὐτοῦ τὸ σαρκίον (1193, D 8) becomes *illius caro tenuis sicut filum facta est* (110, line 16), an absurd exaggeration.

In the remaining sections (δ), (ε), (ζ), the Coptic is either quite new matter, or else such an enlargement of the Greek as to be in effect a different text. These sections will therefore have to be considered in the second part of this chapter. Meanwhile I think it has been shown that in the case of Evagrius also, where the two texts run parallel, the Greek is the original from which the Coptic has been translated.

(5) *The Life of Macarius of Alexandria* (Zoega *Catalogus* 66—71; Amélineau *Monastères de la Basse-Égypte* 235—261; *P. G.* XXXIV. 184—200, and 1050—1065; A 20, 21; B 6).

In making the following synopsis of the Greek and Coptic Lives from the point where the latter begins, I have taken the Greek text which is printed in the Appendix to Floss's edition of the works of the two Macarii[1] (reprinted in Migne, *P. G.* XXXIV. 184 ff.). This text gives the true order of the incidents in the Life, as found also in Meursius and the Latin versions, whereas in A certain dislocations have been introduced. The Coptic begins at the close of the story of Macarius' visit to the enchanted garden of Jannes and Jambres (*P. G.* XXXIV. 188 D).

Greek.	Coptic.
(*a*) Antelope story.	(*a*) Antelope story.
	(*l*) Hyena and sheepskin.
(*b*) The asp.	(*b*) The asp.
(*c*) His various cells.	(*c*) His various cells.
(*d*) Paralytic girl.	(*d*) Paralytic girl.
	Story of Lydia.
(*e*) Visit to Tabennisi.	(*e*) Visit to Tabennisi.
(*f*) Attempted contemplation.	(*f*) Attempted contemplation.
(*g*) Cure of a presbyter.	(*g*) Cure of a presbyter.
(*h*) Cure of a demoniac boy.	(*h*) Cure of a demoniac boy.
	The Libyan robbers.
	Takes nothing to satiety.

[1] *Macarii Aegyptii Epistolae*, &c. (Coloniae: 1850).

Greek.	Coptic.
(*i*) Temptation to travel.	(*i*) Temptation to travel.
(*j*) Story of Marcus.	(*j*) Story of Marcus.
(*k*) Fights self and the devil[1].	(*k*) Fights self and the devil.
(*l*) Hyena and sheepskin.	
(*m*) Not spitting since baptism.	(*m*) Not spitting for seven years.
(*n*) Personal appearance.	(*n*) Personal appearance.
Answer to evil thoughts.	
Conclusion—"This out of much."	
	The broken chalice.
	Seven converted actors.
	Prays for rain in Alexandria.
	Conclusion—"What I could collect about him."
	His day 6th of Pashons.

In order to discover which is the original text, it will be best to compare passages of some length in which the Greek and Coptic most nearly agree. I select therefore the story of Macarius' visit to Tabennisi, the passage marked *e* in the above table. There are flaws in both the Greek texts that are printed in Migne; but on the whole for this particular passage that on column 1057 is the better. The following table schedules the points of difference between the Greek and Coptic (pp. 241—4).

col. 1057

C 6 οἱ Ταβεννησιῶται] + which is a monastery in the South. Abba M. arose. (This breaks the Greek sentence into two.)

8 ἀνῆλθεν εἰς τὴν Θηβαΐδα] he came to the South. } (The order of the Greek
δι᾽ ἡμερῶν δεκαπέντε] + until he came thither. } clauses is inverted.)

9 εἰσελθών] now when he had reached...he came.

10 τῶν Ταβεννησιωτῶν] om.

12 ᾧ ἀπεκρύβη] God did not tell him.

13 Μακάριον] + for he had heard concerning him and he wished to see him (cf. Luke xxiii. 8).

D 1 Παχώμιος] + What dost thou desire, my brother? Behold I see that &c.

2 δοκεῖν σὺ πῶς δύνασαι] Thou art not able πολιτεύεσθαι.

2 ἀδελφοί] + all the.

3 ἀπὸ νεότητος] om.

3–4 καὶ τοῖς τόποις σιναναγατραφέντες φέρουσι τὸν κάματον] om.

4 ἐν ταύτῃ τῇ ἡλικίᾳ] om.

5 τοὺς τῆς ἀσκήσεως πειρασμούς] their persistence.

[1] Floss is certainly right in restoring the name of Macarius in place of Marcus in the last six sections: Marcus is confined rigorously to the short section *j*.

D 7 κακολογεῖς ἡμᾶς]+go to the dwelling of the strangers [who are] husband-men, and dwell there. I will nourish thee there until thou desirest to go forth of thine own accord (or by thyself).

8 ηὐτόνησεν] was weak. 9 νῆστις]+he went again to the abbot.

10 ἐὰν μὴ νηστεύσω κατ' αὐτοὺς) if I do not fast and ἀσκεῖν and do handi-
καὶ ἐργάζωμαι ἃ ἐργάζονται) work like them.

12 πείθει] he sent. 13 ὁ μέγας Π.] om.

13 ἐστι δὲ τὸ σύστημα] Now the number...was. 15 μέχρι τῆς σήμερον] om.

col. 1058

A 1 ἡ Τεσσαρακόστη] the holy Τεσαρακόστη (sic) of the fast. ὁ γέρων Μ.] om.

3 τὸν μὲν ἐσθίοντα ἐν ἑσπέρᾳ,) some fasting till evening each day, others
τὸν δὲ διὰ δύο¹, τὸν δὲ) fasting two two, others fasting five five,
διὰ πέντε) (i.e. two days or five days at a time).

3–5 ἄλλον πάλιν ἑστῶτα διὰ πάσης) and others fasting, standing all night
νυκτός, τὴν δὲ ἡμέραν καθε-) [and] sitting in the day [om. εἰς
ζόμενον εἰς ἔργον) ἔργον].

6 εἰς πλῆθος] om.; +he took them [and] laid them on a high κυρικόν table before him

ἐν γωνίᾳ μιᾷ] +of his cell, plaiting plaited work.

7 καὶ τὸ Πάσχα παραγέγονεν] om.

9 οὐκ ἐκαθέσθη οὐκ ἀνέπεσεν, οὐδενὸς ἄλλου ἐγεύσατο] om.

11 ὡμῶν] om.

12 ἵνα δόξῃ ἐσθίειν] to eat them in their presence, in order that they might know that he used to eat.

καὶ μὴ εἰς αἴησιν ἐμπέσῃ] om.

13 εἰς τὴν χρείαν ἑαυτοῦ] to make water or to moisten palm branches.

14 ἵστατο εἰς ἔργον] om.

μὴ λαλήσας μὴ μικρὸν μὴ μέγα] he used to speak to no one.

15 μηδὲν ἄλλο ποιῶν παρεκτὸς τῆς ἐν καρδίᾳ) praying in his heart, working
προσευχῆς, καὶ τῶν θαλλῶν ὧν εἶχεν ἐν) at the palm branches.
ταῖς χερσίν.)

B 2 τῆς μονῆς ἐκείνης] om.; +in this work.

3 τοῦ ἡγουμένου αὐτῶν] their head of the monastery.

3–5 Πόθεν ἡμῖν ἤγαγες τοῦτον τὸν) Whence hast thou brought this old man
ἄσαρκον ἄνθρωπον, εἰς ἡμε-) hither? Perhaps he was not clothed
τέραν κατάκρισιν) with flesh, [and] thou hast brought him
) here to judge us.

5 ἵνα εἰδέναι ἔχοις] om. 6 σου σήμερον] om.

7–8 ἀκούσας δὲ ταῦτα παρὰ τῶν ἀδελφῶν...ἠρώτησεν τὰ κατ' αὐτόν] om.

10 ἀπεκαλύφθη αὐτῷ] and God revealed to him.

11 ὁ μοναχός] the Alexandrian, he who dwelt in Scete.

12 ὁ κύριος Π.] the head of the monastery.

καὶ ἐξάγει αὐτὸν ἔξω] om.

¹ This clause stands in the text on col. 192. Cf. a parallel passage in the account of the Tabennesiote monks in Α 39: They eat ἄλλοι ἑσπέραν βαθεῖαν· ἄλλοι διὰ δύο· ἕτεροι διὰ τριῶν· ἄλλοι διὰ πέντε (1105 Β). There also σύστημα is used as above in giving the number of the community.

B 14—15 καὶ εἰσαγαγὼν αὐτὸν εἰς τὸν εὐκτήριον οἶκον, ἔνθα ἀνέκειτο αὐτῶν τὸ θυσιαστήριον] [and] brought into the midst of the place-of-making-σύναξις, after that they had ceased from the prayers of the altar +in order that all the multitude of the brethren might see him.

   16 καὶ ἀσπασάμενος αὐτόν] om.

C 2 χάριν σοι ἔχω]+that thou hast edified us all.

   4 ἀσκήσει]+but when they have put forth all their strength, they will not be able to attain to the measure of the forty days of our Lord and our Saviour Jesus Christ, the Son of the living God, [and] μάλιστα [to] thy πολιτείαι, thou that art a man like unto us, καὶ ταῦτα when thou art old.

     παρακαλῶ σε] om.   τόπον σου]+in peace.

   6 τότε ἀξιωθεὶς ὑπ᾽ αὐτοῦ, δεηθέντων αὐτοῦ πάντων τῶν ἀδελφῶν, ἀνεχώρησεν οὕτως.] Then he went, whilst they worshipped him, and all besought him, saying: "Pray for us."

I think a study of this schedule, in regard alike to the additions, the omissions and the alterations, will satisfy the reader that the Greek is the original. But I will call attention to two or three readings which make the matter especially clear. Col. 1057 D, line 8, the Greek is: ηὐτόνησεν παραμείνας νῆστις, 'he held out (till the seventh day), though he had continued fasting'; the Coptic is: 'he was weak, as he had continued fasting.' This would be ἠτόνησεν in Greek. But ηὐτόνησεν is the reading of all the Greek MSS. that I have seen, and is attested by both Latin versions, by Syr. I and by Arm. It therefore follows that the Coptic reading is due either to a mistranslation on the part of the translator, or else to the fact that he used a Greek MS. already vitiated in this point. Either alternative shows the Coptic to be a translation. Again, col. 1058 B, line 4, the monks speak of Macarius as τοῦτον τὸν ἄσαρκον ἄνθρωπον. The Coptic presses the literal meaning of this, and paraphrases "Perhaps he was not clothed with flesh." The Coptic enlargements towards the end are very significant. The Greek story is that Pachomius said, in effect, to Macarius: "Really we have been greatly edified by you; but you are rather too much for us. Please go away, and pray for us." Macarius being thus requested, and all the brethren having alike besought him, he departed; the community being evidently anxious to get rid of him. But in the Coptic it stands thus: "then he went, while they worshipped him, and all

besought him, saying 'Pray for us.'" There is in the Greek a
freshness and a truthfulness to nature which stamps it as genuine;
the Coptic betrays "Tendenz."

We may give another example: In the paragraph marked *i* it
is related that Macarius was grievously tormented by a temptation
of vainglory, the demons pressing him to go to Rome and work
his cures and miracles there. The Greek says (1060 A) that at last
Macarius flung himself down at the doorway of his cell and put
his feet out, saying to the demons: "Drag me along, if you can!
but I will not go away on my own feet." The Coptic says (p. 252)
that Macarius sat at the doorway of his cell and said to the demons:
"If you are able, take me hence by force"; and again: "I have
told you already that I have no feet." Here again it seems that
the Coptic translator has missed the meaning of the Greek. Once
more: the curious compound word πολιοφάγε (1065 c, cf. 1083 c),
"thou white-haired glutton," is absurdly mistranslated in the
Coptic: "thou who eatest thy white hairs" (p. 254).

I shall now take a case in which the Coptic account is much
fuller than the Greek, so that an opportunity may be afforded of
studying the character of the Coptic enlargements. And I select
the instance in which, I think, they may be seen at their best,
the story of the hyena and the sheepskin (*l* in the table). As
both the Greek texts printed in Migne are very unsatisfactory in
this place, I give that of the Paris MS. *ancien fonds grec* 1626,
with one or two corrections from the allied *Coislin* 295.

(Cf. Hervet's translation.)	Amélineau, *Monastères de la Basse-Égypte*, 235 ff. (cf. Zoega, *Catal.* 66 ff.).
1 Διηγεῖτο δὲ ἡμῖν καὶ ὁ δοῦλος τοῦ θεοῦ Παφνούτιος ὁ τοῦ γενναίου τούτου μαθητὴς, ὅτι μιᾶς τῶν ἡμερῶν καθεζομένου τοῦ ἁγίου Μακαρίου 5 ἐν τῇ αὐλῇ καὶ τῷ θεῷ προσομιλοῦντος, ὕαινα λαβοῦσα αὐτῆς τὸν σκύμνον τυφλὸν ὄντα ἤνεγκεν τῷ ἁγίῳ Μακαρίῳ· καὶ τῇ κεφαλῇ κρούσασα τὴν θύραν τῆς αὐλῆς 10 εἰσῆλθεν, ἔτι αὐτοῦ ἔξω καθεζομένου,	And again it came to pass once as he was sitting in his cell, there came unto him a hyena with her young one in her mouth. She carried it and placed it at his door, and knocked with her head at the door. The old man heard her knock, and went out, thinking that a brother was come unto him. But when he opened the door, he saw the hyena, and was

καὶ ἔρριψεν τὸν σκύμνον ὑπὸ τοὺς
πόδας αὐτοῦ.

λαβὼν τὸν σκύμνον ὁ ἅγιος Μακάριος,

καὶ ἐπιπτύσας τοῖς ὀφθαλμοῖς αὐτοῦ,
15 ἐπηύξατο καὶ παραχρῆμα ἀνέβλεψεν·
καὶ θηλάσασα αὐτὸν λαβοῦσα ἡ μήτηρ
οὕτως ἐξῆλθεν.

καὶ τῇ ἑξῆς ἡμέρᾳ κώδιον μεγάλου
προβάτου ἤνεγκεν τῷ ἁγίῳ Μακαρίῳ.

20 καὶ θεασάμενος ὁ ἅγιος τὸ κώδιον
ταῦτα ἔλεγεν τῇ ὑαίνῃ. Πόθεν σοι

astonished, saying: "What doth she seek after here?" And she took her young one in her mouth[1], and held it forth to the old man, weeping. The old man took the young one into his hands, being fearless[2] in his simplicity, and turned it hither and thither, seeking in its body, what was diseased in it. Now when he had considered the young one, behold it was blind in its two eyes. And he took it, and he groaned, and he spat in its face, and signed[3] its eyes with his finger. Straightway it saw, and it went to its mother, and received suck, and followed her; and they went into that river......and into the marsh †where they made their way†[4]. Now the sheep of the Libyans are brought down to the marsh of Scete once a year to eat *shoushet*; and the herdsmen also who dwell in the villages over against Pernouj bring their sheep down to the marsh of Scete once in the year to eat [the] green herb. The hyena waited[5] a day, and on the morrow she went to the old man, a sheepskin being in her mouth, very woolly and fresh, which she carried[6]. And she knocked with her head at the door. Now the old man was sitting in the enclosure; and when he heard the knocking at[7] the door, he rose and opened [it], and found the hyena carrying the skin[8]. He said to the

[1] Lit. *filled her mouth with her young one*

[2] Lit. *established*

[3] Lit. *sealed*

[4] The text from "into that" to "their way," both here and in the copy in the Borgian Museum (see Zoega, *Cat.* pp. 66 f.), appears to be corrupt. Zoega emends his text (which is not the same as Amélineau's), and reads: 'in montana aestu ardentia et inde ad paludem ubi manserunt.'

[5] Lit. *left*   [6] Lit. *placed upon her*   [7] Lit. *of*

[8] Lit. *the skin being placed upon her*

τοῦτο εἰ μὴ βεβρώκεις πρόβατόν
τινος; τὸ οὖν ἐξ ἀδικίας ον ἐγὼ οὐ
δέχομαι παρὰ σοῦ. ἡ δὲ ὕαινα κλί-
25 νασα τὴν κεφαλὴν εἰς τὸ ἔδαφος
ἐγονυπέτει πρὸς τοῖς ποσὶν τοῦ ἁγίου
καὶ ἐτίθει τὸ κώδιον. αὐτὸς δὲ ἔλεγεν αὐτῇ· Εἴρηκά σοι ὅτι οὐ λαμ-
βάνω, ἐὰν μή μοι ὀμόσεις μηκέτι
30 λυπεῖν πένητας κατεσθίουσα αὐτῶν
τὰ πρόβατα. ἡ δὲ καὶ ἐπὶ τοῦτο
διένευσεν τῇ κεφαλῇ αὐτῆς ὡς συντι-
θεμένη τῷ ἁγίῳ Μακαρίῳ. τότε ἐδέ-
ξατο τὸ κώδιον παρὰ τῆς ὑαίνης.

hyena: "Whither hast thou gone, and found this, unless thou hast eaten a sheep? That therefore which thou hast brought to me is from violence[1], I will[2] not take it from thee." The hyena struck her head to the ground and her knees, bending her feet, and beseeching him like a man, that he would take it from her. He said to her: "I have already said that I will not take it, unless thou dost promise me, saying: 'I will not vex the poor by eating their sheep.'" And she made many movements with her head, up and down[3], as though she were promising him. Again he repeated to her: "Unless thou dost promise me, saying: 'I will not take an animal alive.' But thou shalt eat [thy] prey dead from henceforth. If thou be in trouble, seeking without finding, come hither to me, and I will give thee bread. And do no violence[1] from henceforth." The hyena bent her head to the ground...kneeling down, bending her feet, and moving her head up and down[3], towards his face, being as though she promised him. And the old man understood in his heart that it was[4] the dispensation of God, who giveth understanding even to the beasts, for the rebuking of us. And he gave glory to God who giveth understanding even to the beasts. And he praised in the Egyptian tongue God who liveth for ever, †for the soul is honoured†[5]. He said: "I give glory to Thee, O God, who wast with Daniel in the den of lions, and didst give understanding to the beasts: likewise also now Thou hast given understanding

---

[1] Or, wrong
[2] Or, I do
[3] Lit. down and up
[4] Lit. is
[5] The text appears to be corrupt.

35 ὡς δὲ ἡ μακαρία δούλη τοῦ Χρίστου
Μελάνη μοι εἶπεν ὅτι Παρὰ τοῦ
μακαρίου ἐκείνου ἐγὼ ἔλαβον τὸ κώδιον ἐκεῖνο †ξένην†[1] τῆς ὑαίνης ἐπι-
λεγόμενον. καὶ τί τοῦτο θαυμαστὸν
40 παρὰ ἀνδράσιν τῷ κόσμῳ ἐσταυρω-
μένοις ὕαιναν εὐεργετηθεῖσαν εἰς
δόξαν τοῦ θεοῦ καὶ τιμὴν τῶν δού-
λων αὐτοῦ εὐαισθητήσασαν ξένια
τούτῳ κομίσαι; ὁ γὰρ τοὺς λέοντας
45 ἐπὶ τοῦ προφήτου τοῦ Δανιὴλ ἡμε-
ρώσας καὶ ταύτῃ τῇ ὑαίνῃ σύνεσιν
ἐχαρίσατο.

to this hyena also, and Thou hast not forgotten me, but Thou hast made me understand that this ordinance is Thine." And the old man took the skin from the hyena; and she went again to her place. And every few days she came to see him. And when she found no food she came to him, and he threw a loaf to her. She did this many times. And the old man lay on the skin until he died. And I have seen it with my eyes. For when he was about to die, Melania, the queen of the Romans, chanced to visit him, and he gave her that skin for an inheritance. This she had until her death, keeping it faithfully in remembrance of him[2].

I think it will be agreed that in the first half of this passage the Coptic is, from the literary and artistic standpoint, much better than the Greek; it is picturesque, it has local colouring, it has a pastoral air about it, which certainly imparts to it a vividness wanting to the Greek. But on the other hand, equally clear is it that in the second half the Coptic enlargements are thoroughly bad, and have all the signs of being apocryphal additions. So that here again the evidence is in favour of the originality of the Greek. The following words of M. Amélineau throw light on the question:

"L'écrivain copte ne se soucia jamais de la critique, il racontait ce qu'il avait vu, ce qu'on lui avait raconté, employant les ornements du style comme il le pouvait, modifiant à sa guise, croyant parfois qu'une autre phrase, ou même un autre tour de phrase, rendait mieux sa pensée, et les ajoutant l'une à l'autre sans souci de ce qui précédait. De là vient qu'il est presque impossible de rencontrer deux manuscrits semblables, quand même le second a été copié sur le premier....Si l'on traduisait, la traduction ne fut jamais la réproduction fidèle, dans un autre dialecte ou dans une autre langue, de l'œuvre originale. Quand il ne s'agissait pas de l'Écriture, le plus simple copiste pouvait donner carrière à son amour du beau style et changer presque toutes les phrases. Cette année même, il n'y a pas un mois, ayant eu l'occasion de

---

[1] (ξένον)   [2] Lit. *in faith and remembrance*

confier à un jeune homme copte la copie de plusieurs actes de martyrs, je restai stupéfait de l'entendre me dire qu'il me mettrait ces actes '*en meilleur style.*' Je ne pus qu'à grand peine lui faire comprendre qu'il devait bien s'en garder[1]."

The conclusion to be drawn from the evidence, taken as a whole, is that the embellishments introduced by Coptic translators and scribes are by no means always extravagant and grotesque; on the contrary, some of these Copts must have possessed no mean literary sense: we may be prepared to find that they at times introduced a true local colouring into the narrative, and really did in some sense "improve" their texts.

We have gone through the various portions of the Coptic version which have hitherto been printed, and have found in each case that where there is no question of additional matter but only of translation, there can be no reasonable doubt that the Greek is the original. More of the Coptic version will doubtless be recovered in course of time and printed: I suspect from the few lines printed by Zoega, that the Coptic Life of Macarius of Egypt contained in the Vatican Codex LXIV.[2] will prove to be that of the Lausiac History. Any further matter which may come to light will of course demand examination. But there are certain *a priori* difficulties in the way of supposing that Palladius translated Coptic documents, which it may be well to indicate here.

The passages examined make it quite evident that it is a case of actual translation on the one side or on the other: Palladius could not possibly have reproduced the Coptic documents from memory. Now he did not write the Lausiac History till long after his sojourn in Nitria; in the Preface he says that it is the twentieth year of his episcopate, *i.e.* 420; and all through the book he speaks of events that happened after he had left Nitria— the persecution of St John Chrysostom, the Sack of Rome, the death of Melania. It is scarcely conceivable that Palladius should have carried about Coptic documents, or his own translations of them, during the whole of his chequered career; nor does it seem likely that he should have procured them when about to write his

---

[1] *Vie de Schnoudi*, Préface, xiii; cf. *Contes et Romans*, Introduction, lxiv.

[2] *Catalogus* 127: the reader will see the reasons of my belief later on (p. 152).

book[1]. Considerations such as these, drawn from the broad facts of the case, render it in the highest degree improbable that Palladius should have translated or made a direct use of Coptic materials when composing the Lausiac History.

II. *The Coptic Additional Matter.*

We have ascertained that, so far as the printed Coptic Lives agree in matter with the Lausiac History, the evidence leads to the conclusion that the Coptic is a translation of the Greek. We now come to consider the nature of the additional matter found in the Coptic. In the first two fragments there is no additional matter properly so called. We may therefore pass on to

(3) *The Life of Pambo* (for references, cf. p. 111).

The Coptic Life of Pambo is composed as follows :—

Amél. p. 92, l. 1 = *Hist. Laus.*, *P. G.* XXXIV. 1026 D, l. 10.
　　Amél. p. 92, ll. 2, 3 ; not in *Hist. Laus.*
Amél. p. 92, ll. 3—8 = *Hist. Laus.*, *P. G.* 1028 A, ll. 8—14[2].
　　Amél. p. 92, l. 8—p. 94, l. 1 ; not in *Hist. Laus.*
Amél. p. 94, l. 1—p. 99, l. 15 = *Hist. Laus.*, *P. G.* 1028 B init.
　　—1033 B fin.
　　Amél. p. 99, l. 15—p. 103, l. 8 ; not in *Hist. Laus.*
Amél. p. 103, l. 9—p. 104, l. 8 = *Hist. Laus.*, *P. G.* 1033 c.

When we bring together the portions of the Coptic which are not in the Lausiac History, we find that they make a fairly substantial account of Pambo's life : " Abba Pambo succeeded abba Anthony, and they call him abba Pambo ἀληθινόν, that is the truthful. He had a wife and two sons who did not wish to

---

[1] It is true that Palladius was again in Egypt, having been banished to Syene, and perhaps also spent a considerable time at Antinoopolis in the Thebaid ; but that he should have made translations of Coptic writings on these occasions, and should have taken them about with him through Asia Minor and Greece, is only one degree less improbable than the case presented in the text.

[2] *P. G.* XXXIV. 1026 D, l. 10, and 1028 A, ll. 8—14, together make up the full Lausiac History account of Or, the intervening matter being interpolated from the *Hist. Mon.*

become monks. When he first came to the brethren" &c. We may in fact consider this an independent Life, which in the Coptic has been worked up together with the Palladian Life.

Now Socrates tells three stories about Pambo (*Hist. Eccl.* IV. 23). None of these is in the Lausiac History: but all of them, and in the same order, are in our reconstructed second Life. The first of these anecdotes relates how Pambo, being unlettered, went to one of the Fathers whom he asked to teach him a psalm; and after hearing the first verse ("*I said, I will take heed to my ways, that I offend not in my tongue*") said that this would suffice, and going his way spent several years in trying to master thoroughly this one verse (Amél. 92—3). Though the Coptic is somewhat fuller than Socrates' Greek, they both evidently represent the same original. The second story, that of the gold brought to Pambo by Anatolius (p. 100) is given by Socrates very briefly, and with no mention of Anatolius' name. Socrates' text of the third story is printed here, together with a translation of the Coptic. It will be seen that whatever additions may be in the Coptic are mere embellishments. At the end we miss the terseness of the Greek.

(Socrates.)	(Amél. *De Hist. Laus.* 101.)
Οὗτος ὁ Παμβὼς, ᾿Αθανασίου τοῦ ἐπισκόπου παρακαλέσαντος, κατῆλθεν ἐκ τῆς ἐρήμου εἰς τὴν ᾿Αλεξάνδρειαν.	They say also concerning him that abba Athanasius sent for him once and took him into Alexandria. When he entered into the city he
ἰδὼν δὲ ἐκεῖ γυναῖκα θεατρικὴν, σύνδακρυς ἐγένετο.	saw a woman of the theatre (θέατρον) adorned. And straightway he wept[1]. When therefore the brethren who were with him saw him, they said to him: "Our father, we beseech thee,
τῶν δὲ παρόντων πυθομένων διὰ τί ἐδάκρυσε, Δύο με, ἔφη, ἐκίνησεν· ἐν μὲν ἡ ἐκείνης ἀπώλεια·	tell us for what reason are these tears[2]." And he said to them, "There are two things that move me now. The one is concerning the destruction[3] of this soul which I see now.
ἕτερον δὲ	The other is concerning my own soul[4]

[1] Lit. *his eyes wept*
[2] Lit. *tell us these tears that they are those of what thing*
[3] Lit. *The one is the [matter] of the destruction* (emending text)
[4] Lit. *The other is the [matter] of my own soul*

ὅτε ἐγὼ οὐ τηλικαύτην ἔχω σπουδὴν
πρὸς τὸ ἀρέσαι τῷ Θεῷ, ὅσον αὕτη ἵνα
ἀρέσῃ ἀνθρώποις αἰσχροῖς[2].

which is thankless, because it does
not even receive the likeness and
the adornment of this harlot by[1] the
adornment of virtues and the pleasing
of the Lord and His angels."

[1] Lit. *in*

The fact that Socrates gives (as it seems) an abbreviated
extract from the second Life may lead us to suppose that it, as
well as the Lausiac History, was a Greek work—a supposition
which is confirmed by our finding among the *Apophthegmata*
under Pambo's name (*P. G.* LXV. 369) in almost identical words
the anecdote just printed; for Socrates' chapter on the monks
was not one of the sources of the original general collection of
Apophthegmata; it therefore seems reasonable to suppose that the
Apophthegma in question (and very likely some of the others
under Pambo's name which are not derived from the Lausiac
History) may have been derived from this second Life, which
therefore would have been a Greek work. Whether the welding
together of the two Lives was the work of a Greek or of a Copt,
we cannot tell.

It might be expected *a priori* that the two Lives of Pambo
would at some point at least overlap. And it is to be noted that
the compiler who brought these two together failed to observe
that the story of Anatolius and his offering (p. 100) was another
version of the story of Melania and her offering (pp. 94—6).
It is of course conceivable that Pambo acted twice in the same
way; but the request in each case that he should take note of the
amount rather points to the one story being a mere doublet of
the other[3].

It is to be noted that the Coptic is an explanatory edition,
correcting what seems unsatisfactory (as in the case of ὡς μηδὲ
ἀρξάμενος θεοσεβεῖν (*P. G.* XXXIV. 1033 B), which is explained
away in ten lines (pp. 98—99)), and enlarging a story of which

[2] There is a somewhat similar anecdote, but told with much greater detail,
in the *Vita S. Pelagiae Meretricis* (Rosweyd, p. 376); the original Greek has
recently been edited by Usener: *Legenden der h. Pelagia* (Bonn, 1879).

[3] There are several such instances of a story being current in different shapes;
e.g. the story of the Sheepskin in *Hist. Laus.* 20 (above); *Hist. Mon.* (*gr.*) 28;
Rufinus *Hist. Eccl.* II. 4; Sulp. Severus *Dial.* I. 15.

the meaning is a little obscure at first sight (*ἵνα μή σε βαρήσω, ibid.* c), and thereby spoiling it.

(4) *The Life of Evagrius.*

The main interest of the discussion centres round the portion of the Life which is designated (ζ) in the Synopsis on p. 116. Towards the end of the Greek Life mention is made of an apparition of three demons in the guise of clerics, who came and disputed with Evagrius on questions of the faith; and it is merely stated that he overcame them by his spiritual wisdom. The text is as follows:—Τούτῳ τρεῖς ἐπέστησαν ἐν ἡμέρᾳ δαίμονες ἐν σχήματι κληρικῶν, περὶ πίστεως συζητοῦντες αὐτῷ· καὶ ὁ μὲν ἔλεγεν ἑαυτὸν ᾿Αρειανὸν, ὁ δὲ Εὐνομιανὸν, ὁ δὲ ᾿Απολλιναριστήν. καὶ τούτων περιεγένετο διὰ βραχέων τῇ πνευματικῇ σοφίᾳ (P. G. XXXIV. 1194 B).

In the Coptic Life the episode is related at some length, and the arguments are given whereby Evagrius defeated his interlocutors. Cotelier long ago printed a fragment, purporting to be "from the Life of the holy Evagrius written by Palladius," in which the same episode is described[1]. This Greek fragment and the Coptic are the same. Cotelier's Greek is reprinted after the Life of Evagrius in Lami's edition of the *Historia Lausiaca*[2], but not anywhere in the Greek Patrology, either in the Lausiac History (XXXIV.), or in the Appendix containing Cotelier's extra matter (LXV.), or among the *Opera Evàgrii* (XL.). The manuscript in which the Greek is found contains no more of the Life than the fragment printed by Cotelier, which stands among some extracts from the writings of Evagrius[3].

The Greek and Coptic accounts are here printed in parallel columns.

[1] *Eccl. Graec. Mon.* III. 117—120.

[2] *Joannis Meursii Opera Omnia* (ed. Lami), tom. VIII. 556.

[3] The present number of the manuscript is *ancien fonds grec* 1220; it is of the 14th century; the fragment is on f. 271.

Ἐκ τοῦ βίου τοῦ ἁγίου Εὐαγρίου
συγγραφεὶς ὑπὸ Παλλαδίου.

1   Ἐπέστησαν τούτῳ τρεῖς δαίμονες
ἐν σχήματι κληρικῶν ἐν αὐτῇ τῇ
μεσημβρίᾳ. τοσοῦτον δὲ εὐφνέσαντο
ὡς μόλις αὐτὸν γνῶναι, ὅτι δαίμονές
5 εἰσι. καὶ γὰρ ἡ θύρα αὐτοῦ τῆς
αὐλῆς πάντοτε κλεῖθρον εἶχεν· ὅθεν
εὑρὼν αὐτὸ ὡσαύτως ἔγνω, ὅτι δαίμονες οἱ παραγενόμενοι.

ἕκαστος οὖν ἴδιον πρόβλημα ἠρώτη-
10 σεν, εἰπόντες αὐτῷ· Ἐπειδὴ ἠκούσα-
μεν, ὅτι καλῶς περὶ πίστεως διαλέγῃ,
ἤλθομεν, ἵνα πείσῃς ἡμᾶς.

ὁ δὲ πρὸς αὐτούς· Εἴπατε, ὃ βούλεσθε.
λέγει ὁ πρῶτος· Ἐγὼ εἰμὶ Εὐνομια-
15 νός· τοῦτο δὲ ἦλθον, ἵνα μοι εἴπῃς,
ὁ πατὴρ ἀγέννητος ἢ γεννητός;

ὁ δὲ πρὸς αὐτόν· Οὐκ ἀποκρίνομαί
σοι. κακῶς γὰρ ἠρώτησας. ἐπὶ γὰρ
τοῦ μὴ πεφυκότος γεννᾶσθαι οὐδεὶς
20 λέγει γεννητὸν ἢ ἀγέννητον.

ἀπορηθεὶς οὖν ἕλκεται τὸν ἄλλον. ὁ
δὲ ἐλθὼν ἀπωθεῖται τὸν πρὸ αὐτοῦ
ὡς κακῶς ἐρωτήσαντα.

7 αὐτὸ ὡσαύτως] MB: ὡς αὐτὸ αὐτός
10 εἰπόντες] MB. εἰπόντος
15 μοι] MS. με
22 πρό] MB. πρός

(Amélineau, De Hist. Laus. pp. 121—
124.

Again three demons met him
once, being in the form of ministers
of the Church, in the middle of the
day, in the noon-day heat (καῦμα);
and they so adorned themselves that
they did not let him know that they
were[1] demons. Therefore after they
went and he found the door fastened,
he knew that they were[1] demons.
For he did not know at first. And
they were like some discussing[2] with
him concerning the faith from the
scriptures. And each spake with
him his difficulty (πρόβλημα); and
they said to him: "We heard concerning thee that thou dost speak well
touching the orthodox faith. Therefore we came unto thee, that thou
mayest persuade us in that which we
ask of thee." And he saith[3] to them:
"Speak that which ye wish." The
first saith to him, "I am an Eumenian
(Εὐμενιός); and I came unto thee
that thou mightest tell me: 'Is the
Father begotten (γεννητός) or is He
unbegotten (ἀγέννητος)?'" Abba Evagrius saith to him, "I do not[4] answer
thee; for thou didst ask amiss. For
the unbegotten nature (φύσις) must
not be declared to be begotten or
unbegotten." When the first knew
that he was vanquished by him[5], he
drew his companion forward. And
when he came forward, he saith to the

[1] Lit. are   [2] Or, disputing
[3] Or, said (the Coptic word here and
elsewhere may be translated by a Pres.
or Past. It has been translated by
the Present when the Greek has a
Present.).
[4] Or, I will not
[5] Lit. that he vanquished him

ἐρωτᾷ οὖν αὐτὸν ὁ ἀββᾶς Εὐάγριος·
25 Σὺ τίς εἶ; Ἐγώ, φησί, Ἀριανός. Καὶ
τί βούλει; Περὶ τοῦ ἁγίου πνεύματος,
φησί, καὶ τοῦ σώματος τοῦ Χριστοῦ,
εἰ ἀληθῶς τοῦτο ἐκ τῆς Μαρίας.

ἀποκρίνεται ὁ ἀββᾶς Εὐάγριος· Τὸ
30 μὲν πνεῦμα τὸ ἅγιον οὔτε γέννημα
οὔτε κτίσμα. πᾶν γὰρ κτίσμα τόπῳ
περιορίζεται, καὶ τροπὴν ὑφίσταται
καὶ ἐν μετοχῇ ἁγιάζεται. τὸ δὲ
ἅγιον πνεῦμα ἐκ μὲν τοῦ πατρὸς
35 ἐκπορεύεται, τὰ δὲ πάντα πληροῖ—
λέγω δὴ τὰ ἐν τοῖς οὐρανοῖς καὶ
τὰ ἐπὶ τῆς γῆς—αὐτὸ παρ' οὐδενὸς
ἁγιαζόμενον. τὸ ἀπερίγραπτον οὖν
καὶ ἄτρεπτον καὶ κατ' οὐσίαν ἅγιον
40 οὐ δύναται οὔτε κτίσμα εἶναι ἢ λέ-
γεσθαι. περὶ δὲ τοῦ σώματος Μανι-
χαίων ἐστὶ τὸ ἐρώτημα καὶ Οὐαλεντι-
νῶν καὶ Μαρκιανιστῶν· ἢ καὶ Ἀριανῶν;
ἀποκρίνεται ὁ δαίμων· Ναί· ἡμεῖς
45 ἀμφιβάλλομεν, ἀλλὰ δημοσιεύειν οὐ
τολμῶμεν διὰ τοὺς ὄχλους. ἀποκρίνεται ὁ ἀββᾶς Εὐάγριος· Πολλὰ μὲν
οὖν ἐστὶ καὶ λέγεται, ὅτι ἐκ Μαρίας
ἐστὶ τὸ σῶμα· ἥ τε αὔξησις καὶ ἡ
50 περιτομὴ καὶ ὁ ἐν τῇ γαστρὶ ἐνναμη-
ναῖος χρόνος καὶ ἡ γαλούχησις ἥ τε
βρῶσις καὶ ἡ πόσις καὶ ὁ κόπος καὶ
ὁ ὕπνος φθαρτοῦ ἐστὶ σώματος, ἔτι
δὲ ἐξαίρετον ἐπὶ τοῦ σταυροῦ ἡνίκα
55 ἠνύχθη τῇ λόγχῃ καὶ ἔρρευσεν αἷμα
καὶ ὕδωρ. ἀπορηθέντος οὖν καὶ τοῦ
ἄλλου προσέρχεται ὁ τρίτος μετὰ
πολλῆς θρασύτητος, ὥσας τοὺς δύο
ὡς ἀπροσκόπους καὶ λέγει αὐτῷ·
60 Δεδόσθω ὅτι ἐκείνων περιεγένου.
καὶ γὰρ ἡ ἀλήθεια συνηγορεῖ. τί
ἔχεις εἰπεῖν ἐμοί; λέγει αὐτῷ ὁ

first: "Thou didst ask amiss." Abba
Evagrius saith to him: "Thou, what
art thou?" He saith; "I am an
Arian (Ἀριανός)." Abba Evagrius saith
to him: "What dost thou also seek
after?" He saith to him: "I ask concerning the Holy Spirit and concerning
the body of Christ, whether it is truly
that which Mary bare." The holy
Evagrius saith to him: "The Holy
Spirit is neither a thing begotten
nor is He a creature. All creatures
are contained in a place: all creatures
change and are sanctified by Him
Who[1] is better than they."

(The third saith:) "Thou didst
vanquish these, for.... What dost
thou wish to say to me?" The old
man saith to him: "What dost thou

[1] Or, by that which

Εὐάγριος· Σὺ τί ἀμφιβάλλεις; ὁ δὲ ἀποκρίνεται· Ἀμφιβάλλω μὲν οὐδέν,

65 πληροφορίαν δὲ ἔχω, ὅτι ὁ Χριστὸς νοῦν ἀνθρώπινον οὐκ εἶχεν, ἀλλ' ἀντὶ τοῦ νοῦ αὐτὸν τὸν θεόν, τὸ μὴ δύνασθαι ἀνθρώπινον νοῦν ἄρχοντα δαιμόνων νικῆσαι.

70 ὁ δὲ πρὸς αὐτόν· Εἰ μὴ νοῦν εἶχεν ἀνθρώπινον, οὐδὲ σῶμα...εξᾷν...

δύνασθαι μηδὲ Χριστὸν αὐτὸν λέγειν. τὸν τοῦ ἀτρέπτου μὲν οὖν λόγον καὶ τῆς ἀνθρωπίνης ψυχῆς τε καὶ σώ-
75 ματος

διδάσκει Παῦλος ἐν μονάδι ἀνακεφα-λαιῶν τὴν πίστιν καὶ λέγων· Εἷς γὰρ θεός, εἷς καὶ μεσίτης θεοῦ καὶ ἀνθρώπων, ἄνθρωπος Χρι-
80 στὸς Ἰησοῦς.

ὡς ὁρῶ δὲ ὅτι ὑμῶν τῶν τριῶν ἡ

seek after, that thou gloriest before the struggle (ἀγών)?" The demon saith to him: "I indeed do not doubt anything, but my heart is not per-suaded nor assured that Christ took human intelligence; but instead of the intelligence God Himself was in Him. For also human intelligence cannot cast out the prince of de-mons from men, and vanquish him. For also human intelligence is not in the body with God." Abba Evagrius saith to him: "Unless He had taken human intelligence, He would not have taken human flesh also. If[1] therefore He took human flesh from (Mary the) holy Virgin, then He (be-came) man also with soul (and an in-telligence), perfected in all things of mankind save sin only. For the body cannot be (without[2]) soul and intelligence. But if He did not take these, then He is called in vain Christ. The unchangeable Word therefore, the only-begotten Son of the Father, took human body and soul and in-telligence and all things of mankind without sin. Let therefore a single testimony of Paul the Apostle suffice us now, saying—gathering for us the faith into one Unity (μονάς) and one Godhead and one Kingdom, for[3] the coessential Trinity is unchangeable—for he saith: One is God, one is the mediator between God and men, Jesus Christ the Son of God the Father, and the one Holy Ghost, one Catholic Church, one resurrection of the dead, in the time of...even as Paul (said)... ye (deny) all the mystery of the Holy

---

64 ἀμφιβάλλω μὲν] ms. ἀμφιβάλλομεν

[1] Emending Amélineau's text.
[2] Reading ⲁⲧϭⲛⲉ
[3] Or, that

συμφωνία ὅλον τὸ τῆς ἁγίας τριάδος
μυστήριον ἀθετεῖ. εἰ γὰρ ὁ μὲν ὑμῶν
τὸν λόγον κτίσμα λέγει· ὁ δὲ τὸ πνεῦμα τὸ ἅγιον, καὶ τὸ σῶμα τοῦ Χριστοῦ
85 ἀρνεῖται· <ὁ δὲ> καὶ τὴν ψυχήν·
ἐκ τούτου δῆλοι εὑρίσκεσθε Ἰουδαίοις
συντρέχοντες τοῖς τὸν Χριστὸν σταυ-
ρώσασιν. ἐκεῖνοι μὲν ἴσως καὶ συγ-
γνωστοὶ κατὰ σάρκα ἀνελόντες, ὑμεῖς
δὲ τὸ ὅσον ἐν τῇ ἀσεβείᾳ ὑμῶν τὸ
κατὰ πνεῦμα. καὶ ταραχθέντες σφόδρα καὶ ἀπειλήσαντες αὐτὸν παραδειγματισμὸν ἠφαντώθησαν. ὁ δὲ ὡς
ἀπὸ ὕπνου τινὸς ἀνανεύσας περίφοβος
γίνεται. πέμψας οὖν πρὸς Ἀλβῖνον
τὸν γείτονα πραῦτατον ὄντα, ᾧ πάνυ
προσέκειτο, ἀπήγγειλεν αὐτῷ τὸ
δρᾶμα. ὁ δὲ συνεβούλευσεν αὐτῷ
μὴ μένειν μόνῳ, τὸ πολὺ νήφειν τὴν
διάνοιαν καὶ βαρεῖσθαι ὑπὸ τῆς μονό-
τητος.

85 *Addidi* ὁ δὲ

Trinity. One of you has made the
Word [a] creature; another has made
the Holy Ghost [a] creature and[1] the
body of Christ; the other has killed
the soul and the body of Christ"......

(End of MS)

[1] Something is perhaps omitted in
the text.

Here again there can, I think, be no doubt that the Greek is
the original. This follows from considerations both general and
particular. There is throughout a subtlety of theological and
metaphysical speculation, an acuteness in the disputation, a
knowledge of technical terms, which all seem to breathe the
Hellenic spirit. Again (as will be shown in a moment), the
question put by the Eunomian is the very keystone of his system;
the Apollinarist position is accurately represented, and the
argument of its representative is one that might very naturally
have been used by a follower of that heresy; the Arian's question
concerning the Holy Ghost is quite in place in the mouth of an
Arian, while his second question concerning Christ's body sur-
prises Evagrius, who says that he had thought the point raised
was Gnostic rather than Arian. This minute heresiological knowledge seems more akin to the acute Greek mind than to the
Coptic, which appears not to have been versed in metaphysical
speculation.

To come to particulars. The question put by the Eunomian—
ὁ πατὴρ ἀγέννητος ἢ γεννητός; "Is the Father unbegotten or
begotten?"—though at first sight it may appear strange, is just
the way in which a Eunomian might have opened a disputation;
for if Evagrius had returned the obvious answer ἀγέννητος, his
adversary would have gone on to argue that a Being who is
ἀγέννητος and a Being who is γεννητός cannot be ὁμοούσιοι, a
palmary argument of the Eunomians[1]. But Evagrius foils him
by refusing to accept the terms ἀγέννητος or γεννητός as in any
way applicable to a Being μὴ πεφυκὼς γεννᾶσθαι. Here again
the current controversy of the time is accurately reflected; the
line taken by the orthodox was to object to the employment of
the word ἀγέννητος at all[2]. Evagrius' answer is therefore a
dexterous device of living controversy, but it depends on the force
of the Greek πεφυκέναι, in ἐπὶ τοῦ μὴ πεφυκότος γεννᾶσθαι,
which it is difficult to bring out in another language: certainly
the Coptic answer; "the unbegotten nature (φύσις) must not be
declared to be begotten or unbegotten," altogether fails to represent the argument.

Again, in the answer to the Arian, the Greek "Every
creature ἐν μετοχῇ ἁγιάζεται, "is sanctified by participation," is
mistranslated by the Coptic, "are sanctified by Him who is better
than they." In answer to Evagrius' question: "About what dost
thou doubt?" the Apollinarian replies in the Greek: "I do not
doubt anything, but I am certain that" &c.; in the Coptic: "I
do not doubt anything, but my heart is not persuaded or assured

---

[1] St Basil thus represents the Eunomian argument:—Εἰ ἀγέννητος, φασίν, ὁ
πατήρ, γεννητὸς δὲ ὁ υἱός, οὐ τῆς αὐτῆς οὐσίας. ἀγέννητος γὰρ καὶ γεννητὸς οὐκ ἂν εἴη
μιᾶς οὐσίας . . . . . . εἰ ὁμοούσιος, φασίν, ὁ υἱὸς τῷ πατρί, ὁ πατὴρ δὲ ἀγέννητος, ὁ δὲ
υἱὸς γεννητός, ἡ αὐτὴ ἄρα οὐσία ἀγέννητος καὶ γεννητή (c. Eunom. IV. p. 285 Ed. Ben.).

[2] Bp Lightfoot refers to this subject at the end of an Excursus on the terms
γεννητός and ἀγέννητος. "While the orthodox party clung to the ὁμοούσιος as
enshrining the doctrine for which they fought, they had no liking for the terms
ἀγέννητος and γεννητός as applied to the Father and the Son respectively, though
unable to deny their propriety, because they were affected by the Arians and
applied in their own way." And he thus paraphrases a passage of Epiphanius
(Haer. LXXIII. 19), "As you refuse to accept our ὁμοούσιος because, though used by
the fathers, it does not occur in the Scriptures, so will we decline on the same
grounds to accept your ἀγέννητος." He also refers to Basil. (Ignatius and Polycarp, II. 94.)

that" &c. "The unchangeable word" is an evident mistranslation of τὸν τοῦ ἀτρέπτου λόγου. The Coptic enlargement after μονάδι is a gloss, which destroys the meaning of the passage; the change of "the Man Christ Jesus" into "Jesus Christ the Son of God the Father," eliminates the whole controversial point of the citation; and the addition "the one Holy Ghost, one Catholic Church," &c., makes the Coptic here a complete *ignoratio elenchi.* Thus the Greek text of the fragment is convincingly proved to be the original [1].

The title prefixed to the Greek fragment: ἐκ τοῦ βίου τοῦ ἁγίου Εὐαγρίου συγγραφεὶς (*sic*) ὑπὸ Παλλαδίου, must be taken as evidence that a Greek Life of Evagrius, other (and longer) than that of the Lausiac History, circulated under the name of Palladius; and when we find in the Coptic fragment that this identical passage stands as part of a Life of Evagrius connected by some close bond of relationship with that in the Lausiac History,—agreeing in structure, containing the same matter, but considerably longer,—it seems impossible to resist the conclusion that the Coptic version has preserved the greater part of this longer Greek life [2].

The coexistence of two closely allied forms of the Life, both in Greek, both attributed to Palladius, is a phenomenon that claims an attentive consideration. There seem to be four possible hypotheses to account for the fact :—

(i) *Palladius wrote two Lives of Evagrius, a longer as an independent work, and a shorter in the Lausiac History.*

---

[1] There are, however, naturally a few places in which the Greek text may be emended by the aid of the Coptic.

[2] Zöckler apparently dissents from this view. In regard to the Greek fragment indeed, he does not think that this comes "from a late apocryphal Life" ("sieht nicht danach aus, als gehöre es einem Apokryphon späten Ursprungs an," *Evagrius Ponticus* 93): but in the following pages he points out certain features of the Coptic Life, which he believes establish " its late origin and secondary character " (" weist dies alles mit Deutlichkeit auf späten Ursprung und secondären Character dieses koptischen Texts hin, *ibid.* 95). The chief points to which he calls attention will be referred to presently; but they afford no ground whatever for the distinction drawn by him between the Greek and the Coptic fragments, which must stand or fall together. And indeed, on p. 75, Zöckler says that the Life from which the Greek fragment came, exists in a more complete form—"in vollständigerem Texte "—in Coptic.

This is Zöckler's view[1]. He bases it upon the following passage of Socrates, at the end of the long chapter on the Monks (*Hist. Eccl.* IV. 23):

Ἐγένοντο μὲν οὖν κατὰ τὸν αὐτὸν χρόνον ἐν τοῖς μοναστηρίοις καὶ ἄλλοι πλεῖστοι ἄνδρες θαυμαστοὶ καὶ θεοφιλεῖς, ὧν ἐν τῇ προκειμένῃ συγγραφῇ μνημονεύειν μακρὸν ἂν εἴη· ἄλλως τε καὶ ἐκβαίνειν τοῦ προκειμένου ἀνάγκη, εἰ βουλοίμεθα καθ' ἕκαστον τῶν ἀνδρῶν τοὺς βίους, καὶ ὅσα ἐποίησαν θαύματα διὰ τὴν προσοῦσαν αὐτοῖς ἁγιότητα· εἰ δέ τις βούλοιτο τὰ περὶ αὐτῶν μανθάνειν, ὧν τε ἐποίησαν, ὧν τε ἔπραξαν, καὶ ὧν πρὸς ὠφέλειαν τῶν ἀκουσάντων ἐφθέγξαντο, ὅπως τε αὐτοῖς τὰ θηρία ὑπήκουον, πεπόνηται Παλλαδίῳ τῷ μοναχῷ ἴδιον μονόβιβλον, ὃς Εὐαγρίου μὲν ἦν μαθητής. πάντα δὲ ἀκριβῶς περὶ αὐτῶν διεξῆλθεν· ἐν ᾧ καὶ γυναικῶν ἐφάμιλλον τοῖς προειρημένοις ἀνδράσι ἐπανελομένων βίον μνήμην πεποίηται. Εὐάγριος μὲν οὖν καὶ Παλλάδιος μικρὸν ὕστερον μετὰ τὴν Οὐάλεντος τελευτὴν ἤνθησαν.

I am at a loss to understand how Zöckler can see in these words of Socrates any reference to a separate Life of Evagrius; for although the second half of Socrates' chapter is devoted to Evagrius, it is as clear as possible that the concluding passage refers to the monks in general, and that the ἴδιον μονόβιβλον is the Lausiac History and not a Life of Evagrius, as Zöckler would have it[2]. Zöckler hazards the conjecture that the longer Life may be found among the Syriac Lives of Evagrius in the British Museum. As a matter of fact, this is not the case. I have carefully examined them and found them to be substantially the same Life as that contained in the Greek and Latin editions of the Lausiac History. In particular the episode of the interview with the three demons is no fuller in any of the Syriac MSS. than in the standard printed Greek text; and in none of them, as neither in any Greek MS., did I find any of the additional matter of the Coptic Life[3].

The sole evidence that can give any countenance to the theory that Palladius wrote two Lives of Evagrius consists in (1) the existence of the longer form in Coptic; (2) the superscription of Cotelier's Greek fragment, which declares it to be from Palladius'

[1] *Evagrius Ponticus* 93, 96; *Askese und Mönchtum* 219.
[2] "Zwar weiss er vom Vorhandensein eines 'besonderen Buchs' (ἴδιον μονόβιβλον) des Palladius über das Leben des Evagrius."
[3] An account of the Syriac copies of the Life of Evagrius has been given in a former section (§ 10).

Life of Evagrius. But this superscription shows no more than that some copies of the longer form of the Life went under Palladius' name; which would be quite natural and likely even on the hypothesis that it was but an interpolated redaction of the Life in the Lausiac History.

(ii) *The Life of Evagrius did not originally form part of the Lausiac History, but was a separate work, and was afterwards incorporated in an abridged form in the Lausiac History*[1].

The evidence of the manuscripts tells as strongly as such evidence can tell in favour of the Life of Evagrius having stood, in its present form and position, in the original Lausiac History. The Greek MSS., so far as I have been able to examine them, fall into three main groups, which I designate a, β and γ. a represents the type of text found fused with the *Historia Monachorum* in A (*e.g.* Paris 1626, &c.); the Life of Evagrius is found in these MSS. β is made up of a large number of MSS. presenting certain textual phenomena akin to those of the Palatine MS. printed by Meursius (*e.g.* Paris 1596, 1600, &c. &c.). In this particular MS., and in some others of the same group, the Life of Evagrius is wanting, but in a greater number of the MSS. of the group it is found. Moreover, in every case of its absence known to me, the Life of Didymus the Blind is also absent. But this latter Life certainly belongs to the true text; and the absence of both from certain MSS. of the group is clearly due to an anti-Origenistic tendency. There can therefore be no doubt that the Life of Evagrius stood in the archetype of group β. The group γ preserves an early tradition of the text, independent of a and β. Its chief representative is the Paris MS. 1628, in which Evagrius is wanting, though Didymus is found. But a considerable fragment of the same text is preserved also in the curious MS. *Coislin* 282, where the block of Lives from Pachon to Moses the Libyan presents distinctive readings of the aforesaid MS. 1628;—the critical apparatus to the extracts from the Life of John of Lycopolis (pp. 24—28) illustrates the affinity. In *Coislin* 282 the Lives run on in consecutive series from John of Lycopolis to Moses the Libyan,—John, Posidonius, Serapion, Evagrius, Pior,

---

[1] This I see is Dr Preuschen's position.

Moses,—just as in the good MSS. of the other groups. Seeing that the other five Lives are of the γ text, it may safely be concluded that that of Evagrius, which is one of the series, also belongs to that text; especially as it presents just the same sort of differences from the α and β texts as are found throughout the work. It thus appears that the Life of Evagrius existed in the archetypes of each of the three groups of Greek MSS. It also stood in the copy of the Lausiac History used by Sozomen (VI. 30). It is found in both the Latin versions. The evidence of the Syriac versions is neutral: on the one hand, the Life is not found in organic connection with clearly Palladian matter in any copy known to me; on the other, the Syriac MSS. are so incomplete, and in Anan-Isho's *Paradise* the book has been so tampered with, that the negative evidence to be drawn from them is worthless. The Syriac and Armenian copies of the Life are found in Collections of Evagrius' Works, or of Lives of Saints: but the Lausiac History Lives of John of Lycopolis and others are found in similar places; and it is but natural that, when a Life was required for such purposes, it should be taken out of a work so popular as the Lausiac History. This does not afford any reason for supposing that the Life of Evagrius was originally written to be prefixed to his works, and only afterwards put into the Lausiac History[1].

---

[1] Dr Preuschen deals with the question on pp. 255—259 of his *Palladius und Rufinus*, and it is right to take account here of the reasons that have led him to his conclusion. They may be summarised as follows: (1) The formal introduction to the Life of Evagrius (cf. p. 116), which seems to point to a separate existence; also the reference to general readers—εἰς οἰκοδομὴν τῶν ἐντυγχανόντων,—whereas usually throughout the History Lausus alone is contemplated. But it seems to me that elsewhere in the book similar subsidiary introductions are found,—as to the account of the two Macarii and to that of the holy women (P. G. xxxiv. 1043 and 1220), and in particular the remarks on those who fell away, referred to by Dr Preuschen himself, which seem to afford a perfect parallel to the piece under discussion: ἀναγκαῖον δ' ἐστὶν καὶ τοὺς τῶν ἡττημένων βίους ἐνθεῖναι τῷ βιβλιδαρίῳ τούτῳ πρὸς ἀσφάλειαν τῶν ἐντυγχανόντων (ibid. 1091; cf. also 995). (2) Dr Preuschen is disposed to see in the Syriac and Armenian copies of the Life evidence of its separate existence: but I think that what has been said by Professor Robinson in the preceding section (p. 101), and by myself in the text, shows that there is no sufficient reason for doubting that all these copies are taken from the Lausiac History. (3) The ending of the Life—ἕως ἐνταῦθα ὁ ἄκρος βίος τῆς ἐναρέτου πολιτείας τοῦ ἀοιδίμου Εὐαγρίου—is a trace of its previous independent existence. This

(iii) *The original Lausiac History was a longer work than ours,
and only an abridged copy has come down to us in Greek; but the
Coptic version has preserved in part the original unabridged form
of the work.*

This hypothesis is put forward by Amélineau as a possible
alternative to his theory of Coptic originals[1]. Here again the
manuscript evidence is against such a theory. In none of the
Greek MSS., nor in Sozomen, nor in the earliest versions, Syriac or

ending belongs to the MSS. of the α and β groups; but it is absent in *Coislin* 282,
the representative here of the γ text; and it is also absent in the versions. In
many other places somewhat similar conclusions are found (*e.g.* A 18, 28, 35, 36,
104, 108, 113), and some of these conclusions are similarly absent in the γ text.
(4) In one group of MSS. (Vienna 9 and 84, and Paris 1532, to which must be added
Arundel 527) the Life of Evagrius stands at the end of the Lausiac History; in
this circumstance Dr Preuschen sees the first stage of the process whereby he
conceives that an abridgment of the longer separate Life made its way into the
Lausiac History. My study of the textual phenomena of these MSS. has convinced
me that they are but a sub-group of β, and that their archetype was an ordinary
β MS. that had undergone an arbitrary literary revision. I am therefore unable
to attach importance to any of their readings; to put them higher up in the
pedigree of the text than groups α and γ and the Latin versions (in all which
the Life of Evagrius stands in its usual place) is in my judgment altogether impossible. I therefore regard as a mere accident the position of Evagrius at the
end of the work. Of course it will be incumbent on me to make good my statements when I come to deal with the MSS. in the *Introduction* to the Text.
(5) Lastly, Dr Preuschen thinks that Sozomen, in his sketch of Evagrius, used
the long form of the Life rather than that found in the Lausiac History: his
reason is the resemblance between Sozomen's words: ἀλλ' οἷος μὲν περὶ λόγους ἦν
ἐπιδείξουσι αἱ γραφαὶ ἃς κατέλιπεν (VI. 30), and those of the Coptic Life: *the books
which he wrote testify to his knowledge and excellent mind* (cf. *infra*, p. 144).
The contexts of the two passages are wholly different: in the Coptic the words
occur in the very middle of the Life; in Sozomen they occur after a passage which
Dr Preuschen agrees was derived from the *Historia Monachorum*; they are followed immediately by a passage describing his modesty and meekness, ἐλέγετο δὲ
καὶ τὸ ἦθος μέτριος κ.τ.λ., not found in either form of the Life by Palladius; and
then comes the story of his departure from Constantinople, from the beginning
of the Life in both redactions. Thus its position in Sozomen would lead us to
suppose the passage was not taken from the Life in either its longer or its shorter
form. After all, the resemblance is not close, beyond the mere ground idea, which
is a very obvious one to anyone who knew Evagrius' writings. It has been shown,
moreover, in § 8, and here again Dr Preuschen agrees, that in this very part of his
History, as elsewhere, Sozomen has been making free use of the Lausiac History.

What Dr Preuschen has brought forward does not lead me to modify the conclusions at which I had previously arrived.

[1] *De Hist. Laus.* 39 and 72.

Latin, have I found anything to suggest a text of the work longer than that which has come down to us;—unless indeed it be an addition found in Lat. II to the story of Evagrius' interview with the three demons. The body of the story agrees with the ordinary Greek text of the passage (printed above, p. 131); but after the words: καὶ τούτων περιεγένετο διὰ βραχέων τῇ πνευματικῇ σοφίᾳ, the Latin goes on: dum de testimoniis sanctarum Scripturarum concluderet, illi subito conturbati et magnum strepitum facientes, phanthasma schematis eorum dissolutum est et nusquam comparuerunt (Rosweyd, 997). Now in the long redaction of the episode it is by texts from holy Scripture that Evagrius confutes the heretics, and at the end we read: καὶ ταραχθέντες σφόδρα καὶ ἀπειλήσαντες αὐτὸν παραδειγματισμὸν ἠφαντώθησαν, which certainly resembles the Latin addition. In the Armenian version, too, as Professor Robinson has pointed out, it is said that the three demons became invisible. But seeing that the whole narrative in Lat. II is unquestionably the Short Life, and that no other trace of any affinity with the Long can be detected, and having regard to the phenomena of Lat. II as a whole, and its relations to the other texts, I think it is impossible to suppose that the addition in question can be due to any survival from a longer text of the Life of Evagrius. The resemblances, though at first striking, may safely be put down as curious coincidences. And after all, it is but natural that Evagrius when controverting with heretics should have had recourse to holy Scripture; similarly, it is but natural that the demons when put to confusion should make a noise and disappear:—it is what they always did under such circumstances[1].

---

[1] The Sermon on "the Faithful Departed," included among the works of St John Damascene, quotes as from "the historic book of Palladius to Lausus" an anecdote of Macarius of Egypt and a skull (P. G. xcv. 256). The anecdote is not in the Lausiac History, but is to be found among the *Apophthegmata* (P. G. LXV. 280, also XXXIV. 257). I do not think that this citation lends any support to the theory that the original text of the Lausiac History contained matter not in ours; for it has already been pointed out that in Syria, the country of St John Damascene, the *Apophthegmata* were attributed to Palladius, and currently spoken of as part of the Lausiac History. And there were interpolated Greek copies: as a matter of fact this very apophthegm, along with several others, is found in the chapter on Macarius in the Paris MS. 1627.

Thus, beyond the bare existence of the longer form of the Life, which has to be accounted for in some way, there is no direct evidence producible in support of any one of these three hypotheses; and although none of them have been proved to be untenable, the external evidence is against them all.

(iv) *The Life in the Lausiac History is the genuine one, and the longer Life is an interpolated and secondary redaction.*

This is the view to which I have been led after a prolonged study and comparison of the two texts. In the Table given a few pages back (p. 116) the Life was divided into certain sections; it is on the sections there marked (δ) and (ε), describing Evagrius' manner of life in Cellia, that the question has mainly to be decided. In order to enable the reader to form his own judgment on the case, it is necessary to lay before him the Greek text of this portion of the short Life, and a fairly full synopsis of the long Life. In the Coptic column only those portions which represent the Greek are given in full, and they are printed in italics; in the Greek column those portions of the text which are not represented in the Coptic are enclosed in square brackets.

(P. G. xxxiv. 1194.)

Ζήσας οὖν δεκατέσσαρα ἔτη ἐν τοῖς λεγομένοις κελλίοις, [ἤσθιε μὲν ἄρτου λίτραν τὴν ἡμέραν· ἐν τριμηνιαίῳ δὲ χρόνῳ ξέστην ἐλαίου]

ἀνὴρ ἀπὸ ἀβροδιαίτου καὶ τρυφηλοῦ βίου καὶ ὑγροτάτου ἡγμένος. ἐποίει δὲ εὐχὰς ἑκατὸν, [γράφων τοῦ ἔτους τὴν τιμὴν μόνον ὧν ἤσθιεν·] εὐφυῶς γὰρ ἔγραφεν [τὸν ὀξύρυγχον χαρακτῆρα.]

[ἐντὸς οὖν πεντεκαίδεκα ἐτῶν] καθαρεύσας τὸν νοῦν, κατηξιώθη

(Amél. De Hist. Laus. 111—121.)

He went to the desert of the cells. *He was there fifteen years*, passing his life there in many ascetic practices (πολιτεῖαι), and he died there, being sixty years old, without the sorrows of the old age of the body, as it is written: In a short time, &c. One day he asked Macarius how to overcome fornication; M. replied that at the time he should not eat fruit or any thing cooked in a fire. *Now he was a wonderful man, having come from a life full of repose and enjoyment. It is right to tell in the first place of his old age.* Every day *he used to make a hundred prayers, and he was a very skilful scribe* (γραφεὺς τεχνίτης). After eight years he began to suffer from the stone, and his elders made him abate his austerities. Until his death he ate no bread, but a few vegetables, etc., until he had fulfilled his short time. He neither ate, nor allowed his disciples to eat, fruit or anything pleasant. Such was his asceticism in matters of food. In regard to sleep, he slept the third part only of the night and never by day. During the greater part of the night and at midday he used to pace up and down the enclosure to keep himself awake, forcing himself to contemplate the visions presented to his mind. *His mind became very pure, and he was worthy of a grace of wisdom and knowledge*

χαρίσματος γνώσεως καὶ σοφίας
καὶ διακρίσεως πνευμάτων.

συντάττει οὖν οὗτος τρία βιβλία,
'Ιερὰ (sic ; but there seems to
be some early corruption in the
Greek texts) Μοναχὸν,

'Αντιρρητικὸν, οὕτω καλού-
μενα,

τὰς πρὸς τοὺς δαίμονας ὑποθέμενος τέχνας.
τούτῳ ὤχλησέ ποτε εἰς βάρος
ὁ τῆς πορνείας δαίμων, ὡς αὐτὸς
ἡμῖν διηγεῖτο, καὶ διὰ πάσης νυκτὸς γυμνὸς ἔστη ἐν τῷ φρέατι,
χειμῶνος ὄντος, ὡς παγῆναι αὐτοῦ
τὰς σάρκας. ἄλλοτε πάλιν ὤχλη-
σεν αὐτῷ πνεῦμα βλασφημίας,
καὶ ἐν τεσσαράκοντα ἡμέραις ὑπὸ
στέγην οὐκ εἰσῆλθεν, ὡς καὶ τὸ
σῶμα αὐτοῦ, καθάπερ τῶν ἀγρίων
ζώων, κρότωνας ἐκβράσαι.

and judgment, discerning the works of demons.
He was accurate in the Scriptures and the orthodox traditions of the Catholic Church, and the
books which he wrote testify to his knowledge
and excellent mind. For he wrote three books of
instruction, one about the monks of monasteries,
another about the monks who dwelt in the cells
of his desert, another about the priests of God,
that they might be vigilant in the holy place.
The three books taught all men to live profitably
according to the traditions of the Church. The
brethren used to assemble to him on Sabbaths
and Sundays, and during the night would discuss their thoughts with him and listen to his
words of comfort until dawn, and so departed
from him praising God, for his teaching was
very sweet. But he urged them, if any one had
a troublesome thought, not to disclose it till
they were alone, lest he should destroy a little
one by his thought. He every day admitted to
his cell five or six pilgrims who came from afar,
attracted by his wisdom and asceticism ; every-
thing that was sent to him was kept by the
steward, who always served in his house. Abba
Theophilus the Archbishop often wanted to
seize him and make him bishop of Thmoui, but
he fled away [to Palestine, it is stated p. 118,
where the fact is again referred to]. One day
the demons wounded him ; we heard his voice
but we did not see them. During the night they
scourged him with bull's hide whips ; we saw the
wounds on his body, God is our witness. But
if you wish to know the temptations he suffered
from the demons, read the book which he wrote
against the contradicting of demons, and you will
see all his power and different temptations. He
wrote it that the readers might be comforted, and
he taught us by what methods different thoughts
are overcome. This great man was at first unknown. At one time the demons so multiplied
fornication upon him that the thought entered his
heart: "God has forgotten me," as he told us, and
he spent the whole night standing in the well, being
naked in the winter praying, until his flesh had
dried up like a stone. Another time again the
spirit of blasphemy troubled him, and for forty
days he did not enter under the roof of a cell,
until all his body was full of ticks like a brute
beast. And a few days afterwards he told us
revelations which he had seen, and he never
concealed them from his disciples. "For it
came to pass," said he, "as I was sitting in my
cell by night, with my lamps burning, as I was
meditating on one of the prophets ; at midnight
I was in an ecstasy, and I found myself as
if in a dream." [The vision is described at
some length.] It was impossible to find a worldly
word in the mouth of abba Evagrius, or a quar-
relsome word ; nor would he hear such from
another. We heard also this miracle about him.

[A cure he wrought in Palestine when fleeing from the bishopric.] [A story told to Evagrius by an old man concerning some hot loaves he had·found in the desert.] For I also chanced to be there, and while he was saying these things and telling the prodigy to abba Evagrius I was sitting there. [Evagrius tells a similar story, how he had found a purse in the way, and explains how in such cases it may be known whether it be the handiwork of angels or demons.] ἐπέστησαν τούτῳ τρεῖς δαίμονες ἐν σχήματι κληρικῶν, ἐν αὐτῇ τῇ μεσημβρίᾳ κ.τ.λ. (Cf. *supra*, p. 132.)

τούτῳ τρεῖς ἐπέστησαν ἐν ἡμέρᾳ δαίμονες ἐν σχήματι κληρικῶν κ.τ.λ. (Cf. *supra*, p. 131.)

I think there can be no question that the general impression produced by a perusal of the longer account is a favourable one. The picture drawn of Evagrius is very graphic, and the personal details and anecdotes about him are such as we should have no difficulty in believing to have come from the pen of Palladius. But the first and the important question to face is this: Which account is the primary one, and which the derived? And here I am clearly of the opinion that, whatever view may be taken of the intrinsic character of the additional matter in the long Life, that form of the Life bears the marks of being an expansion of the short form, whereas the short Life could not have been abridged from the long. This is a mere question of literary criticism, and the reader has before him the materials for controlling my conclusions. In the first place, certain passages in the Greek, which have all the appearance of being authentic information about Evagrius, are not found at all in the longer account. The portions of the longer Life which are printed in italics are mere *disjecta membra*, and could hardly have been picked out and built up into the compact Greek of the short Life; on the other hand, there is little difficulty in understanding how additional matter might have been inserted in different places into the framework of the short Life, thus breaking it up into the detached fragments that are found scattered about in the long Life. I would direct special attention to the parallel passages naming Evagrius' works. The short account says: "He composed three books, Ἱερά, Μοναχὸν, Ἀντιρρητικόν." There is some difficulty about the first title, which probably is not the true reading; but the three titles given in the long account quite baffle Zöckler, who has devoted nearly forty pages to the investigation of the lists of Evagrius' writings[1], and who declares these titles to be simply erroneous[2].   But it is something more than a mere error; for after a considerable interval the long Life reverts to the question of Evagrius' writings, and picks up again the last title, 'Αντιρρητικόν, which it correctly describes as Contradictions of Demons; so that it mentions four works of Evagrius in all. Here I think it is evident that the notice in the short Life cannot have been made up out of the twofold reference in the long Life.   It is to be noted, too, that the first sentence in this portion of the long Life (*he passed his life there in many ascetic practices, and he died there, being sixty years old,...as it is written, &c.*) is a doublet, repeated almost verbally, and with the same text of holy Scripture, from the passage at the beginning of both forms of the Life, already printed (p. 116).   Doublets are usually a mark of secondary character.   Lastly, in the earlier passage just referred to, there is an addition in the longer Life of exactly the same personal character as those under consideration here; and it was shown (p. 117) that this passage has all the appearance of having been violently inserted into the Greek text.   This must suffice to indicate, so far as is possible in such subject-matter, the nature of the considerations which finally satisfied me of the priority of the short form of the Life, and of the fact that in the Greek of our Lausiac History we have the genuine Life of Evagrius as originally written by Palladius[3].

When this result has been ascertained, further questions as to the additional matter of the long Life become of less interest. I do not see that it could be precisely proved that Palladius

---

[1] *Evagrius Ponticus*, c. 2.

[2] *Ibid.* 95. (This is one of his proofs of the secondary character of the long Life.)

[3] Zöckler gives certain reasons, different from the above, which have led him to the same conclusion (*Evagrius Ponticus* 94—95): and the Bollandist reviewer considers that he has made good his position: "Il montre fort bien que le fragment copte sur Evagrius est postérieur au texte de Palladius" (*Analecta Bollandiana*, XIV. 120 (1895).   But to one of his arguments no value can be allowed, viz. that the passage at the end of the Greek Life (1194 D) savouring of ἀπάθεια, is not found in the Coptic Life : for the MS. of the latter is incomplete, and breaks off before this point is reached.

himself did not expand the original Life; but it has already been seen that no evidence of any value can be adduced in support of such a hypothesis. The personal details, indeed, and the close relationship with Evagrius claimed by the inter- polator, would seem to point to a member of Evagrius' circle of disciples: in particular there is at the end of the interview with the three demons, the mention of Albinius as the neighbour of Evagrius and the friend on whom he chiefly relied for support; and in different places in the Lausiac History Albinius is men- tioned as a disciple and companion of Evagrius (*P. G.* xxxiv. 1113, 1196; cf. 1091). On the other hand it is possible that all this personal element may be the invention of a clever interpolator, who kept up the character consistently to the end. A limitation, however, must be made: he must have been familiar with the general conditions of life in Nitria; and he must have known something of Evagrius' writings, for the brief note which he adds explaining the nature of the Ἀντιρ- ρητικόν is quite correct. There may have been in the writings of Evagrius information concerning himself which is not acces- sible to us. There exist, moreover, among the Syriac MSS. at the British Museum copies of a collection entitled "Sayings of the Disciples of Evagrius[1]," which however I have not examined. Socrates appears to have had access to sources of information not open to us, concerning Evagrius as well as others of the monks; and he says that Theophilus wished to make him a bishop, but he escaped by flight[2]. This circum- stance is related in one of the interpolated passages of the long form of the Life, with the additional information (possibly a mere invention) that Thmoui was the see in question, and that Palestine was the place to which he fled. It seems likely that the interpolator and Socrates may have derived their information from the same source.

Until this whole range of literature has been scientifically investigated, it would, I think, be premature to express any posi- tive view as to the age and character of the interpolations.

In regard to the long account of the interview with the

---

[1] Wright's *Catalogue*, DCCXXXVI. and DCCLXXXIX.
[2] *Hist. Eccl.* iv. 23.

demons, there is nothing at all like it, nothing of the same theological character, anywhere in Palladius. But it is evident that the brief reference to the episode found in the Lausiac History would readily suggest possibilities of a little theological writing, and would be a temptation to one theologically minded to improve the occasion.

(5) *The Life of Macarius of Alexandria.*

If the reader refers back to the table printed on pp. 119—20, where a comparative synopsis is given of the Greek and Coptic Lives, he will see that the additional matter of the Coptic occurs in three places. It will be convenient to deal with them in reverse order.

At the close of that portion of the Coptic material which corresponds to the Greek, three anecdotes are added, and then comes the conclusion of the Life, quite different from the Greek. This conclusion is so worded as to give rise to the suspicion that the Coptic Life of Macarius, like the other Coptic fragments, was intended for liturgical use: "Now I wished, O my beloved (*plural*), to tell you much concerning abba Macarius; these are what I have been able to find of him (they are very little); now in his practices and acts of asceticism he was perfect in his old age. And the day of his perfecting when he died was the sixth of the month of Pashons....What we have said is enough for the profit of those who hear, and that they may do it, that they may obtain the part and the lot of this truly valiant abba Macarius," &c.[1] The three stories that immediately precede these concluding words I have been unable to identify: one of them purports to have been told the narrator by Paphnutius, the disciple of the saint. They are all such as might have been current in collections of *Apophthegmata.*

The two Coptic insertions between *h* and *i* may actually be traced to Greek sources of this kind, but belong really to his namesake, Macarius of Egypt. The original of the story about the Libyan robbers (Amél. p. 249) is to be found among the Greek *Apophthegmata* of Macarius of Egypt (*P. G.* LXV. 281 or XXXIV. 260), but not among the Coptic set printed by Amélineau in

---

[1] *Monastères de la Basse-Égypte,* 260.

this same volume: the story has been considerably embellished and "improved" in the Coptic, but there can be no doubt that the more prosaic Greek account is the original. The next paragraph of the Coptic, which tells how he encouraged some young brothers by saying: "From the day that I became a monk, I have not eaten bread unto satiety, and I have not slept unto satiety," is derived from a saying of Macarius of Egypt to Evagrius, recorded in the Μοναχός of the latter, and cited by Socrates (IV. 23): Θάρσει, ὦ τέκνον· ἐν ὅλοις εἴκοσιν ἔτεσιν, οὔτε ἄρτου οὔτε ὕδατος οὔτε ὕπνου κόρον εἴληφα.

The remaining additional piece, the story of Lydia, presents some curious features. It is necessary first to print the Greek and the Coptic of the preceding story *d* (the Paralytic Girl), and then the Coptic story of Lydia.

(*P. G.* xxxiv. 1059.)

[Ὁ φιλόθεος]¹ οὗτος τοσοῦτον πλῆθος ἐθεράπευσε δαιμονιζομένων, ὡς μὴ ῥᾳδίως ἀριθμῷ ὑποβάλλεσθαι τούτους. παρόντων δὲ ἡμῶν πρὸς τοῦτον [τὸν ὅσιον ἄνδρα] παρθένος τις [φοράδην] ἐκομίσθη ἀπὸ Θεσσαλονίκης [ἐνορία τῆς Ἀχαίας,] εὐγενὴς τῷ γένει, πλουσία ἐν βίῳ, πολυετίαν ἔχουσα ἐν παραλύσει. καὶ τούτῳ προσενεχθεῖσα ἐρρίφη πλησίον τῆς αὐτοῦ κέλλης. εἰς ἣν σπλαγχνισθεὶς καὶ ἐπευξάμενος ἐλαίῳ τε ἁγίῳ ἀλείφων αὐτὴν ταῖς ἑαυτοῦ χερσὶν [καὶ συνεχῶς μᾶλλον δὲ νουνεχῶς ὑπὲρ αὐτῆς προσευχόμενος] ἐν εἴκοσι ὅλαις ἡμέραις, ταύτην ὑγιῆ εἰς τὴν ἑαυτῆς ἐξαπέστειλεν πόλιν.

(*Amél. op. cit.* 240 f.)

And this holy old man abba Macarius healed multitudes of men possessed with demons, exceeding many, innumerable. So then when we were there, there was brought to him a virgin that was palsied and exceeding sick. She heard the report of him¹ in her country and caused them to bring her unto him; and when he had prayed over oil, he anointed all her body with his holy hands many times during² twenty days. God healed her through his prayers, and he sent her to her house healthy and made whole³, glorifying God. And when she had come to her city [at] the end of three days she died, and left 300 gold pieces. When she came to die⁴, she made [a] testament that they

---

¹ The Greek words enclosed in square brackets are omitted in some mss. (cf. Hervet's trans.).

¹ Lit. *his report*
² Lit. *through*
³ The same root is used in Coptic for "healthy" and "made whole."
⁴ Lit. *rest*

ἥτις τοῖς ἰδίοις ποσὶν ἀπελθοῦσα πολλὴν καρποφορίαν ἀπέστειλεν τοῖς ἁγίοις.

should be taken to the holy abba Macarius, because of the manner in which she was made whole. For the report of the holy abba Macarius was spread abroad. And another maiden heard concerning him, and came unto him from Thessalonica, whose name was[1] Litia. She was a scribe writing books[2] and living in great asceticism in the manner of men[3]. And she spent a full year[4], being in a great cave. She met the old man once every day. And no other saw her in all the mountain, save the day that she went from the mountain to depart to her country. And [as for] her hidden thought concerning which she came unto the old man, God gave rest to her from it through the prayers of the old man; and she went to her country, glorifying God, because He gave her rest through her coming unto the old man.

As contrasted with the Greek, the statements in the Coptic that the girl who had been cured died three days after her return home, and when dying left to Macarius a large bequest out of gratitude for her cure, are certainly strange, and not the sort of alteration that we should expect in this class of literature. Still more strange is the fact that, though the second story is not found in the Greek at all, the circumstance that the heroine came from Thessalonica is recorded in the Greek of the heroine of the first story. Were nothing to be considered except the two texts before us, an obvious explanation of the difficulty would be that someone's sense of ascetical propriety may have been offended by the second story, which accordingly was suppressed; and that it left just a trace of its former existence in the transference of Thessalonica as the heroine's birthplace to the story which was retained. But when all the facts of the case are kept in view, it seems altogether more likely that the second

---

[1] Lit. *is*   [2] Lit. *books of reading*
[3] Lit. *practising asceticism exceedingly in a masculine life*
[4] Or, *a year, being perfect,*

story was interpolated and that this one item of the Greek text found its way into it by some accident.

Two or three short pieces of the Coptic version deserve to have attention directed to them:

In the story of the cure of the demoniac boy (*h*), instead of the extra-ordinary and grotesque statement of the Greek that the boy himself was raised into the air (*P. G.* xxxiv. 1059 D, to be cited hereafter, § 15), the Coptic has "the demon was raised into the air, crying out and saying" &c. (p. 248).

In the Greek the story about Marcus is introduced by the words ἡμῖν διηγήσατο, but in the Coptic it is told on the following authority: "Now his disciple, who ministered to him in his old age, who entrusted to him the son of the *dux*, for he had believed, who came to the old man and now dwells in the holy mountain, working at his manual labour, eating by his toil, greatly loving strangers—this faithful disciple told me," &c. (p. 253). I am unable to offer any explanation of the reference to "the son of the *dux*"; but the whole passage seems to be very circumstantial.

The third passage is that in which Palladius relates that he came to Macarius' cell, and found the presbyter of a neighbouring village lying there (1059 A, but the text in 193 B is better); the Coptic has: "And again it came to pass whilst I was with him and the holy Albinius, there came a presbyter of a village" (p. 246). Here, as before, the mention of Albinius should be noted, for he was one of Palladius' fellow disciples under Evagrius. But this may very well be due to some scribe who had noted the circumstance in the Lausiac History; for in the story of the hyena and the sheepskin the Greek ἡμῖν is similarly turned into 'the holy Evagrius and I,' in Syriac Version I. as found in Anan-Isho's Paradise [cf. Bedjan, 79], whereas in the MSS. that preserve the more primitive form of this version, the Syriac is here the same as the Greek (cf. nos. i, iv, x and xi, in the list of MSS. on p. 84); so that Syriac scribes no less than Coptic made "improvements" of this kind in their texts.

In the case of the Life of Macarius of Alexandria more than in any of the others the establishment of the priority of the Greek Life is of critical and historical importance. The two forms of the Life contain the same personal reminiscences and experiences of the narrator, so that the biographer is the same man in both. This is indeed one of the chapters of the Lausiac History in which the personal element is most strongly marked. Palladius again and again relates incidents as having happened to himself or in his presence. In the Coptic Life these incidents are similarly related in the first person; so that if Palladius be not the author, we have a flagrant case of the offence wherewith

Lucius charges him—the appropriating and retailing as his own the personal experiences of others.

In the first division of this section it has been shown from a number of linguistic considerations that the Coptic was certainly translated from the Greek; and in the present division some of the additional Coptic matter has been traced to Greek sources: so that I think the Palladian authorship of the Life has been solidly established. But such is the importance of the question in its bearing on the whole historical character of the book, that I here supplement what has already been said by a further argument based on considerations quite different from those which have gone before.

In the Lausiac History the Lives of Macarius of Egypt and Macarius of Alexandria form a single account, and the transition from the account of the former to the account of the latter is in the shape of an autobiographical note or reminiscence, as follows: "I did not meet Macarius of Egypt, for he died a year before I entered the desert; but I did meet Macarius of Alexandria, for I spent nine years in Cellia, during three of which he was still alive" (P. G. xxxiv. 1049, 1050). As the beginning of the Coptic Life of Macarius of Alexandria, printed by M. Amélineau, is wanting, we do not know whether the autobiographical notes existed in the MS. But in a Coptic Life of Macarius of Egypt, described by Zoega, the corresponding notes which stand at the end of that Life in the Lausiac History are found, though divided into two fragments, one being given at the beginning and the other at the end of the Life. This leads me to surmise that the Life will prove to be that of the Lausiac History, although neither Zoega nor Amélineau has identified it as such. I print the Greek and the Coptic as given by Zoega in parallel columns.

P. G. xxxiv.	Zoega (Cat. 127—9).
(*Beginning of Life*, 1043). Καὶ τὰ μὲν πρῶτα διηγήσομαι τοῦ Αἰγυπτίου Μακαρίου τὰς ἀρετὰς,	(*Beginning of Life*). Now I will narrate concerning the Egyptian first of all, and he also died in body before the Alexandrian. And he it is who buried the body of abba Anthony. He spent sixty-five years in the
ὃς ἔζησεν τὰ σύμπαντα ἔτη ἐνενήκοντα. ἀπὸ τούτων ἐν τῇ ἐρήμῳ πε-	desert, and he died being ninety-seven

πρίηκεν ἐξήκοντα ἔτη.

(*End*, 1049). τῷ ἁγίῳ τούτῳ ἐγὼ οὐ
συντετύχηκα· πρὸ ἐνιαυτοῦ γὰρ τῆς εἰς
ἔρημον εἰσόδου ἐμῆς...ἐκεκοίμητο, τῷ δὲ
ὁμοζύγῳ τούτου... τῷ ἁγίῳ Μακαρίῳ
Ἀλεξανδρεῖ συντετύχηκα πρεσβυτέρῳ
ὄντι τῶν λεγομένων Κελλίων. εἰς ἃ
Κελλία παρῴκησα ἐγὼ ἐνναετίαν· ἐν
οἷς τρία ἔτη μοι ἐπέζησεν ὁ Μακάριος
οὗτος.

years old[1]. And two years after he
went forth from the body I came
into the Mount and I found the
Alexandrian living for two years
more.

(*End*). For I did not see him
with my eyes, for before I came to
the Mount he died; but his disciples
told me concerning these miracles
which God wrought through him.

As the two sets of autobiographical notes occur together in the
Greek and knit the two lives into one story, and as those referring
to Macarius of Egypt are found in the Coptic version of his life,
it is but reasonable to suppose that those referring to Macarius of
Alexandria, which are organically connected with the others,
must have stood also at the beginning of the Coptic version of that
Life. Now these form only part of a whole series of such autobiographical notes found scattered throughout the Lausiac
History. And it will be shown (§ 15) that when these notes are
brought together they yield a chronology of Palladius' life
perfectly consistent, and fit into one another in a way that
would be most extraordinary, except on the hypothesis that they
afford the actual chronology of his life. It is impossible to
suppose that some of them should be genuine, while others are
merely taken over by him from other writers. And this, it seems
to me, furnishes almost a demonstration that the Life of Macarius
of Alexandria was written by Palladius himself; and that, whatever be the solution of the critical problems involved, the Coptic
is not the original language of the Life. The only other alternative would seem to be, that not merely parts of the Lausiac
History but practically the whole book was a mere translation of
Coptic works: an extravagant theory, which certainly is not put

---

[1] The difference between the figures in the Greek and the Coptic is probably
due to those in the Coptic having been harmonised with the data of the Coptic
Synaxarium (cf. Amélineau *Monuments* III., *Musée Guimet* XXV. *Introd.* XXXVIII.).
The identification of Macarius of Egypt with the Macarius who buried St Anthony
is probably an error, though a very common one (cf. Amélineau, *ibid.* XXXI.): Palladius does not fall into it.

forward by M. Amélineau, who holds that large portions are undoubtedly the original work of Palladius[1].

With a few remarks on the age of the Coptic version this long section will be concluded.

Mai's authority has already been cited (p. 110) for the statement that the MS. containing the introductory pieces and the lives of Pambo and Evagrius dates from the tenth century, and that the MS. containing the Life of Macarius was written in 1153. But there are indications that the version is much older than the tenth century.

(a) In the Greek Life of Pambo mention is made of a Dracontius, who is merely described as ἀνὴρ ἔνδοξος καὶ θαυμασ-τός (*P. G.* XXXIV. 1028 B). But in the Coptic, in place of this quite vague clause, the precise statement occurs that he was Bishop of Timinhor, the modern Damanhour, identified with the Greek Hermopolis Parva. Now a Dracontius, bishop of Hermo-polis Parva, attended the Council of Alexandria held in 362[2]; and this date fits in very well with the statement of the Lausiac History that Dracontius was the uncle of one of Pambo's disciples. It is to be noted that this passage occurs in that portion of the Coptic Life which M. Amélineau recognises as a translation from the Greek of the Lausiac History. Either then the Coptic trans-lator had a very good and early Greek MS. of the Lausiac History; or, as seems more likely, he altered his text in accordance with his knowledge of the local ecclesiastical history. But either alterna-tive points to the antiquity of the Coptic version.

(b) In the Coptic version one of the reasons held out to Macarius to induce him to go to Rome is this: "For the Romans agree with the Egyptians in their ascetical practices and their orthodox faith" (p. 252). These words do not occur in the Greek MSS. or in the other versions: they are a Coptic addition; and it

---

[1] Cf. the passages collected from his *De Hist. Laus.* in § 15, on the *Histo-ricity* of the Lausiac History. In the Introduction to the *Monastères de la Basse-Égypte* he uses the whole series of Palladius' autobiographical memoirs as authentic (XXXIII. ff.).

[2] Among the bishops present was Δρακόντιος Ἑρμουπόλεως μικρᾶς (Mansi, ed. 1759, III. 353).

is difficult to suppose that a Coptic translator or scribe should have inserted them after the Council of Ephesus (450), the occasion of the excommunication of Pope Leo I. by Dioscorus of Alexandria, and the accomplishment of the Monophysite Schism.

§ 13. THE ETHIOPIC AND ARABIC VERSIONS OF THE RULE OF PACHOMIUS.

In the Lausiac History (A 38—42) the Rule of St Pachomius is given, together with a description of the manner of life followed in his monasteries, and two anecdotes of the great convent of women founded by the saint. Portions of this matter are found in Ethiopic and in Arabic; and it is necessary to consider the bearing of these fragments on the question discussed in the preceding section,—the original language in which the material of the Lausiac History was written.

It will be convenient to have first an analysis of the contents of what Palladius gives us:—

(a) *P. G.* xxxiv. 1099 c. Brief account of Pachomius, who he was, where he lived, &c.

(β) *P. G.* xxxiv. 1099 c. An angel appears to him, tells him to found monasteries, gives him a Rule written on a tablet of brass.

(γ) *P. G.* xxxiv. 1099 c—1100 c. Epitome of the Rule.

(δ) *P. G.* xxxiv. 1100 c, D. Brief general account of the monasteries he founded, and of Aphthonius, the friend of Palladius.

(ε) *P. G.* xxxiv. 1100 D—1105 B. Special account of the monastery at Panopolis (Akhmîm) which Palladius had visited.

(ζ) *P. G.* xxxiv. 1105 B, c. Short account of the convent of nuns.

(η) *P. G.* xxxiv. 1105 c—1106 A. Distressing story of two of the nuns.

(θ) *P. G.* xxxiv. 1106 A—1107 c. Story of abba Pitirum and the nun who pretended to be foolish.

The Ethiopic Version.

It is quite likely that much more of the Lausiac History may exist in Ethiopic than the fragment that has been printed. Wright's *Catalogue* of the Ethiopic MSS. at the British Museum contains a number of entries that might upon examination prove to contain Palladian matter, such as "Histories of our holy Fathers," "Garden of the Monks[1]." But the only portion of the Lausiac History in Ethiopic that has been printed consists of sections (a) to (ζ) of the analysis just given. It stands as the first of three "Rules of Pachomius," edited in 1866 from two MSS. by Dillmann in his *Chrestomathia aethiopica* (pp. 57—69). No more editing appears to have been done; but a German translation has been made by König (*Th. Studien u. Kritiken*, 1878, p. 323), an English one by Schodde (*Presbyterian Review*, 1885, p. 678), and quite recently a French one by Basset in his series of *Apocryphes Éthiopiens* (no. VIII., Paris, 1896). This last edition, in which the translation is at any rate roughly confronted with the chief of the other authorities for the text, has been used for the present investigation.

It has been said that the Ethiopic texts contain three "Rules of Pachomius." These are :—

I. The matter corresponding to sections (a) to (ζ) of the Lausiac History in the analysis of the Greek text given above.

II. A short redaction of the collection of minute rules and regulations found in Greek and translated by St Jerome from Greek into Latin.

III. A miscellaneous collection : it begins with eight brief regulations resembling those in II ; then follows an allegorical discourse, purporting to be an address by St Pachomius to his monks.

The Third Rule exists only in Ethiopic. Weingarten[2], and also Mangold[3], held it to be the most primitive of the three Rules ; but Basset altogether rejects the idea and declares it to be the latest of them all, and to have been composed in Ethiopic[4].

The Second Rule exists in two Greek redactions: a shorter, printed by the Bollandists (*Acta SS.* Tom. III. Maii, Ap. 53*, reprinted *P. G.* XL. 948), and a longer, printed by Pitra from a St Petersburg MS. (*Analecta Sacra* V. 113). St Jerome's Latin version of it also exists in two redactions, one in Gazaeus' edition of Cassian (cf. *P. L.* L. 271), the other in Holsten's *Codex Regularum* (ed. 1663), pars I. 32 (cf. *P. L.* XXIII. 61); the translation is

---

[1] Cf. the series of MSS. CCLIX.—CCLXV.; also CCCXXXV. and CCCXLVIII.; all modern and dating from the sixteenth to the eighteenth century.

[2] *Ursprung*, 51.   [3] *Herzog-Plitt*, XI. 159.

[4] *Les Règles attribuées à Saint Pakhome*, 14 ; Dillmann also pronounces Rule III the most recent (*op. cit.* XII).

the same, and the matter nearly the same, the differences for the most part lying merely in the arrangement. The Ethiopic Second Rule agrees most closely with the shorter of the Greek redactions, but numbers 18—26 of the Greek are missing. This document has in its successive redactions all the appearance of an ever-growing body of minute regulations, framed to meet the emergencies constantly arising in the everyday life of a great monastery. The burden is "let no one do this," "let no one do that." In other words, it seems to be a collection of "declarations" or "rules of the house," lesser regulations for the domestic economy of the monastery, rather than the original Rule of Life. St Jerome in the Preface to his translation speaks of these regulations as "praecepta Pachomii et Theodori et Orsiesii" (the three first superiors); and the redaction printed by Gazaeus begins with the title: "Haec sunt praecepta vitalia tribus a majoribus tradita" (*P. L.* L. 277; cf. no. 8 in the other redaction, *P. L.* XXIII. 66).

The First Rule, *i.e.* the form found in Palladius, has much more the appearance of preserving, if not the actual form of the original Rule, at any rate a correct and substantial epitome of it[1].

We may now pass on to consider the bearings of the Ethiopic First Rule on the various problems that have been engaging our attention.

---

[1] This view of the nature and relations of the three Rules is shared by Grützmacher (*Pachomius u. das älteste Klosterleben* 117—129), Zöckler (*Askese u. Mönchtum* 200—203), and Basset (*op. cit.* 11—14). Weingarten's main ground of objection to Rule I is the passage wherein it is stated that the monks were to be divided into twenty-four classes according to the letters of the Greek alphabet, and a Greek letter imposed on each class: it is clear that at the beginning St Pachomius did not know Greek. Grützmacher in answer points out that the Copts used the Greek letters (*op. cit.* 125). Basset says this is not fully satisfactory, as the Coptic alphabet contains thirty-one letters (*op. cit.* 12). The restoration of the true Greek text lessens the difficulty: ἐκέλευσεν εἰκοσιτέσσερα τάγματα εἶναι τῶν ἀδελφῶν· καὶ ἑκάστῳ τάγματι ἐπέθηκεν στοιχεῖον ἑλληνικὸν ἀπὸ α καὶ β καὶ γ καὶ δ καὶ τῶν καθ' ἑξῆς (omitting ἕως τοῦ ω). Palladius may be describing the system as he found it a century after its first institution: or he may have modified the terms of the Rule so as to make them more easily intelligible to Greek readers. Notice, however, the reference to the use of Greek letters in St Pachomius' "mystic Epistles," in the Greek *Vita Pach.* c. 63 (not in the Coptic redactions).

Grützmacher and Zöckler, who are infected with the theory of Coptic originals, consider that in the Ethiopic text we have a translation of the original Coptic, independent of the Greek of Palladius and better than it. Basset, on the other hand, while also believing that the original language of the piece was Coptic, takes it for granted throughout his *Notes* that the Ethiopic version was made not from the Coptic but from the Greek as found in the Lausiac History. And in this he is certainly right, whatever may be the solution of the further problem as to the original language of the *Vita*. For the Coptic theory supposes that the passage originally stood in the *Vita Pachomii*. As a matter of fact it does now stand in two redactions of the Life, one in Arabic, the other in Latin; but naturally the introductory portion (a) of the Greek, giving elementary information about Pachomius, is not found in either of these redactions, for it would be quite out of place in a full Life. But it is found in the Ethiopic, exactly as in Palladius. Again, not only (a), but also (β) and (δ) are missing in both redactions of the Life, and between (γ) and the subsequent sections (ϵ), (ζ), varying quantities of matter occur; whereas in the Ethiopic the sections (a) to (ζ) succeed each other as in the Greek. Lastly, the description of the manner in which funerals were conducted in the convent of nuns (Basset, 27) agrees closely with the Greek of Palladius, but differs altogether from the account given in the Arabic and Coptic forms of the Life (the texts will be found below, p. 162). It is therefore clear that the Ethiopic version of the Rule was made not from any supposed Coptic original, but from the Greek of Palladius.

Thus, though this fragment is of use for the purposes of textual criticism, it throws no light upon the more fundamental question under discussion in this and in the preceding section. It is, perhaps, right to observe that, apart from manifest corruptions, in nearly all the points wherein it differs from the printed Greek text, the Ethiopic has the support of some one or other extant Greek MS., often the Paris MSS. 1627 and 1628.

The Arabic Version.

As in the case of the Ethiopic version, so here, there is ground for supposing that the Lausiac History exists in an Arabic dress. Not to speak of an Arabic copy of the Syriac *Paradisus* mentioned by Assemani (*Bibl. Mediceae Laurent. et Palat. Cat. Cod.* LIX.), Mrs Gibson's *Catalogue of the Arabic MSS.* in St Katharine's, Mount Sinai, appears to contain references to copies and fragments of the Lausiac History, as do other catalogues also of the chief oriental collections.

But the only portions of the Lausiac History so far printed in Arabic are the portions relating to St Pachomius and his monks and nuns, which occur in an Arabic version of the *Vita Pachomii.* The interest of this Arabic Life lies in the fact that it was without doubt translated from a Coptic Life; so that we are here once again brought face to face with the question whether Coptic documents were translated by Palladius.

In order to render the following discussion intelligible it is necessary to mention the various redactions of the *Vita Pachomii.* The extant redactions of the Life fall into two groups, a Greek and a Coptic, with a clear line of demarcation between them, and no less clearly marked affinities between their respective members:

Greek Group.

1. The Greek Life printed by the Bollandists (*Acta SS.* Tom. III. Maii, App. 22*), together with the *Asceticon Pachomii* (called by the Bollandists *Paralipomena*) (*ibid.* 44*) . . . . $=gr+asc$

2. A Latin version printed by Lipomanus and Surius (May 14th) . . . . $=lat^1$

3. Another Latin version, printed by Rosweyd (cf. *P. L.* LXXIII.) . . . . $=lat^2$

Coptic Group.

4. A Sahidic Life; existing only in fragments . . . $=sah$
5. A Bohairic Life . . . . $=boh$
6. An Arabic version . . . . $=ar$

The documents of the Coptic group have been printed for the first time by M. Amélineau[1]. He supposes that *sah* was the primitive form of the Life, from which the others, both later Coptic and Greek, were derived. Only fragments of *sah* exist; but Amélineau holds that in *ar* we have a faithful reproduction of *sah*, *boh* being but an abridgment. In *ar* are found certain portions of the Lausiac History account of Pachomius—viz., (γ) (ϵ) (ζ) (η) of the analysis on p. 155. Accordingly Amélineau holds that these passages were originally written in Coptic and were simply translated and adopted by Palladius; and in this he is followed by Grützmacher and Basset[2].

Before proceeding to the consideration of this position, we must take cognisance of *lat*[2], in which (γ) and (ζ) are found, and found at the same points of the Life as in *ar*. This fact has been put forward as a confirmation of the theory, not indeed by Amélineau himself, but by Grützmacher and Basset, who say that *lat*[2] was derived from a copy of the Life not mutilated in these places. It is necessary to examine with care the case of *lat*[2]; for if it gives a real attestation to *ar* in regard to the Palladian passages, the united testimony of the two redactions would go far to prove Amélineau's theory. Fortunately the problem admits of an absolute demonstration, in so far as *lat*[2] is concerned.

(1) In *lat*[2] (c. XXII.) one of the rules reads as follows: "Qui uero semel ad hoc intraret monasterium ut ibi iugiter permaneret, per tres annos a studiis sacratioribus arceretur: operaretur tantum opera sua simpliciter, et ita post triennium stadium certaminis introiret." This is a literal translation of the ordinary Greek as found in Meursius and in Migne: Τὸν μέντοι εἰσελθόντα εἰσάπαξ συμμεῖναι αὐτοῖς ἐπὶ τριετίαν εἰς ἀγῶνα ἀδύτων αὐτὸν οὐ δέξῃ, ἀλλ' ἐργατικώτερα ἔργα ποιήσας, οὕτως εἰς τὸ στάδιον ἐμβαινέτω μετὰ τὴν τριετίαν (*P. G.* XXXIV. 1100). But the words ἀγῶνα and εἰς τὸ στάδιον (in the Latin, *studiis* and *stadium certaminis*) do not occur in any of the versions of the Lausiac History, neither in Latin I, nor in Syriac I[3]; nor again in the Ethiopic, nor in the Arabic itself (but the latter in this place departs widely from all

---

[1] *Monuments,* Tom. II. (*Musée Guimet,* XVII.); Tom. I. Fasc. II.
[2] *Opp. citt.,* 118, 11 respectively.
[3] This whole portion is wanting in Latin II. and Syriac II.

other copies). The evidence of the versions makes it certain that, at any rate in regard to these particular words, the genuine text of the Lausiac History must have been that preserved in the Paris MSS. 1627 and 919[1], namely:

ΕΙϹⲰΤⲰΝΑΔΥΤⲰΝ,

which got corrupted into

ΕΙϹΑΓⲰΝΑΔΥΤⲰΝ.

Then εἰς τὸ στάδιον, which is not in MSS. 1627, 919 at all, was inserted in the next line to carry on the metaphor of ἀγών.

Thus the passage in *lat²* contains a corruption which demonstrably arose among the Greek MSS. of the Lausiac History; and therefore the text in *lat²* cannot possibly be carried back independently of the Lausiac History to any supposed Coptic common source of Palladius, *lat²* and *ar*.

(2) In other places *lat²* shows unmistakable signs of alteration under the influence of the Lausiac History. As a particularly apposite instance let us take the passage which describes the manner in which the funerals of the nuns were carried out, and let us compare the various texts.

(See Table on next page.)

The present question is not whether the Coptic account, as found in *ar* and *boh*, or that of the Greek Life is the more primitive; it is whether the Greek underlying *lat²* in this place has borrowed directly from the Lausiac History. It is evident at a glance that Palladius' account has been substituted bodily for that of the *Vita*; and thus the fact is established that this redaction of the *Vita Pachomii* has been interpolated by passages taken straight from the Lausiac History. We are therefore justified in concluding that any Palladian matter found in *lat²* is to be accounted for in the same way.

---

[1] MS. 919 contains only a few fragments taken from *Hist. Mon.* and *Hist. Laus.* The section on Pachomius (f. 42) contains A 38—42 in the same text as MS. 1627. Preuschen makes a slip in saying that it is the chapter on Pachon, A 29 (*op. cit.* 151). 1628 omits the whole passage.

TABLE.

(Arabic and Bohairic Lives; *Musée Guimet* XVII. 382 and 38.)

(N.B. Words within [ ] are omitted in *ar*)

If one of them died they took her into the oratory and their mother wrapped her in the shroud; then abba Peter informed our father Pachomius, and he chose wise men [from among the brethren] and took them [with him to the convent]. They entered the enclosure and stayed in the porch and chanted becomingly until they had shrouded her and placed her on the hearse (*ar* in the coffin) [and carried her towards the mountain. The virgin sisters walked behind the hearse]. Their father walked behind them and their mother preceded them until they had buried (the deceased) and had prayed over her [and had returned to their home with great sorrow].

(Lausiac History, *P. G.* XXXIV. 1105.)[1]

Ἐὰν τελευτήσῃ παρθένος, ἐνταφιάσασαι αὐτὴν αἱ λοιπαὶ παρθένοι φέρουσι καὶ τιθέασιν αὐτὴν εἰς τὴν ὄχθην τοῦ ποταμοῦ. περάσαντες δὲ οἱ ἀδελφοὶ μετὰ πορθμοῦ, μετὰ βαΐων καὶ κλάδων ἐλαιῶν, μετὰ ψαλμῳδίας διαφέρουσιν αὐτὴν εἰς τὸ πέραν καὶ θάπτουσιν εἰς τὰ μνήματα ἑαυτῶν.

(Greek Life, c. 22—Boll. p. 26*.)

καὶ τελεουμένης δὲ ἀδελφῆς, συνάγονται μέχρι νῦν οἱ ἀδελφοὶ κατά τινα ὡρισμένον τόπον καὶ οὕτως ψαλλόντων αὐτῶν, αἱ λοιπαὶ κατὰ τὸ ἕτερον μέρος ἐνταφιάσασαι ταύτην καλῶς τιθέασιν ἐν τῷ μέσῳ· εἶθ᾽ οὕτως λαμβάνοντες οἱ ἀδελφοὶ μετὰ σεμνῆς ψαλμῳδίας, θάπτουσιν αὐτὴν ἐν τῷ ὄρει μετ᾽ εὐλαβείας πολλῆς καὶ φόβου θεοῦ, ὡς προσῆκεν δούλοις Χριστοῦ.

(*lat*[1] § 29, Lipomanus p. 87, ed. 1581.)

Quando autem consummatur soror, usque ad hodiernum diem congregantur fratres in aliquo loco definito, et ita iis psallentibus, ceterae in alia parte, cum eam pulchre ad sepeliendum composuerint, ponunt in medio. Deinde sic eam accipientes fratres, cum graui et ueneranda psalmodia in monte sepeliunt cum magna pietate ac Dei metu, ut decet seruos Christi.

(*lat*[2] § 28, Rosweyd p. 124.)

Quod si defuncta esset uirgo, curantes funus ejus reliquae, cunctaque quae ad sepulturam pertinent adimplentes, deferebant usque ad ripam fluminis quod utraque monasteria dividit, psalmos ex more canentes. Tunc transeuntes monachi cum ramis palmarum et oliuarum frondibus, psallentes transuehebant eam, et in sepulchris suis cum hilaritate condebant.

---

[1] The Ethiopic in Rule I. (Basset, 27) agrees exactly with the Greek of Palladius.

(3) On the hypothesis that *sah* was the original Life, and that *ar* is its best representative, the only possible pedigree of the redactions of the *Vita* is:

1. *ar* (= *sah*, ex hypothesi)
2. *boh*
3. *gr* + *asc*
4. *lat*¹ (*i.e.* its Greek original)
5. *lat*² („   „   )

This fact is so obvious to any one who takes the trouble to compare the various redactions, that I shall not delay to prove it: indeed even from the Tables given on p. 167 and in Appendix IV it is abundantly evident.   Whether it be *ar* or *gr* + *asc* that represents the original, on either hypothesis beyond all question *boh* represents the link between them.   Similarly *lat*¹ represents the link between *gr* + *asc* and *lat*².   To suppose, as Grützmacher does, and also Basset¹, that the Greek original of *lat*² should have come from the Coptic (*ar* = *sah*) without passing through *boh*, *gr* + *asc* and *lat*¹, is to postulate a literary impossibility.   The presence of the Palladian passages in *lat*² is therefore wholly independent of their presence in *ar*, and affords no confirmation whatever of the theory that they stood in the earliest Coptic redaction of the *Vita Pachomii*.

These three arguments demonstrate superabundantly that the passages in question are interpolations in *lat*² from the Lausiac History: the circumstance that they occur at the same points of the Life as in *ar* is due merely to the fact that these are the natural points for their occurrence.

Having thus cleared away complications arising from supposed attestations of *ar* by *eth* and *lat*², we are in a position to consider the question of the Palladian passages as they stand in *ar*.   It has been seen that they must be judged simply on their own merits, as their presence there is unsupported by any external evidence. The following is a list of the passages in question, with the references to the pages of M. Amélineau's volume (*Annales du Musée Guimet* XVII.); he has supplied French translations of all the documents edited therein.

---

¹ *Opp. citt.* 8 and 11 respectively.

Arabic *Vita*

 pp. 366—369. The Rule, (γ) in the analysis, p. 155.

 pp. 376—378. Account of the monastery (at Panopolis), the two parts in inverted order, (ϵ).

 pp. 382—384. The convent of nuns, (ζ) (much shorter) and (η).

We are not here directly concerned with the question whether the *Vita Pachomii* was first written in Coptic or in Greek; but merely with the much narrower question whether the Pachomian portions of the Lausiac History were translated by Palladius from Coptic documents. Of course the affirmative answer to this latter question involves the priority of the Coptic form of the *Vita*; but it also assumes the truth of the two following propositions :—

(*a*) that the earliest Coptic Life—*sah*—is more faithfully preserved in *ar* than in *boh*; and (*b*) that *ar* has accurately preserved the type of *sah*, without many or serious changes and interpolations.

I think it will be possible to arrive at conclusions concerning these two propositions, which will render unnecessary for present purposes any discussion of the more general question. I shall take (*b*) before (*a*).

(*b*) M. Amélineau himself recognises that *ar* has been in places interpolated and worked up from other documents—indeed the actual words occur in the text: "I will tell you another story concerning our Father which I have found in another volume[1]." And Grützmacher shows that this is the case even more than Amélineau supposed. He points out the existence of doublets, and it would be possible to add to his list: he shows too that a twofold stream of tradition may be detected, manifested by differences in matters of fact, of idea and of treatment, in the second part of *ar* as compared with the first[2]. And in all this what he says is endorsed by Zöckler[3]. As a matter of fact Grützmacher's second document is not far to seek: it is neither

---

[1] *Musée Guimet*, XVII. 599: Amélineau remarks in a note: "Ce passage prouve que cette vie de Pakhôme a été faite un peu de pièces et de morceaux"; and on p. 651 he says that another passage "prouve qu'il y a là une interpolation postérieure."

[2] *Pachomius*, 15, 16.

[3] *Askese u. Mönchtum*, 194.

more nor less than the second Greek work, the *Asceticon Pachomii*, the *Paralipomena* of the Bollandists, in which may be found two of the three passages (*ar* 613 and 628) cited by Grützmacher in proof of the presence of a second document[1]. Still more significant from our point of view is the presence in *ar* 426 of five of the rules from the collection called the *Second Rule* in the Ethiopic, a manifest interpolation to illustrate and give point to the text. Thus the composite and secondary character of *ar* is clearly demonstrated, and we can have no confidence in any passage in it which is not attested by some other redaction of the *Vita*. But the Palladian passages are wholly unattested. And not only so; there are positive grounds for believing that the Greek form as found in Palladius is the original, and the Arabic is a form that has undergone intentional alteration. Let one instance suffice: in the Greek (*P. G.* XXXIV. 1100 B) it is stated that there were twelve prayers at evensong; we know from Cassian (*Inst.* II.) that it was the early and normal usage in Egypt to have at the evening prayer, as at the nocturns, twelve psalms, each followed by a prayer; and one Ammon who had spent three years at St Pachomius' monastery about A.D. 350, a short time after the death of the saint, and who some fifty years later wrote out his recollections of what he had seen there, incidentally mentions the fact that in his time there were twelve prayers at the evensong[2]. On the other hand the latest redaction of the collection of lesser house-rules (that translated by St Jerome) says more than once that the number of psalms and prayers at vespers was six. Whence we may conclude that the primitive number was twelve, but that by the end of the century it had been reduced to six. Now in this passage in the Arabic Life (p. 369) the number is given as six. Thus it appears that in Palladius the text is correct, whereas in *ar* it is found in an altered form. Of another passage (the one that names some of the Greek letters) Basset declares that the Arabic "n'est qu'un commentaire développé de ce qui est dans le grec de Palladius et l'éthiopien" (p. 12). Thus the secondary character of the

---

[1] Pp. 605—639 of *ar* are from the *Asceticon*; the chapters occur in the following order: 5, 6, 13, 15, 16, 7, 17—27, 29, 30, 32, 33, 12, 34—36.

[2] Ἐπιστολὴ Ἀμμῶνος, § 14 (Boll. Tom. III. Maii 58*;) (cf. *infra* § 17).

passages as they actually stand in the Arabic Life, as compared
with their form in the Lausiac History, seems to be quite established. And this affords yet another presumption that they must
be regarded as later interpolations in the Arabic redaction of the
Vita Pachomii.

(*a*) I now approach the more fundamental question as to
whether there are good grounds for the view that the earliest
Coptic Life—*sah*—is better preserved in *ar* than in *boh*. And
here I must protest that it is only possible to deal with the facts
that are actually before us: documents and redactions that may
have existed, but of the existence of which there is no evidence,
cannot be considered. We must take the printed documents
as we find them, and base our conclusions on them as they
stand. M. Amélineau in one place says that three different
redactions of *sah* are known to him[1]. One of them, however,
turns out to be *ar*, which he christens the *Great Life;* the
second redaction is represented by only two fragments, and on
p. 485 he had spoken of one of these as being from "a different *Life*" of Pachomius,—not merely a different *redaction*
of the Life; the third redaction is the one represented by the
great body of Sahidic fragments, which both by their number
and extent afford ample materials for comparison with the other
documents[2]. It is obviously only this last Sahidic Life that can
be considered here; and we have to ask the plain question
whether the Arabic Life, as printed by M. Amélineau, or the
Bohairic Life agrees the more closely with the Sahidic fragments
before us? To this question only one answer can be given. Let
us turn to Fragment I. in the volume of the *Monuments* last referred to: it opens with these words: "She went to the south in
great sorrow, because not only Theodore had not come to her, but
also her younger son Paphnutius had gone away and had gone to
live with him" (p. 521). These words are the conclusion of the
account of the visit paid to the monastery by Theodore's mother
after he had become a monk; and it is evident that his brother

---

[1] *Monuments* &c. I. Fasc. ii. 488 (*Mémoires de la Mission archéologique
française au Caire*).

[2] A full list of the *sah* fragments is given *infra* in Appendix IV., together with
their correspondence with the other Lives.

Paphnutius is represented as having accompanied their mother on the journey, and as having stayed at the monastery when she went home. This agrees exactly with the account of the episode given in *boh* (*Musée Guimet* XVII. 53—56); but not with that given in *ar* (ibid. 405—6), where (as in *gr* 26) there is no mention at all of Paphnutius having accompanied his mother. The subject-matter immediately following this incident is quite different in *ar* and *boh*, and here again *sah* agrees closely with *boh*.

To take another case, the long *sah* fragment V in the *Musée Guimet* XVII. (pp. 317—328) agrees closely in matter and structure with *boh* (pp. 91—103); while the corresponding section of *ar* (pp. 411—442) differs very widely, as the following comparative table will show :—

[The figures in columns *ar boh sah* give the pages in vol. XVII. of the *Musée Guimet*; those in *gr* the chapters in the Greek Life. The sign + in *ar* signifies additions or alterations, and the sign − denotes notable lacunae in *ar*, as compared with *boh-sah*. In *gr* the signs * and † signify that *gr* approximates to *boh-sah* or to *ar* respectively; $^1/_2$ and $^2/_2$ indicate the early and late portions of the chapter.]

ar	boh	sah	gr
411—12+	91—2	317—18	*44
412			
413+and−	92—3	318—19	†45
414—16			
416—20+	93—5	319—21	*46
420—24+	(88—91)	(vac)	(*43)
424—26+	95—6	321—22	*47$^2/_2$
426—27 (5 rules from "Rule II")			
427—29+	96—9	322—24	*48
429—30			
430—32+	99—101	324—26	*49
432—33			
434−	101	326	*50$^1/_2$
	102	327	*52$^2/_2$
434—39			
439—40			†54
440	(104)	(vac)	(*56$^1/_2$)
441—42+	102—3	327—28 (fin.)	*55$^1/_2$

[Other similar instances might be given.]

In structure (as appears from the Table), and also in subject-matter (as any one will discover who takes the trouble to read the portions of the documents indicated), *sah* and *boh* run perfectly parallel; but in *ar*, as compared with *sah*, there are transpositions and omissions, and many very considerable additions; and even where the matter is the same, in almost every case there are notable alterations of the text.   This one set of parallel passages, even if it were unsupported by similar instances, would suffice to dispose of the only argument brought forward by Amélineau in support of the claims of *ar* to represent *sah*.   Having printed from the three documents the (in this case) closely parallel accounts of St Athanasius' visit to Tabennisi (cf. *gr* 20), he comments as follows (in 1889): "Comme il est facile de le voir, ce second récit (*ar*) ne diffère du premier (*boh*) que par quelques légères différences échappées à l'inadvertence du copiste, et cependant il est plus clair et semble mieux traduit de l'original thébain (*sah*).......Ce fragment (*sah*) se continue par un récit qui, dans les deux versions, se trouve aussi à la suite de ce fait et qui est identiquement le même dans les trois œuvres.   Comme on l'a pu voir, le fragment qui représente pour nous l'original thébain (*sah*) est à peu de chose près le même que les deux versions.   J'en peux donc conclure, autant qu'une conclusion est possible, que la version arabe représente sans doute la *vie* originale, mais qu'elle a été traduite avec cette liberté d'allures dont les auteurs coptes ont toujours usé dans tout ce qu'ils faisaient[1]."   The idea seems to be that as *ar* followed *sah* closely in this particular passage, there is a good presumption that it followed it equally closely throughout.   It is curious that, with the other Sahidic fragments before him, Amélineau should have drawn such a conclusion; and indeed six years later (1895) he seems to have become doubtful as to the substantial identity of *ar* and *sah*[2]. But if so, what becomes of the only reason put forward to make us believe in *ar*?

Still more unaccountable is it that Grützmacher, who criticizes Amélineau's methods somewhat severely (*e.g. op. cit.* 7), should

---

[1] *Musée Guimet*, xvii., *Introd.* lxvi.

[2] *Sah* "était peut-être faite elle-même par abrégé de la grande vie de Pakhôme" (= *ar*). (*Mémoires* &c. Fasc. ii. 488.)

declare that a comparison of the fragments of *sah* with the other recensions shows that *sah* was a fuller Life that any of them, and that of all the recensions *ar* is the one that most closely resembles *sah*[1]. He appears indeed to have been unaware of the many considerable fragments of *sah* published by Amélineau in 1895, the year preceding the publication of his own *Pachomius*, as also of those published by Mingarelli long ago.

The whole question has nothing recondite in it; it turns on the merest matters of fact, whether the Sahidic fragments come from a redaction of the *Vita* which more closely resembled *boh* or *ar*. The following conclusions in regard to the inter-relations of the various documents are suggested by a study of the passages analysed on p. 167, and I have no hesitation in saying that they are amply borne out by the phenomena of the different Lives as a whole:—

(1) *sah* and *boh*, while often differing from *gr*, on the whole agree very closely with one another;

(2) *ar* differs from them very considerably, especially in regard to additions; the additional matter, when judged by ordinary canons, being often of a character unmistakably apocryphal;

(3) each one of the redactions (*sah, boh, ar, gr*) contains matter not found in any other redaction;

(4) if we compare the three Coptic texts in detail, we find agreements usually between *sah* and *boh*, but sometimes between *sah* and *ar*, and sometimes between *boh* and *ar*;

(5) usually *sah-boh* are much nearer to *gr* than is *ar*; but sometimes *ar* is nearer to *gr* (see cases in Table p. 167; also the instance of Theodore's mother given above, p. 166).

---

[1] "Die Richtigkeit dieser Annahme (*i.e.* that *sah* was the original *Vita*) lässt sich noch durch einen Vergleich der wenigen Fragmente der koptisch-thebanischen Vita (*sah*) mit den übrigen Rezensionen erweisen; darnach war die k.-th. Vita (*sah*) die ausführlichste Darstellung des Lebens des Pachomius und seiner Nach-folger...Aber so richtig es ist, dass diese Vita (*ar*), wie aus einem Vergleiche der Fragmente der k.-th. Vita (*sah*) mit dieser Rezension hervorgeht, genauer als alle anderen Rezensionen sich an das Original (*sah*) hält, so ist sie doch keineswegs als absolut wortgetreue Uebersetzung zu bezeichnen" (*Pachomius* 14).

The general inferences to be drawn from these facts seem to be that *sah, boh* and *ar* are independent derivatives from a Coptic archetype, which approximated more closely than any of them to the archetype of the Greek Lives; and that *sah-boh* preserve this archetype much more faithfully than *ar*.

It has I think been sufficiently demonstrated that the Pachomian passages of the Lausiac History formed no part of the *Vita Pachomii;* and therefore it is unnecessary to enter upon the question of the original language of the *Vita.* But it did seem necessary to thresh out in this and the preceding section the whole question of the alleged Coptic originals of portions of the Lausiac History, and to show that there is as yet no reason for supposing that Palladius made direct translations from Coptic documents, the Greek having so far in each case turned out to be the original.

NOTE. I had hoped, as stated in a note on p. 108, to be able to indicate here the reasons which, after a careful study of the various redactions of the *Vita Pachomii,* have convinced me that the Greek *Vita* and *Asceticon* are the original documents from which the others have been derived. I find however that it would be impossible to do this within the limits of a page or two. I shall therefore only state my belief that an overwhelming case might easily be made out. When the Coptic Life is reconstructed from its three representatives (*sah, boh, ar*) it is seen that many of the parts wherein it differs from *gr* present the features of a secondary document—apocryphal character, "tendenz," and unmistakable doublets. In three passages of *gr* (cc. 6, 31, 62) the writer speaks as the actual author, and specifies as his sources of information the elder monks who had known Pachomius, and states expressly that before him no one had written a biography of the saint. Of course such passages might well stand in a translation: but they do not stand in the Coptic redactions;—so far as it is possible to judge, the whole contexts of *gr* 31 and 62 never had a place in the Coptic Life; the context of *gr* 6 is found in *boh* 22 and *ar* 356, but in both the particular passage in question is wanting. It must be concluded, therefore, either that a Coptic translator omitted the passages, or that a Greek translator invented them. The first is the obvious alternative to adopt in the absence of any good reason for holding the priority of the Coptic. This evidence of *gr* in its own favour receives support from a statement in a Coptic *Vita Theodori,* which in part corresponds with the later sections of *gr* (88—96), to the effect that the first biography of Pachomius was written by the monks who acted as Greek interpreters to those who did not know Egyptian (*sah* 302, *boh* 258).

I know of only one passage that might give countenance to the idea that the Coptic was the original: in *gr* 48 mention is made of a monk having been guilty of theft; in *ar* 428 it is represented as an act of impurity. It might be argued that *gr* here shows "tendenz" in softening down the offence. But *sah* 323 (also *boh* 97) agrees with *gr*; so that it is in *ar* that the alteration has been made.

It is probable from the nature of the case that the Coptic version was almost contemporary with the Greek; and M. Amélineau says that many of the actual fragments of *sah* date from the fourth century, or the beginning of the fifth (*Mémoires* Fasc. II. 484). It was made in an entourage familiar with the early traditions about Pachomius; and therefore I am prepared (with obvious limitations) to accept the supplementary historical data of the Coptic as being of practically the same value as those of the Greek. In the Coptic the Life of Theodore seems to have been greatly enlarged and sometimes separated from the Life of Pachomius.

Summary of Results of Part I.

At the conclusion of Part I. it may be convenient to sum up the main results of the investigation. I conceive that the following positions have been made good:—

I. The currently received text of the Lausiac History—the Long Recension—must be rejected: it is a fusion of that work and the *Historia Monachorum.*

II. The early versions, chiefly Latin I. and Syriac I., bear witness to the fact that the Latin *Paradisus Heraclidis,* as printed in Rosweyd, substantially represents in matter and structure the original work of Palladius: if a printed Greek text be sought, recourse must at present be had to that of Meursius, but certain lacunæ must be filled up from the later editions.

III. There is no ground for supposing that Palladius made use of any Greek documents.

IV. Nor is there any sufficient reason for thinking that he translated Coptic documents.

The book when restored to its true shape may rightly claim to be the authentic and original handiwork of its author. The textual and literary difficulties with which it has been encompassed have been removed.

It remains to enquire whether the Lausiac History in its restored form is better able to face the historical criticism to which it has been subjected; and whether it now affords a firmer foothold than has hitherto been attainable for the investigation of Christian Monastic Origins.

PART II. HISTORICAL CRITICISM.

§ 14. The Theological Character of Palladius.

Before we enter upon the discussion of the historical problems opened out by the Lausiac History, it may be well briefly to touch upon our author's theological and ecclesiastical character. In this regard Palladius has borne a bad name; he is commonly spoken of by Church historians as one gravely suspected of Pelagianism and Origenism, if not altogether compromised. This section contains a few notes on the broad facts of the case.

A reader of the Lausiac History, even one who does not sympathise with Palladius' ideas or respect his judgment, will, I think, carry away the impression that the author was, according to his lights at all events, a man sincere and pious. He was moreover the trusted friend of St John Chrysostom, suffering deprivation of his see, and an exile of several years' duration for his fidelity to the Saint, and travelling to Rome as his envoy to secure the favourable hearing of his case before the Pope[1]. This intimate connection with St John Chrysostom must raise a strong presumption in favour of Palladius' orthodoxy.

Yet we find his contemporaries St Epiphanius of Salamis (*P. L.* xxii. 527) and St Jerome (*Vall.* ii. 681, *P. L.* xxiii. 497) accusing Palladius of Origenism; and we have it on the authority of Photius (*Bibl. Cod.* 59, *P. G.* ciii. 109) that the alleged Origenism of Palladius was used as a weapon against St John Chrysostom.

---

[1] All that is stated in the text holds good, whether Palladius who wrote the Lausiac History be identified or not with the writer of the *Dialogue* on St John Chrysostom. Tillemont refuses to identify them (*Mémoires*, xi. 530 and 642); Zöckler inclines the other way (*Herzog-Plitt*, xi. 174), and probably he is right. [Dr Preuschen also favours the identification (*Palladius und Rufinus*, 246, note).]

It is to be noted that in regard to such accusations, Palladius does not stand alone. He shares the charge of Origenism with a whole group of well-known personages—Dioscorus bishop of Hermopolis, Ammonius Parotes, and their two brothers (the famous four Tall Brothers), Heraclides bishop of Ephesus, Isidore the Almsgiver, and above all Evagrius; in short the group of monks opposed to and persecuted by Theophilus, Patriarch of Alexandria. Into the story of this quarrel it is unnecessary to enter. Suffice it to say that it appears to have been a question of ecclesiastical politics quite as much as of doctrine. At the beginning of the fifth century the Eastern Church was divided into two bitterly opposed parties, the leaders of which ·were Theophilus of Alexandria and St John Chrysostom. Few will now be found either to admire or defend Theophilus and his proceedings: "unscrupulous" is the epithet which Newman applies to him: and elsewhere he asks: "Who can speak with patience of the enemy of St John Chrysostom, that Theophilus, bishop of Alexandria?"[1] It was Theophilus and his partisans who violently expelled St John Chrysostom from his see, and were responsible for the exile and the outrages that caused his death; and the extent to which party spirit carried away even good men may be gauged from the fact that St Cyril of Alexandria, nephew and successor of Theophilus, "did not hesitate, in a letter still extant, to compare the great Confessor [St John Chrysostom] to Judas, and to affirm that the restoration of his name to the episcopal roll would be like paying honour to the traitor instead of recognizing Matthias. For twelve years did he and the Egyptians persist in this course."[2] Theophilus accused his opponents of Origenism; and Origenistic sympathies formed one of the charges levelled against St John Chrysostom. It seems strange that their zeal against Origenism should have induced St Epiphanius and St Jerome to make common cause with such a man as Theophilus, and to support him and look to him as their leader, even though they did not take actual part in his violent deeds. Without question it is mainly owing to their adverse judgment

[1] *Theodoret* (*Hist. Sketches*, II. 341): *Apologia* (orig. ed.) 399.
[2] Newman, *Theodoret* (ut sup.); cf. *P. G.* LXXVII. 356.

that the ecclesiastical reputation of Palladius and the others has suffered.

But it is necessary to ask whether St Jerome's verdict on the doctrine and character of Theophilus' opponents must needs be accepted. And even if he may often have judged rightly as to the real tendency of their writings, may it not be that his estimate of their persons was biassed by the party spirit that ran so high at the time? For it is a fact that cannot be gainsaid that St Jerome was a thorough-going partisan of Theophilus; he even translated into Latin a scurrilous invective by Theophilus against St John Chrysostom (*Vall.* I. 750—754, *P. L.* XXII. 931—5, and LXVII. 676—8). St Jerome's opinions in regard to Rufinus were not shared by St Augustine or St Paulinus of Nola (*P. L.* XXXIII. 248, and LXI. 311, 371, 397, 398); and the same two saints extol in the highest terms the virtues and good deeds of the elder Melania (*P. L.* LXI. 315—321, 392—3), of whom St Jerome said, even after her death, that "the blackness of her name indicated the darkness of her perfidy" (*Vall.* I. 1023, *P. L.* XXII. 1151). John bishop of Jerusalem, too, one of the chief objects of the attack of St Jerome and St Epiphanius, was very highly spoken of by St Augustine, St John Chrysostom, Theodoret, and Pope Anastasius (Tillemont *Mémoires*, XII. 342). It is thus clearly seen that St Jerome's unfavourable estimate of several of the more prominent so-called Origenists was not at all the view of other contemporaries, whose words and opinions must carry as great, if not greater weight. Indeed, as Abbé Duchesne says: "On diminuerait notablement le nombre des Pères de l'Église s'il fallait en déduire tous ceux qui ont provoqué les vivacités de St Jérôme."[1]

To say this is no real disparagement of St Jerome. What Newman says of St Cyril of Alexandria, "I don't think Cyril himself would like his historical acts to be taken as the measure of his inward sanctity,"[2] may surely be said of St Jerome in his controversial writings. And it may well be that, in spite of outbursts and mistakes, the bringing of that rugged and impetuous

---

[1] *Revue des Sciences Ecclésiastiques* (1882). *Les Témoins ante-nicéens du dogme de la Trinité.*

[2] *Theodoret* (ut sup.).

nature under control, bespeaks a greater virtue and was a more admirable conquest than the perfect serenity of other saints in whom human passions raged less boisterously at first.

When we turn to the specific charges against Palladius and those who suffer with him from the accusation of Origenism, we find that the chief rock of offence is their use of the term ἀπάθεια, or *impassivity*, to describe the state attained by various ascetics. The term was later on used by the Pelagians to express one of their tenets—a state of complete mastery over sensuality and of entire freedom from temptation.   Tillemont, however, shows that the word was freely used in the generation before Palladius by writers of unquestionable orthodoxy, and therefore was susceptible of a sound meaning[1].   As employed in the Lausiac History it seems to be used in this earlier sense[2].

Another of the counts against Palladius rests on the two bitter attacks he makes upon St Jerome (A 78—82 and 125): if we make allowance, however, for the party feeling natural under the circumstances, we shall see that this is only what might be expected from a prominent adherent of St John Chrysostom against a prominent adherent of Theophilus.

But the great cause of suspicion at a later date against Palladius individually is undoubtedly the fact that he was the disciple and friend of Evagrius, who was named along with Origen and Didymus in lists of teachers of heresy drawn up at the sixth and seventh General Councils.   The evidence concerning Evagrius' orthodoxy or the reverse is brought together and discussed by Zöckler (*Evagrius Ponticus* 80—91).   It appears that the only points in his teaching ever condemned explicitly were certain fantastic ideas as to the origin of souls and spirits[3].   That

---

[1] *Mémoires*, x. 381.

[2] Such was clearly the opinion of Rosweyd (Prol. § xv.).

[3] The following fragments are quoted by Maximus (*Schol. in Dion. Areopag. De Ec. Hier.* vi., *P. G.* iv. 173) from a work of Evagrius: Ἕκαστον τάγμα τῶν οὐρανίων δυνάμεων ἢ ὅλον ἐκ τῶν κάτω, ἢ ὅλον ἐκ τῶν ἄνω, ἢ ἐκ τῶν ἄνω καὶ ἐκ τῶν κάτω συνέστηκε.   And immediately after: Ἐξ ἀγγελικῆς καταστάσεως καὶ ἀρχαγγελικῆς ψυχικὴ κατάστασις γίγνεται· ἐκ δὲ τῆς ψυχικῆς δαιμονιώδης καὶ ἀνθρωπίνη· ἐκ δὲ τῆς ἀνθρωπίνης ἄγγελοι πάλιν καὶ δαίμονες γίγνονται.   In the Acts of the Synod held at Constantinople in 543, these propositions are recited word for word and anathematised among a series of Origenistic propositions (*Mansi* ix. 397); and it

Evagrius' doctrine on these points was derived from Origen seems plain; but of the more fundamental errors that go under the name of the great Alexandrian, especially those in regard to the Holy Trinity and the Incarnation, Zöckler declares that not a trace is to be found in the extant writings of Evagrius. The same is the witness of Tillemont: "Ce qui nous reste des écrits d'Évagre ne le fait condanner de personne que nous sachions"[1]: and his verdict was endorsed by the Bollandist reviewer of Zöckler's *Evagrius* only four years ago[2]. That Evagrius, Palladius, and their friends, read Origen's works and admired and defended them is unquestionable; but so did Athanasius, and Basil, and the two Gregories. In those days his teaching had hardly as yet fallen under the suspicion, much less the ban of the Church. And as there is a disposition on all hands to rescue the memory of the master, whatever may have been his misbeliefs, from the charge of having been a heretic, may not the like indulgence be extended to his disciples also?

Tillemont well sums up the case, so far as Palladius is concerned: "Un soupçon si peu appuyé ne nous doit pas empescher de respecter un évesque, dont la vie n'a rien que d'édifiant, dont les écrits ne portent qu'à la piété, qui paroist avoir eu beaucoup de simplicité et d'humilité, qui a mérité très justement le titre de Confesseur pour avoir défendu avec une générosité extraordinaire la cause de la vérité et de l'Église dans l'innocence de St Chrysostome, et pour avoir enduré beaucoup en la défendant; à qui les auteurs contemporains attribuent l'esprit de prophétie; qui, nonobstant l'accusation d'Origénisme, a esté receu à Rome comme un prélat très Catholique, quoique les *Origénistes* y eussent esté

is probable that the fifth General Council, held at Constantinople ten years later, repeated the condemnation. To Zöckler belongs the merit of identifying the passages, and thus making clear the precise teaching of Evagrius condemned by the Church (*op. cit.* 78, 86), and justifying Tillemont's verdict on the great body of his writings.

[1] *Mémoires*, x. 381.

[2] "Tillemont a eu raison de dire que (*ut supra*), et que 'le crime d'Origénisme est commun à beaucoup de personnes qu'on peut croire avec fondement avoir été très bons catholiques'." (*Analecta Boll.* xiv. 120). Particularly hard is the case of abbot Or of Nitria: through having been identified by the redactor of A with his namesake of the Thebaid, who rightly or wrongly is set down by St Jerome as an Origenist, he himself has gone down to posterity as a heretic.

condannez trois ou quatre ans auparavant, et qui sans doute a
de mesme esté reconnu pour Catholique par tout l'Orient, puisqu'après avoir souffert avec patience durant beaucoup d'années
la perte de son évesché, on lui en a confié un autre."[1].

§ 15. Historicity of the Lausiac History.

We now enter upon the consideration of the question for the
sake of which all the foregoing discussions have been undertaken.
Is the Lausiac history a mere romance, or is it a work of genuine
historical character?

Those who condemn the book are very much influenced by the
miraculous element which so largely pervades it, and which to
their minds proves the wilful mendacity of the writer. This point
I shall not touch upon for the present, but shall allow it to stand
over till the end of this section. My immediate task is to subject
the book to the ordinary tests of historicity and truthfulness, to
examine its chronology and geography, and to supply some
material for judging whether its statements accord with those of
the accredited documents of the time.

It will be well in the first place to consider the specific reasons,
apart from miracles, put forward by Dr Weingarten as justifying
his extremely unfavourable verdict as to the trustworthiness of the
Lausiac History. He calls attention to two cases wherein the
Lausiac History is in contradiction of the ascertained history of
the time[2].

(1)   In A 136 Palladius relates that he had seen at Alexandria in her old
age a certain virgin, and that the city clergy had told him that St Athanasius
fled to her house in 356 as a refuge from his pursuers, and abode there in
concealment for six years, until the death of Constantius. Now it is known
from St Athanasius' own writings that on that occasion he fled to the desert,
and lived there among the monks during the period in question—a proof,
says Weingarten, of the shamelessness with which Palladius falsified the
history of his time.

---

[1] *Mémoires*, xi. 530. The imputations made by Baronius in regard to Palladius'
private character, and reprinted by Rosweyd as an introduction to Book VIII., are
in some points based on palpable errors of the Annalist himself, and in others are
mere inferences wholly unwarranted by the evidence.

[2] *Ursprung des Mönchtums*, 28—30.

On the question of fact, viz. that it is not true that Athanasius stayed all these years in Alexandria, Tillemont agrees with Weingarten ; but he suggests that there may have been some foundation for the story, as, *e.g.* that on the night of the search made for him Athanasius may have gone to the young virgin's house as the safest place, and may have stayed there for a time, until he found an opportunity of slipping away[1]. This suggestion has commended itself as likely to Cave and Montfaucon, and in our own day to Canon Bright, who considers that there are independent reasons pointing to the conclusion that Athanasius did not at once withdraw to the desert[2]. It is to be noted that although Palladius tells us that he saw this virgin, then in her seventieth year, he heard the story not from her, but from the clergy of Alexandria. There is little difficulty in supposing that, in an age when written records were necessarily scarce, some exaggeration or error may have crept into the popular tradition of an event that had happened some forty years previously[3].

(2) The Greek text of A 20 makes Melania say that she had seen St Athanasius in Egypt ; but she did not come to Egypt till after his death.

Here it is enough, waiving all discussion of the chronology of Melania's life, a somewhat intricate question, to inform the reader that only one family of Greek mss. introduces St Athanasius' name in this place ; that it is absent from all the versions ; and accordingly is a certain interpolation.

Thus Weingarten's case against Palladius, in so far as it rests on alleged historical misstatements, may safely be said to break down[4].

We now pass on to test the chronology of the Lausiac History.

Palladius' Chronology of his own life[5].

At the outset of his work, in the prefatory Διήγησις (beginning Πολλῶν πολλά), Palladius tells Lausus that at the time he writes he is in the thirty-third year of his monastic life, the twentieth of his episcopate, and the fifty-third of his age (*P. G.* xxxiv. 1001). There is no variation in these figures[6]. From them we learn that

---

[1] *Mémoires*, viii. 698. [2] *Dictionary of Christian Biography*, i. 194.

[3] Palladius was in Alexandria in 388—390, and again in 400.

[4] Dr Lucius also rejects the historical character of the book ; his argument is a corollary of his theory as to its composition, viz. that Palladius' accounts of the Egyptian monks were not his own. This theory has already been shown to be untenable (cf. § 8) ; and with the theory falls also the whole superstructure built upon it. Therefore Palladius' character as an historian is unaffected by Dr Lucius' particular line of attack.

[5] Cf. note, p. 182.

[6] The Paris ms. 1628 gives the fifty-sixth year of his age ; but Dr Preuschen puts this down without hesitation as a paleographical error (*op. cit.* 234).

Palladius became a monk in his twentieth year, and bishop in his thirty-third; and that therefore he had been a monk for some thirteen years when he was made bishop;—the data allow a margin of nearly two years, practically covering any period from over twelve to under fourteen years. We learn also that, as the greater part of the Lausiac History is concerned with what took place before Palladius was a bishop, most of the book is made up from the writer's memory of events from which he was separated by an interval of from twenty to thirty years. A reasonable elasticity must therefore be allowed to the notes of time he gives, and his figures must not be strained by an undue arithmetical precision; he must be allowed the privilege of speaking now and then in round numbers.

In the body of his work Palladius in various places gives sufficient details as to his movements to render it possible to construct a chronology of his life. Fortunately he supplies a determinate starting-point; for he begins by telling us that he first came to Alexandria in the second consulate of Theodosius the Great, i.e. in the year 388 (A 1). He remained in the neighbourhood of Alexandria from two to three years (A 2 and 7), and then betook himself to Nitria, probably towards the end of 390 or the beginning of the following year; there he spent a full year, ἐνιαυτὸν ὅλον (A 7), after which he passed into the more remote desert of "the Cells," where he remained for nine years (A 20, P. G. xxxiv. 1050). Towards the close of this period his health broke down, and at last he was sent by his brethren to Alexandria; the physicians there sent him on to Palestine, whence he passed to Bithynia, and there he was consecrated bishop (A 43, P. G. xxxiv. 1114). These figures would point to the year 400 or 401 as that in which Palladius left the desert; and A 4 implies that his absence from Alexandria covered a period of just ten years. But it must have been in 400, and in the very beginning of it, that he left the desert; for he was present as bishop at a synod held by St John Chrysostom at Constantinople in the May of that year. This makes up the period of twelve or thirteen years mentioned in the preface.

Without unduly straining the figures it might be possible to suppose that Palladius quitted Egypt in 399; but the set of dates he gives in A 86, in connection with the facts of Evagrius' life, prevents us, I think, from thus anticipating his departure from Egypt; for Palladius there practically tells us that he was present at Evagrius' death. Now the starting-point for the chronology of Evagrius is the fact that he was present at the Council of Constantinople, and was left by St Gregory Nazianzen with his successor Nectarius, to aid him by his preaching in the suppression of Arianism. This was the summer of 381. At least a year must be allowed for Evagrius' activity at Constantinople and for the episode that led to his withdrawal to Jerusalem. . His sojourn at Jerusalem lasted more than six months; so that it cannot have been before the summer or autumn of 383 that he arrived at Nitria. At Nitria he spent two years, and then entered the desert of "the Cells," where Palladius' various statements would lead us to infer that he lived for a period of fifteen or sixteen years, his entire monastic life extending over seventeen or eighteen years: Palladius' details do not demand more than a full seventeen years. This would place his death in 400; and as he died on the Epiphany, there was just sufficient time for Palladius to have travelled to Bithynia and to have been consecrated by May in that year[1].

I exhibit the two sets of figures in tabular form :—

EVAGRIUS.	PALLADIUS.
381 at C. of Constantinople.	
1 year at Constantinople.	388 came to Alexandria.
1 year at Jerusalem.	2½ years at Alexandria.
2 years in Nitria.	1 year in Nitria.
15 years in Cellia.	8½ years in Cellia.
400 (Epiphany) died.	400 (Epiphany) left the desert.

One point there is which seems to place earlier than 400 the date of Palladius' leaving the desert. He says (A 43) that it was three years after his visit to John of Lycopolis that the illness came upon him which compelled him to repair to Alexandria.

---

[1] Tillemont places Evagrius' death twelve months earlier (*Mémoires*, x. 379); but I do not think this is compatible with Palladius' narrative, and in this view I have the support of Zöckler, who thinks Evagrius' death cannot have taken place earlier than the Epiphany in 400, and that there is no reason for putting it later. (*Evagrius Ponticus*, 17.)

Now John of Lycopolis died (if any credit is to be attached to the *Historia Monachorum in Aegypto*, c. I. *fin.*) at the end of 394 or early in 395, shortly after the victory of Theodosius over Eugenius; and Palladius' visit to him cannot be placed later than the summer of 394. Now his illness came upon him a full three years after this; and it is not to be supposed that he should at once have made up his mind to relinquish his monastic life without struggling for some time against the malady. And so there does not seem to be any real inconsistency between this statement and the others[1].

At another point also Palladius' chronology of his own life touches that of the *Historia Monachorum*, and so it is possible to make the two works test each other. He tells us that Macarius of Alexandria was alive for three years after his coming to Cellia (A 20). From what has been said above it would seem that Palladius came to Cellia towards the end of 391, or early in 392. This would place Macarius' death in 394 or 395; and as his feast is kept in January by both East and West, there seems to be reason in Tillemont's surmise that he died in January 395 (*Mémoires*, VIII. 648). But he was already dead when the party, whose tour is narrated in the *Historia Monachorum*, reached Nitria and Cellia (cc. 28, 29); and as they were with John of Lycopolis about the end of September 394, when the news of Theodosius' victory reached Egypt (c. I. *fin.*), the question arises whether the tour described in that book can reasonably be supposed to have extended over some four or five months. It took Palladius eighteen days to travel direct without any stoppage from Nitria to Lycopolis (A 43). The narrative of the *Historia Monachorum* supplies

---

[1] Dr Preuschen says that the disentanglement of the two texts in the account of John of Lycopolis makes 394 an impossible date for Palladius' visit to John (*Palladius und Rufinus*, 243). I cannot see anything in the restored text of the Lausiac History that militates against this date. It was necessitated by the interpolated text: it is not necessitated by the true text; but neither is there any intrinsic ground for rejecting it. I have carefully studied Dr Preuschen's ample and quite fresh treatment of the chronology of Palladius' life (*op. cit.* 233—246). After full consideration I am not led to alter what I had already written. I see the force of some of the difficulties he raises; but I think his own system is encompassed by difficulties of a higher order. The question demands further treatment, and I shall deal with it in Appendix V.

evidence that the seven made their journey in a leisurely way; it is expressly stated that they stopped three days with John of Lycopolis (c. 1, *fin.*), and a week with abbot Apollonius or Apollos (c. 7, *fin.*); and it is reasonable to suppose that similar stoppages were made at other places. Accordingly it is not surprising to read in the *Epilogue* that the Epiphany (A.D. 395) found them still on their travels, and apparently not yet arrived at Nitria. So that there is no difficulty whatever in reconciling Palladius' dates with the fact that Macarius of Alexandria was already dead when the writer of the *Historia Monachorum* reached Nitria.

It thus appears that the general statement in the Preface to the Lausiac History, the various autobiographical notes scattered throughout the body of the work, the set of chronological data given for Evagrius' Life, and the points of time fixed by the *Historia Monachorum*, all tally with sufficient accuracy. This raises a presumption that both books have at any rate an historical framework[1].

---

[1] In regard to the *Historia Monachorum* Tillemont raises some chronological difficulties :—

(1) It is stated (c. 7, *init.*) that Apollonius or Apollos was about eighty years of age (in the Greek ὀγδοηκοστοῦ ὢν ἔτους, cf. A 52) at the time the writer saw him, *i.e.* at the end of 394. But it is stated in the same place that he retired to the desert at the age of fifteen and passed forty years in solitude, until "the times of Julian" (361—3); which would make him at least eighty-five in 394. Tillemont devotes a whole page to the discussion of this difficulty (*Mémoires*, x. 721);—and yet it is but reasonable in such cases to take the ages assigned to the solitaries as being but approximations.

(2) According to Palladius (A 43) John of Lycopolis was thirty years of age when he enclosed himself in his cell, and seventy-eight when he died; according to the Latin *Historia Monachorum* (c. 1, *init.*) these dates should be forty and ninety respectively (*Mémoires*, x. 718). Here again it is unreasonable to press too closely such figures, based on hearsay and mere recollections. On the one point, however, which Palladius professes to have learned from John himself, the figures of the two accounts practically agree, giving forty-eight and fifty years respectively as the period of John's inclusion.

(3) The Latin *Historia Monachorum* (c. 27) says that Evagrius abstained altogether from bread, *i.e.* in 395; but according to Palladius (A 86) it seems as if it was not until the last two years of his life that he so abstained, *i.e.* 397—8 (*Mémoires*, x. 795). There are textual uncertainties about both passages. In any case, when we recollect that Palladius did not write his account of Evagrius till

General Chronology of the Lausiac History.

To test one by one all the statements of Palladius which bear upon chronology, and to bring the whole of his narrative into contact with the contemporary documents, would be a long and wearisome task. Fortunately a more compendious method is at hand which will suffice for our present purpose. It will probably be admitted that not many historians, if any, have rivalled Tillemont's extraordinarily minute and accurate knowledge of the whole body of great sources for the history of the fourth and fifth centuries. The preceding foot-note affords examples of the scrupulous care, at times even bordering upon excessive fastidiousness, with which he collects scattered statements and exposes discrepancies no matter how trifling. The wonderful *Notes et Éclaircissemens* attached to each volume of his great work are, in spite of incidental errors, a monument to all ages of labour, of scholarship, of sagacity, and of exquisite tact. In the *Notes* to several of the volumes the Lausiac History is freely used and is diligently compared with all other sources of information. At times it is shown that Palladius is in error—as is only to be expected of any historian in any age, and especially of a writer who records his reminiscences of what took place a quarter of a century before[1]. But on the whole Palladius emerges from this searching ordeal unscathed; and he has won from the prince of historical critics

---

some twenty years after his death, it will not be a matter of surprise should it appear that he was in error upon such a point by two or three years.

Chronological difficulties such as these are not of a nature to deserve further consideration.

On the other side we may note the following as an instance of accuracy: the *Historia Monachorum*, in the Latin version (c. 23), speaks of Dioscorus the Tall as being already a bishop in the beginning of 395. Now we know from the Lausiac History (A 13) that in 391 he was but a priest; in September 394, however, he sat as bishop of Hermopolis at the Council held at Constantinople (cf. Tillemont, *Mémoires*, XI. 447). So that here again the *Historia Monachorum* fits in with the history of the time in a matter where owing to the small margin it would have been easy to go astray.

[1] One of the most serious difficulties is in regard to Pambo (A 10); it is discussed by Tillemont, VIII. 788.

the high encomium already quoted in full in the Introductory paragraph of this Study.

I had intended to have worked out as a test case Palladius' account of the two Roman ladies who bore the name of Melania (A 117—121); but it soon appeared that such an undertaking would outrun my available space. I therefore content myself with referring to the *Notes* (*Mémoires*, x. 821—3), wherein Tillemont discusses the chronology etc. of the elder Melania's life; it will there be seen how consistently Palladius' different pieces of information hold together; and when in two important points the united authority of St Jerome and St Paulinus of Nola stands against him, Tillemont still holds that Palladius is right. And if Palladius' account of the early years of the elder Melania be compared with that given by her other friend St Paulinus[1]; or his account of the younger with the recently printed contemporary *Vita S. Melaniae Junioris*[2]; it will appear that the accounts are substantially the same, while there are those natural discrepancies in detail which are ever to be looked for in the most authentic independent accounts of the same series of events[3]. Palladius in connection with Melania (A 117) makes reference to a number of bishops and others banished under Valens from Egypt to Diocaesarea in Palestine; and this is supported by contemporary letters of St Peter of Alexandria, and St Basil, and by St Epiphanius[4].

M. Amélineau's special knowledge of the early Christian literature and history of Egypt makes the following testimony an important corroboration, from an independent standpoint, of what has here been put forward: "Nihil in illius (*sc.* Palladii) scriptis inveni quod ab aliorum scriptorum dictis discrepet[5]."

---

[1] Ep. xxix. (*P. L.* lxi. 316).

[2] *Analecta Bollandiana*, viii. 16—63.

[3] To give one instance, compare Palladius' statement (A 121) that when at Rome on St John Chrysostom's business he was hospitably entertained in Campania by Pinian and Melania the Younger, with the following passage of the *Vita* of the latter, referring to the very period of Palladius' visit to Rome: "Sanctis etiam episcopis et presbyteris et omnibus aduenientibus peregrinis in suburbano urbis Romae in rure constituentes non paruam humanitatem exhibentes administrabant" (p. 25).

[4] Tillemont, *Mémoires*, vi. 586—7.

De Hist. Laus. 8.

One point, however, only recently raised, must be noticed in detail. I refer to the statement that John of Lycopolis was a bishop. Were this the case, it would tend to shake our confidence in the credibility of the *Historia Lausiaca,* and also of the *Historia Monachorum*; for the writers of both claim to have visited and interviewed John a short time before his death, and what they say is quite irreconcilable with the idea that he was a bishop. Mr Evetts, in a note to his edition of Abu Salih's Arabic History, writes: "On the approach of the officers of Theodosius to Lycopolis, the bishop John gave orders for their reception,"—thus making him bishop of Lycopolis or Asyut[1]. But in the Coptic fragment in Zoega referred to as the authority, he is spoken of not as "bishop," but as "abbot" John[2]; and M. Amélineau assures me in a letter that there is nothing in the original document to suggest that John was a bishop. But in the title of a Coptic sermon attributed to Theophilus, it is said that the sermon was preached "in the presence of abbot John the anchorite, the Archimandrite of the mount of Lycopolis, who afterwards became bishop of the town of Hermopolis Magna[3]." In the Introduction to his volume published in 1895, M. Amélineau briefly discusses the point, and he declares the statement to be very doubtful[4]; and in a letter to me, dated May 15th, 1896, he altogether rejects it[5]. He tells me further that the Coptic *Synaxarium,* "la meilleure autorité que nous avons à ce sujet," does not know of John having been a bishop; and the same is the case with the wide circle of contemporary writers who make mention of John, some of whom claim to have met those who had come into contact with him:—St Augustine, Cassian, Rufinus, Sulpicius Severus, Theodoret, Sozomen, St Jerome, St Eucherius: the references may be found in Tillemont (*Mémoires,* x. 9—29). The statement accordingly may be rejected without hesitation.

[1] *Churches and Monasteries of Egypt, attributed to Abu Salih (Anecdota Oxoniensia,* Semitic Series, vii. 1895), 6, note 2.

[2] *Catalogus,* 540.

[3] *Ibid.* 107.

[4] *Monuments,* Tom. i., Fasc. ii., 504.

[5] "Je regarde le sermon de Théophile comme apocryphe ; par conséquent le titre qui a été ajouté peut n'avoir pas grande valeur, et n'en a pas en effet." And when referring to Mr Evett's statement, M. Amélineau says that John never was

Geography of the Lausiac History.

In the case of the chronology of the Lausiac History Tillemont saved us from the inconvenience of a detailed examination, and now in regard to its geography M. Amélineau will do us the same good service. Indeed, seeing that he knows the ground thoroughly, having travelled over it several times, and that he is an expert on the geography of Christian Egypt—for he has produced a standard work upon the subject[1]—it is clear that his judgment is of peculiar value. M. Amélineau gives it as his deliberate conviction that Palladius must have spent a long time in Egypt and have seen much of the country. The reason on which he relies is the accuracy of the geography of the Lausiac History: "Multa sunt quae, nisi vidisset, tam accurate describere nequivisset. Quaedam enim apud illum inveniuntur locorum descriptiones quibus ab illo visa fuisse ipsa loca demonstratur. Cujus rei ut exempla referam, accuratissime arenosa loca Alexandriae circumjecta (A 2), et iter Alexandria ad Nitriae montem perducens describit": and he quotes the passage from A 7, remarking that the reference to Ethiopia, which would now be erroneous, is in strict accord with the nomenclature of Palladius' time. The local descriptions of Nitria and Scete, found in A 20 and 33, are also instanced in evidence of Palladius' accuracy in point of topography; and then M. Amélineau concludes: "Itaque Palladius quod omnia loca, ut supra dixi, accuratissime describit, non debet dubitari quin omnia suis ipse oculis perspexerit[2]."

Palladius' general picture of Monastic Life in Egypt.

The point I wish to examine is this: whether the *mise-en-scène*, the background of the Lausiac History, in which the various sketches given by Palladius are set, is conformable to that derived from other sources of information: whether the general impression of life in the Desert conveyed by Palladius' book is true.

bishop of Lycopolis, "pas plus d'ailleurs, je crois, que Jean n'a été évêque d'Eschmounein" (Hermopolis Magna).

[1] *Géographie de l'Égypte à l'époque Copte.* Cf. *supra*, p. 108.

[2] *De Hist. Laus.* 8–9. (These examples are all from the true Lausiac History. Not understanding the composite nature of the A redaction, M. Amélineau later on treats of the geography of the *Historia Monachorum* as if it also was due to Palladius.)

In regard to the austerities which Palladius records of so many of the solitaries, M. Amélineau writes: "As often as he describes localities, or names monks, or relates their practices, fasts, and *crucifixions*, as they called them, he is worthy of credit[1]." And indeed what is known of oriental asceticism at the present day must go far to remove any hesitation in accepting what Palladius relates. It may be of interest to point out that the mortifications recorded of the Egyptian solitaries, extraordinary and appalling as they were, were all of a kind that may be called natural, consisting in privation of food, of drink, of sleep, of clothing; in exposure to heat and cold; in rigorous enclosure in cell or cave or tomb; in prolonged silence and vigils and prayer; in arduous labour, in wandering through the desert, in bodily fatigue: but of the self-inflicted scourgings, the spikes and chains, and other artificial penances of a later time, I do not recollect any instances among the Egyptian monks of the fourth century.

The long fasts spoken of by Palladius may, indeed, be thought to present a special difficulty; and therefore it may be well to adduce two corroborative testimonies drawn from sources quite outside the range of writings dealt with in this Study. The first is from the treatise *De Vita Contemplativa*, in which we read that the Therapeutae never partook of food until sunset, and that many of them would altogether abstain from food for three days together, and some even for six days[2]. The value of this evidence is unaffected by any question as to whether the *D. V. C.* was written in the first century or the third. Whether the treatise describes Jewish ascetics of the first century, or Christian monks of the third, there cannot, I think, be any reasonable doubt that it portrays the actual manner of life of a real community in Egypt. A still more unimpeachable witness is St Dionysius of Alexandria, who, in his Canonical Letter to

---

[1] *De Hist. Laus.* 18.

[2] Σιτίον δὲ ἢ ποτὸν οὐδεὶς ἂν αὐτῶν προσενέγκαιτο πρὸ ἡλίου δύσεως, ἐπειδὴ τὸ μὲν φιλοσοφεῖν ἄξιον φωτὸς κρίνουσι εἶναι, σκότους δὲ τὰς τοῦ σώματος ἀνάγκας· ὅθεν τῷ μὲν ἡμέραν, ταῖς δὲ νυκτὸς βραχύ τι μέρος ἔνειμαν. ἔνιοι δὲ καὶ διὰ τριῶν ἡμερῶν ὑπομιμνήσκονται τροφῆς, οἷς πλείων ὁ πόθος ἐπιστήμης ἐνίδρυται· τινὲς δὲ οὕτως ἐν- ευφραίνονται καὶ τρυφῶσιν ὑπὸ σοφίας ἑστιώμενοι, πλουσίως καὶ ἀφθόνως τὰ δόγματα χορηγούσης, ὡς καὶ πρὸς διπλασίονα χρόνον ἀντέχειν, καὶ μόλις δι' ἓξ ἡμερῶν ἀπογεύεσθαι τροφῆς ἀναγκαίας (Mangey 476; Conybeare 71). Quoted by Eusebius, II. 17.

Basilides on the time for breaking the fast on Easter Day, states that at Alexandria in the middle of the third century many of the faithful partook of no food whatever for two whole days preceding Easter, some for three days, and some for four, while some used even to keep an unbroken fast for the entire week; and he says that if these latter, all but dead from their prolonged fast, take food on Easter Day at an earlier hour than the others, they are not to be criticised for so doing[1]. With these authentic and independent witnesses before us, even the great fast of Paul the Simple ceases to be very wonderful; for according to Palladius (when restored to his true form) it lasted but for four days, and according to the Greek text of the *Historia Monachorum* for no more than a week;—that it extended over twelve days is the fiction of the redactor of A, who has combined the two versions of the story.

This is perhaps the most suitable place to refer to an anecdote vouched for by Palladius, which, though not claiming to be in any sense supernatural, is certainly wonderful, and has been seized upon by both Weingarten and Lucius as a proof of Palladius' mendacity and the fabulous character of the Lausiac History[2]. Palladius assures us (A 13) that he himself saw abbot Benjamin suffering from dropsy to such a degree that his little finger could not be spanned by the fingers of Palladius' two hands; and that, when he died, the door-posts of his cell had to be moved in order to allow the body to be carried out. There is nothing incredible in the second statement; for the doorway may have been narrow. In regard to the first, I consulted a competent physician, and he said that such an enlargement of the finger would be quite impossible in dropsy; but that in certain forms of elephantiasis, especi-

---

[1] Ἐπεὶ μηδὲ τὰς ἓξ τῶν νηστειῶν ἡμέρας ἴσως μηδὲ ὁμοίως πάντες διαμένουσιν· ἀλλ' οἱ μὲν καὶ πάσας ὑπερτιθέασιν ἄσιτοι διατελοῦντες, οἱ δὲ δύο, οἱ δὲ τρεῖς, οἱ δὲ τέσσαρας, οἱ δὲ οὐδεμίαν· καὶ τοῖς μὲν πάνυ διαπονηθεῖσιν ἐν ταῖς ὑπερθέσεσιν, εἶτα ἀποκάμνουσι καὶ μόνον οὐκ ἐκλείπουσι, συγγνώμη τῆς ταχυτέρας γεύσεως. εἰ δέ τινες οὐχ ὅπως οὐχ ὑπερτιθέμενοι, ἀλλὰ μηδὲ νηστεύσαντες ἢ καὶ τρυφήσαντες τὰς προαγούσας τέσσαρας, εἶτα ἐλθόντες ἐπὶ τὰς τελευταίας δύο ἢ μόνας ἡμέρας, αὐτὰς ὑπερτιθέντες, τήν τε παρα- σκευὴν καὶ τὸ σάββατον, μέγα τι καὶ λαμπρὸν ποιεῖν νομίζουσιν, ἂν μέχρι τῆς ἔω δια- μείνωσιν, τούτους οὐκ οἶμαι τὴν ἴσην ἄθλησιν πεποιῆσθαι τοῖς τὰς πλείονας ἡμέρας προησκηκόσι (P. G. x. 1277).

[2] It is cited by M. Amélineau also as a specimen of the reckless exaggeration at times indulged in by Palladius (*De Hist. Laus.*, 18).

ally in a tropical country, very extraordinary enlargements may
occur; and that in former times elephantiasis and any other
forms of disease in which the symptom was an abnormal swelling
were often spoken of as dropsy. So that, if we make allowance
for some exaggeration in the narrative of thirty years later, I do
not think that even this anecdote affords ground for a general
charge of wilful untruthfulness.

Nor, again, is the Lausiac History a mere idealising and glori-
fication of the monastic life. It is by no means an unvaried record
of extraordinary virtue. Even in the case of the most illustrious
monks, the difficulties, temptations, and struggles which they
underwent are narrated with a simplicity at times verging on
crudeness; and the weaknesses, failures and falls of many are
freely chronicled. If anywhere, we should look for an ideal state
of things in the great convent for women established a generation
previously by St Pachomius[1]; but Palladius' picture of the inner
life of this convent is by no means ideal (A 40—42): a nun there
committed suicide on account of a calumny wilfully uttered against
her by a sister; another, who pretended to be foolish, was treated
with great unkindness by several of the sisters, and made the object
of rude practical jokes[2]. Again, it may be thought that there is
a curious touch of nature in Palladius' account of Dorotheus
(A 36), who was chaplain or director of another convent of nuns,
and used to sit without ceasing at a window that overlooked the
convent, and strive to keep the peace among them: ἀδιαλείπτως
παρακαθεζόμενος τῇ θυρίδι τὴν ἀμαχίαν αὐταῖς ἐπραγματεύσατο
(P. G. XXXIV. 1098). Indeed it can be clearly seen from Palladius' pages that, in the midst of the prevalent asceticism and
together with much real holiness, a great deal of human nature
survived even in the desert.

To sum up the results of the investigations instituted in this
section: the Lausiac History does not at all present the charac-

---

[1] When Grützmacher says (Pachomius, 4 and 138) that Palladius erroneously
places this convent at Panopolis (Akhmīm) instead of at Tabennisi, it is he himself who is in error: the τούτων in P. G. XXXIV. 1105 B, line 14, refers not to the
particular monks of Panopolis, but to the Tabennesiote congregation in general.

[2] Ἐγὼ τοῦ πίνακος τὸ ἀπόπλυμα πολλάκις αὐτῇ κατέχεα. Ἄλλη· Πληγὰς αὐτῇ ἐγὼ
ἔδωκα....Ἄλλη πάλιν· Ἐγὼ πολλάκις τὴν ῥίνα αὐτῆς ἐσυνάχθησα (P. G. XXXIV. 1107).

teristics of a "Gulliver's Travels," or of a romance. Quite the reverse: its chronology holds well together, its geography and topography are minutely accurate, its statements accord with well ascertained history and with the general conditions of the time. In other words, it is found to possess the ordinary marks of an authentic and veracious document. And as such it is received, with certain obvious limitations, by critics so little liable to the suspicion of credulity as Amélineau and Zöckler, who, after a special study of the book from very different standpoints, declare their belief that it contains a solid and ascertainable kernel of fact[1].

I am pleased to be able to add that this is also the conclusion to which Dr Preuschen's investigations have led him: the closing words of his recent book express his belief that the Lausiac History is on the whole a true picture of the monachism it professes to describe, and that anyone who undertakes to write of early monachism must rely without hesitation on the general presentation of it given in the *Historia Lausiaca* and the *Historia Monachorum*[2].

---

[1] Amélineau: "Sunt *Historiæ Lausiacæ* loca quæ ab auctore ipso esse excogitata apparet [*i.e.* not borrowed from Coptic or other sources], nemo enim nisi ille talia scribere potuit. Itinera quæ fecerit non solum recte indicat amicosque nominibus suis designat, sed etiam intimas mentis cogitationes adultique corporis concupiscentias confitetur." And after quoting in illustration A 29, he goes on: "Quæ nemo, nisi ille qui fuerit expertus, scribere potuisse, neque ad hæc scribenda ullo alio scripto opus fuisse videtur." (*De Hist. Laus.* 10.) Elsewhere: "In priore *Historiæ Lausiacæ* parte [sc. A 1—37] multa scripta sunt quæ Palladium ipsum spectant. Auctor enim ipse suas peregrinationes, suam agendi rationem, mali ingenii ad peccatum sollicitationes, quas tentationes nunc vocant, describit, neque illa respuenda mihi esse videntur" (*Ibid.* 6). Zöckler: after saying that without doubt the account is "stark gefärbt und mit verschiedenen wunderhaften Zutaten bereichert," he continues: "Aber an ein willkürliches Erdichten nach moderner Romanschriftstellerart oder auch nur in der Weise mittelalterlicher Legendenschmiede ist bei ihnen [*i.e.* both the *Historia Lausiaca* and the *Historia Monachorum*] noch nicht zu denken. Die Angaben betreffs der Lebensumstände, Aussprüche und Taten der grössten Mehrzal der geschilderten Heiligen lauten viel zu konkret und genau, als dass jene extreme Fiktionshypothese sich durchführen liesse" (*Herzog-Plitt*, XI. 174).

[2] His words are that, apart from incidental errors, "werden wir in der *Historia Lausiaca* einen ziemlich treuen Spiegel der Stimmungen und Empfindungen innerhalb der Mönchskreise zu erblicken haben. Und insofern ist sie uns, wie der *Historia Monachorum*, von hohem Wert. Wie uns in diesen Darstellungen das Mönchtum entgegentritt, so muss es im wesentlichen damals gewesen sein. Wenn

The Miracles of the Lausiac History.

It remains to consider how far the credibility of the Lausiac History is affected by the frequent record of miracles and wonders. It is not my intention to institute any discussion as to the credibility of miracles in general, or of those of the Lausiac History in particular. But as the whole book has been discredited and declared to be altogether unhistorical on account of the miraculous element found in it, it becomes necessary to consider whether this extreme view is really dictated by a sober criticism. A moment's reflection tells us that the Lausiac History and the other records of early Egyptian monachism do not stand alone in this regard : the severest historical schools of our day construct the history, on all hands received as scientific, of the early Middle Ages out of documents in which the supernatural element is as strongly marked as in the Lausiac History. This is obvious, and needs no illustration. The question therefore arises : Is there anything in the Lausiac History to differentiate it from the great body of documents just referred to, and to demand special methods of treatment ? I am unable to see any such difference. I repeat, there is no question here of the objective truth or falsehood of the miraculous occurrences recorded ; but merely whether, even from the most sceptical standpoint, it is reasonable to set them down as wilful inventions on the part of Palladius, and to look on him as a writer so mendacious that his book must forfeit all claim to an historical character.

I cannot help thinking that such views are due to the want of a proper exercise of the historical imagination, a failure to realise and throw oneself back into the conditions and surroundings of the writer. And in truth it is no easy thing to enter in this way into the modes of thought reflected by the literature to which the Lausiac History belongs. The Copts, whether monks or laymen, lived in an atmosphere of the supernatural ; they expected miracles at every turn, and were ready to see the direct operation of angels and demons in the everyday occurrences of life, and they believed

man daher das Mönchtum jener Zeit zu schildern unternimmt, so darf man sich unbedenklich auf die beiden Darstellungen des Rufin und des Palladius stützen" (*Palladius und Rufinus*, 260).

with avidity whatever wonders were suggested to them. The Coptic spirit revelled, and still revels, in the marvellous. On this subject I would direct attention to two of M. Amélineau's writings, *Le Christianisme chez les anciens Coptes (Revue de l'Histoire des Religions*, 1887), and the *Introduction* to the *Contes et Romans de l'Égypte Chrétienne*, where this side of the Coptic character is illustrated very fully. Thus it came to pass that stories of all kinds circulated freely in the desert relating the virtues, the penances, and above all the miracles of the great solitaries. It is but natural that a Greek or Roman living for ten years, as Palladius did, in this environment, should have been carried away by the *genius loci*, and have given credence to all that he heard of the wonders wrought by the servants of God. Nay, it does not even argue any extraordinary credulity in him. The *Zeitgeist* in both East and West was only a degree less prone than in Egypt to accept the marvellous in whatever guise it came. It was not Christians only who admitted supernatural occurrences; the belief in magic and sorcery was universal among pagans, even the most highly educated and cultured. I offer as a single example Gibbon's account of his favourite Julian. I might also refer my readers to the first portion of Mr Lecky's chapter on *Magic and Witchcraft* (*History of Rationalism*, c. I.).

Therefore, that there should have been current in the Egyptian deserts a vast floating tradition of marvellous stories, some of a type merely magical, and that Palladius should have believed every thing of the kind that he heard, and should have recorded it in his book, is only what might have been expected; and it cannot be taken as a sign of any want of truthfulness on his part, or as a reason for questioning the substantial worth of his history. It is not easy to see why Palladius should be judged in this matter by a different standard from St Augustine; and it may safely be said that the single well-known chapter in the *De Civitate Dei* (XXII. 8) presents a problem at least as remarkable as the whole of the Lausiac History[1].

---

[1] Mr Lecky thus epitomises the chapter: "St Augustine, the ablest and most clear-headed of all the Fathers, and a man of undoubted piety, solemnly asserts that in his own diocese of Hippo, in the space of two years [*i.e.* the two years immediately preceding the time at which he wrote], no less than seventy miracles

The Lausiac History contains some seventy references to miraculous occurrences, if we include dreams, visions, apparitions, and readings of the heart, as well as cures and prophecies. The large majority are reported upon hearsay, and, after what has been said, I do not think that these ought to present any difficulty. Palladius vouches for about ten on his own personal authority; and the accounts of some of them are no less circumstantial than startling. I had drawn up a table of these first-hand narratives of miracles, but on reflection it seemed unnecessary to print it[1]. The most intellectual and the most upright of Palladius' contemporaries make similar claims to have witnessed miracles,—*e.g.* St Augustine, Theodoret, Sulpitius Severus. The Lausiac History and the kindred works dealing with Egyptian Monachism are therefore only particular instances of a very wide question; and unless special reasons can be shown, they should be judged by the same canons and interpreted by the same methods as prevail in analogous cases. So long, indeed, as the Lausiac History was encompassed by special literary and historical difficulties, it was natural that the marvels it relates should attract undue attention; now, however, that the literary problem has been disentangled, I do not think that the question of the miracles should any more be raised.

Weingarten's own view is that the Lausiac History and its fellows—*Historia Monachorum, Vita Antonii,* Cassian and the rest—are all mere imitations of the Greek romances so popular

had been wrought by the body of St Stephen.......He gives a catalogue of what he deems undoubted miracles, which he says he had selected from a multitude so great that volumes would be required to relate them all. In that catalogue we find no less than five cases of restoration of life to the dead" (*History of Rationalism* (ed. 7), I. 163 note); cf. also *Supernatural Religion* (complete ed.) I. 170—186, where the facts concerning St Augustine are brought together.

[1] They may be found in A 2, 20 (3), 43, 77, 86, and 103. Perhaps it is right to print the most extraordinary of these accounts (A 20). Palladius says : ὑπ' ὄψεσιν πάλιν ἐμαῖς προσενέχθη τῷ Μακαρίῳ παιδαρίσκος ἐνεργούμενος ὑπὸ πνεύματος χαλεποῦ. ἐπιθεὶς δὲ αὐτῷ τὴν δεξιὰν ἐπὶ τὴν κεφαλὴν, καὶ τὴν εὐώνυμον ἐπὶ τὴν καρδίαν, ἐπὶ τοσοῦτον ὁ ἅγιος τούτῳ ἐπηύξατο, ἕως οὗ αὐτὸν ἐπὶ ἀέρος ἐποίησεν κρεμασθῆναι. οἰδήσας οὖν ὁ παῖς ὡς ἀσκὸς ὅλῳ τῷ σώματι τοσοῦτον ἐφλέγμαινεν, ὡς γενέσθαι πολυτάλαντον τῷ σηκώματι. καὶ αἰφρίδιον ἀνακράξας διὰ πασῶν τῶν αἰσθήσεων ὕδωρ ἤνεγκεν· καὶ λωφήσας γέγονεν εἰς τὸ μέτρον ὃ ἦν ἀπ' ἀρχῆς. (*G. P.* XXXIV. 1059.) Cf. the Coptic account, *supra* p. 151.

at the time. This position he maintains at some length in the *Ursprung* (47—49, 58—63), and reasserts in the *Mönchtum*[1]. He appeals for illustration and proof to the various collections of Θαυμάσια (especially that of Phlegon) in Westermann's *Paradoxographi*, and to the Μεταμορφώσεις of Antonius Liberalis in the same editor's *Mythographi*.

Let the reader look through these collections and judge for himself. Here are the titles of some of the chapters in Antonius' *Metamorphoses:*—1, "Ktesylla into a Pleiad after her death"; 8, "Lamia the Sybarite into a fountain named after her"; 15, "Meropis into an owl." Anyone who knows his Ovid will be able from these specimens to form a just idea of the nature of the book. It is especially to c. 17, "Leucippus from a woman into a man," that Weingarten refers, as in it he finds a parallel to a repulsive anecdote in the Latin *Historia Monachorum* (c. 28), how a girl was not only cured of a disease by Macarius of Egypt, but at the same time turned into a man. As this is the particular piece on which Weingarten especially fastens in support of his hypothesis, I remark :—

(1) the story is reported only on hearsay;

(2) it is not found in the Greek, nor have I anywhere met with it in Greek;

(3) the text of the Latin is here doubtful: it stands as in Rosweyd (p. 480) in all copies of the *Hist. Mon.* known to me; but it is one of the passages interpolated in c. 9 of Latin Version II. of the *Hist. Laus.*, and there the passage is so worded as to suggest no such grotesque idea (Rosweyd 989). In our present want of knowledge in regard to the Latin text of the *Hist. Mon.* it is impossible to say which reading is the true one.

---

[1] "Die *Mythographi* und *Paradoxa* der antiken griechischen Sage sind die Vorbilder und Quellen der christlichen Legenden und Mythen, die Rufinus, Hieronymus, Palladius, und ihr Gefolge geschaffen. Eine wesentliche, bis jetzt übersehene, aber sehr wichtige Grundlage für den christlichen Heroenroman bildet auch des Philostratus' Leben des Apollonius von Tyana, dessen vielfach überraschende Beziehungen zur pseudoathanasianischen *Vita Antonii*, zu des Hieronymus *Vita Hilarionis* und zu *Cassians* Tendenzgesprächen die Ergänzung dieses Artikels im nächsten Heft der Zeitschrift für Kirchengeschichte dartun wird" (*Herzog-Plitt*, x. 788). The supplementary article here promised I have not been able to find.

Weingarten appeals also to the epitomes of the chief Greek romances in Rohde's *Griechische Romane* (361 ff.), and in particular to the Life of Apollonius of Tyana as the prototype of the *Vita Antonii* and of Cassian. I invite the reader with confidence to compare the two classes of literature and to judge for himself. Let him even only read Mr Baring Gould's article "Early Christian Romances" (*Contemporary Review*, Oct. 1877), and he will be able to realise in some measure how essentially Palladius and Cassian and the others differ from the Christian romances of the time, and much more from the heathen romances.

Unquestionably there are myths and romances in the *Vitae Patrum*: Rosweyd pronounces the story of "Macarius the Roman, who travelled to Paradise" to be a "fabula"; the Bollandists declare the Life of Postumian to be "fabulosissima"; "Barlaam and Josaphat," concerning which Rosweyd expresses some cautious doubts, is now known to be a religious novel; and there are other instances. But the line of demarcation between a fourth century romance and the Lausiac History, marvels and all, is as clear cut and distinct as that between Sinbad the Sailor and Christopher Columbus.

§ 16. Other Sources of Early Egyptian Monastic History.

The historical value of the foregoing investigations into the problems, literary and other, that encompass Palladius' book, consists mainly in the light which they shed upon the origin and early development of Christian monachism. But there are other sources, akin to the Lausiac History, which give rise to similar problems. The enquiries which it has been our duty to make in regard to the various points raised concerning the Lausiac History, suggest certain broad principles of criticism that should guide us in dealing with this whole cycle of literature. It is therefore germane to the scope of this Study to indicate the application of these principles to three or four of the other chief sources of Egyptian monastic history, with a view to the establishment on firmer foundations of this whole department of study.

A list of the more important sources will be of use.

Primary Sources.

1. The *Vita Antonii* (cf. § 17).
2. The *Vita*, the *Asceticon*, the *Regulae* of Pachomius, and the *Epistola Ammonis* on Theodore (cf. §§ 13 and 17).
3. The *Historia Lausiaca*.
4. The *Historia Monachorum in Aegypto*.
5. The *Institutes* and *Conferences* of Cassian.
6. The *Apophthegmata Patrum*.

Subsidiary Sources.

7. The Coptic documents relating to Schnoudi (printed by Amélineau) (cf. *supra* p. 107).
8. The Life of Macarius of Egypt by Serapion, in Coptic (Amélineau) and Syriac (Bedjan) (cf. § 17).
9. The chapter in Socrates (*Hist. Eccl.* IV. 23) (cf. § 12).
10. The *First Dialogue* of Sulpitius Severus (cf. § 18).
11. Statements by Rufinus, chiefly *Hist. Eccl.* II. 4, 8; and *Apol.* II. 12.
12. The *Regula Antonii*, *Regula Macarii*, and similar Rules, printed by Holsten (*Codex Regularum*) (cf. *P. G.* XXXIV. 967 ff.).

NOTE. The list does not claim to be exhaustive : there are various *Vitae*, Letters, Sermons, and ascetical treatises, some of which no doubt are authentic ; but this literature has not yet been properly investigated (cf. *P. G.* XL. and XXXIV.). Nor have the Rules (No. 12) been subjected to criticism as yet, except the *Regula Antonii*, on which Dom Gontzen of Metten has recently published a careful study[1]: the *Regula* exists in Latin and Arabic versions (*P. G.* XL. 1067) ; it is not by St Anthony, but is made up out of the *Vita*, *Apophthegmata* and writings attributed to him. Sozomen's information on the Egyptian monks has no independent value, as it is wholly based on known extant sources (except the second half of VI. 31) ; what he tells, however, concerning the monks of Asia Minor, Syria and the East (*Hist. Eccl.* VI. 32—34) is of great value, being based for the most part on sources that are at present unknown ; while, from the manner in which he has used his Egyptian sources, we can see that he was careful and accurate in the work of abridgement.

[1] *Die Regel des h. Antonius* (1896).

The Historia Monachorum in Aegypto.

This book has been constantly before us in the preceding investigations. It bears, as we have seen already, a bad character with the critics; Weingarten and Lucius are as severe in their judgments on it as they are on the Lausiac History, and Professor Gwatkin declares it to be "past defence except as a novel[1]." Dr Preuschen's views on the nature of the book, being the outcome of careful study, must claim our best attention. He has arrived at the conclusion that the Latin is the original form of the work, and that Rufinus is the author in the full sense of the word. He thus rejects Tillemont's Petronius-hypothesis, revived by Zöckler and Grützmacher (cf. *supra*, p. 12)[2]; but he is alive to the chronological difficulties, and in view of them he does not believe that Rufinus himself ever made the journey described, or, indeed, that any such tour ever took place. His view is that Rufinus, during his prolonged sojourn in Egypt, visited a number of the solitaries—this we know on his own authority—and thus acquired a thorough knowledge of the character and working of Egyptian monachism about the year 375. A quarter of a century later (c. 402—3) he set himself to draw a picture of the monastic system in Egypt for the benefit of the brethren of his monastery on the Mount of Olives: the picture which he drew is a faithful one; but he has thrown it into the popular form of a narrative of travels. Thus the book is true in the sense that a good historical novel is true, and is a most valuable source for the general history of Egyptian monachism; but the framework of the story is the invention of the writer[3].

Dr Preuschen's theory of the character of the *Historia Monachorum*, which thus preserves the substantial truthfulness of the book—on this point he is uncompromising—is on the face

[1] *Studies of Arianism* 93.
[2] *Palladius und Rufinus* 174—6.
[3] *Op. cit.* 178 ff. and 205 ff. In regard to St Jerome's statement that Rufinus wrote a book "quasi de monachis," but that many of them "nunquam fuerunt" (op. sup., p. 11 note), Dr Preuschen points out that St Jerome had passed far too short a time in Egypt to be able to say with competent knowledge what monks did or did not exist in the remoter regions (p. 205).

of it a reasonable one, and it fairly meets many of the difficulties of the case. But it is evidently a corollary of the view that the Latin, not the Greek, is the original form of the work. After a renewed survey of the ground, I am confirmed in my previous conviction that the Latin is a translation from the Greek. The really substantial reasons that move me are based on a variety of linguistic and textual considerations, and I hope to be able in Appendix I. to establish from such evidence the truth of my view. But questions of this kind must usually be determined by a number of converging probabilities; and I therefore propose to develope in this place certain aspects of the problem, which will at once reveal difficulties in the way of Dr Preuschen's theory of the nature of the book, and furnish illustrations of its true origin and historical character.

(1) M. Amélineau declares that the description of the mountain overhanging the Nile on which Pityrion dwelt (*gr.* 17, *lat.* 13, cf. A 74) is so accurate that anyone who has been over the ground will easily recognise it as the present Gebel-el-Ter[1]. If this be the case, it is evident that the writer of the *Historia Monachorum* must have seen the spot; and the question arises, Did Rufinus ever make his way so far south? In three places in his works (*Apol.* II. 12, *Hist. Eccl.* II. 4 and 8) he gives lists of the celebrated monks whom he had seen, and all the names he mentions, whether of monks or of places, so far as they can be identified, are confined to Nitria and Scete and to the district of Pispir. The details given in the Lausiac History (A 25; *P. G.* XXXIV. 1073) indicate that Pispir was situated by the Nile, somewhere between Babylon and Heracleopolis; and Amélineau identifies "the Mount of Anthony in Pispir" with Der-el-Mêmûn, half way between Aphroditopolis (Atfih) and Beni Suef, some seventy miles north of Gebel-el-Ter[2]. In his *Hist. Eccl.* II. 8, however, Rufinus says that among persons whom he had seen were "Scyrion (*al.* Quirtori) et Helias et Paulus in Apeliote." No place is known of the name Apeliote: and Preuschen conjectures that it is a corruption of Antinoite or

---

[1] *De Hist. Laus.* 47, 48. The mountain is there called Gebel-el-Ataka; but on the page of Isambert to which reference is made, as also in the handbooks of Baedeker and Murray, it is called Gebel-el-Ter.

[2] *Géographie de l'Égypte* 353.

Hermopolite, and further that Scyrion is a corruption of Pityrion[1]. If these conjectures are well grounded, it follows that Rufinus was at Gebel-el-Ter.   But I cannot help thinking that Amélineau is wiser in declaring himself unable to offer any suggestion in regard to the name Apeliote[2].   As a matter of fact, it must have been some place in the neighbourhood of Scete; for Scyrion can be no other than the Ἰσχυρίων of the *Apophthegmata* (called Cyrion, Squirion and Histirion in the Latin MSS.), who is stated to have dwelt near Scete[3].   Thus there is no reason for supposing that Rufinus ever set eyes on Gebel-el-Ter, or ever was further south than the Faiyum; and, as he more than once gives lists of the districts of Egypt which he had visited, the argument from silence is valid and cogent.

(2)   In any case, it may safely be said that he never was at Lycopolis; otherwise he surely would have mentioned the great John, the Seer of the Thebaid, as among the monks whom in his *Apology* and *Ecclesiastical History* he says he had been privileged to see.   For a like reason, he can hardly have visited Hermopolis Magna, or he would have mentioned that Apollonius or Apollos, of whom so long an account is given in the *Historia Monachorum*. Now in the *Historia Monachorum* eleven localities are mentioned by name as having been successively visited by the tourists; and M. Amélineau thinks that in addition to Gebel-el-Ter it is possible to identify a second place visited but not named, and that the monastery of Tabennesiote monks presided over by Ammon (c. 3) may be placed at Schmoun, a village which stood on the bank of the Nile, half way between the neighbouring towns (on opposite banks of the river) Hermopolis Magna (Eshmunēn) and Antinoë[4].

---

[1] *Palladius und Rufinus* 179.

[2] *Géographie* 54. [Professor Robinson remarks: "ἀφηλιώτης (Att. ἀπ.) is of course a good word. It comes several times in the Berlin papyri in describing the boundaries of properties. But I do not know an instance of it as a place-name."]

[3] The statement that he lived in Scete occurs in some Greek MSS. (*P. G.* LXV. 241); in the Coptic version (Zoega, *Cat.* 358); and in the Latin version found in Bks v. and VI. of Rosweyd (p. 646), but not in Bk III. (p. 529).

[4] Amélineau's words are: "Quem Ammonem monasterium Schmoun incoluisse coptici libri affirmant, neque enim ullum aliud erat in hac regione coenobitarum monasterium" (*De Hist. Laus.* 45).   For Schmoun cf. his *Géographie* (168 and 208).   Preuschen (*op. cit.* 207) seems to me to create an unnecessary difficulty by interpreting the expression 'Tabennesiotes' quite literally as meaning monks of

We thus have thirteen localities fixed, and it will be of interest to compare with the strict geographical sequence the order in which they occur in the respective itineraries of the Greek and Latin *Historia Monachorum.* The journey is represented as beginning from the south and working northwards. I add in col. 1 the modern names from the maps in the *Archaeological Report* of the "Egyptian Exploration Fund," 1896—7; and in cols. 2 and 3 the numbers of the chapters in which the names occur.

True geographical order.	Greek Itinerary.	Latin Itinerary.
S. Lycopolis (Asyut)	Lycopolis (1)	Lycopolis (1)
[1] (Schmoun)	[1] (Schmoun) (3)	[1] (Schmoun) (3)
Hermopolis (Eshmunēn)	Oxyrhynchus (5)	Oxyrhynchus (5)
Antinoë (Sheikh Abadeh)	Antinoë (7)	Hermopolis (7)
Akoris (Tehneh)	Hermopolis (8)	Antinoë (12)
[1] (Gebel-el-Ter)	Akoris (14)	[1] (Gebel-el-Ter) (13)
Oxyrhynchus (Behneseh)	Heracleopolis (16)	[Akoris (15)]
Heracleopolis (Abnas)	[1] (Gebel-el-Ter) (17)	Heracleopolis (16)
Arsenoitis (Faiyum)	Arsenoitis (20)	Arsenoitis (18)
Memphis (Tel Monf)	Babylon and Memphis } (20)	Memphis and Babylon } (18)
Babylon (Fostat)		
Nitria (Wady Natron)	Nitria (23)	Nitria (21)
N. Diolcos (Sebennytic Mouth in Lake Burlus)	Diolcos (32)	Diolcos (32)

Oxyrhynchus is seriously displaced in both itineraries, being several places too far to the south[2]. There is also in both a

the monastery of Tabennisi, and thus making his author place Tabennisi north of Lycopolis. It seems more natural to suppose that the term designated in general monks of the Pachomian observance (cf. the later terms Cluniac and Cistercian). Preuschen says that there is no evidence of any Pachomian monastery so far north: but the Arabic *Vita Pachomii* (p. 676) distinctly says that Theodore founded a monastery at Eshmunēn : *sah* and *boh* here fail us: but in the Bohairic *Vita Theodori* (p. 269) the existence of more than one Pachomian monastery in the district of Schmoun is implied (cf. *ar* 693, *sah* vac). Amélineau's "libri coptici" must be further witnesses, as they mention Ammon by name.

[1] It must be remembered that Schmoun and Gebel-el-Ter are but conjectures, however well founded, of Amélineau's; also that the name Akoris does not stand in the Latin text, though it unquestionably should be there (cf. *sup.* p. 14).

[2] The recent literary finds at Behneseh have brought into unwonted prominence the description of Oxyrhynchus in the *Hist. Mon.*, and what is there found has excited some scepticism and criticism of the book, especially the statement that there were in the place ten thousand monks and twenty thousand virgins. It is to be noticed, however, that these figures are given on the authority of the bishop of Oxyrhynchus; and it seems to be a well-established fact that Orientals, and

further displacement of Gebel-el-Ter, to the north in the Greek, to the south in the Latin. The fact that the Greek seems to invert Hermopolis and Antinoë, and also Memphis and Babylon, is of no significanĉe: the two former are so near to one another (on opposite sides of the Nile) that it is impossible to say which of them would be' visited first; the latter are merely named together. I say "seems to invert H. and A.", because one of the Syriac versions makes it practically certain that in this point the Greek order was originally the same as that of Rufinus and Sozomen (cf. Appendix I. iv.). Thus neither itinerary has a perceptible advantage over the other. The point, however, to which I wish to call attention is the substantial accuracy of the itinerary in both forms. In those days, when the helps which we now enjoy were not available, it would have been a matter of extreme difficulty—indeed an extraordinary feat of memory—to draw up in proper order this list of places visited more than twenty years previously. Still more difficult would it have been for one who never had been over the greater part of the ground to construct such an itinerary out of current sources of information, either written or oral; and it seems pretty certain that Rufinus never traversed the country between Lycopolis and Heracleopolis.

(3) Dr Preuschen's theory postulates that Rufinus, writing in 402—3, fixed on the winter of 394—5 as the period in which to place the journey; and though he had not set foot in Egypt for some twenty years (not since 385), he deliberately set himself to reproduce the circumstances of the year he had thus arbitrarily chosen[1]. Thus he calculated the approximate ages of the chief solitaries, as John and Apollonius, and represented the Macarii as deceased, Evagrius as still living, and Dioscorus as already a bishop. I doubt whether fiction was so understood or so written in the year 400.

(4) I would direct attention to the Epilogue and the enumeration it contains of the eight dangers encountered by the travellers on their journey—e.g. their wading through a deep marsh and through an overflow from the Nile; their thinking a crocodile

above all Copts, have very vague ideas on numbers. That Oxyrhynchus was a great Christian and monastic centre about the year 400 seems to be beyond doubt.

[1] Op. cit. 178.

was dead, and being attacked by it on approaching unwarily; their being pursued by robbers along the sea-bank of Lake Burlus (at Diolcos) "until the breath almost failed from their nostrils." The account appears to me to have all the freshness and circumstantiality and simplicity of a narration of facts, and not at all to present the characteristics of a made-up piecé.

These are among the reasons which make me think that the journey was a real one, that the writer himself was one of the party, and that the story was written while the recollection of the incidents was still fresh in his mind. Rufinus' authorship would thus be excluded, and a strong additional presumption raised in favour of the Greek being the original; for if Rufinus was not the author of the book, the natural alternative is that he was the translator[1].

Cassian's Institutes and Collations.

The writings of Cassian are the most important source of information, if not as to the lives of individual monks, yet certainly as to the general spirit and the practical working of early Egyptian monachism. But Weingarten has passed the same verdict on Cassian as on Palladius and the *Historia Monachorum*:—the cities and caves and old men are all mythical; the geographical details must be treated as we treat the geography of Homer; and the dialogues are merely expressions of Cassian's own dogmatic views; they are his personal contribution to the Semi-pelagian controversy, and never were spoken by the monks into whose mouths he puts them[2].

In considering such a view, it is necessary to remember that Cassian's life from the year 400 onwards is bound up with historical personages, such as St John Chrysostom, St Leo the Great, and certain Gallic bishops. I do not know whether Weingarten questions the fact of Cassian's having been in Egypt; but the most recent editors, Petschenig in the Vienna *Corpus*, and Gibson in the *Nicene Library* (a translation), accept the

---

[1] I see that in his review of Dr Preuschen's book, Dr Grützmacher indicates that he too feels difficulties of the kind developed above in the way of accepting Dr Preuschen's theory (*Theol. Lit. Zeitung*, 1898, no. 4).

[2] *Ursprung des Mönchtums* 62; cf. his Article *Mönchtum* in Herzog-Plitt x. 788.

framework of his earlier life as contained in his writings. According to this, Cassian was twice in Egypt, about the Delta and in Scete or Nitria, and must have spent there the greater part of the years 390—400, and perhaps even a longer period. As to his geography, it is limited to descriptions of two localities: on two occasions (*Coll.* VII. 26 and XI. 1—3) he describes the district about Thennesus or Tanis, the modern San, at the mouth of the Tanitic branch of the Nile in lake Menzaleh; the two pictures agree very well with one another, and with the accounts of the same district given by Murray (*Egypt*, 311—313) and Baedeker (*Lower Egypt*, 213 and 227), who describe it as a territory once very rich, but through an inundation of the sea now a brackish marsh, with here and there lakes and islands on which stand the ruins of towns. These modern authorities do not describe in the same detail the district at the Sebennytic mouth, in lake Burlus, where stood Diolcos, the other locality described by Cassian (*Inst.* v. 36); but it seems possible to judge from the maps that what he says must be fairly correct.

As compared with his compeers, there is in Cassian a marked sobriety in regard to supernatural occurrences; I do not recollect that he anywhere claims to have himself witnessed a miracle. Cassian's general picture of the life and manners of the Egyptian monks, their discourses, their visits to one another, their austerities and self-drill in virtue, agrees with that presented by Palladius and the other contemporary sources of information.

But there is one point special to Cassian, to which I would invite attention. He claims to have practised the monastic life not only in Egypt but also in Palestine; and in various passages he draws a sharp contrast between the observances which obtained in the two countries, above all in regard to matters liturgical (*Inst.* II. and III.). Here his information is of the most minute character, so that he is perhaps the most important single authority for the early history of the Canonical Office. The chief points of difference which he notes are that in Egypt at the public offices the psalms were recited by a single voice, and that the hours of tierce, sext and none were not said publicly or in common; whereas in Palestine and Mesopotamia antiphonal singing was in vogue, and the three day-hours formed part of the regular public office. The statements of Cassian are in one way or another borne out by authorities on either side: on the side of Egypt by the Lausiac History, the *Vita* and *Regulae Pachomii*, the Rules of Serapion and three other Fathers, the *Apophthegmata*, pseudo-Athanasius *de Virginitate*, and St Jerome: on the side of Palestine by SS. Basil, Ephraim, Chrysostom, Jerome and Theodoret, and the *Peregrinatio Sylviae*[1]. This accuracy of Cassian in the minutiae of liturgical practice is a sign that he is recounting what he had seen, and that he had a practical knowledge of monasticism both in Egypt and the East.

For such reasons as these, I think it is impossible to doubt the substantial truth of Cassian's picture of Egyptian monastic life, based, as it appears to be, upon the writer's personal observation. But an interesting question arises, how far the Conferences are to be taken as historical, *i.e.* as actually spoken by those into whose mouths they are put. Cassian left Egypt within a year or two of 400, and he did not write his Collations till 426. It is not likely that he had any shorthand notes; probably he had nothing but his memory to rely upon. Under these circumstances it is, as Dr Gibson says, "impossible to determine with certainty how far they really represent the discourses actually spoken by the Egyptian Fathers, or how far they are the ideal compositions of Cassian himself" (*Prolegomena* 188). I am ready, too, with Dr Gibson (*ibid.* 191), to believe that the thirteenth Conference was written to combat some of St Augustine's positions on free-will, grace and predestination, and that its language is coloured by the Semi-pelagian controversy which was then raging. But I observe that this need only imply that the teaching Cassian had imbibed in Egypt should be brought to a point and cast in the terminology of the actual controversy; for St Augustine's teaching was not that which had been current in the East and in Egypt. St Pachomius, indeed, is represented in his Life as a strong opponent of Origen and as banishing Origen's works from his monasteries; but in those parts of Egypt where Cassian had dwelt Origen was a dominant influence. Now within the range of questions connected with the controversy on grace, Origen's teaching seems to

---

[1] This list of authorities is mainly based on the passages brought together by Dom Bäumer, *Geschichte des Breviers* 69—130.

have resembled that of a prominent theological school in modern
times, which has found itself unable to follow St Augustine to the
later fully matured and characteristic positions which he took up[1].
That there were in Nitria and Scete certain initial tendencies
which in antagonism to St Augustine's system would easily have
been repelled in the direction of Semi-pelagianism, is, I think, a
fact that is established by the general circumstances of the case;
accordingly I do not think that even in this matter Cassian is
merely inventing[2].

On the Conferences in general my own view is that, without
regarding them as literal reports of what was spoken, we may
accept the historicity of Cassian's matter;—we may believe that he
really saw and conversed with the monks he claims to have known,
and that the Conferences truly represent the teaching current in
the desert; and that in some cases Cassian's account reproduces
with substantial accuracy what actually was said and done.   There
are throughout the Conferences a number of passages which seem
to have all the freshness and life that mark a true narrative.   I
single out at random the "sumptuous repast" wherewith abbot
Serenus regaled his guests,—it consisted of parched vetches with
salt and a more liberal allowance of oil than was usual, together
with three olives, two prunes and a fig for each (*Coll.* VIII. 1).
But in this regard the picture of abbot Sarapion stands out pre-
eminent (*Coll.* X. 2 and 3): the occasion of the episode is
historical,—the promulgation in 399 of the Festal Letter of
Theophilus against Anthropomorphism, which caused such a dis-
turbance in Nitria and Scete.   Cassian writes[3]:

And this was received by almost all the body of monks residing in the
whole province of Egypt with such bitterness owing to their simplicity and
error, that the greater part of the Elders decreed that on the contrary the
aforesaid Bishop ought to be abhorred by the whole body of the brethren as

[1] Cf. Origen, *De Oratione* §§ 5 and 6, and *Philocalia* (ed. Robinson) c. xxv.   For
a brief and clear statement, from the historical standpoint, of St Augustine's teaching, see the Study entitled *Der Augustinismus* (Munich, 1892) by Dom Rottmanner
of Munich, whom Wölfflin has styled "der beste Kenner Augustins."

[2] I do not wish to express any opinion on the authorship or provenance of the
Homilies &c. attributed to St Macarius of Egypt; but it is worth noting that Tillemont perceives in them distinct Pelagian tendencies (*Mémoires* VIII. 810).

[3] I avail myself of Dr Gibson's translation.

tainted with heresy of the worst kind, because he seemed to impugn the teaching of Holy Scripture by the denial that Almighty God was formed in the fashion of a human figure, though Scripture teaches with perfect clearness that Adam was created in His image. Lastly this letter was rejected also by those who were living in the desert of Scete, and who excelled all who were in the monasteries of Egypt, in perfection and in knowledge, so that, except Abbot Paphnutius the presbyter of our congregation, not one of the other presbyters, who presided over the other three churches in the same desert, would suffer it to be even read or repeated at all in their meetings. Among those then who were caught by this mistaken notion was one named Sarapion, a man of long-standing strictness of life, and one who was altogether perfect in actual discipline, whose ignorance with regard to the view of the doctrine first mentioned was so far a stumbling block to all who held the true faith, as he himself outstripped almost all the monks both in the merits of his life and in the length of time (he had been there). And when this man could not be brought back to the way of the right faith by many exhortations of the holy presbyter Paphnutius, because this view seemed to him a novelty, and one that was not ever known to or handed down by his predecessors, it chanced that a certain deacon, a man of very great learning, named Photinus, arrived from the region of Cappadocia with the desire of visiting the brethren living in the same desert : whom the blessed Paphnutius received with the warmest welcome, and, in order to confirm the faith which had been stated in the letters of the aforesaid Bishop, placed him in the midst and asked him before all the brethren how the Catholic Churches throughout the East interpreted the passage in Genesis where it says "Let us make man after our image and likeness." And when he explained that the image and likeness of God was taken by all the leaders of the churches not according to the base sound of the letters, but spiritually, and supported this very fully and by many passages of Scripture, and showed that nothing of this sort could happen to that infinite and incomprehensible and invisible glory, so that it could be comprised in a human form and likeness, since its nature is incorporeal and uncompounded and simple, and what can neither be apprehended by the eyes nor conceived by the mind, at length the old man was shaken by the numerous and very weighty assertions of this most learned man, and was drawn to the faith of the Catholic tradition. And when both Abbot Paphnutius and all of us were filled with intense delight at his adhesion, for this reason; viz., that the Lord had not permitted a man of such age and crowned with such virtues, and one who erred only from ignorance and rustic simplicity, to wander from the path of the right faith up to the very last, and when we arose to give thanks, and were all together offering up our prayers to the Lord, the old man was so bewildered in mind during his prayer because he felt that the Anthropomorphic image of the Godhead, which he used to set before himself in prayer, was banished from his heart, that on a sudden he burst into a flood of bitter tears and continual sobs, and cast himself down on the ground and exclaimed with strong groanings : "Alas ! wretched man that

I am! they have taken away my God from me, and I have now none to lay hold of; and whom to worship and address I know not." By which scene we were terribly disturbed, and moreover, with the effect of the former Conference still remaining in our hearts, we returned to Abbot Isaac, whom when we saw close at hand, we addressed with these words : &c.

It is impossible to read this impressive passage without the conviction that Cassian must have witnessed the scene he so graphically describes. By its circumstantiality, its realism, its pathos, its bare humanism as contrasted with anything like "tendenziös" idealising, it is stamped with the stamp of truth: it is separated by an impassable gulf from the fiction written in the fourth and fifth centuries.

The Apophthegmata Patrum.

Dr Preuschen in a review of one of M. Amélineau's volumes declared that it was impossible in that place to say anything on the Apophthegmata Patrum, as the subject is practically uninvestigated[1]. This statement of a specialist emboldens me to make some beginning of an investigation into this highly interesting group of documents by registering the results to which I have been led in the course of my studies on Palladius. Weingarten declares with confidence that the Apophthegmata are wholly unhistorical in character, were written later than the fourth century, and belong to the period of the best mystics of the Greek Church[2]. He does not explicitly define that period; but from what he says elsewhere I gather he would place it even after the fifth century[3]. And so Zöckler seems to understand him; for he says that the Apophthegmata are "in any case of much later origin" than the writings of Palladius, and in support of this

---

[1] "Ueber diese Sammlungen etwas zu sagen, scheint mir z. Zt. unmöglich, da die in den Hss. stehenden, an Umfang sehr verschiedenen Rezensionen so gut wie gar nicht untersucht sind." (Deutsche Litt. Zeitung 1896, No. 12.)

[2] The Apophthegmata "sind überhaupt keine historische, sondern eine ethische Schrift, die einer späteren Zeit als dem vierten Jahrhundert angehört, von einer über alle Wertlegung auf mönchische Askese und auf das Mönchtum überhaupt so erhabenen, so reinen und anziehenden Gesinnung, wie man sie nur bei den besten Mystikern der griechischen Kirche findet. Sie bieten keine Geschichte, sondern die Kritik und Ueberwindung der Mönchsgesinnung." (Der Ursprung des Mönchtums, 25, note.)

[3] Cf. Herzog-Plitt x. 788.

statement he merely refers to Weingarten; and in his most recent work he repeats that the collection is undoubtedly late, though it contains individual points of value[1]. When we go back to Weingarten and examine the basis of his opinion, it turns out to be as follows: he clearly perceives the spirituality and beauty of the apophthegmata, but he has a fixed idea as to the low and debased character of Egyptian monachism in the fourth century, so that he does not believe it possible that the apophthegmata can have emanated from it. It may be gathered from Weingarten's language that he supposes the apophthegmata were composed by a Greek writer in the sixth century as a moral and spiritual treatise. If however we are to consider the questions of origin and date as matters to be determined by the evidence, it must in the first place be observed that there were at least three Greek collections or redactions of apophthegmata:—

(i)   Alphabetical: the apophthegmata connected with each Father are brought together, and the collection is arranged alphabetically according to the names of the Fathers; so that under A come in groups the apophthegmata of Anthony, of Ammonius, of Arsenius, and so on; and it is in this shape that the only printed Greek text exists[2].

(ii)   Topical, or according to subject matter: this form has not hitherto been printed in Greek, nor do I know that a complete copy exists; but Photius possessed one, and he has preserved the titles of the chapters[3]: moreover translations of the book exist in various languages:

(a)   Latin, printed by Rosweyd, Books V. and VI., which in reality form but a single work (as Rosweyd himself points out, p. 644); since c. 1 of Book VI. is really part of c. 18 of Book V.

---

[1] The apophthegmata "sind jedenfalls viel späteren Ursprungs" (*Herzog-Plitt*, xi. 174). "Eine zwar späte und in manchen Partien stark apokryphen Charakter tragende, aber doch auch einzelnes Wertvolle umschliessende Kompilation" (*Askese und Mönchtum*, 224).

[2] Cotelier, *Ecclesiae Graecae Monumenta*, i. 338—712; reprinted in Migne, *P. G.* lxv. 71—440. A more ample collection on the same alphabetical principle exists in the British Museum, *Burney* ms. 50.

[3] Photius gives as the title of the work Ἀνδρῶν ἁγίων βίβλος (*Bibliotheca*, Cod. cxcviii.; *P.G.* ciii. 664); then follow the titles of the sections or Books (cf. Rosweyd, p. 559; *P. L.* lxxiii. 852).

When the true form is thus restored, we get a work in twenty chapters, the titles whereof correspond to those given by Photius, —his cc. 21 and 22 are not found in any MS. or version that I am acquainted with, and are probably an addition.

(β)   Armenian, in the Venice *Lives of the Fathers* (cf. *supra*, p. 97).

(γ)   Coptic, printed by Zoega (*Catal.* 287—361) from a Vatican MS., but in a very fragmentary state.   The titles however of sections XVI, XVII, and XVIII are preserved and are the same as those of sections XVII, XVIII, and XIX of the Greek, as given by Photius.

(iii)   Another topical collection in forty-four chapters: this redaction, so far as I know, exists only in the Latin version, which is printed by Rosweyd as Book VII. of his *Vitae Patrum*.   But the Latin book was broken up and reconstructed in various fashions: thus we find in Book III. of Rosweyd 220 of these apophthegmata, in no special order either of names or of subject matter; and in Appendix III. a similar miscellaneous selection of 109 apophthegmata[1].   These three Latin collections present the same translation: see *e.g.* Bk. III. 201, Bk. VII. c. 37 No. 3, and App. III. 14 (cf. Bk. V. xvii. 10).   The Prologue of Book VII. sets forth that it was translated by Paschasius the deacon at the request of Martin the presbyter and abbot; the name of St Martin of Dumes is given in two Spanish MSS. as the translator of Appendix III., but this must be an error; and Rosweyd's attribution of Book III. to Rufinus is certainly wrong[2].

These three great collections are for the most part made up of the same materials, but each contains apophthegmata not found in the others.   The Preface to the alphabetical collection explicitly states that it was formed from a number of small collections (the narrative in most of them being συγκεχυμένη καὶ ἀσύντακτος) by a process of heaping together the apophthegmata that belonged to each Father; it adds that the anonymous apophthegmata were inserted in arbitrary blocks at the end of

---

[1] The 19 apophthegmata attached to Latin Version II. of the Lausiac History are also from this collection.

[2] Photius (*loc. cit.*) speaks of another collection called the Μέγα Λειμωνάριον.

each letter of the alphabet[1]. And there can be little doubt that the other two redactions were similarly made up out of much the same materials[2]; so that (as is but natural) a number of minor sets of apophthegmata preceded the great Greek collections. Therefore if we can determine the date at which the latter were formed, we shall have fixed the posterior limit for the date of the composition of the apophthegmata in their primitive state. Could we be certain that Paschasius the deacon really was the translator of Redaction iii., we should be able to fix the date of the translation at about 500. But in regard to Redaction ii., an absolutely certain posterior limit is supplied by the fact that the Latin version is older than St Benedict's Rule; for St Benedict says: "Licet legamus uinum omnino monachorum non esse," evidently quoting this Latin translation of Abba Poemen's apophthegm, which runs: "quia uinum monachorum omnino non est[3]." Now some year about 530 may be taken as the probable date at which St Benedict wrote his Rule; so that the Latin version of Redaction ii. of the apophthegmata must have existed in the early years of the sixth century, and the redaction itself in the fifth[4].

When we come to consider the earlier materials out of which the great collections were made up, it has to be pointed out that Evagrius made collections of apophthegmata which were used by Socrates in the second half of his long chapter on the monks (IV. 23); and that for the first half Socrates evidently had at hand one or more similar collections. I am glad to find that on this point Dr Preuschen has arrived at the same conclusion as myself[5]. Thus minor Greek collections may be traced in the

[1] *P. G.* LXV. 73.

[2] I do not think that any weight can be attached to Photius' statement (*loc. cit.*) that Redaction ii. is an abridgment of the Μέγα Λειμωνάριον.

[3] *St Benedict's Rule*, c. 40; Rosweyd, Bk. V. libellus IV. No. 31. St Benedict's manner of introducing the saying, "licet legamus," makes it certain that he is quoting the apophthegm—which is found too in the Greek: ὁ οἶνος ὅλως οὐκ ἔστι τῶν μοναχῶν (*P. G.* LXV. 325). So that it could not with any show of reason be suggested that the saying in the book of apophthegmata was borrowed from St Benedict.

[4] The points noticed by Dietrich (*Codicum syriacorum specimina* 6), as indicating a somewhat later date, are based on apophthegmata found in the alphabetical Redaction only. Historical references in some of the apophthegmata in Redaction ii. show that it cannot have been put together until a period later than 450.

[5] *Palladius und Rufinus*, 225, 226, cf. 180.

early years of the fifth century. I think that the early Syriac
sets of apophthegmata must represent such primitive smaller Greek
collections. The apophthegmata themselves are in the main the
same as those of the Greek: this appears from the numerous
examples printed by Dr Budge, which may nearly all be identified
with apophthegmata in the Greek and Latin collections[1]. But I
have not succeeded in detecting among the Syriac MSS. any trace
of the great Greek collections: on the contrary, there is an almost
endless variety of minor collections of every shape and form.
And these multitudinous Syriac sets of apophthegmata were in
wide circulation at the beginning of the sixth century: they are
found in one MS. dated 532, and in another dated 534[2], and in
very many MSS. assigned by Wright to the sixth century. Therefore they probably were translated in the previous century; and
the narrow margin of time, no less than the internal evidence of
the MSS., forbids us to look on them as the *débris* of Syriac
translations of the greater Greek collections: they rather represent the earlier unredacted forms in which the apophthegmata
first circulated.

As to the original lesser sets, I believe they came from Egypt.
Some of the sayings may be traced to Evagrius, Palladius, and
the *Historia Monachorum*. Greek-speaking monks resident in
Egypt would naturally make collections of the anecdotes and
sayings that were in circulation concerning the leading solitaries.
They may have translated such collections already existing in
Coptic: it is shown however in Appendix III. that the actual sets
of apophthegmata in Coptic printed by Amélineau cannot be
regarded as such primitive Coptic collections. Moreover evidence can be adduced to prove that apophthegmata did circulate
in Egypt at the end of the fourth century. Let the reader
compare the following anecdotes:—

Cassian (*Inst.* v. 27).	Sulpitius Severus (*Dial.* i. 12).
Apud senem Paesium in heremo uastissima commorantem cum senex Ioannes magno coenobio ac multitu- dini fratrum praepositus aduenisset,	In hoc monasterio duos ego senes uidi, qui iam per quadraginta annos ibi degere, ita ut nunquam inde dis- cesserint, ferebantur. quorum prae-

---

[1] *Book of the Governors* and *Laughable Stories of Bar Hebraeus.*
[2] Wright's *Catal.* Nos. DCCCCXXIV. and DCCXXVII.

et ab eodem uelut antiquissimo sodali perquireret, quidnam per omnes quadraginta annos, quibus ab eodem separatus in solitudine minime a fratribus interpellatus est, egisset, Numquam me sol, ait, reficientem uidit. et ille, Nec me, inquit, iratum (ed. Petschenig[1]).

tereunda mihi commemoratio non uidetur, siquidem id de eorum uirtutibus et abbatis ipsius testimonio et omnium fratrum audierim sermone celebrari, quod unum eorum sol numquam uidisset epulantem, alterum numquam uidisset iratum (ed. Halm).

Now the differences in the two recitals are such as to make it clear that Cassian (who wrote the later of the two) did not derive the story from Sulpitius; and I have not perceived elsewhere in Cassian any trace of a dependence upon him. Nor have I been able to find among the apophthegmata any story that might have been their common source. It remains then that Cassian and Postumian (whose travels Sulpitius records) heard some such story in Egypt[2].

I cite one other apophthegma which seems to bear upon the obscure question of the consecration of the early patriarchs of Alexandria[3], and which can hardly have originated out of Egypt or after the fourth century: Ἦλθόν ποτέ τινες αἱρετικοὶ πρὸς τὸν Ποιμένα, καὶ ἤρξαντο καταλαλεῖν τοῦ ἀρχιεπισκόπου Ἀλεξανδρείας, ὡς ὅτι παρὰ πρεσβυτέρων ἔχοι τὴν χειροτονίαν. ὁ δὲ γέρων σιωπήσας ἐφώνησε τὸν ἀδελφὸν αὐτοῦ, καὶ εἶπε· Παράθες τὴν τράπεζαν καὶ ποίησον αὐτοὺς φαγεῖν, καὶ πέμψον αὐτοὺς μετ᾽ εἰρήνης (P. G. LXV. 341).

Thus it seems to be established that the apophthegmata passed through the following stages:—

(1) Isolated anecdotes current in Egypt during the second half of the fourth century.

---

[1] A Greek translation stands in the alphabetical collection of apophthegmata as one out of eight περὶ τοῦ ἀββᾶ Κασιανοῦ (P. G. LXV. 244); it has been retranslated into Latin in c. iv. of Redaction ii. (Rosweyd, 569); six out of the eight extracts are similarly retranslated in various parts of the collection.

[2] I have not thought it necessary to discuss the *Dialogue* of Sulpitius: in spite of a "traveller's story" by Postumian that in Egypt water commonly boils and food is cooked by the heat of the sun, I think the same general verdict may be passed on it as on the other documents; and I see that such is Dr Preuschen's opinion also (*op. cit.* 177). Cf. *infra*, p. 231.

[3] Cf. Lightfoot, *The Christian Ministry* (*Philippians*, 231). The apophthegma printed in the text is not there cited among the evidence; nor does Canon Gore refer to it when treating of the same question (*Christian Ministry*, Note B).

(2) Groups of such anecdotes, sometimes centring round a special Father, sometimes dealing with a particular virtue or vice, often quite miscellaneous; also sets of extracts from writers such as Evagrius, Cassian, etc.: all these were in continual process of formation during the fifth century.

(3) Great collections, whereof three are known to have existed in Greek; in these the lesser groups were sorted out and co-ordinated on various principles, alphabetical or topical. They were made towards the end of the fifth century[1].

(4) These collections were often broken up, and detached pieces of them circulated widely: thus most of the Greek MSS. that I have seen are fragments of this kind, and the apophthegmata of Anthony, or of Macarius, etc., are frequently found by themselves.

Dr Kattenbusch has occasion in his work on the Creed to examine the series of apophthegmata brought together under the name of Macarius of Egypt (*P. G.* LXV. 257, or XXXIV. 232, 236), which certainly are second to none in regard to the apocryphal element they contain. His verdict is that the marvels are not of a sort to be set down as simply "unhistorical," when due allowance is made for all the circumstances of the case; and he evidently sees no reason for doubting that on the whole they emanated from Macarius himself and his disciples[2].

This is my own position in regard to the *Apophthegmata* in general: without for a moment questioning that there are apocryphal additions, I believe that on the whole the *Apophthegmata* are substantially genuine, and represent the ideas and the teaching of those to whom they are attributed; and that therefore they are a true record of Egyptian monachism.

Of the six sources entered as "principal" in the list given at the beginning of this section, the *Vita Antonii* will be referred

---

[1] Quite analogous is Anan-Isho's collection of Syriac apophthegmata, made at a later date.

[2] "Wer die Apophthegmata des Macarius liest, findet auch Wundergeschichten, aber doch nur solche die nicht 'unhistorisch' klingen, wenn man einmal annimmt, dass der heilige Mann visionär war und dass anderseits im Munde seiner Jünger manches sich drastischer gestaltet hat, als es geschehen" (*Das apostolische Symbol*, II. i. 246).

to again in the ensuing section: of the Pachomian documents it seems unnecessary to treat specifically,—they are freely accepted as historical by the French and German scholars who in recent years have had occasion to deal with them: but in regard to the other four principal sources—viz. the *Historia Lausiaca*, the *Historia Monachorum*, Cassian, and the *Apophthegmata*—enough has, I hope, been said in vindication of their substantially historical character, to warrant their use in the investigation of monastic origins, according to the recognised methods of historical criticism.

§ 17. RECENT THEORIES CONCERNING ST ANTHONY.

The traditional view concerning St Anthony is that he was born about A.D. 250, embraced the monastic state in his early manhood, and died about 356. Dr Weingarten was the first to challenge the tradition. He maintained that there were no Christian monks earlier than the year 340; and that the *Vita Antonii* was not written by St Athanasius, but was a mere romance composed for the purpose of expounding and propagating the monastic ideal[1]. He was understood to question St Anthony's very existence; but this position he repudiated. While holding that Paul the Hermit and Hilarion were absolute myths, he declared his belief that St Anthony did exist, but not until a century later than the time fixed by tradition; and that beyond his mere existence nothing whatever is known about him[2].

The more extreme position has, however, been taken up by writers who have popularised Weingarten's theories in England. Dean Farrar in an article entitled "Was there a Real St Antony the Hermit?" (*Contemporary Review*, Nov. 1887) hesitates indeed to return a simple negative to the question he proposes; but he discredits the *Vita*, and says that if it "be spurious or a novel, there is no contemporary evidence that St Antony ever existed." Two years later in his *Lives of the Fathers* he writes: "I must

---

[1] *Ursprung des Mönchtums* (1877).

[2] Article *Mönchtum* (*Herzog-Plitt*, x. 774), "Ich habe nicht, wie ich misverstanden bin, die Frage aufgeworfen, ob es überhaupt einen Antonius gegeben,—als historische Persönlichkeit ist er auch durch...bezeugt."

reluctantly acknowledge a deepening uncertainty about any single fact in the life of Antony" (I. 451). Professor Gwatkin in his *Studies of Arianism* (pp. 98—103) summarises the controversy, and gives a useful list of the literature it called forth up to the year 1882. He concludes: "Christian monks there were none" in the supposed date of Anthony's lifetime. This last position he was led to modify in his *Arian Controversy* (1889), where he says: "There may have been Christian monks [in Egypt] by the end of the third century" (p. 123); but he speaks of St Anthony as "the great hermit Antony who never existed" (p. 48).

The necessary preliminary for any satisfactory consideration of monastic origins is obviously a settlement of the question raised concerning St Anthony. The controversy has hitherto been made to turn almost wholly on the *Vita Antonii*. The discussion involves numerous points of detail, minute and technical; but it is not my purpose to enter on this branch of the subject at all. I propose to leave the *Vita Antonii* on one side, and to see how the case stands without it.

Weingarten's rejection of the *Vita* and his whole position in regard to St Anthony are but a corollary of his general theory as to the date at which Christian monachism originated. He says categorically that before 340 there were not yet any Christian hermits, whether in Egypt or out of it[1]. The reasons for fixing this date are: (1) St Athanasius' Festal Letter of 338, in which when speaking of the desert he refers not to any monks or hermits, but to Elijah[2]; and (2) the fact that nowhere in his writings does Eusebius make any mention of the monks. This last is the point on which Weingarten really relies: he urges that Eusebius never once mentions St Anthony's name, and that there are places in his writings, especially in the Life and the Panegyric of Constantine (written 337—340), in which he certainly would have referred to St Anthony and the monks, had he known of them[3].

---

[1] "Um das Jahr 340 hat es noch keine christlichen Eremiten gegeben" (*Ursprung*, 45).

[2] *Ibid.* The passage in question runs: "As also Elijah when he thought he was alone in the wilderness lived with troops of angels" (Larsow, 108).

[3] *Ursprung*, 6—10; *Mönchtum*, 764—6.

We are here in the presence of another instance of the "Silence of Eusebius," to use the phrase made famous by Bishop Lightfoot. To justify Weingarten's inferences it would have to be established:

(1) that Eusebius nowhere throughout his voluminous writings makes any mention of Christian monks;

(2) that had he known of the institution he would surely have spoken of it;

(3) that had the institution existed Eusebius must have known of it.

It is evident that (2) and (3) are very difficult and uncertain ground, and I do not intend to enter on it[1]: (1) however is a question of fact, and Weingarten's statement has been formally challenged by Nestle and by Zöckler, who believe that Eusebius does betray an acquaintance with the monastic institute[2]. It is my purpose to look at the matter from the other side, and to call attention to the wholesale clearing of the ground that has to be effected in order to make way for the new theory of the late origin of Christian monachism. Weingarten labours manfully at the task in his article in *Herzog-Plitt*. Not to speak of certain

---

[1] In regard to (3) it is perhaps worth remarking, as the subject-matter happens to be so entirely analogous, that we have it on St Augustine's own authority that he had been at Milan for two years before he knew of the existence of St Ambrose's great monastery just outside the city walls (*Conf.* VIII. c. 15). Mr Conybeare in his Excursus on the authorship of the *De Vita Contemplativa* collects some very curious examples of "Silence" (346—9).

[2] In Brieger's *Zeitschrift für Kirchengeschichte* (1882, pp. 504 ff.) Nestle called attention to passages in the Commentary on the Psalms which is printed by Montfaucon as that of Eusebius. The following expressions occur: Τὸ γοῦν πρῶτον τάγμα τῶν ἐν Χριστῷ προκοπτόντων τὸ τῶν μοναχῶν τυγχάνει. σπάνιοι δέ εἰσιν οὗτοι... τοιοῦτοι δὲ πάντες εἰσὶν οἱ τὸν μονήρη καὶ ἀγνὸν κατορθοῦντες βίον, ὧν πρῶτοι γεγόνασι οἱ τοῦ Σωτῆρος ἡμῶν μαθηταί, οἷς εἴρητο· Μὴ κτήσησθε χρυσόν κ.τ.λ. (*Comm. in Ps.* lxvii. 7; cf. *in Ps.* lxxxiii. 4; P. G. XXIII. 689 and 1008). Zöckler (*Ask. u. Mönchtum*, 181) agrees with Nestle and Montfaucon in accepting these words as written by Eusebius, and in seeing in them a reference to Christian monks: Bishop Lightfoot also accepts the Commentary as genuine, and from internal evidence fixes the date at c. 330 (*Dict. Christ. Biog.* II. 336): Bardenhewer (*Patrologie*, 1894, p. 232) gives no indication that it has been suspected. Preuschen, however, expresses a grave doubt, but gives no reasons beyond saying that the question has not as yet been sufficiently investigated for a final judgment to be formed (ap. Harnack, *Altchristl. Lit.* I. 575). Zöckler (*loc. cit.*) refers also to other but less clear passages in Eusebius' writings.

obscure cases referred to by Eusebius, or of the Hieracitae, or of
the Novatian hermit Eutychian spoken of by Socrates (I. 13),
Weingarten has to explain away the references to the μονάζοντες
in St Athanasius' writings previous to 340; and when he comes
to Aphraates' Homilies, he has to declare the whole range of
questions—who Aphraates was, when he lived, and whether the
Homilies are really his,—to be so uncertain, that any evidence
based upon them is valueless (p. 776). It may have been possible
to write thus in 1882; but Dr Nestle's article on Aphraates in
the new edition of *Herzog* (vol. I. 1897) shows that these questions are no longer open, and that Aphraates' Homily VI. is proof
that by the year 336 monachism had spread from Egypt to the
East, and had already acquired a certain organisation in Mesopotamia[1]. The testimony of Aphraates is confirmed by the recently
published Syriac Life of Mar Awgin (Eugenius), the introducer
of the monastic system into Mesopotamia[2]. Although it abounds
in marvels beside which anything found in the Lausiac History
pales, Dr Budge has no scruple in believing that true history
may be extracted from it. He writes:

"It is a notorious fact that Christian monachism was first introduced into
Mesopotamia by Mar Awgin the Egyptian, who forsook his occupation as a
pearl-fisher in his native place on the 'island of Clysma' near the modern
Suez, and went to live at the monastery of Pachomius in Egypt. After a
short time he departed for Mesopotamia, and built a monastery in the
mountains near Nisibis. The period of this saint's life is well known, for he
was a friend of James of Nisibis, he watched the siege of Nisibis by Sapor,
and in his days the Emperor Constantine died; Mar Awgin himself died
A.D. 362, being an old man[3]."

Now Mar Awgin lived in his monastery at Nisibis for more
than thirty years[4]; so that it was founded before the year 333.
Assemani, relying on various Syriac authorities, says it was

---

[1] *Herzog-Hauck*, I. 611. "Die ersten 10 (Homilien) aus dem Jahr 336/7." "Die
6 Homilie von den 'Bundes-Kindern' d. h. Mönchen und Einsiedlern setzt schon
eine gewisse Organisation des Mönchtums voraus."

[2] Bedjan, *Acta* III. 376 ff. Dr Budge gives an epitome of the Life (*Book of the
Governors*, Introduction, cxxv—cxxxi).

[3] *Book of the Governors*, Introduction, xliv (362 appears to be a misprint for
363, cf. cxxviii and cxxxi).

[4] *Ibid.* cxxvi; cf. cxxiv and cxxxi.

founded before the Council of Nicea (325)[1]. Thus Mar Awgin's sojourn at St Pachomius' monastery must be placed c. 320.

In an article on St Epiphanius of Salamis Lipsius places the birth of that Father in the decade 310—320; he says: "much of his early life was spent among the monks of Egypt....At twenty years of age [*i.e.* between 330 and 340] he returned home and built a monastery near Besanduke" in Palestine[2].

Up to this we have been dealing with non-Egyptian evidence. When we turn to Egypt, we find that, in order to make room for the new theory, it is necessary to reject the whole set of dates implied in the cycle of Pachomian literature. But among the scholars who of late years have occupied themselves with St Pachomius, the only question in debate is whether the year of his death was 348 (Amélineau and Mangold), 345 (Krüger, Grütz-macher, Preuschen, and Zöckler), or 340 (Achelis). The monastery of Tabennisi was founded forty years before his death, and there-fore probably in 305, certainly before 310. To place the founda-tion after 340 would be inconsistent not only with the chronology but with the whole framework and substance of the cycle of documents dealing with Pachomius and Theodore[3]. It is neces-sary to reject also the independent cycle of Coptic documents relating to Schnoudi. Schnoudi was born in 333; he was taken at the age of nine (342) to the great monastery presided over by his uncle Bgoul, at that time advanced in years, but formerly a disciple of Pachomius[4].

[1] Dissertation on the Syrian Nestorians (*Bibl. Orient.* III. ii. c. XIV.). He shows that Mar Awgin is to be identified with the Aones mentioned by Sozomen (VI. 33).

[2] *Dict. Christ. Biog.* II. 149.

[3] Grützmacher's chapter on the Chronology (*Pachomius*, 23 ff.) shows that the dates are not obtained solely from the *Vita*, but from a careful process of confront-ing the statements of the *Vita* with facts of external history, and in particular with the Festal Letters of St Athanasius: the *Epistola Ammonis* bears independent witness to the fact that St Pachomius was dead before 350.

[4] Amélineau, *Vie de Schnoudi*, 15, 29, 41, 83. In the Schnoudi documents we find ourselves in another atmosphere than that of the Greek documents. M. Amélineau's judgment on such purely Coptic sources is valuable: "Toujours ces inventions merveilleuses reposent sur un fait réel: ce sont ces faits qui recueillis et analysés un à un permettent de reconstruire l'histoire. Le plus souvent il est facile de retrouver sous l'enveloppe merveilleux la réalité qu'on cache en voulant l'orner; d'autres fois la chose est assez difficile....Les écrivains de cette nation n'ont jamais inventé de toute pièce" (*S. Pachôme*, 3).

The evidence so far adduced, to prove that Christian mona-chism existed in Egypt long before 340, is quite independent of all question of St Anthony. I now proceed to examine the statement that apart from the *Vita* "there is no contemporary evidence that St Antony ever existed."

(1) Since those words were written, a Life of Macarius of Egypt by Serapion or Sarapamon has been published, in Coptic and French by Amélineau, and in Syriac by Bedjan[1]. In the Life a passage occurs in which the writer speaks in the first person, using the words "I, Sarapamon," and describing the personal intercourse between himself and Macarius[2]. On the strength of this Amélineau declares: "Je regarde l'attribution de cette vie à l'auteur nommé comme parfaitement certaine, et nous sommes en présence d'une œuvre réellement authentique" (*Introd.* xxvii). This may be so; but the biographer cannot have been, as is stated in the title of the Coptic Life, the well-known Serapion bishop of Thmoui, for he was dead by 370 at the latest, whereas the Life includes the death of Macarius (390) and various subsequent events. It may be that additions have been made to the Life, which in its extant shape is a lection for litur-gical use; but more probably the statement in the Coptic title, that Serapion the writer was the bishop of Thmoui, is a gloss, for it does not occur in the Syriac title. It seems then that in this document we have a Life of Macarius written by a monk Serapion or Sarapamon who actually knew him, and that the narrative is authentic and contemporary. But Sarapamon was a disciple of St Anthony, and in various places in the Life he speaks of his personal connection with him[3]. If then M. Amé-lineau's judgment on the nature of the Life be correct, we have, quite independently of the *Vita Antonii*, not merely contemporary evidence to St Anthony's existence, but the evidence of one who knew him intimately.

---

[1] *Monuments*, III. (*Musée Guimet*, xxv. 1894); *Acta* v. (1895).

[2] Amélineau, 79; Bedjan, 205. In one of the Coptic mss. the third person is found; but the Syriac attests the use of the first person, which may safely be taken as correct (cf. Preuschen, *Deutsche Lit. Zeitung*, 1896, No. 12).

[3] Serapion the bishop also is represented as a disciple of Anthony; but the name was very common.

But there is a great body of evidence of a more satisfactory character, in my judgment, than that of Sarapamon.

(2)   Palladius (A 4) claims to have visited and conversed with the famous Didymus the Blind. He declares that on one occasion Didymus said to him: "Thrice did the blessed Anthony come into this cell to see me"; and that he related to him an anecdote about what St Anthony had done on one of these occasions. I can see no reason for supposing that Palladius is less trustworthy in what he relates concerning his intercourse with Didymus than in regard to his intercourse with the Melanias[1].

(3)   Another anecdote of Didymus' intercourse with St Anthony is told by St Jerome (Ep. LXVIII). Canon Bright believes that St Jerome "probably heard it from Didymus' own lips," during the month which he passed at Alexandria mainly in order to see Didymus[2]. This probability is heightened when we notice that Rufinus also tells the same story, but in a slightly varied form (*Hist. Eccl.* II. 7). Of course it is possible, but it seems hardly likely, that Rufinus should have seen St Jerome's *Epistola ad Castrutium*, written in 397 to console Castrutius on his blindness. Rufinus' intercourse with Didymus was much longer and more intimate than was St Jerome's. It seems altogether reasonable to suppose that each of them heard the story from Didymus himself.

(4)   In A 3 Palladius tells us that Isidore, the Xenodochus or Hospitaller of the Alexandrian Church, had met St Anthony, and related to Palladius a story he had heard from St Anthony. This Isidore is an historical personage no less than Didymus, and played a conspicuous part in the quarrel between Theophilus and the monks[3].

---

[1] Weingarten (*Ursprung*, 29 note) says that this piece of evidence is rendered suspicious by the fact that Palladius immediately goes on to relate that Didymus told him he had learned in a dream the death of Julian at the very time it occurred, and had been directed to give information thereof to St Athanasius; this is but a case of the supernatural occurrences already sufficiently discussed. Weingarten compares a similar revelation of the same event to two other monks, who communicated it to St Athanasius. His reference is to the *Opera Athanasii* (ed. Ben. I. ii. 869); but the story is in reality an extract from the *Epistola Ammonis ad Theophilum* § 23 (cf. *infra*, p. 223).

[2] *Dict. Christ. Biog.* I. 827.

[3] *Dict. Christ. Biog.* III. 315.

(5)   Palladius mentions a Stephen "the Libyan" as having known St Anthony: Palladius never saw this Stephen; but his friends Evagrius and Ammonius went to visit him, and told Palladius about him (A 30).

(6)   Chronius a presbyter of Nitria told Palladius that he had gone to St Anthony's monastery in Pispir, and had seen him, and had acted as interpreter between St Anthony and the Greek Eulogius, as St Anthony did not know Greek (A 25, 26); and in another place (A 89—91) Palladius again makes mention of this Chronius (and also of a Jacob) as having been known to St Anthony and seen by himself.

(7)   In the *Historia Monachorum* (*gr.* 26, *lat.* 25) the author says that he saw in Nitria a Chronius (so Rufinus and Sozomen) or Kronides (so the Greek and Syriac), one of the surviving disciples of Anthony.   This Chronius may safely be identified with the preceding; so that Palladius and the author of the *Historia Monachorum* corroborate each other.

(8)   Two other disciples of St Anthony were seen by this same writer, Pityrion at Gebel-el-Ter (*gr.* 17, *lat.* 13), and a certain Origen in Nitria (*lat.* 26).   The latter chapter does not occur in the Greek, but it is attested by Sozomen (cf. *supra*, p. 54), and I have no doubt its absence is due to anti-Origenistic tendencies (cf. *supra*, p. 113).

(9)   The conclusion of Cassian's First Conference, with the opening of the Second, are among the passages I had marked for citation in proof of the actuality and truthfulness to nature that characterise so many of his accounts.   These two Conferences are given by abbot Moses of Scete, and he thus begins the second chapter of the Second Conference: "And so I remember that while I was still a boy in the region of Thebaid, where the blessed Antony lived, the elders came to him to enquire about perfection: and though the conference lasted from evening till morning, the greatest part of the night was taken up with this question.   And when each one gave his opinion according to the bent of his own mind,...then at last the blessed Antony spoke and said," etc. [1]

---

[1] Dr Gibson's translation, 308.

(10) The biographer of St Pachomius relates that Zacchaeus, one of the disciples of the saint, and some others of the brethren visited St Anthony after the death of Pachomius; he gives an account of the interview, and also of an address which Theodore made to the community in commemoration of the event (*gr* cc. 77 and 87; cf. *sah* 297, and *ar* 657). He does not say that he was present on the occasion; but he was one of the Pachomian monks at the time, and was well informed of all that went on.

(11) Ammon, however, the writer of the *Epistola ad Theophilum*, does claim to have been present, and gives a much fuller account of Theodore's discourse, and also what purports to be a translation of a Coptic letter sent by St Anthony to the community (c. 20). He states further that he had heard St Athanasius and other bishops speaking in his presence about St Anthony (c. 23)[1].

(12) In his *Hist. Eccl.* II. 8, Rufinus says that he had seen "Poemen et Joseph in Pispiri, qui appellabatur Mons Antonii." We have already seen that Palladius bears witness to the fact that St Anthony had a monastery in the district of Pispir (p. 199); and the *Apophthegmata* represent Poemen as having lived in contact with St Anthony. Rufinus' visit took place about 375; and Weingarten considers the existence of a monastery of Anthony at so early a date a sufficient proof of the existence of Anthony himself[2].

The Table subjoined exhibits the various threads connecting St Anthony with writers who vouch for his existence, not indeed (except Sarapamon) as having themselves seen him, but as having heard about him from those who had come into personal contact with him.

---

[1] *Acta SS.* die xiv Maii, App. 54* ff. As the *Epistola Ammonis* professes to have been written some forty or fifty years after the events narrated, the question arises how this letter of St Anthony can have been reproduced. I do not know that the *Epistola Ammonis* has as yet been subjected to adequate critical examination. The names of the monks that occur in it, both Pachomian and Nitrian, are for the most part attested by other documents, and I do not see on the surface any reason for suspecting the *Epistola*. This seems to be the attitude also of Amélineau (*Monuments,* etc. Tome II; *Musée Guimet,* xvii. *Introduction,* xliii), Grützmacher (*Pachomius,* 13, 32), and Preuschen (*Palladius u. Rufinus,* 208); indeed they tacitly accept it as a valuable historical source. I therefore give for what it is worth Ammon's twofold testimony to St Anthony's existence.

[2] *Mönchtum,* 774.

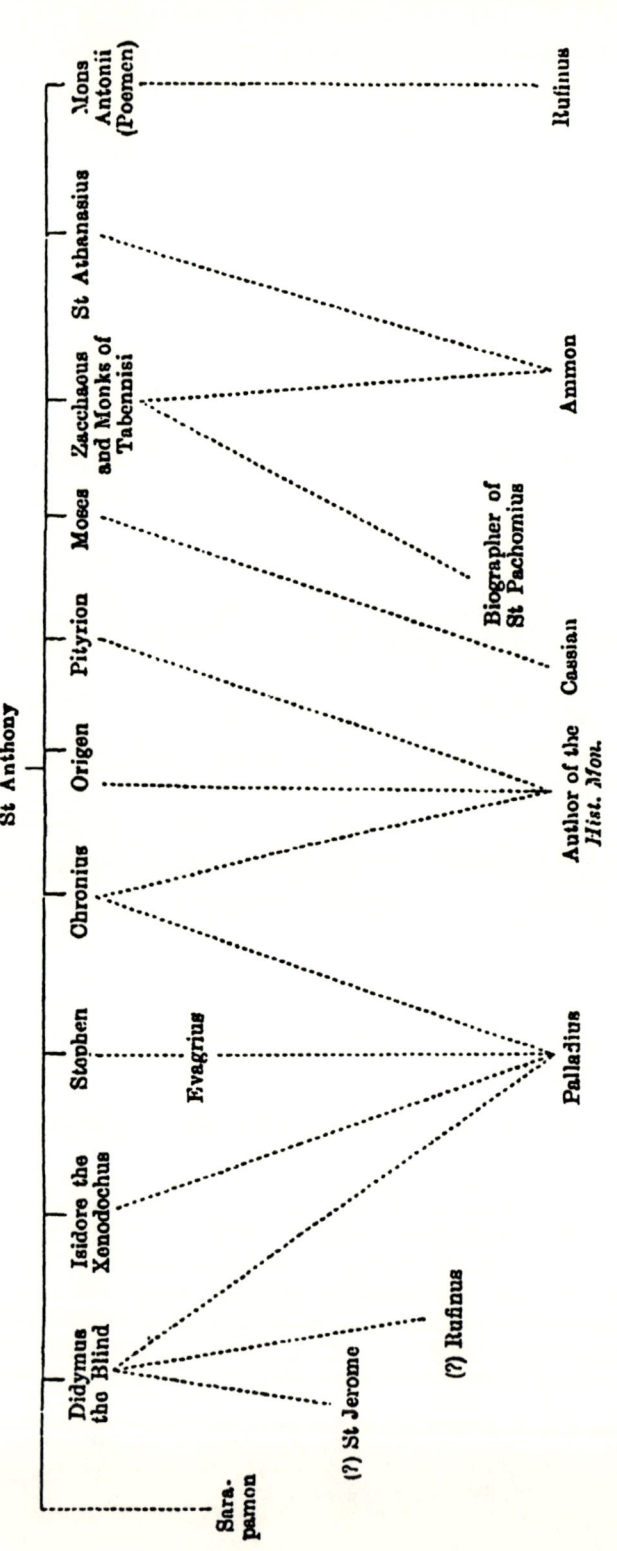

I do not say that all these testimonies are of equal authenticity or authority; but the evidence of Palladius, of Cassian, and of the author of the *Historia Monachorum*, seems to be beyond reasonable suspicion. It is quite likely that in a law court this body of evidence would not be admitted as "contemporary evidence"; but if it be not admitted as such at the bar of history, it will have to be confessed that no contemporary evidence can be produced for many historical facts that have hitherto been accepted without scruple by the scientific historians of the day.

But stronger than the testimony of any individual witness is what may be called the "Nitrian tradition." Macarius of Egypt lived the greater part of his life in Nitria, and there was a fixed tradition there during his own lifetime that he had been "the disciple of Anthony[1]." This tradition is attested by the *Apophthegmata*; by Rufinus (*Apol.* II. 12), who had himself seen Macarius and gives to him alone, out of several whom he mentions, the title "discipulus Antonii[2]"; by the *Historia Monachorum* (*gr.* 28, *lat.* 27). It seems impossible to suppose that such a tradition should have grown up around Macarius, had St Anthony never existed, or had Macarius not really been his disciple.

Strongest of all is the broad fact that, turn where we will in the monastic literature that has its roots in Egypt between the years 370 and 400, the lofty figure of Anthony rises up in the background of the history. Whether in works which may claim to be history, or in the vaguer traditions enshrined in the *Apophthegmata*, or in the pure romances, a firmly set tradition ever looks back to Anthony as the inspirer, nay even the creator, of that monastic system which, on Weingarten's own showing, had by the

---

[1] Tillemont's perplexities (*Mémoires*, VIII. 806), as to which of the two Macarii was "the disciple of Anthony," arose from the fact that two paragraphs from the Greek account of Macarius of Egypt in the *Hist. Mon.* had been interpolated in Palladius' account of Macarius of Alexandria by the Redactor of the Long Recension. The difficulty no longer exists. On the other hand, I think Amélineau is certainly right in distinguishing Macarius of Egypt from Macarius "the disciple of Anthony," who is so often spoken of in this literature as having, along with Amatas, buried St Anthony. This is a third Macarius (*Monuments*, III.; *Musée Guimet*, XXV. *Introd.* XXXI).

[2] In another place (*Hist. Eccl.* II. 4) he speaks in a more vague manner.

year 370 attained to vast proportions in Egypt and elsewhere. Such a tradition, so early and so widespread, is a historical fact, and behind it must stand historical facts. To suppose that a fictitious "character of the novels of the day" should have grown within a few years into such an 'Antonius-myth' as this: or that a real Anthony should have gone to the desert and done his life's work and died, and his work have grown to such magnitude, and himself have come to occupy such an overmastering position in the monastic world, all in a short thirty years: or that his very contemporaries should, as by common consent, have put back his date by a whole century; these, one and all, are suppositions that do not commend themselves by any intrinsic probability.

It is necessary now to say a brief word upon the *Vita Antonii*[1]. Concerning this document two distinct questions have been raised:

(1)   Is it a genuine work of St Athanasius?

(2)   Is it history or romance?

On the first of these questions it would be obviously out of place to enter in any detail; nor have I made such a careful textual study either of the works of St Athanasius or of the *Vita* itself as would entitle me to express any opinion on the subject. Weingarten denied the authenticity[2]; and he has been followed by a number of scholars: other scholars no less distinguished, and belonging to various schools of thought, have taken the opposite view, and the question must be declared to be still open. The tendency, however, seems to be in the direction of connecting the *Vita* with St Athanasius. The most recent summary of the controversy is by Zöckler in his *Askese und Mönchtum* (1897), and he inclines to the view that, at the least, St Athanasius had a hand in the work, editing it and publishing it in his own name[3]. And Grützmacher, in reviewing Zöckler's book, expresses a regret that St Athanasius' full authorship had not been maintained[4].

---

[1] *Opera Athanasii* (ed. Ben. I. ii. 793, *P. G.* xxvi. 837); the contemporary Latin version by Evagrius is given in Rosweyd and *P. L.* lxxiii.

[2] *Ursprung*, 10—22; *Mönchtum*, 767—774.

[3] *Op. cit.* 188—192.

[4] *Theol. Literaturzeitung*, 1897, No. 9.

On the second point, the historical character of the *Vita*, something more definite may here be said. In addition to arguments of the same kind as those employed against the Lausiac History and the rest, Weingarten brings forward certain difficulties proper to the *Vita Antonii* which claim serious consideration. They are mainly based upon the long discourse on the theory and practice of asceticism (cc. 16—43) and the disputation with certain Greek philosophers (cc. 72—80), both which passages betray an acquaintance with the LXX. and with Greek philosophy and mythology impossible in St Anthony, who is uniformly represented as ignorant of Greek. In regard to the ascetical discourse, there seems no need to believe that it represents an actual sermon preached by St Anthony on any given occasion: it may rather be regarded as an orderly exposition of his general teaching, brought together from divers sources by the Greek biographer and co-ordinated in language of his own. Such a view in no way compromises the historicity of the *Vita*. In regard to the disputations with the philosophers, it has to be noticed that Dr Schulthess has recently edited a portion of the *Vita* in Syriac with a critical Introduction, in which he comes to the conclusion that the Syriac MSS. are evidence that the extant Greek text (early though it is shown to be by the Latin version made within a year or two of St Athanasius' death) is not the primitive Greek *Vita*. For the Greek that underlies the Syriac differed notably from our Greek; and in particular in the passages in cc. 75, 76, instead of the detailed lists of Greek gods and goddesses, the simple question is found: "What are these beasts and reptiles that you reverence as gods?" The ascetical discourse, too, is much shorter [1]. Without a very careful study of both the Greek and the Syriac forms of the *Vita*, it would be premature to express an opinion on this point. It is not impossible that a

---

[1] *Probe einer syrischen Version der Vita S. Antonii* (Leipzig, 1894). Only cc. 1—15 of the Syriac are there printed; but the whole has been published by Bedjan, *Acta* v. Schulthess says: "Vielmehr scheint aus der syrischen Version hervorzugehen, dass der uns vorliegende griechische Text nicht der ursprüngliche zu sein braucht, sondern dass die Vita Antonii des Athanasius oder Pseudo-Athanasius schon sehr frühe in zwei, vielleicht auch mehreren, z. T. stark abweichenden Gestalten existiert hat " (p. 14 ; cf. 19).

Syriac translator might abbreviate the longer discourses. I merely call attention to the existence of this shorter redaction.

For the rest, the general verdict to be passed on the Lausiac History, on Cassian, on the *Vita Pachomii*, and the other works of the class, must be extended to the *Vita Antonii* also; there seems to be no intrinsic reason for placing this last on a lower historical level.

It may perhaps not be out of place to conclude with Newman's appreciation of the Anthony of the *Vita*: "His doctrine surely was pure and unimpeachable; and his temper is high and heavenly,—without cowardice, without gloom, without formality, without self-complacency. Superstition is abject and crouching, it is full of thoughts of guilt; it distrusts God, and dreads the powers of evil. Antony at least has nothing of this, being full of holy confidence, divine peace, cheerfulness and valorousness, be he (as some men may judge) ever so much an enthusiast[1]."

§ 18. ORIGIN AND CHARACTER OF EARLY CHRISTIAN MONACHISM IN EGYPT.

I venture to hope that the investigations which have been undertaken in the foregoing pages will help to place on a firmer footing the study of the early history of Christian monachism. It is no part of my plan to enter into details iu regard to the origins and characteristics of the monastic life as it is presented to us in the various documents with which we have had to deal: but the familiarity with the documents which has resulted from my attempts to solve some of the problems which they present has enabled me to observe certain clear lines of distinction, the recognition of which may, I believe, be of value to other students. I propose therefore to record some of the impressions left on my mind as the result of a somewhat prolonged acquaintance with a literature which is peculiarly bewildering from its wealth of details and from the total absence of method in its presentation of them.

---

[1] *The Church of the Fathers* (1840): "Antony in Conflict."

It will be necessary to say a few words at the outset as to what appears to be the actual history of the first beginnings of Christian monachism in Egypt.

Precursors.

Asceticism and mysticism are the expressions of a deeply seated instinct of human nature. This fact is abundantly attested by the first part of Dr Zöckler's *Askese und Mönchtum*, which deals with pre-Christian asceticism and shows how widespread are the indications of it, and that among races the most distinct (pp. 1—135).

According to Mr Flinders Petrie a love of asceticism was not one of the marks of the early Egyptian character[1]; but the tendency had manifested itself already in the time of the Ptolemies, before the Roman occupation of Egypt: for in the temples of Serapis, and especially in the great Serapeum at Memphis, the priests lived a severe monastic, or rather, eremitical life of seclusion, abstinence and austerities. Chaeremon gives an account of the priests' settlement at Heliopolis. These Egyptian ascetics were called κάτοχοι: and there is reason for believing that the institution was widespread, and that it survived into the Christian period. This monachism was indigenous, and grew out of the old Egyptian religion[2]. It is remarkable, too, that it was on Egyptian soil, among the Neo-platonists of Alexandria, that Hellenist asceticism reached its fullest development. It appears however to have remained a purely personal matter, and not to have led to the practice of the eremitical life or the formation of religious communities. But such communities were formed among the Jews resident at Alexandria. I am not going to speak of the Essenes, or of the Therapeutae of the *De Vita Contemplativa*. It is enough for my purpose to call attention to a catena of passages from the undoubted works of Philo, which is given by Mr Conybeare in his able defence of the Philonic authorship of the last-named work. From these it appears that many Alexandrian

---

[1] *Religion and Conscience in Early Egypt* (1898), 122—3.

[2] Fuller information on the κάτοχοι, with references to the original sources, will be found in Weingarten's *Ursprung*, 30—36, and *Mönchtum*, 784.

Jews in his day used to leave parents and property, and go forth
into the country there to make their abode, each in his own
cottage, ἐν μοναγρίῳ, leading a solitary and austere life of poverty,
of chastity, of silence and labour, of watching and prayer[1]. When
these facts are kept in mind, when it is remembered that both
pagan and Jewish religious communities existed in Egypt during
the first and second centuries, there ceases to be any difficulty in
explaining the origin of Christian monachism. It might have
been predicted that tendencies which found expression in forms
of monastic life among Egyptian pagans and Egyptian Jews,
would soon find a similar expression in the case of Egyptian
Christians.

Beginnings of Christian Monachism.

The earliest practice of asceticism in the Christian Church did
not lead its votaries to withdraw from the world; they carried
out the ascetical life in the midst of their families, keeping fasts,
abstaining from marriage, devoting themselves to prayer and good
works.

When Dionysius of Alexandria writes that under the stress of
the Decian Persecution (c. 250) a great number of Christians fled
from the cities of Egypt to the deserts and mountains, and lived
there for a time in solitude (Eusebius, *Hist. Eccl.* VI. 42), it is
quite clear that he is talking of a merely passing episode, and not
of any inauguration of the monastic life. He does not even imply
that any of these fugitives in the desert took up their permanent
abode there, and became the first Christian hermits. On the
other hand, there is nothing unlikely in the supposition that some
of the more ascetically inclined may have done so; and when we
find a later tradition, attested by Eusebius (?), St Jerome and
Sozomen[2], that such was the case, there seems to be no good
reason for hesitating to accept what might *a priori* be expected.

---

[1] Philo's *De Vita Contemplativa* (ed. Conybeare), 261—275. Mr Conybeare's
learned edition of this most interesting treatise is a welcome contribution to the
study of the history of asceticism.

[2] Euseb. *Comm. in Ps.* lxxxiii. 4, P. G. xxiii. 1008 (cf. *supra*, p. 217, note); Jer.
Vita Pauli (*init.*); Soz. *Hist. Eccl.* I. 12 (*fin.*).

Nor is there anything unreasonable in supposing that one of these
first hermits was named Paul, that he lived in a cave near the
shore of the Red Sea, and that a short time before his death
(c. 340) he was visited by St Anthony.

A few words are necessary on St Jerome's *Vita Pauli*.

(1) In the first place it has to be said that this work contains a distinctly
mythological element quite different from what is to be found in Palladius or
the other writers whose works have been before us. Thus in the *Vita Pauli*
a hippocentaur and a satyr are introduced as meeting St Anthony in the
desert and conversing with him. The style of the work, too, is highly
rhetorical, and the whole tone is different from that of the writings whose
substantial historicity has been maintained in these pages. The *Vita Pauli*
was written in 374, before St Jerome had ever been in Egypt. Accordingly
he cannot have received his information at first hand from Macarius and
Amatas, the disciples of Anthony, who are cited at the beginning as the
authorities for the whole story. It is evident from the Introduction to
St Jerome's *Vita Hilarionis* that in his own day some had questioned the
very existence of Paul the Hermit—"detrahentes Paulo meo...ut qui semper
latuit non fuisse"; and the same view has been maintained by various
modern critics.

(2) Were there nothing else besides the *Vita* to be considered, there
would perhaps be no difficulty in supposing that it was a religious romance
written by St Jerome for purposes of edification, and that Paul was an
absolute fiction of his own imagination: no reasonable blame could attach to
the writing of such a piece. But it is hardly conceivable, were it all a pure
invention of St Jerome's own, that when writing to Eustochium of the
anachoretical life he could have said : "Hujus vitae auctor Paulus, illustrator
Antonius[1]"; and still less that in his Chronicle he should have written
(A.D. 359) : "Antonius monachus...in eremo moritur, qui solitus multis ad
se uenientibus de Paulo quodam Thebaeo mirae beatitudinis uiro referre
quam plurima." It seems altogether more in accord with probability that
St Jerome had heard at any rate the broad outlines of the story from others.
How far he may have worked it up, and adorned it with details, must remain
a matter of conjecture[2].

(3) The *Vita* is not the only evidence that is forthcoming for the
existence of Paul the Hermit. We have a statement regarding him recorded
by Cassian as that of Abbot Piamun of Diolcos (*Conf.* XVIII. 6), and one of
Postumian recorded in the First Dialogue of Sulpitius Severus (c. 17).
There is no reason whatever for the assertion that these two statements are
based upon the *Vita*. The passage in Sulpitius is important; Postumian
says : "I visited two monasteries of St Anthony which are at the present

[1] Ep. XXII (*Vall.* I. 119; *P. L.* XXII. 421).
[2] It is shown in Appendix III. that the Latin, not the Coptic, is the original.

day occupied by his disciples. I also went to that place in which the most blessed Paul, the first of the hermits, had his abode. I saw the Red Sea and the ridges of Mount Sinai." There were two monasteries of St Anthony (cf. *Vita Antonii*), one in Pispir (cf. *supra*, p. 199), and one near the Red Sea, the present Deir Mar Antonios ; at some distance from the latter stands the Deir Mar Boulos, and from these two monasteries, as Isambert says, "on a une belle échappée de vue sur le désert, la Mer Rouge, et les montagnes sinaitiques[1]." It will be seen how correct are the topographical details of Postumian's account. At the present day this would have little or no significance ; but in a work written about 400 A.D. it is a strong proof that he who gives the description had seen the spot[2]. If the existence of a monastery of Anthony in 375, as vouched for by Rufinus, is satisfactory evidence of the existence of St Anthony (cf. *supra*, p. 223), it is hard to see why the existence of a monastery of Paul in 400 should not be evidence of the existence of St Paul the Hermit[3].

But Paul must have been an almost unique example of a hermit living in complete isolation at so early a date ; for the *Vita Antonii* says that when St Anthony became a monk (c. 270), men leading the eremitical life had not yet gone out into the desert, but built for themselves huts in the neighbourhood of the towns and there practised the ascetical life. St Anthony at first followed their example ; but after fifteen years, at the age of thirty-five, he withdrew to the desert (c. 285) and lived a life of strict enclosure in a cave for some twenty years. Many followed his example, and came and settled near his own retreat ; and at last, in compliance with their importunities, he came forth and undertook the direction and organisation of the multitude of monks that had grown up around him. This was about the year 305 ; almost at the same time Pachomius founded his proto-monastery at Tabennisi in the far south.

This is but a restatement of the old familiar story ; and I have made it for the purpose of indicating my belief that the

---

[1] *Itineraires de l'Orient*, 2ᵉ partie, p. 460 (ed. 1878).

[2] The internal evidence of the *Dialogue* fixes c. 400 as the date of Postumian's journey ; and we know from the Letters of St Paulinus of Nola that about that time Postumian did travel to the East (*Dict. Christ. Biog.* IV. 447).

[3] It is a not unfrequent error among modern writers to suppose that the Deir Mar Boulos was the monastery of Paul the Simple, the disciple of Anthony. On the question of Paul the Hermit Dr Zöckler's view appears to be much the same as mine (*Askese u. Mönchtum*, 183—4).

critical study of the documents issues in the confirmation of the traditional account in all its main features.

Two types of Egyptian monachism: (a) the Antonian or semi-eremitical.

It is not my purpose to make any study of the monastic ideal—the scientific treatment of ideals is a territory in which Englishmen as a rule do not feel at home—but I wish to point out certain salient features of primitive Egyptian monachism, a recognition of which appears to be necessary for a right understanding of monastic history.

It is to be noted, then, that monachism developed along two lines in Egypt, the Antonian and the Pachomian. The former took its rise among those monks who settled around St Anthony's mountain, and whom he organised and guided. This was the form of monachism which by the end of the fourth century had come to prevail from Lycopolis (Asyut) to the Mediterranean. But it is in Nitria and Scete that it can best be studied; for the system was carried out on a larger scale and we have more accurate pictures of its working there than elsewhere. We learn a great deal about it from Cassian, and minute details are given in the Lausiac History (A 7) and in the *Historia Monachorum* (*lat.* 21, 22); the latter passage is printed in full in Appendix I. iv.; the chief passages of the former are here given in a footnote [1]. The close agreement between the two passages is evidence of their authentic and accurate character. From them we learn that there was a vast number of monks in Nitria, some of whom dwelt in the inner desert of "the Cells." These last were hermits in the strict sense of the word, living out of earshot of one another, and coming together for divine worship only on the

---

[1] Ἐν ᾧ ὄρει οἰκοῦσιν ἄνδρες ὡς πεντακισχίλιοι, οἵτινες διαφόρους ἔχουσι πολιτείας, ἕκαστος ὡς δύναται καὶ ὡς βούλεται· ὡς ἐξεῖναι καὶ μόνον μένειν καὶ δεύτερον καὶ πολλοστόν. ......κἀκείνοις καὶ τοῖς εἰς τὴν πανέρημον ἀναχωρηταῖς, ἀνδράσιν οὖσιν ἑξακοσίοις.......ἐν τῷ ὄρει τούτῳ τῆς Νιτρίας ἐκκλησία μία ἐστὶ μεγίστη.......καὶ τῆς ἑσπέρας καταλαβούσης ἔστιν ἑστάναι καὶ ἀκούειν ἀφ' ἑκάστης μονῆς ὕμνους καὶ ψαλμοὺς τῷ Χριστῷ ἀδομένους, καὶ προσευχὰς εἰς οὐρανοὺς ἀναπεμπομένας, ὡς νομίσαι τινὰ μετάρσιον ἐν τῷ τῆς τρυφῆς παραδείσῳ μετοικισθῆναι. τὴν δὲ ἐκκλησίαν σαββάτῳ καὶ κυριακῇ καταλαμβάνουσι μόνον (*P. G.* xxxiv. 1020).

Saturdays and Sundays. In Nitria itself the monk might at choice live either by himself or in the same dwelling with one or two or with several of his brethren. Here also the monks assembled in the great church for divine worship only on Saturdays and Sundays; on other days they celebrated the office apart in the separate cells and monasteries, so that at evening one might stand and hear the psalms and hymns arising from all the cells around, and, as Palladius says (*loc. cit.*), "believe oneself to be in Paradise." Cassian too (*Inst.* II. 11) illustrates this practice by showing that it was common for two or three or four to perform the services together.

On this system every man was left very much to himself and his own discretion—"they have different practices, each as he is able and as he wishes[1]." There was no Rule of Life. The elders exercised an authority; but it was mainly personal, and was but a supremacy of greater spiritual wisdom. The society appears to have been a sort of spiritual democracy, ruled by the personal influence of the leading ascetics; but there was no efficient hold upon individuals to keep them from falling into extravagances. The monks used to visit one another frequently and discourse, two or three or more together, on holy Scripture or on the spiritual life. At times too there were general conferences in which a large number took part. Moreover, as occasion arose, one would give another a broad hint or a practical rebuke, if he observed anything of which he disapproved. A young man would put himself under the guidance of a senior and obey him in all things; but the bonds between them were wholly voluntary. The purely eremitical life tended to die out (Cassian, *Conf.* XIX.); but what took its place continued to be semi-eremitical, at any rate until after the period with which we are dealing.

(b) *Pachomian or cenobitical type.*

South of Lycopolis the monastic institute underwent a different development. There too the eremitical life was the first, and it was under the hermit Palaemon that Pachomius

---

[1] Palladius, *loc. cit.*; Cassian also affords many illustrations of what is here said.

began his career. About the year 305, almost at the same time that St Anthony came forth from his seclusion to win for himself the title of "Father of Monks," St Pachomius, still a young man, founded his first monastery at Tabennisi near Denderah, a locality not to be confounded with the island of Tabenna in the Nile near Syene[1]. The institute spread with astonishing rapidity, and by the time of Pachomius' death, c. 345, it reckoned eight monasteries and several hundreds of monks. The most remarkable feature about it is that (like Citeaux in a later age) it almost at once assumed the shape of a fully-organised congregation or order, with a superior general and a system of visitation and general chapters,—in short all the machinery of centralised government, such as does not appear again in the monastic world until the Cistercian and the Mendicant orders arose in the twelfth and thirteenth centuries.

The internal organisation of the Pachomian monasteries had nothing of the family ideal: the communities were too large for this. It was on a military system; and St Pachomius' Rules resemble a code of discipline. In the different monasteries there were a number of separate houses, each containing thirty or forty monks, and having a praepositus, a cellarer, and other officers of its own. Many of the liturgical services were performed in them, and only for the more solemn offices did the whole community assemble in the church. The houses were organised on the basis of trades,—the fullers being gathered together in one, the carpenters in another, and so on (St Jerome, *Pref. in Reg. Pach.*, P. L. XXIII. 63). There is besides mention of one house being set apart for Greek-speaking monks (*Epistola Ammonis* § 4). One of the features which distinguished the monasteries of St Pachomius from those of Nitria and northern Egypt was regular and organised work, not merely for the sake of providing occupation or as a penitential exercise, but as an integral part of the life. Palladius tells us that at the monastery at Panopolis

---

[1] I do not think that there is any solid ground for a view put forward by Revillout (*Revue Égyptologique*, 1880, p. 160), and adopted by other writers, that Pachomius before his conversion to Christianity had been a monk of Serapis (Grützmacher, *op. cit.* 39 ff.). In this opinion Dr Preuschen agrees with me (*Deutsche Lit. Zeitung*, 1896, no. 23).

which he visited, all sorts of trades were practised—agriculture,
gardening, carpentry, iron-work, dyeing, tanning, boot-making,
and so forth: he says too that caligraphy was practised, and that
"they learned the Scriptures by heart[1]."

The author of the *Historia Monachorum* (Epilogue) says that the
Pachomian monks were more wonderful—θαυμασιώτεροι—than
those of Nitria; and Cassian says the same (*Inst.* IV. 1); but this
certainly is a case of *omne ignotum pro magnifico*. It is quite clear
that in regard to austerities and ascetical practices of all kinds the
Nitrian and Antonian monks surpassed those of St Pachomius. The
fundamental idea of St Pachomius' Rule was to establish a moderate
level of observance which might be obligatory upon all; and then
to leave it open to each—and to indeed encourage each—to go
beyond the fixed minimum, according as he was prompted by his
strength, his courage, and his zeal. This idea comes out clearly
in Palladius' account (A 38, 39). That the leading ascetics of
Nitria far surpassed in their austerities even the most forward of
the Tabennesiotes, appears from the story of the visit paid to
Tabennisi by Macarius of Alexandria, and the murmurs of the
monks there at the admission among them of such "a man
without flesh" (ἄσαρκος ἄνθρωπος) who put them to shame
(*supra*, p. 122). The aim of Bgoul and Schnoudi in their great
monastery at Athribis was to combine with the cenobitical life the
austerities of Nitria[2].

The most authentic and detailed account we possess of the
manner of life in the Pachomian monasteries is that which
Palladius gives of the monastery at Panopolis (Akhmīm). I
can see no reason whatever for doubting its authenticity and
truthfulness. It is known that there was a Pachomian monastery
at Panopolis (*Vita Pachomii gr.* 51); it is known that Palladius
was sent in banishment to Syene; both in going there and on the
return journey he must have passed through Panopolis. Why

---

[1] The following is the full text of this passage (cf. *P. G.* xxxiv. 1105 B): ὁ μὲν
ἐργάζεται γῆν γεωργῶν, ἄλλος κῆπον, ἄλλος χαλκεῖον, ἄλλος ἀρτοκοπεῖον, ἄλλος τεκτο-
νεῖον, ἄλλος γναφεῖον, ἄλλος βυρσεῖον, ἄλλος σκυτοτομεῖον, ἄλλος καλλιγραφεῖον, ἄλλος
πλέκων σπυρίδας τὰς μεγάλας, ἄλλος τὰ λεγόμενα μαλάκια τὰ σπυριδάλια τὰ μικρά.
ἀποστηθίζουσι δὲ πάσας τὰς γραφάς.

[2] Amélineau, *Vie de Schnoudi*, 42, 83.

need we have recourse to any theory of Coptic documents? What more natural, more certain, than that he should have visited the monastery? Palladius tells us that the tables were laid and a meal was prepared at midday, so that the delicate monks might have their dinner then; dinners were provided at each successive hour until evening, for some of the monks kept the fast till the late evening. Some he tells us ate only every second day, others only every third day, and some only every fifth day. St Jerome also speaks of their voluntary abstinence from the common food provided, and says that if any liked to absent themselves altogether from the common table they were free to do so, and might if they preferred have bread and water and salt provided for them in their cells every day or every second day[1]. The Rule said "Allow them either to eat or to fast[2]."

This voluntariness, or system of private venture, even in the monasteries of St Pachomius, this absence in Egyptian monachism of what is now understood by Common Life and living according to the Rule, is an important feature of the whole system which is not, I think, commonly noticed or understood.

The spirit of Egyptian monachism.

After what has been said, it is possible to indicate what appears to be the spirit, the dominating principle, that pervaded Egyptian monachism in all its manifestations—whether the purely eremitical, the semi-eremitical of Nitria, or the cenobitical. It was a spirit of strongly-marked individualism. Each worked for his personal advance in virtue; each strove to do his utmost in all kinds of ascetical exercises and austerities,—in prolonging his fasts, his prayers, his silence. The favourite name used to describe any of the prominent monks was "great athlete." And they were athletes, and filled with the spirit of the modern athlete. They loved to "make a record" in austerities, and to contend with one another in mortifications; and they would freely boast of their spiritual achievements. The author of the *Historia Monachorum* describes the Nitrian monks as "surpassing one another in virtues,

---

[1] *Preface* to his trans. of the *Reg. Pach.* (*P. L.* XXIII. 64).

[2] Μήτε νηστεῦσαι κωλύσῃς μήτε φαγεῖν (Palladius, A 38; *P. G.* XXXIV. 1099).

and being filled with a spirit of rivalry in asceticism, showing
forth all virtue, and striving to outdo one another in manner of
life[1]." But it is in Palladius' account of Macarius of Alexandria
that this spirit stands out most conspicuously: "if he ever heard
of any one having performed a work of asceticism, he was all on
fire to do the same[2]"; and Palladius illustrates it by examples.
Did Macarius hear that another monk ate nothing but one pound
of bread a day? For three years he ate each day only what he
could extract in a single handful through the narrow neck of a
jar. Did he hear that the Tabennesiotes ate nothing cooked by
fire throughout Lent? He did the same for seven years. Did
he hear that their general observance was "great"? He did not
rest satisfied until he had gone to see, and had beaten them all.

The idea of individual effort, of surpassing one's brethren, was
the dominant note in the Pachomian monasteries also; but there
it was confined within narrower limits[3]. A strange system it
was, and often leading to extravagances, eccentricities, and
worse.

But that is only one side of the picture; there is another side.
If it be true that "by their fruits ye shall know them"; if the
system is to be judged by the men and the teaching it produced;
if the great beauty and the deep spiritual sense of the *Apophthegmata* and of Cassian's *Conferences* are to be taken, as surely
they must, as the measure of holiness and true Christian spirit in
those whose teaching they embody; if they breathe a mysticism
as high and pure as any that has since been seen; then must the
system be justified when it is judged. At any rate a more easy
Christianity can ill afford to criticise the Egyptian monks.

---

[1] 'Αλλήλους ταῖς ἀρεταῖς ὑπερβάλλοντας καὶ φιλονικώτερον πρὸς τὴν ἄσκησιν διακειμένους, τᾶσάν τε ἀρετὴν ἐνδεικνυμένους καὶ ἀγωνιζομένους ἐν τῇ πολιτείᾳ ἀλλήλους ὑπερβάλλειν (c. 23, Preuschen p. 83; cf. also the account of the monks with Apollos,
πειρᾶσθαι ἀλλήλους ὑπερβάλλειν ταῖς ἀρεταῖς, μή τις ἐλάττων ἐν ταῖς εὐδοκιμήσεσι ταύταις
τοῦ ἑτέρου φανείη, c. 8, p. 36).

[2] Εἴ τι ἀκήκοεν πώποτέ τινα πεποιηκότα ἔργον ἀσκήσεως, διαπύρως πάντως τοῦτο
κατώρθωσεν (A 20; P. G. xxxiv. 1051).

[3] Cf. the passages of Palladius already referred to; and the description in the
Hist. Mon. (c. 3) of the Tabennesiote monastery of Ammon; also St Jerome's
Preface to the Reg. Pach. (P. L. xxiii. 63).

This closes what I have to say concerning the ancient monks of Egypt. The Deir Mar Antonios and the Deir Mar Boulos still stand by the shore of the Red Sea; along the banks of the Nile there are several monasteries inhabited by monks; in Nitria and Scete there are four, and the ruins of many others lie about the desert. An account of many of these will be found in Curzon's *Monasteries of the Levant*. A more recent visitor to the Wady Natron is Mr A. J. Butler. He tells us that the body of Macarius of Alexandria still reposes in the church of the Deir Mar Makar. There are but twenty monks in the monastery. The old spirit of austerity survives: every evening the monks perform the "Metanoe" or Penance, making a hundred and fifty prostrations, falling flat on the ground with outstretched arms; and in the course of each day they make three hundred such prostrations. For the rest Mr Butler says: "The life, in its outer guise at least, is scarcely altered since the dawn of monasticism, though the high ideals of the early recluses are long since levelled with the dust, though their heroic enthusiasms have sunk down to a dull stagnation, though the lamp of their knowledge is extinguished, and the pulse of their devotion is still [1]."

§ 19. Epilogue.

In the preceding section certain great features of the monastic system in Egypt have been singled out as in a special way characteristic of the spirit of the institute in the land of its birth: in this *Epilogue* I propose rapidly to sketch the main developments and modifications which these fundamental ideas underwent when monachism was transplanted to other climes. I do this in the hope of supplying some suggestions that may prove useful to the student of later monastic history.

Early Oriental Monachism.

The chief sources are :—

(1) Certain chapters in the second half of the Lausiac History (A 102—104, 106—115).

---

[1] *Ancient Coptic Churches of Egypt* (Clarendon Press, 1884), i. 287.

(2)   Sozomen, *Hist. Eccl.* VI. 32—34.
(3)   Various parts of Cassian.
(4)   Theodoret, *Philotheus* (Rosweyd, Bk. IX.) ; also *Hist. Eccl.* IV.
(5)   The *Book of the Governors* by Thomas of Marga (ed. Budge).

In this section the term " Oriental " is used of Syria, Palestine
and Mesopotamia : for in monastic matters, as in others, Egypt is
not to be regarded as an eastern land ; it holds its own place
apart, midway between East and West. Monachism was at an
early date introduced from Egypt into Syria by St Hilarion, and
into Mesopotamia by Mar Awgin[1]. It has been stated already
that there was in Egypt during the second half of the fourth
century a tendency to give up the purely eremitical life for a
form of life which, though called cenobitical, in most places
remained in effect semi-eremitical. In Syria and Mesopotamia
the opposite tendency set in, and the practice of the eremitical
life was strongly emphasised. This appears above all from Theodoret's *Philotheus*, which shows how common a strictly eremitical
life became : I may mention also in illustration the account given
by Palladius of St John Chrysostom's sojourn with the hermit
near Antioch (*Dialogus*, c. 5). The details given by Theodoret
and the other authorities show, moreover, that the austerities
practised by the Oriental hermits surpassed anything that is read
of in Egypt[2]. The institute, too, underwent certain strange developments unheard of there, the most remarkable being the life of
the pillar-hermits[3]. Sozomen tells us (VI. 33) that some of the
Syrian monks were called " Shepherds "—βοσκοί—because " they
had no houses but dwelt on the mountains, and ate neither meat
nor bread ; but when meal-time came they took sickles and went
forth to cut grass, and on this they made their repast, as though
they were cattle." Here too we find frequent references to mortifications of a character not met with in the records of primitive

---

[1] On St Hilarion see an excellent article by Zöckler, "Hilarion von Gaza"
(*Neue Jahrb. f. deutsche Theologie*, 1894); on Mar Awgin, cf. *supra* § 17.

[2] Cf. *supra*, p. 188.

[3] Cf. Nöldeke, *Sketches from Eastern History: Some Syrian Saints* (trans.). The
pillar of the monophysite hermit mentioned in the *Book of the Governors* (II. 330 ff.)
seems to have been like an Irish round tower, and it had a window; he is spoken
of as dwelling *in* the pillar, not *on* it. But St Simeon's pillar seems to have
been a pillar in the strict sense (Nöldeke, *op. cit.* 214).

Egyptian monachism: St Simeon Stylites, before ascending a pillar, had dwelt in an enclosure on a mountain, his right leg fastened to a large stone by an iron chain twenty cubits long[1]; Theodoret relates that some of the hermits constantly carried on their shoulders heavy weights of iron[2], and that he had seen another who had passed ten years in a tub suspended in mid-air from poles[3]; Palladius tells us of a hermit in Palestine who dwelt in a cave on the top of a mountain, and for the space of twenty-five years never turned his face to the west[4]; St Jerome solemnly declares that he knew a Syrian hermit who lived in an old cistern on five figs a day[5]; St Gregory Nazianzen speaks of Syrian hermits who wore iron fetters, slept on the bare ground, fasted for twenty days together, and stood immovable in prayer in the rain and wind and snow[6]; Sozomen mentions by name one Syrian monk who ate no bread for eighty years, and another who abstained and fasted to such an excess ὥστε σκώληκας ἐκ τῶν ὀδόντων ἕρπειν (VI. 34)[7].

It is evident from the writings of Cassian that he had a deeply rooted belief in the superiority of Egyptian (*i.e.* Antonian, for he never encountered Pachomian) monachism over that of Syria[8]. At first sight he might be supposed to mean that Oriental monachism was less austere than Egyptian; but a closer inspection shows that Cassian falls into line with the other witnesses that have been cited, and testifies that there was in Syria a tendency to increase the bodily austerities. Thus we learn from *Conf.* XXI. 11, 12, that the monks of Syria fasted during Paschal time, whereas those of Egypt did not; and from *Inst.* II. 2, III. 1, 4, 8, that in Syria the night office was much longer than in Egypt, and several new offices were instituted at different hours

---

[1] Nöldeke, *op. cit.* 213.
[2] *Philotheus*, 10, 15, 23, &c.
[3] *Ibid.* 28.
[4] *Hist. Laus.* A 108; cf. 104.
[5] *Vita Pauli*, c. 5.
[6] *Poemata*: πρὸς Ἑλλήνιον (*P. G.* XXXVII. 1455).
[7] At a later date (c. 600), if we can rely on John Climacus, such austerities were practised in Egypt also, at any rate in the monastic penitentiary which he describes (*Ladder, Degrees* 4 and 5).
[8] Cf. especially *Conf.* XVII. and *Pref.* to *Inst.* (*ad fin.*)

of the day, whereas the Egyptian monks adhered to the two offices of evensong and nocturns, each consisting of only twelve psalms.   And there is, I think, discernible on the side of Egypt a certain irritation and jealousy at practices which appeared to the superficial observer more austere and perfect.   Thus abbot Piamun speaks bitterly of certain monks who had come from Syria to visit the Egyptian solitaries, and had gone back and changed " neither their method of fasting, nor their scheme of psalms, nor even the fashion of their garments" (*Conf.* XVIII. 2). Thus Cassian too enables us to see that in Syria there was an increase of the fast days, and a multiplication and prolongation of the canonical offices—in other words, a development of the physical side of the life ; and in *Conf.* XVII., where the comparative merits of Egyptian and Syrian monachism are discussed and summed up in favour of the former, it seems that the advantage is made to lie on the spiritual side, and to consist in " the inimitable purity of life," "the concentration of mind and aim," the perfection in virtue, and the continual prayer of the Egyptian monks.

I do not know of any detailed account that gives a picture of life in an Oriental monastery during the fourth or fifth century. But Thomas of Marga's *Book of the Governors* supplies us with adequate materials for the sixth and two following centuries. What he describes is the life of the Nestorian monastery at Beth Abhe in Mesopotamia ; but doubtless this is typical of them all. During the first three years of their monastic life, the noviciate, the inmates lived in separate huts in the vicinity of the church, and came together daily for all the canonical offices and for meals, and were under the direction and control of elder monks. At the end of the three years the monk, if he had shown himself fit, went to dwell alone in a cell at some distance from the church ; otherwise he was dismissed.   Once the monk had retired to his solitary cell he lived as a hermit for the rest of his days, coming to the services in the church only on Sundays and festivals.   Thomas of Marga relates various astonishing austerities practised by these solitaries of Beth Abhe,—one of them kept his legs bent by leather thongs and stood on one leg "like a crane" while he prayed, resting on a crutch, till he fainted from sheer exhaustion ; and when he recovered consciousness he would begin again, standing on the other leg.

It is important to observe that this account describes the monastic life in Mesopotamia under the influence of a great reform effected in the middle of the sixth century by Mar Abraham of Kashkar[1]. It appears that in the second half of the fifth century considerable laxity had crept into the Nestorian monasteries of Mesopotamia, the monks being even allowed to marry[2]. However, Mar Abraham and his colleagues restored the institute to its earlier type, and the account of Beth Abhe may safely be taken as a sample of the normal spirit and working of purely Oriental monachism.

From all that has been said, we may conclude that when monachism was transplanted from Egypt to Oriental lands it lost nothing of its original character as exhibited mainly in the Antonian model;—indeed the most characteristic features, the craving for austerities, the individualism, the love of the eremitical life, became more strongly emphasised.

Early Greek Monachism.—St Basil.

The monastic institute underwent some changes under the influence of St Basil, and to him the Greek and Russian Churches look back as the founder of their monachism. It was about the year 360 that St Basil withdrew to his solitude on the Iris near Neocaesarea in Pontus, and began to gather disciples around him and to form his first monastery. The early letters that passed between him and St Gregory Nazianzen give a graphic picture of St Basil's monastic life. Gregory paid a visit to his friend in the early days of his retirement, and describes the dwelling, without roof and without floor, the hearth without fire and without smoke, the sad and hungry banquet. "I have remembrance," he says, "of the bread and the broth (so they were named); how my teeth got stuck in your hunches, and lifted and heaved themselves as out of paste." He tells of the

---

[1] The Monastic Rule of Mar Abraham in eleven Canons is printed in English, from Mai's Syriac, by Budge (op. cit. I. cxxxiv ff.).

[2] Cf. Budge, op. cit. I., Introduction, cxxxi—cxlvi.

"rivalry in virtue," and of the bodily labours of the day, the wood-drawing and the stone-hewing, the plantings and irrigations; and, again, of the psalmodies and vigils, and departures to God through prayer[1]. And Basil on his side explains to Gregory his idea of the life:—unkempt hair, a single coarse garment, one meal a day of bread, vegetables and water; broken sleep; a daily round of public prayer in the church, of study of holy Scripture, and of labour in the fields accompanied by constant prayer (Ep. ii). So far there is little to justify the statement that St Basil introduced modifications into the monastic life as practised in Egypt and the East; but there were notable differences in his conception of it[2]. In the first place, St Basil set his face against the eremitical life; and Sozomen tells us that in fact in Galatia, Cappadocia and the neighbouring provinces, the monks lived in communities and there were no hermits (VI. 34). It was a true community life, in a fuller sense than that of St Pachomius' monasteries:—it was not possible to choose one's dinner time at any hour of the afternoon; meals were in common, work was in common, prayer was in common seven times a day. In their ascetical exercises the monks were under the control of the superior, and they were not allowed to undertake austerities without his sanction. In this matter St Basil introduced quite new principles: he lays it down in various places that to fast or practise austerities to such an extent as to wear out the body and make it unable for work is a misconception and unscriptural: work is more important than fasting: it is the duty of the superior to see that each individual combines fasting and labour to such an extent as his bodily forces will allow.

Such was the form which the monastic institute assumed in the hands of St Basil; the modifications are the result of the contact of the primitive ideas of monachism, as they existed in Egypt and the East, with European culture and modes of thought. But although St Basil's Rules and teaching have

---

[1] Cf. Newman, *Church of the Fathers:* "Basil and Gregory." St Gregory's Letters v. and vi.

[2] I assume the genuineness of the *Rules, Constitutions* and other ascetical works attributed to St Basil; but if they are really by Eustathius of Sebaste, this does not materially affect the questions here discussed.

become the norm for monastic life in the Greek Churches, there long survived a tendency to revert to the primitive type, and to make provision for the cremitical life and the accompanying practice of personal asceticism[1].

Early Monachism in Western Europe.

Although monachism was first introduced from Egypt into Europe at Rome, and took root in Italy first of the European countries, still it will be convenient to begin with a rapid survey of the character of early monastic life in Gaul, since the records of Gallic monachism are much fuller than those of Italy.

(1) The first monastery in Gaul seems to have been that founded at Ligugé near Poitiers by St Martin, c. 360. When he became bishop of Tours he formed a monastery outside that city and made it his ordinary residence. Sulpitius Severus gives an account of the manner of life. The monastery was situated two miles from the city, in a spot so secret and retired that Martin enjoyed in it the solitude of a hermit; his cell was a wooden hut; he had eighty disciples, most of whom dwelt in caves hollowed out of the rocks in the overhanging mountain; they were clothed in coarse garments; they rarely left their cells except to assemble for prayer, or for the daily meal when the hour of fasting was over; no art was practised except that of transcribing, and this by the younger monks only, the elders giving themselves up wholly to prayer[2]. It is evident that this was a simple reproduction of the Antonian monachism of Egypt.

The most famous organiser of the monastic life in Gaul was Cassian. His monastic policy is definitely set forth in the *Prefaces* to the *Institutes* and to the three Parts of the *Conferences*. It was to adhere as closely as possible to the rules and practices of Egypt; yet in the *Preface* to the *Institutes* he says, "Where I find anything in the rule of the Egyptians which, either because of the severity of the climate, or owing to some difficulty or diversity of habits, is impossible in these countries, or hard and difficult, I

---

[1] The Abbé Marin has recently published a work entitled *Les Moines de Constantinople*, A.D. 330—898 (Paris, 1897), which gives a very full account of the character and working of Greek monachism.

[2] *Vita Martini*, c. 10.

shall to some extent balance it by the customs of the monasteries which are found throughout Pontus and Mesopotamia." Thus certain mitigations are admitted, though under protest, in the *Institutes*; but Cassian nowhere conceals his conviction that the full Egyptian system and the eremitical life is the true type of the monastic life, and the whole tendency of the *Conferences* is to extol and to propagate the primitive Egyptian ideals. We learn from the *Prefaces* that throughout the south-eastern corner of Gaul the monastic life was inaugurated by various bishops under Cassian's inspiration, and he rejoices that a rule has been established "with the strictness of ancient virtue," and that many are embracing the eremitical life.

The fame of Lerins has eclipsed that of the other early monasteries of Gaul. I have not made a study of the monastic literature of Lerins, as found in the writings of Hilary, Eucherius, Faustus and Caesarius; but the purposes of the present survey will be fully served by a passage from the standard work on St Caesarius by the Abbé Malnory, one of the best living authorities on the early monachism of France. After remarking that the details have to be gathered from many sources and pieced together so as to form a picture of the life at Lerins, he continues:

En voici les grandes lignes. On voit tout d'abord un mélange de la vie cénobitique avec la vie érémitique....Les cellules séparées sont réservées aux Anciens....Libres de s'enfoncer dans les solitudes de l'île, mais circonscrits par le cercle que la mer forme autour d'eux, ils restent ainsi sous l'œil de l'abbé et des préposés, et on les retrouve mêlés de nouveau à la communauté pour célébrer l'office ou entendre les instructions de l'abbé. Pour ces solitaires sont les veilles et les jeûnes prolongés, les macérations exceptionnelles, les extases de la dévotion, ou les études approfondies [1]. [And in another place :] Chaque frère qui le désirait, et qui était jugé assez avancé dans la perfection pour ce nouveau genre de vie, pouvait se former un petit ermitage séparé du groupe des religieux, auxquels il ne se trouvait plus mêlé que pour la récitation commune de l'office, et passait ainsi, sans sortir de l'île, du régime de la Trappe à celui de la Chartreuse [2].

This reference to La Trappe shows that the general impression on Malnory's mind is of an austere life at Lerins; and it is evident

---

[1] *Saint Césaire Évêque d'Arles*, par A. Malnory (Bibliothèque de l'École des Hautes Études: Paris, 1894), p. 249.

[2] *Ibid.* p. 12.

that the eremitical life was regarded as the ideal to be aimed at. The Second Part of Cassian's *Conferences* is dedicated to Honoratus, the founder of Lerins, and Eucherius, a prominent monk there; and from what he says it may be seen that they, like Cassian himself, looked to Egypt for the model of the monastic life.

Could we rely on the Lives of SS. Romanus and Lupicinus we should be able to point to the monastery of Condat in the Jura as another illustration of the Egyptian character of primitive French monachism : but Malnory has shown reason for questioning the genuineness of this whole set of Lives, and Krusch, who had formerly accepted them, now says that they must be given up[1].

The *Liber Vitae Patrum* of Gregory of Tours, however, supplies authentic information concerning the monks of Auvergne and central France in the sixth century. From his pages we learn that there also the eremitical life was common, and the practice of severe personal austerities much in vogue[2]: he mentions one hermit who kept a huge stone on his back whilst he was at prayer; and another who wore iron chains on his hands and feet and neck[3].

The evidence rehearsed amply justifies the statement that Gallic monachism during the fifth and sixth centuries was thoroughly Egyptian in both theory and practice.

(2) The most recent work dealing with Irish and Celtic monachism is Mr Willis Bund's *Celtic Church in Wales* (1897). In the long chapter on *Monasteries* he discusses the origin and character of the monastic system in Ireland and Wales: he considers it to have been a purely indigenous Celtic growth, and rejects the idea of any connection with Gallic or Egyptian monachism. He maintains that the first " monasteries" were merely settlements where the Christians—priests and laity, men, women and children—lived together. After a time monasteries for men and for women were formed, and then the eremitical life came into vogue as a later development. It seems to be probable that

---

[1] *Monumenta Germ. Hist. Scriptorum Rerum Merov.* III. 126 (1896).

[2] Cf. cc. 3, 9, 10, 11, 12, 13, 14, 15, 18, 20 (ed. Krusch, *Mon. Germ. Hist. Scriptorum Rerum Merov.* I. ii. (1885)).

[3] Pp. 715, 721, ed. Krusch.

these later stages of Irish monachism may have been influenced and modified by the monastic ideas and literature of Egypt: at any rate the external manifestation was identical in the two countries. The tendency to embrace the eremitical life always continued a marked feature of Irish monachism, and also the craving for an extreme form of corporal austerities. On the latter point Mr Bund says: "The Celt never did anything by halves, and his devotions and austerities, both in the monasteries and the hermitages, would have astonished even the monks of the Eastern Church[1]." It has generally been supposed that the Rule of St Columbanus gives a picture of Irish monachism: Mr Bund seems to question this; but even if the Rule does not embody the manner of life at any particular monastery, it certainly is an expression of the tendencies that prevailed. Mr Bund justly observes that St Columbanus' Rule "would, if carried out in its entirety, have made the Celtic monks almost, if not quite, the most austere of men[2]." The Lives of St Columbanus and his companions by Jonas bring out, too, their ingrained love of the solitary life. Dom Bäumer has occasion, while discussing the celebration of the divine office in the Irish monasteries, to refer to the character of Irish asceticism and monasticism; he calls attention to the love of the eremitical life and of extraordinary mortifications, and says that on the ascetical and mystical side the Irish nature was closely akin to the Egyptian[3].

(3) The leading facts concerning the introduction and spread of monachism in Italy, and its history up to St Benedict's time,

---

[1] *Op. cit.* 159. Under the word *Austeritas* in the *Index Moralis* to Colgan's *Acta SS. Hibern.* a number of examples are given which amply bear out Mr Bund's statement.

[2] *Op. cit.* 166. On St Columbanus and his Rule cf. Malnory, *Quid Luxovienses Monachi etc.* (Paris, 1894), and Seebass, *Ueber Columba v. Luxeuils Klosterregel* (1883), and a series of articles in Brieger's *Zeitschrift f. Kirchengeschichte* (1893 onwards).

[3] *Geschichte des Breviers*, 163. A short time before his death I had a conversation on the subject with that eminent Celtic scholar and antiquarian the late Fr. Denis Murphy, S. J.; and when I had laid before him the characteristic features of Egyptian monachism—the leaning towards the solitary life, the hankering after austerities, the strongly personal and individualistic spirituality,—he at once declared that these were the very tendencies met with among the Irish monks.

have been brought together in an excellent Study by Dom Spreitzenhofer of Vienna[1]. He dwells upon the thoroughly Egyptian character of primitive Italian monachism. Not only were the first monks who came to Rome Egyptians, but the *Vita Antonii* was at an early date (c. 380) translated into Latin, and it became the recognised embodiment of the monastic ideal. There was a tendency, too, among Italians who wished to give themselves up to an ascetical life, to repair to Egypt and Palestine, as the places where the monastic life could be most perfectly carried out,—witness St Jerome and Rufinus, Paula and Eustochium, and the Melanias. And in Italy itself, as appears from several texts collected by Spreitzenhofer, the monastic institute throughout the fourth century maintained its primitive character, especially in the matter of fasting (*op. cit.* 84 ff.): perhaps the most striking single illustration is a passage in which St Augustine declares that in monasteries of both sexes in Rome it was not uncommon to pass three days and more altogether without food or drink[2].

Information concerning Italian monachism during the fifth century is meagre. Nevertheless certain indications are forthcoming. Rufinus translated into Latin an abridgment of St Basil's Rules, in the hope that the "Cappadocian observance" might make way in Italy; and St Jerome translated the Rule of Pachomius. There is evidence that both Rules made their influence felt here and there, and in varying degrees, among Italian monasteries: but I do not know of any evidence that would lead us to suppose that the life of any monastery in Italy (or Western Europe) was organised on the lines of either system. Italian monachism in the fifth century seems to have been eclectic in character, and to have freely borrowed ideas and regulations from these two Rules, and from other documents of Egyptian origin— from Cassian, the *Historia Monachorum*, the *Apophthegmata*, the *Regula Orientalis*, the *Regula Serapionis*, the *Regula Macarii*, the

---

[1] *Die Entwicklung des alten Mönchtums in Italien* (Wien: 1894).

[2] Romae etiam plura (sc. diuersoria sanctorum) cognoui in quibus......ieiunia prorsus incredibilia multos exercere didici non quotidie semel sub noctem reficiendo corpus, quod est usquequaque usitatissimum, sed continuum triduum uel amplius saepissime sine cibo ac potu ducere. neque hoc in uiris tantum sed etiam in feminis (*De Mor. Eccl.* I. 70, *P. L.* XXXII. 1340).

Regula SS. Patrum. St Benedict shows a familiarity with all these documents; and this goes to prove that they were all in current use in the monasteries of central Italy at the end of the fifth century. Thus, in spite of the fact that by this date monastic life in Italy had become indefinitely diversified, each monastery having practically its own rule, it is seen that the authoritative documents were of Egyptian origin, and that Italian monachism still drew its inspiration from Egypt. This inference is verified by the few glimpses of the actual working of the survivals of pre-Benedictine monachism which are afforded by St Gregory's *Dialogues* (c. 600). There are casual mentions of monks leading an eremitical life (Bk. III. 15, 16, 18; IV. 9, 36); the most circumstantial account is that of Marcius, the hermit of Monte Marsica in Campania, who for many years together never left his narrow cave, having chained himself to the rock. And in regard to St Benedict himself, St Gregory relates that on his resolving to become a monk he retired almost as a matter of course to the wilderness, and lived alone in a cave, practising great austerities.

What has been said will suffice to show that in Italy, as in Gaul and Ireland, the early monachism was thoroughly Egyptian in its ideals and in its working.

In one important particular, viz. the method of celebrating the divine office, the monasteries of Western Europe, even those of Ireland, appear to have departed from the Egyptian model, and to have followed that of Syria and Cappadocia; but in other matters the dominant feeling was that the more nearly the life could be made to approximate to that of the Egyptian monks the more perfectly was the monastic ideal being carried out; and the great object of European monks was to emulate those of Egypt.

In Ireland this system worked successfully for a long time. But in Gaul great difficulties were experienced. We have already seen that even Cassian thought it necessary to make mitigations in the Egyptian manner of life. And in the *Dialogues* of Sulpitius Severus one of the interlocutors is Gallus, a Gallic monk, one of St Martin's disciples, who makes several half-comical protests that such fasting as is possible in the East cannot be expected of Gauls: "the love of eating is gluttony in the case of the Greeks, whereas among the Gauls it is due to their nature" (*Dial.* I. 8). There can be no doubt that in Italy, too, the same difficulties came to be felt, and that in the course of the fifth century considerable and widespread laxity had made its way into the monastic system. It is evident that St Benedict's descriptions of the Sarabaitae and Gyrovagi (*Reg.* c. 1) are no mere antiquarian reproductions of what St Jerome and Cassian had said before, but depict a state of things that existed around him. We have moreover the instance of the relaxed monastery that St Benedict was called to govern before he had founded any monastery of his own[1].

This falling away may no doubt have been largely due to the fact that the monks of Italy and Gaul were trying to live up to an ideal which the climatic and other conditions of the country rendered impossible or, at any rate, extremely difficult; and to the discouragement and demoralisation consequent on an abiding sense of failure.

St Benedict.

Such was the danger that threatened monasticism in Western Europe at the opening of the sixth century, when St Benedict wrote his Rule[2]. To meet the case he did not gather up what remained still in exercise of the primitive austerities, and attempt a restoration of the old ascetic life; but struck out a new line, such as seemed to him more fitting for the times and circumstances. He prescribed for his monks proper clothes, sufficient food, ample sleep; he reduced the time of prayer, and discouraged private venture in asceticism.

It is important to observe that all this was the result of mature experience. He began his monastic career by practising in its extremest form the prevailing type of monachism, which I have called the Egyptian, first for a period of three years, and then again for a period of time not specified by St Gregory (*Dial.*

---

[1] St Gregory, *Dialogues*, II. 3.

[2] St Benedict's life fell about the period 480—550. The current chronology is mere approximation and surmise: only one date can be accurately determined— Totila's visit to Monte Cassino in 543, described in St Gregory's Dialogues, Bk. II. cc. 14 and 15. (This Book is practically the *Vita S. Benedicti*: it will be referred to in the following pages as *Dial.* II.)

II. 1 and 3). He dwelt in a cave without conversing with men; his food was the bread let down by the monk Romanus from the high rock that overhung the cave; his drink was water; his garments were the skins of beasts; the shepherds took him for a wild beast; on one occasion at least he was famishing; on another he overcame carnal temptations by rolling himself naked in the thicket of briars and nettles (*ibid.* 1 and 2)[1].

And yet when in the maturity of his spiritual wisdom St Benedict came to write a Rule for his monasteries, we find that he deliberately turned his back on the austerities that had hitherto been regarded as the chief means for attaining the spiritual end of the monastic life. He calls his Rule "a very little rule for beginners"—*minima inchoationis regula*—(c. 73), and says that, though there may be in it some things "a little severe," still he hopes that he will establish "nothing harsh, nothing heavy[2]." In this he is not speaking the language of false humility, but the very truth, as will appear from a number of antitheses between his regulations and those of the previously fashionable Egyptian monachism[3].

St Benedict says: "although we read that wine is not at all the drink of monks" [*i.e.* in the *Apophthegmata*, cf. *supra*, p. 211], yet "because in these times monks will not be persuaded of this," he allows a *hemina* (= ½ pint) daily to each (c. 40).

He allows to each daily a pound of bread, and orders two dishes of cooked food, and a third of fruit or young vegetables [contrast Cassian's "sumptuous repast," *supra* p. 206], "so that he who cannot eat of one may

---

[1] Abbot Tosti and Dom Amelli accept the view put forward by Dom Schmidt of Metten (*Studien und Mittheilungen O. S. B.* 1888) that St Benedict was not a mere boy, but a young man, when he left Rome. And certainly we would gladly believe that the story of *Dial.* II. 2 was not told of one who was but a child when he fled from Rome. Dom Schmidt's theory is preferable from every point of view: the only difficulty is the mention of the *nutrix*; but in the case of two grown-up women (*ibid.* 23) a *nutrix* is similarly mentioned.

[2] Constituenda est ergo a nobis dominici schola seruitii. in qua institutione nihil asperum nihil graue nos constituros speramus. sed et si quid paululum restrictius dictante aequitatis ratione propter emendationem uitiorum uel conseruationem charitatis processerit, non illico pauore perterritus refugias uiam salutis, quae non est nisi angusto initio incipienda (*Prol.*).

[3] The contrasts are made with the Antonian form of Egyptian monachism rather than with the Pachomian; for the former was the type prevalent both in East and West.

make his meal of the other" (c. 39)—a concession altogether foreign to Egyptian notions. During the greater part of the year there were two such meals in the day. Though the flesh of four-footed animals was forbidden, except to the sick and delicate "for their recovery," it was the tradition at Monte Cassino in the eighth century that the flesh of birds was allowed by the Rule[1]. In a word the advice and practice of the Egyptian monks was ever to reduce the quantity of food and drink almost to a minimum: St Benedict prescribes only frugality, and the avoidance of surfeiting and gluttony (cc. 39, 40).

Abba Pambo laid it down that a monk's clothes should be such that if they were left out on the road no one would think of taking them (*Apophthegmata*, P. G. LXV. 369). St Benedict directs the abbot to see that the monks' clothes fit them; they are to get new clothes while the old ones are still fit to be given to the poor; they are to have warmer clothes in winter, lighter in summer; they are to change their clothes for the night, and the clothes are to be washed (c. 55). St Benedict (*ibid.*) considers a monk's outfit to consist of two cowls, two tunics, shoes and stockings, girdle, knife, pen, needle, handkerchief and tablets—a great contrast with the poverty and nakedness practised in Egypt.

In Egypt the monks slept on the bare ground with stones for pillows, or, at best, on papyrus mats (Cassian *Conf.* I. *fin.*); St Pachomius made his monks sleep in a sitting or reclining posture (*Hist. Laus.* A 38); and whereas abba John in Cassian (*Conf.* XIX. 6) deplores the degeneracy of the times in that a blanket may be found in hermits' cells—"a thing which I cannot mention without shame,"—St Benedict allows not only a blanket, but coverlet, mattress, and pillow as well (c. 55).

In Egypt there was a constant straining to reduce the quantity of sleep to the narrowest possible limit and such battling with sleep was one of the favourite forms of asceticism. St Benedict, on the other hand, allows his monks during the greater part of the year eight hours, and even more, of unbroken sleep each night; and in the summer six hours by night and a siesta in the middle of the day[2].

Even in the matter of prayer St Benedict preserves the same moderation. The canonical office, indeed, was moulded after the Oriental type and was longer than in Egypt, where it consisted of only twenty-four psalms each day. But in Egypt the monks aimed, and with considerable success, at an almost continual prayer throughout the whole day (cf. Cassian, *Inst.* III. 2; and many other illustrations). It appears that in St Benedict's monasteries

---

[1] Calmet, *Comment. in Reg. S. Ben. (in loc.)*; Herrgott, *Vetus Disciplina Monastica*, Preface.

[2] It is commonly but mistakenly supposed that midnight office is what St Benedict enjoined: the usual hour for the night office was 2 a.m.; in the height of the summer it began about 1.30, but never earlier.

at the end of the office the monks used to pray in silence for a time (*Dial.* II. 4); but in his Rule he says that the prayer made in common is to be cut quite short—*omnino brevietur*—and that when the sign is given all are to rise and leave the oratory; and of private prayer he says it should be short and pure—*brevis et pura*—"unless it be prolonged by the inspiration of Divine grace" (cc. 20, 52). The daily psalmody consisted of forty psalms with canticles and lections, and can hardly have taken more than from four to five hours: the gradual multiplication of psalms, offices, devotions, and conventual masses, which absorbed the greater part of the working day in the Benedictine houses during the later Middle Ages, began to set in only with St Benedict of Aniane in the ninth century, and reached its full development at Cluni[1].

Thus from whatever side we look at the matter, we see that St Benedict deliberately eliminated austerity as it had been understood and practised before his time. No doubt a life according to the letter of the Rule would be held to be a very austere one at the present day: but in the eyes of St Benedict's contemporaries it would not have appeared so. The regime stood between the life of good Christians in the world and the life in severe monasteries; and when compared with the common law of the Church (*e.g.* for Lent), or the usual monastic observances of those days, St Benedict's Rule cannot have appeared to be anything else than what he said it was, a *minima inchoationis regula*.

But, besides the elimination of austerity, there was in St Benedict's reconstruction of the monastic life a positive element; and this too took the form of a break with the past. I have shown that a strong individualism was the key-note of Egyptian monachism in all its phases, in Western Europe hardly less than in Egypt. St Benedict was a collectivist in the spiritual order. In place of rivalry in ascetical achievement, he established a common mode of life, made up of a round of objective duties,—public common prayer, work, and reading; and the sanctification of the monk was to be sought by living the life of the community. St Benedict made it a point of virtue "that a monk do nothing but what the common rule of the monastery and the example of

---

[1] Bishop, *Origin of the Prymer* (Early English Text Society, Original Series, 109).

seniors exhorts" (c. 7); and that "in all things all follow the rule as their master" (c. 3). In Lent indeed, as in St Pachomius' monasteries, each one is exhorted to add something voluntarily to his ordinary service of God; but, the monks are not left, as there (*Hist. Laus.* A 20), to pit themselves one against the other, but each one is obliged to obtain the abbot's blessing on what he undertakes, "else it will be deputed unto pride, not unto reward" (c. 49). There is no suggestion in the Rule of what are now called "penitential exercises": if exhortations and warning failed, corporal chastisement was resorted to in the case of refractory monks; but it was a punishment, not a mortification, and it was not self-inflicted. When a neighbouring hermit chained himself to a rock, St Benedict rebuked him, saying: "If thou be God's servant, let the chain of Christ, and not any chain of iron hold thee" (*Dial.* III. 16).

St Benedict says, indeed, that the observance of his Rule will only show that "we possess in some measure uprightness of manners and the beginning of a good life[1]," adding that those who press forward to the perfection of holy living will find the height of perfection in the lives and teaching of the Egyptian Fathers; and he orders the frequent reading of Cassian, the *Vitae Patrum* and St Basil's Rules (c. 73). But though he thus holds out higher possibilities, they do not enter into the practical scope of his Rule. Similarly St Benedict speaks with admiration of the eremitical life, which then formed an integral part of European monachism, and was commonly regarded not only as the most perfect realisation of the monastic life, but as the goal to be aimed at in practice by those who had the necessary courage and strength in virtue; but he expressly excludes it from his Rule, and says that he legislates for cenobites alone (c. 1).

This twofold break with the past, in the elimination of austerity and in the sinking of the individual in the community, made St Benedict's Rule less a development than a revolution in

---

[1] Ut hanc obseruantes in monasteriis aliquatenus uel honestatem morum aut initium conuersationis nos demonstremus habere.

monachism. It may be almost called a new creation; and it was destined to prove, as the subsequent history shows, peculiarly adapted to the new races that were repeopling Western Europe. The fundamental changes effected by St Benedict in the conception of the monastic life go far to explain why, on the one hand, the Benedictine form of monachism easily and generally made its way among populations Teutonic or partially Teutonised; while, on the other hand, it never found a congenial home among purely Celtic races.

APPENDIX I.

Historia Monachorum in Aegypto (supra, p. 15).

The subjects to be dealt with in this Appendix fall under the following heads:

(i) The original language—Greek, not Latin.
(ii) The Latin version.
(iii) The Syriac and other Oriental versions.
(iv) The History of the Text.
(v) The Authorship.

(i) *The Original Language—Greek, not Latin.*

This is a point which does not at all affect the validity of any view put forward in these pages concerning the Lausiac History. Still it has an important bearing on the general question of the sources of early monastic history; and as I have on p. 15 expressed my belief that the Greek is the original, while Dr Preuschen has arrived at the opposite conclusion (*Palladius u. Rufinus*, 196), it will be in place to show reason for adhering to my former judgment. For this purpose it will be best to institute a careful comparison of the two texts in some one of the longer Lives in which the Greek and Latin run closely together. I select the Life of Apollos or Apollonius (*gr.* 8, *lat.* 7), which possesses this advantage for purposes of comparison, that the Greek text stands in Migne free from all foreign accretions (*P. G.* xxxiv. 1137 ff.).

In the following references P = Preuschen, M = Migne, R = Rosweyd.

Ἀπολλῶ, ἀπολῶ διά σου τὴν σοφίαν τῶν ἐν Αἰγύπτῳ σοφῶν.　　　P 33
Apolloni, per te perdam sapientiam sapientium in Aegypto.　　　M 1137
The play of words on Apollos' name, which obviously suggested the R 460
citation (1 Cor. i. 19), is lost in the Latin. (M and some mss. repeat the name; but P's reading is certainly correct.)

γεννήσεις μοι λαὸν περιούσιον ζηλωτὴν καλῶν ἔργων.　　　P 33
generabis mihi populum substantialem et perfectum, aemulatorem M 1137
operum bonorum.　　　R 460

Cf. Tit. ii. 14 καθαρίσῃ ἑαυτῷ λαὸν περιούσιον ζηλωτὴν καλῶν ἔργων. The regular Latin renderings of περιούσιον are O. L. *abundantem* and Vg. *acceptabilem* : nowhere except here is *substantialem* found in Tit. ii. 14; but it is worth noting that at this time St Jerome was translating ἐπιούσιον by *supersubstantialem*. *Substantialem et perfectum* is an attempt on the part of Rufinus to translate the difficult Greek λαὸν περιούσιον. A Latin writer simply quoting the text would not have thus gone out of his way to try to bring out the force of the Greek, but would have used a current version. The *perfectum* may have been suggested by Lk. i. 17 *parare Domino plebem perfectam*. In Deut. xiv. 2 λαὸν περιούσιον is rendered *populum peculiarem* in Vg.; O. L. vac.

P 34
M 1138
R 460

ἡ τροφὴ δὲ αὐτοῦ τέως καθάπερ πρῶτον παρὰ θεοῦ ἐξ ἀμηχάνου ἐχορηγεῖτο. ἐν τῇ ἐρήμῳ γὰρ αὐτῷ δι' ἀγγέλου ἡ τροφὴ ἐκομίζετο.

Cibo autem magis coelesti quam humano utebatur.

The Latin appears to be a paraphrase; it is vague and common-place compared with the Greek.

P 34
M 1138
R 460

τὸ δὲ ἔνδυμα αὐτοῦ ἦν ὁ λεβιτών, ὅνπερ τινὲς κολόβιον προσαγορεύουσι, καὶ λέντιον μικρὸν ἐπὶ τὴν κεφαλὴν αὐτοῦ.

Indumentum ejus stuppeum colobium erat, quod apud illos lebetes appellatur, et linteum quod collum et caput obuolueret.

The Latin explains the material of the garment, but puts in the first place the name *colobium*, which was a latinised word, and then says it is called *lebetes* (*i.e.* *lebiton*) by the Egyptians. Similarly in St Jerome's Preface to the *Reg. Pach.* (*P. L. L.* 276), and in the Latin *Vita Pach.* (Rosw. 117), a clause is inserted explaining the word *lebiton*. Cassian employs *colobium*, not *lebiton*.

P 35
M 1138
R 460

ὁ δὲ οὓς μὲν πρὸς θεωρίαν προσεκαλεῖτο, οὓς δὲ τὴν πρακτικὴν συνεβίβαζε μετελθεῖν ἀρετήν.

alios ad bene operandum, alios ad bene intelligendum prouocabat.

The recognised Greek antithetical terms θεωρία and πρακτική are paraphrased in the Latin.

P 35—6
M 1138
R 460

μηδὲ ἄχρι ἀκοῆς παρακληθῆναι ὑπ' αὐτῶν ἀνασχόμενος.

om. Lat.—the meaning of the Greek was perhaps obscure.

P 36
M 1138
R 460

λαμπαδηφόρος ἄγγελος.

angelus ingenti luce resplendens.

P 36
M 1138
R 461

ἢ τὴν θεόθεν ἐλθοῦσαν τοῖς ἀλόγως κατεχομένοις ἐλευθερίαν παριδεῖν.

quam diuinae uirtuti obsistere, quae eorum cura gerebat.

The Greek here can hardly have arisen from the very common-place Latin.

P 37
M 1139
R 461

ὅταν τὴν ἀπάθειαν καὶ τὴν ἀνορεξίαν κτήσησθε.

si nulla uobis passio fuerit erga mundana desideria.

The pithy and technical Greek seems clearly the original.

ἀποκαλύψεις ἰώρα τινάς.　　　　　　　　　　　　　　　　　　　P 37
reuelationes ei *plurimae* ostendebantur.　　　　　　　　　　M 1139
　　　　　　　　　　　　　　　　　　　　　　　　　　　　　　R 461

Apollos' monks are compared to ἀγγελικήν τινα στρατιὰν κεκοσμημένων P 38
κόσμῳ παντὶ λευκοφοροὺντων.　In the Latin this is prosaically rendered: M 1139
caelestem quendam et angelicum cernebamus exercitum, in omnibus R 461
uirtutibus adornatum.　nullus sane in eis sordidis utebatur indumentis,
sed splendore uestium pariter atque animorum nitebant.

εἰφράνθητι ἔρημος διψῶσα.　　　　　　　　　　　　　　　　　P 38
ut laetaretur eremus sitiens.　　　　　　　　　　　　　　　　M 1139
In. xxxv. 1 (O. L.) *laetare desertum sitiens;* there is no authority for R 461
eremus in this passage; an original Latin writer would have quoted a
current version. The Latin goes on: et multi filii ejus uiderentur in
deserto; this seems to be based on Is. liv. 1 (=Gal. iv. 27), which is
quoted in full in the Greek.

ὑπὲρ τοῦ ποταμίου ὕδατος.　　　　　　　　　　　　　　　　P 40
pro aquis pluvialibus.　　　　　　　　　　　　　　　　　　　M 1140
I do not regard this as evidence of the Latin being a translation, as R 462
plucialibus is in all probability a Latin corruption of *fluvialibus*: it is
impossible to suppose that Rufinus, who had been in Egypt, would speak
of prayers for rain there.

ὥστε ἀπαλλαγέντας ἐκεῖθεν ἀποστῆναι τῆς πλάνης.　　　P 41
pollicentes ut si eos resoluat his uinculis pariter quoque erroris in eis M 1140
uincula dissolueret.　The Latin is a paraphrase.　　　　　　R 462

τοὺς ἰδίους εἰς τὰ ἴδια ἀπέστρεψεν.　　　　　　　　　　　P 42
fecit omnes cum pace discedere.　　　　　　　　　　　　　　M 1145
　　　　　　　　　　　　　　　　　　　　　　　　　　　　　　R 462
δυνατὸν εἶναι τὸν θεὸν λέγων τοῦτο αὐτῷ παρασχεῖν.　　P 42
omnia enim possibilia dicebat esse credenti.　　　　　　　　M 1145
The Latin is a formal citation (Mk. ix. 22); the Greek is not a citation R 462
at all.　The citation is easily suggested by the Greek; on the other hand
it is unlikely that the Latin citation should have been dropped by a Greek
translator.

κεχάρισται σοι ὁ ὀψιγόνος οὗτος πρόσφυξ.　　　　　　　P 42
donatur tibi salus istius pro quo supplicasti.　　　　　　　M 1145
The Latin is a paraphrase to avoid the difficult words.　　　R 462

ὁ οὐκέτι ἀνδροφόνος.　　　　　　　　　　　　　　　　　　　P 43
latro ille iam sanctus.　　　　　　　　　　　　　　　　　　　M 1145
　　　　　　　　　　　　　　　　　　　　　　　　　　　　　　R 462

σὺν πέντε τισὶν ἀδελφοῖς.　　　　　　　　　　　　　　　　P 44
cum paucis fratribus.　　　　　　　　　　　　　　　　　　　M 1145
　　　　　　　　　　　　　　　　　　　　　　　　　　　　　　R 463

σύνθετά τινα λάχανα.　　　　　　　　　　　　　　　　　　　P 44
olera ex his quae sale aspersa reponi apud eos solent.　　　M 1146
σύνθετα λάχανα is a regular phrase in the Greek text; it occurs in the R 463

17—2

account of abbot Hor, where in the Latin it is given as *olera composita*,
without any explanation (cf. P 25, M 1027, R 457).

P 45
M 1146
R 463

    ἐξ ἀμηχάνων ἐτρέφοντο.
    sine cibo per gratiam Domini pascebantur.

P 46
M 1147
R 464

    ἑαυτὸν ἐξαπλώσας (M *ἐναπλ.*).
    om. Lat.; the Greek is unusual.

P 47
M 1147
R 464

    The monks of Apollos' monastery did not partake of food till they had
received the Eucharist at the ninth hour (*i.e.* about 3 p.m.) daily. The
Greek continues: *οὕτω διαιτηθέντες* (having taken food in this way [*i.e.*
after the Eucharist]) they sat and were taught till *τὸ πρωτοϋπνίον.*
Then they separated as described. The Latin takes *διαιτηθέντες* as if it
were *διατεθέντες* and translates: *sic usque ad uesperam permanebant,* and
so has to give them a meal after their lessons are learnt, *post haec iam
cibo sumpto.*

P 47
M 1147
R 464

    οἱ τὰ γήϊνα μὲν φρονοῦντες ἐπὶ τοῖς γηΐνοις εὐφραίνονται.
    hi qui terrena diligunt super fragilibus et caducis rebus laetantur.
    The forcible repetition disappears in the Latin.

P 48
M 1147
R 464

    In the Greek there is an incidental allusion to 1 Thess. v. 17 ff.; in
the Latin it is an actual quotation.

P 48
M 1148
R 464

    δι' ὑπερβολὴν θαύματος ἐσιωπήσαμεν, i.e. "we lost all power of speech
through wonder" every time we heard them. In Lat. "silere de his melius
censeo quam parum digne proloqui."

    I set the two following passages side by side:—

P 48
M 1148
R 464

Πολλάκις καὶ περὶ τῆς ὑποδοχῆς τῶν ἀδελφῶν

ἔλεγεν, ὅτι· Δεῖ ἐρχομένους τοὺς ἀδελφοὺς προσκυνεῖν. οὐ γὰρ αὐτούς, ἀλλὰ τὸν θεὸν προσεκύνησας. εἶδες γάρ, φησί, τὸν ἀδελφόν σου, εἶδες κύριον τὸν θεόν σου.

καὶ τοῦτο, φησί, παρὰ τοῦ Ἀβραὰμ παρειλήφαμεν.

καὶ ὅτι δεῖ ἐσθ' ὅτε τοὺς ἀδελφοὺς πρὸς ἀνάπαυσιν παραβιάζεσθαι, παρὰ τοῦ Λὼτ μεμαθήκαμεν παραβιασαμένου τοὺς ἀγγέλους.

Multa de hospitalitatis studio
disserebat, et praecipiebat attentius
ut aduentantes fratres quasi Domini
suscipiamus aduentum. nam et
adorari fratres aduentantes prop-
terea, inquit, traditio habetur, ut
certum sit in aduentu eorum aduentum Domini Jesu haberi, qui dicit:
'Hospes fui et suscepistis me' (Mt.
xxv. 35, O. L.). sic enim et A-
braham suscepit eos qui homines
quidem uidebantur, Dominus autem
in eis intelligebatur. interdum autem etiam contra uoluntatem cogere
fratres ad corporalem requiem sancti Lot exemplum proponebat, qui
angelos ui compulsos ad hospitium
domus suae perduxit.

It will be seen at a glance that the beauty of the Greek is wholly gone in the Latin, and I think that literary considerations by themselves make it clear that in this passage the Greek is the original. The Greek owes its superiority very much to the striking quotation εἶδες γάρ κ.τ.λ.; and Professor Robinson has pointed out to me that this is an Agraphon cited twice by Clement Alex. in the same words: εἶδες γάρ, φησί, τὸν ἀδελφόν σου, εἶδες τὸν θεόν σου (Strom. I. 19, 94 and II. 15, 71), and also by Tertullian: uidisti, inquit, fratrem, uidisti dominum tuum (De Orat. 26)[1]. Rufinus did not recognise the citation, and so paraphrased it, substituting a biblical text for the apocryphal saying; it will hardly be suggested that a Greek translator or copyist inserted the Agraphon,—indeed, although it has disappeared, its echo is still plainly discernible in the Latin.

ἐμέμφετο δὲ πολλὰ τοὺς τὰ σίδηρα φοροῦντας καὶ τοὺς κομῶντας.

P 49
M 1148
R 465

The Greek of this whole passage is somewhat obscure. Not so the Latin, which makes Apollos attack in the most direct manner ostentatious asceticism: a citation from the Sermon on the Mount is introduced to bring out the point. It seems unlikely that a passage so perfectly plain as the Latin should have been obscured in the process of translation into Greek. In the Latin we read ferrum in collo circumferent; a Greek would hardly have rendered this by τὰ σίδηρα φοροῦντες, for σιδηροφορεῖν means "to bear arms."

Finally, in seven passages of the Greek (P 39. 9, 20; 40. 8; 41. 13; 43. 10, 12; 47. 19) Ἕλληνες is used in the sense of "pagans": in the Latin it is always altered, usually into gentiles, but once into Aegyptii, and once into eos qui caerimoniis daemoniacis agebantur.

The thirty passages to which attention has been called supply arguments based on considerations of many different kinds, and of very varying force. Some are almost decisive in themselves; others are mere indications. But they all point the same way; and taken together they amount, I think, to a full demonstration that in the Life of Apollos the Greek is the original. And this Life, of course, carries with it the rest of the book. Still, in order to show that similar evidence is producible from other portions also, I shall call attention to three or four additional passages.

σχολάσατε καὶ γνῶτε, κ.τ.λ.

uacate et cognoscite.

P 11
M 1116
R 453

The Greek follows the LXX., Ps. xlvi. (xlv.) 11. The ordinary Latin reading, both O. L. and Vg., was uacate et uidete. Cyp. Testim. indeed has cognoscite; but Mr Burkitt informs me that this text of the Psalms was quite African, and that it is most unlikely that Rufinus should have had it: he considers that the probabilities are entirely in favour of

---

[1] Resch, Agrapha 296 (Texte u. Untersuch. v. 4).

cognoscite in this place, being a direct translation of γνῶτε. It was necessary so to translate it, for the context turns on γνῶσις and *cognitio*.

P 14
M 1121
R 454

ἄφρων ἤδη καὶ θηλυμανὴς ἵππος γενόμενος.

sicut equus et mulus quibus non est intellectus.

The Greek is an indirect citation of Jer. v. 8, ἵπποι θηλυμανεῖς ἐγενή- θησαν. In the Latin a more familiar and obvious, but far less appropriate text, is substituted, Ps. xxxii. (xxxi.) 9. Ἄφρων may have suggested *quibus non est intellectus*.

P 16
M 1123
R 454

ἡμιθανῆ καταλιπόντες.

seminecem reliquerunt.

The allusion is to Lk. x. 30, ἀφέντες ἡμιθανῆ. But the only Latin word used in this text, whether O. L. or Vg., is *semiuiuus*, and if the allusion were due to a Latin author, he would certainly have used it here: *seminecem* can only be a translation of ἡμιθανῆ.

I may refer also to the case of Ἀχώρεως and *uicina*, already discussed (p. 14). Dr Preuschen admits that, on the face of it, the readings tell in favour of the Greek being the original (*op. cit.* 192); but he thinks it not decisive,—the name Akoris may have been inserted by a Greek from his own knowledge of the geography of Egypt; or it may have been omitted by a Latin copyist. Were there grave reasons for holding the priority of the Latin, and were Akoris only a "difficulty," it might be right to sweep it away in this fashion: but when no strong case has been made out in favour of the Latin, it is not allowable so to deal with this word Akoris.

And here I am bound to say that Dr Preuschen's treatment of the question of the original language seems very inadequate (*op. cit.* 191—6). Apart from certain *à priori* considerations, he advances but one argument based on internal evidence: in the account of Copres and Patermuthius (*gr.* 11, *lat.* 9) it is related that while Copres was speaking one of the party fell asleep, and while asleep had a vision; on awaking he told the vision to his companions "in the Latin tongue." From this Dr Preuschen argues that Latin is represented as being the natural language of the travellers, and he thinks that the statement would hardly have been made in a book written in Greek. He sees a confirmation of the latter surmise in the fact that in some Greek mss. ρωμαιστί has been altered into ρῆμα, thus showing that the statement seemed strange to a Greek. He points out, too, that the work was written in Rufinus' monastery near Jerusalem, which was largely, if not predominantly, a Latin community. He considers that these facts make it certain that the book was written in Latin[1]. For my own part, I cannot see the matter in this light: the

---

[1] "Es musste wol auffallen, dass in einer griechischen Schrift, die von Erlebnissen mehrer Mönche erzählte und von einem Augenzeugen verfasst sein wollte, diese Mönche lateinisch mit einander redeten. Für das Empfinden

course of the narrative makes it clear that at least some of the travellers could speak Greek, and this Dr Preuschen allows (p. 195, note); the party of travellers was very likely of mixed nationality, and the one who spoke in Latin may not have been familiar with Greek; or perhaps (as the context may fairly suggest) he did not wish Copres (or the interpreter) to understand what he was saying to his companions. In short, there are so many alternatives and possibilities, that I do not think any conclusion can be got out of the passage; certainly not any conclusion that will stand against the body of internal evidence that has just been adduced, backed as it is by the external evidence adduced in § 3 (p. 13) and § 16 (pp. 198—203).

I had prepared a list of the Greek mss. that have come under my inspection (some twenty in number); but in view of the much fuller descriptive list given by Dr Preuschen (*op. cit.* 137—152) there seems to be no need for me to give one that of necessity would be much less perfect.

It may, however, be of use to indicate the structure of the Greek book by giving the titles of the chapters: references are added, by means of which the work may be reconstructed out of two volumes of Migne's Greek Patrology. (Numbers in Roman figures refer to the chapters as incorporated in the Long Recension of the Lausiac History, *P. G.* xxxiv.: those in Arabic figures to the columns of *P. G.* lxv., where the fragments edited by Cotelier (*Eccl. Graec. Mon.* iii. 171 ff.) are reprinted. The numbers prefixed to the chapters are those of Dr Preuschen's edition.)

Prologue, 441; 1 John Lycop. (cf. *sup.* pp. 25—29); 2 Hor (cf. *sup.* p. 38); 3 Ammon, xlviii.; 4 Be, xlix.; 5 Oxyrhynchus, 445; 6 Theonas, l.; 7 Elias, li.; 8 Apollos, lii.; 9 Ammoun, liii.; 10 Copres, liv.; 11 Patermuthius, 448; 12 Surus, Esias, Paul and Anuph, lv.—lviii.; 13 Helle, lix.; 14 Apelles, lx.; 15 John, lxi.; 16 Paphnutius, lxii.—lxv.; 17 Pityrion, lxxiv.; 18 Eulogius, lxxv.; 19 Isidore, lxxi.; 20 Sarapion, lxxvi.; 21 Apollonius, lxvi., lxvii.; 22 Dioscorus, lxviii.; 23 Nitria, lxix.; 24 Ammonius the Tall, lxx.; 25 Didymus, 456; 26 Chronides and Three Brothers, 456; 27 Evagrius, 448; 28 Macarius Aeg. (§§ 2, 3, 5 on col. 1050, *P. G.* xxxiv.; and other matter); 29 Amoun of Nitria (a short introduction; §§ 1, 2 on col. 1026; and cf. *sup.* p. 37); 30 Macarius Alex. (an introduction; and § 4 on col. 1050); 31 Paul the Simple (cf. *sup.* pp. 31—35);

griechischer Leser lag es unzweifelhaft weit näher, sie sich griechisch redend zu denken. So korrigierte man mit leiser Änderung ῥωμαιστί in ῥῆμα und der Anstoss war beseitigt. Aus dieser Stelle und der Geschichte, die der Text an dieser Stelle gehabt hat, scheint sich mir mit Sicherheit zu ergeben, dass die griechische Form secundär ist und nur als eine Bearbeitung des lateinischen Originales zu gelten hat " (p. 196).

32 Piammon, lxxii.; 33 John of Diolcos, lxxiii.; 34 Epilogue, cl. (2nd §, cf. col. 1252 D).

(ii)   *The Latin Version.*

It has been shown in § 3 (p. 11) that the Latin version was made by Rufinus. At the end of c. 29 of the Latin there is a reference to Rufinus' own *Eccl. Hist.*, which was not written before 400. Therefore the date of the version may be fixed between 400 and 410, the year of Rufinus' death; Dr Preuschen considers 402 or 403 to be a probable date (*op. cit.* 203—5). Thus the version was made within six or eight years of the writing of the book.

In regard to the Latin text, Rosweyd's edition (with which Vallarsi's, reprinted in *P. L.* xxi., is identical) is based on twenty MSS., one of which was written in 819 (*Prolegomenon*, xxiv). The numerous authorities for the version which have come under my notice present the same text. Dr Preuschen, however, informs us that a Munich MS. of the ninth century (*cod. lat.* 6393) contains a better text (*op. cit.* 163).

When we compare the Latin with the Greek, it appears that in c. 1 (John Lycop.) there are two enlargements (cf. *sup.* p. 22, note 1); from c. 2 to c. 22 (*lat.* c. 20), the portion describing the monks of the Thebaid, the Latin and Greek agree on the whole very closely; but in the concluding portion of the book, that which deals with the monks of the Nitrian desert, great divergencies exist, the Latin being considerably longer than the Greek, and in certain Lives (*e.g.* the two Macarii and Paul the Simple) almost wholly different from it, while the Latin conclusion of Amoun of Nitria is much shorter[1]. Professor Robinson in the *Introduction* to his edition of the *Philocalia* has occasion to examine Rufinus' character as a translator of Origen; he finds that his translations are usually paraphrastic, clauses being repeated or inserted to bring out the meaning, so that it is the general thought that is reproduced rather than the individual sentence; in one case "he has expanded his author into nearly twice the original compass, adding much explanatory matter of his own"; in others the original is abbreviated almost beyond recognition (pp. xxxi—xxxix). There would therefore be little difficulty in attributing to Rufinus most of the differences that exist between the Greek and Latin forms of the *Hist. Mon.* But some of the differences must, I think, be attributed to other causes.

In the first place, there is reason to believe that the Latin text has been interpolated here and there by later copyists. In the additional matter at the beginning of c. 1, we read: "*Soli Deo uacans, non diebus non noctibus a colloquiis Dei et oratione cessabat*" (p. 450). There is nothing

---

[1] Cf. *supra*, p. 37, where the two texts are printed; on pp. 31—35 the two texts may be compared in the beginning of Paul the Simple.

corresponding to these words in the Greek; but they occur more than once
in the office of St Cecilia's day, being taken from the Old Latin Acts of
that Saint.   In regard to these Acts, the date at which they were written
is the only point of interest here; and there seems to be a consensus of
opinion among modern writers of all schools that they are not older than
about the beginning of the fifth century.   De Rossi holds that they are
not even a re-edition of earlier Acts, but were newly composed towards
the year 400 from traditions embodying a story true in its main outlines[1].
Erbes discusses De Rossi's theory, and places the composition of the Acts
after 486[2].   Thus it seems that these Acts were not even written during
Rufinus' lifetime; in any case it is in the highest degree unlikely that he
ever read them; still less likely is it that he should have known the words
in question through their liturgical use in St Cecilia's office.   Whoever
introduced them into the Latin *Historia Monachorum* can hardly have
taken them directly from the Acts, but must have been familiar with
them through their frequent occurrence in the liturgy on St Cecilia's day.
This familiarity would not have been gained from the primitive liturgical
use of such Acts, viz. to be read out publicly as a continuous narrative in
the Church where the Martyr's feast was being celebrated; but from the
later custom, which selected striking sentences from the Acts, and repeated
them again and again in antiphons and responsories, as at the present
day.   But such a practice brings us to a date certainly later than Rufinus.
Lastly, it will hardly be suggested that the words were introduced into
the Acts from Rufinus' translation of the *Historia Monachorum*: the Acts
are clearly their original place.   It seems therefore certain that this
sentence, and probably along with it the whole Latin enlargement in
which it occurs, must be credited to a later copyist.

Again, in the account of Paul the Simple (c. 31) the following short
homily is found in the Latin but not in our Greek text:

Ex cuius exemplo docebat beatus Antonius, quod si quis *uelit ad perfectionem
uelociter peruenire*, non sibi ipse fieret magister, nec propriis *uoluntatibus
obediret*, etiam si rectum uideatur esse quod uellet; sed secundum mandatum
Saluatoris obseruandum esse, ut ante omnia unusquisque *abneget semetipsum
sibi*, et renuntiet propriis *uoluntatibus*, quia et Saluator ipse dixit: *Ego ueni
non ut faciam uoluntatem meam, sed eius qui misit me.* et utique uoluntas
Christi non erat contraria uoluntati Patris; sed qui uenerat obedientiam docere,
non inueniretur obediens, si propriam faceret uoluntatem.   quanto ergo magis
nos non iudicabimur inobedientes, si faciamus proprias uoluntates.

Now the following expressions occur in St Benedict's Rule:—

"Si ad exaltationem illam caelestem *uolumus uelociter peruenire*" (c. 7),
cf. "*ad perfectionem* conuersationis qui *festinat*" (c. 73); *uoluntatibus*

---

[1] *Roma Sotterranea*, II. xl sq.   Bishop Lightfoot gives a *précis* of De Rossi's
theory (*Ignatius and Polycarp*, I. 516—522).

[2] *Zeitschr. f. Kirchengesch.* 1888, p. 1 ff.

oboedientes (c. 5, ed. Wölfflin ; Vulg. *uoluptatibus*) ; "*abrenuntians propriis uoluntatibus*" (Prol.). Moreover the two texts are cited in the Rule, and with the same peculiarities of reading :—*abnegare semetipsum sibi* (c. 4) ; and *non ueni facere uoluntatem meam sed eius qui misit me*, twice (cc. 5 and 7). The *sibi* does not occur in the Vg. in Luke ix. 23, nor in the parallel passages ; but it may be seen from Sabatier that it was an O. L. reading, though not a common one. The second text, John vi. 38, stands thus in the Vulgate : *Descendi de caelo non ut faciam uoluntatem meam, sed uoluntatem eius qui misit me;* and this is the reading also of the Old Latin. So that the *Historia Monachorum* and St Benedict's Rule agree in having *ueni* in place of *descendi de caelo*, and in omitting *uoluntatem* in the second clause[1]. The agreements between this passage of the *Historia Monachorum* and St Benedict's Rule, both in regard to these unusual readings of N. T. texts, and in regard to the other three forms of expression verbally identical in both, establish beyond question a relation of dependency between the two works. That St Benedict should quote this work of Rufinus need cause no surprise ; he does so in several places. But it seems unlikely that he should have used this one passage in six different parts of his Rule, adopting words and thoughts not particularly striking, and especially taking from it unusual readings of the Scripture. On the other hand, some monk copying the work, and wishing to introduce a little homily on obedience, and having St Benedict's Rule imprinted on his memory by daily use, would quite easily and naturally string together the familiar words and phrases : *propria* is used with *uoluntas* four times in this passage and seven times in the Rule. The little dogmatic excursus on the Will of Christ is unlike anything else found in the book. Indeed the whole passage has the air of an interpolation.

I think the two passages just discussed are evidence that the Latin text has suffered interpolation at the hands of copyists. Nor will anyone familiar with the phenomena encountered in the handing down of texts find any difficulty in the idea that the extant Latin mss. are all descended from a single interpolated ancestor. But even if the theory of interpolation be admitted, it must not be hastily assumed that all the differences between the Greek and the Latin are to be attributed to Rufinus and his copyists ; the question will be further investigated when we treat of the History of the Text.

(iii)   *The Syriac and Oriental Versions.*

There are among the Syriac mss. at the British Museum copies of three versions of the *Hist. Mon.* and remnants of a fourth.

---

[1] Phaebadius of Agen cites the text in the same way, and a few authorities are given for one or other of the variants : but the readings were not common O. L. (cf. Sabatier, and Wordsworth and White).

Manuscript	Reference	No. in Wright	Century	Remarks
Version I				
Add. 17176	ff. 2—57	DCCCCXXIV.	A.D. 532	Complete, except Helles
Add. 12173	ff. 58—117	DCCCCXLIII.	VI or VII.	First half very incomplete
Add. 14648	ff. 48—58	DCCCCXLIII.	VI.	Helles to end
Add. 14579	ff. 79, 148—165	DCCCVIII.	A.D. 913	Extracts
Add. 12175	ff. 200—210	DCCXXVII.	A.D. 534	Ends with Paphnutius
Add. 12174	ff. 190—200	DCCCCLX.	A.D. 1197	cc. 8, 9, 16, 10, 11, 21 of the Greek
Add. 17177	ff. 94—130	DCCCCXXV.	VI.	cc. 10, 11, 12 of the Greek[1]
Version II				
Add. 14650	ff. 30—68	DCCCCXLIX.	VI or VII.	Complete
Version III				
Add. 14646	ff. 80—133	DCCCCXXXVII.	VI.	Ends with Helles
Add. 14609	ff. 44—90	DCCCCXLI.	VI.	Complete
Add. 14732	ff. 159—166	DCCCCLXIII.	XIII.	John of Lycopolis
Version IV				
Add. 14597	ff. 122—136	DCCXXX.	A.D. 569	Extracts
Add. 17177	ff. 86—94	DCCCCXXV.	VI.	John of Lycopolis

In the first four copies of Version I. the *Hist. Mon.* is closely connected with a great set of *Apophthegmata* entitled "Histories of the Egyptian Monks." It is Version I. that Anan Isho used for Book III. of his *Paradise*: this is accordingly printed in Bedjan's edition: certain lives, however, are wanting in the *Paradise* (the two Macarii and Paul the Simple); and there are some displacements—the *Epilogue* has been transferred to the middle of the book (c. 19) and is called "The triumphs of the blessed Fathers who worked miracles." In all three Syriac versions the concluding (Nitrian) portion of the work agrees with the Greek, not with the Latin.

The Armenian *Vitae Patrum* (vol. I.; cf. *sup.* p. 97) contains a number of the Lives from the *Hist. Mon.*, some in two versions. Dr Preuschen records the important readings in his critical apparatus; he believes that the Armenian is derived from the Syriac (*op. cit.* 160).

In his volume of *Mémoires* (Fasc. ii., 1895, pp. 650—3) M. Amélineau has published two short Sahidic fragments of the account of John of Lycopolis in the *Hist. Mon.*, corresponding to *P. G.* XXXIV. 1107 D—1108 B, and 1113 B, 1115 B and C (omitting all the *Hist. Laus.* matter, cf. *sup.* pp. 26—9). These fragments have escaped Dr Preuschen's notice, but they are of little importance: they represent an ordinary Greek text (cf. Appendix III.).

[1] I am responsible for Dr Preuschen's statement that these Lives belong to Version IV.; but it is only the Life of John of Lycopolis, which immediately precedes them, that belongs to Version IV.

(iv) *The History of the Text.*

It is right to state that the following investigation was written out long before the appearance of Dr Preuschen's book; I avail myself, however, of his careful work on the subject (*op. cit.* 163—170 and 180—191). I shall first present by means of a diagram what I believe to be the general outline of the history of the text and of the mutual relations of the textual sources, as indicated by the authorities that I have been able to examine. I shall then make some comments in explanation of the diagram.

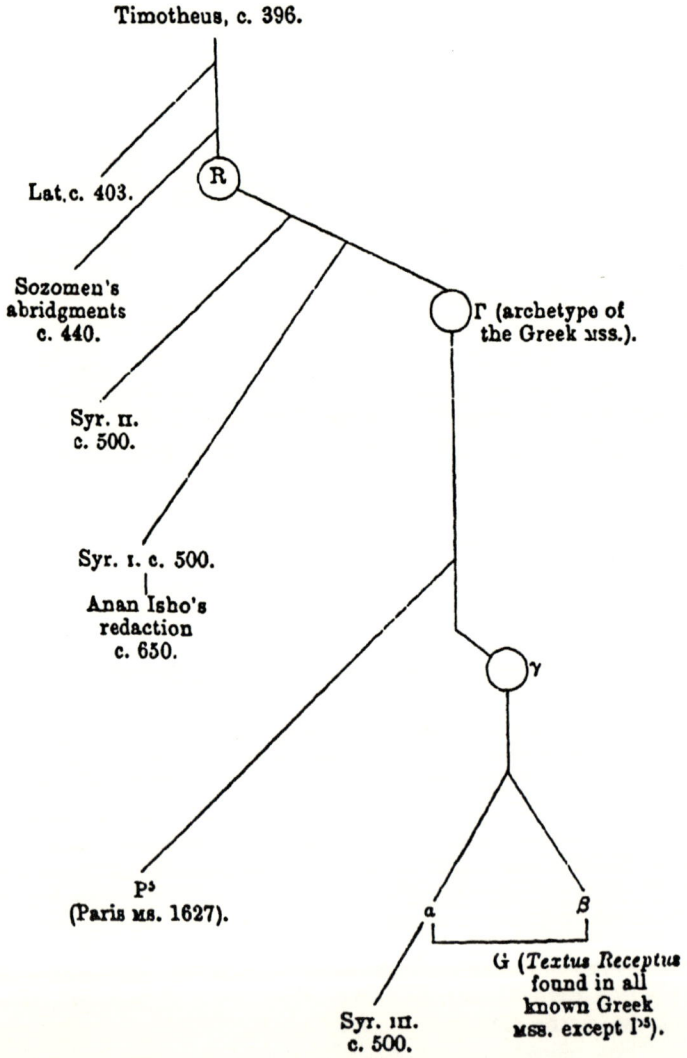

Timotheus, c. 396.

Lat. c. 403.

R

Sozomen's
abridgments
c. 440.

Γ (archetype of
the Greek mss.).

Syr. ɪɪ.
c. 500.

Syr. ɪ. c. 500.

Anan Isho's
redaction
c. 650.

γ

P⁵
(Paris ms. 1627).

a

β

G (*Textus Receptus*
found in all
known Greek
mss. except P⁵).

Syr. ɪɪɪ.
c. 500.

In commenting on this Table I shall begin from the bottom and work upwards. (1) I use the letter G to denote the *Textus Receptus*, which is found in all the Greek MSS. known to me (and to Dr Preuschen), with the single exception of the Paris MS. 1627, which I designate by Dr Preuschen's sign, P[5]. A common feature of all these G MSS. is that the name Piammon (c. 32) is corrupted into Ammonas: Piammon is attested by *lat., Soz., syr.* I. (Philemon), *syr.* II. (Pomnos), and it is found in P[5]. All the MSS. containing the text G are therefore descended from a single archetype, γ, in which the corruption in Piammon's name had been made. Dr Preuschen shows that they fall into two groups a and β; and in a had occurred the further corruption of ῥῆμα for ῥωμαιστί (cf. *sup.* p. 262). In *syr.* III. this same corruption is found, and Piammon is called Amōn. Therefore *syr.* III. is derived from a MS. of the type G.

(2) If the reader will turn back to § 5 and compare col. A line 15, p. 26, and col. A line 25, p. 28, he will see that the words οἰκείῳ θανάτῳ ὁ βασιλεὺς τελευτήσει occur in both places. It is unlikely that this repetition can be genuine; and when the contexts are examined, I think it will be felt that the words are in place the second time they occur, but out of place the first. This impression is confirmed by the fact that in *lat., syr.* I. (cf. Bedjan 334), and *syr.* II., the clause occurs only in the second place[1]. I think it may be taken that the twofold occurrence of the clause is a doublet, and that at the beginning of the chapter it is an interpolation. In P[5] the clause occurs in the first place; in the second, as pointed out in the critical apparatus (p. 29) a page had evidently been lost at this very point in one of the ancestors of the MS. We are therefore justified in concluding that this common corruption runs through all known Greek MSS. of the *Hist. Mon.*, and that therefore they are all derived from a common ancestor, Γ.

Dr Preuschen has not noticed this point; but he has been led to the same conclusion by another common corruption, μικρῶν instead of μιαρῶν (cf. *lat.* and *syr.* I.), towards the beginning of the account of Patermuthius (c. 11). (*Op. cit.* 169.)

(3) From what has been said it appears that we have two independent representatives of Γ, namely the single MS. P[5], and γ, the archetype of the other Greek MSS. Unfortunately P[5] is a late MS. (cent. xiii.) and is in a very corrupt condition: probably Dr Preuschen is correct in his surmise that its text has undergone a literary revision. Dr Preuschen points out (p. 167) that there are a number of remarkable agreements between P[5] and *syr.* I. I have indicated on p. 27 (col. C, lines 22—25) an agreement with *lat.*; and many other instances are to be found throughout the book.

---

[1] In *syr.* III. the passage occurs in the first place only: but this version has been shown to be derived from γ: probably the translator did not care to repeat the passage. In *syr.* IV. it occurs in the first place; the second vac, as the only copy is imperfect at the end of the Life. There are not sufficient materials for locating *syr.* IV. in the Table.

Where P[5] is thus attested by *syr.* I., *syr.* II. or *lat.* (all independent of Γ) its readings evidently must claim our best attention[1].

(4) *Syr.* I. and *syr.* II. represent Greek MSS. that take us behind Γ, but still are in substantial agreement with it. Where Γ differs from *lat.*, especially in the shorter form of the Nitrian portion of the book (*gr.* 23, *lat.* 21, to end) both Syriac versions support Γ. I have placed *syr.* II. a step higher in the pedigree than *syr.* I., because *syr.* II. agrees with *lat.* and Sozomen in placing Elias after Helles, whereas *syr.* I., along with Γ, places him earlier in the book, next to Theonas. The Syriac versions are evidence that the Greek text represented by Γ existed, and was widely current, before the close of the fifth century, *i.e.* within a century of the date at which the book was written.

(5) A still earlier witness to the text is Sozomen. It has, I think, been amply demonstrated in § 8 that Sozomen had in his hands the *Hist. Mon.*, and further details on the subject will be found in Appendix II., with all the references, which need not be repeated here[2]. Sozomen's *History* was completed between the years 439 and 450; so that his copy of the *Hist. Mon.* was written probably not later than 430. Most of his abridgments are so curt as to be of little use for textual criticism; *e.g.* VI. 28 is only about one-twentieth of the length of the corresponding parts of the source. But here and there he is available and highly useful as an authority for the text.

(6) The Latin version, being by Rufinus, must have been made within ten years or so of the composition of the work. It was not made from the

---

RUFINUS, CC. 21 AND 22.

Venimus autem et ad Nitriae famosissimum in omnibus Aegypti monasteriis locum, qui quadraginta fere milibus abest ab Alexandria, ex nomine uici adiacentis in quo nitrum colligitur, Nitriae uocabulum trahens, prospiciente hoc, credo, tunc iam diuina prouidentia, quod in illis locis peccata hominum, tamquam nitro sordes, abluenda essent et abolenda. in hoc igitur loco quinquaginta fere, aut non multo minus cernuntur uicina sibi, et sub uno posita patre, tabernacula, in quibus aliqui plures simul, aliqui pauci, nonnulli etiam singulares habitant, et mansione quidem aliqui diuisi, animo autem et fide et charitate coniuncti et inseparabiles manent.

---

[1] What Dr Preuschen has given us is in effect γ; he has seldom adopted even the attested special readings of P[5]..

[2] In this main thesis Dr Preuschen concurs (cf. *infra*, App. II.).

author's autograph, for into the copy used by Rufinus had already crept a corruption in the word Ἀχώρεως, from which Sozomen, the Syriac versions, and Γ and γ were free; it therefore did not enter into the line of descent of our Greek MSS., though other corruptions of the same word found their way into some of them at a later stage,—after γ (cf. *supra*, p. 14).

(7) It is important to note that in a number of easily recognisable points Rufinus and Sozomen agree together against the Greek and Syriac[1]. A few examples will bring out this point. Concerning Anuph:

Ruf. (c. 10) ex quo nomen Saluatoris in persecutione confessus sum.

Soz. (iii. 14) ἀφ' οὗ πρῶτον ἐν τοῖς διωγμοῖς ὑπὲρ τοῦ δόγματος ὡμολόγησε.

Gr. (c. 12; cf. A 58) ἐξ οὗ τὸ τοῦ σωτῆρος ὄνομα ἐπὶ τῆς γῆς ὡμολόγησα.

(Compare the whole of the passages. *Syrr.* agree with *gr.*)

Concerning Apelles:

Ruf. (c. 15) in silentio noctis......aufugit.

Soz. (vi. 28)   νύκτωρ......ἀπέδρασεν.

Gr. (c. 14; cf. A 60)   om.   om.

Syr. L (Bedjan 397)   om.   om.

(It is only the particular words indicated that are wanting in *gr.* and *syr.* I.)

Dr Preuschen has gone over the ground very carefully, and has fully demonstrated the close relation between Ruf. and Soz. (*Op. cit.* 183 ff.) But the palmary case is the description of the desert of Nitria, the three-fold text of which is here given in full.

SOZOMEN, VI. 31.

Καλοῦσι δὲ τὸν χῶρον τοῦτον Νιτρίαν, καθότι κώμη τίς ἐστιν ὅμορος ἐν ᾗ τὸ νίτρον συλλέγουσιν. οὐ τὸ τυχὸν δὲ πλῆθος ἐνταῦθα ἐφιλοσόφει· ἀλλὰ μοναστήρια ἦν ἀμφὶ πεντήκοντα ἀλλήλοις ἐχόμενα, τὰ μὲν συνοικιῶν, τὰ δὲ καθ' ἑαυτοὺς οἰκούντων.

GREEK, c. 23 (Preuschen).

Κατήχθημεν δὲ καὶ εἰς Νιτρίαν,

ἔνθα πολλοὺς καὶ μεγάλους ἀναχωρητὰς ἑωράκαμεν, τοῦτο μὲν ἐγχωρίους, τοῦτο δὲ καὶ ξένους, ἀλλήλους ταῖς ἀρεταῖς ὑπερβάλλοντας, καὶ φιλονικώτερον πρὸς τὴν ἄσκησιν διακειμένους, πᾶσάν τε ἀρετὴν ἐνδεικνυμένους, καὶ ἀγωνιζομένους ἐν τῇ πολιτείᾳ ἀλλήλους ὑπερβάλλειν. καὶ οἱ μὲν αὐτῶν περὶ τὴν θεωρίαν, οἱ δὲ περὶ

----

[1] A statement in the Note on p. 57 *supra* is not quite correct: the monk named Apollos in *gr.* 8 and Apollonius in *lat.*, is named in *syr.* I., II., III., Apolo and Apolon, but not Apollonius.

RUFINUS, CC. 21 AND 22.

huic ergo cum appropinquaremus loco, ubi peregrinos fratres aduenire senserunt, continuo uelut examen apum, singuli quique ex suis cellulis proruunt, atque in obuiam nobis laeto cursu et festina alacritate con- tendunt, portantes secum quamplurimi ipsorum urceos aquae et panes, secundum quod propheta corripiens quosdam dicit: Quia non existis filiis Israel in obuiam cum pane et aqua. tunc deinde susceptos nos adducunt primo cum psalmis ad ecclesiam, lauant pedes, ac singuli quique linteis quibus utebantur abstergunt, quasi uiae laborem leuantes, re autem uera uitae humanae aerumnas mysticis traditionibus abluentes. quid ergo nunc de humanitate eorum, quid de officiis, quid de caritate loquar, cum omnes gestirent nos ad suam quisque introducere cellulam, et non ea solum quae hospitalitati debentur explere, sed insuper aut de humilitate, qua ipsi pollebant, docere, aut de mansuetudine atque aliis huiusmodi bonis, quae apud illos, uelut ad hoc ipsum de saeculo seques- tratos, diuersa quidem gratia, uua tamen eademque doctrina discuntur. nusquam sic uidimus florere caritatem, nusquam sic uidimus opus feruere misericordiae, et studium hospitalitatis impleri. scripturarum uero diuinarum meditationes et intellectus, atque scientiae diuinae nus- quam tanta uidimus exercitia, ut singulos paene eorum oratores credas in diuina esse sapientia.

Post hunc uero alius est locus in deserto interiori, decem fere ab hoc milibus distans, quem locum pro multitudine dispersarum in eremo cellu- larum, Cellia nominauerunt. ad hunc locum hi, qui ibi prius fuerunt imbuti, et secretiorem iam depositis indumentis ducere uolunt uitam, secedunt : eremus enim est uasta, et cellulae tanto inter se spatio diremp- tae, ut neque in conspectu sibi inuicem, neque in uocis auditu sint positae.

singuli per cellulas commanent, silentium ingens et quies magna inter eos est : die tantum sabbati et dominica in unum ad ecclesiam coeunt, et ibi semetipsos inuicem tamquam caelo redditos uident. si quis forte in conuentu illo defuerit, intelligunt statim eum corporis aliqua inaequalitate detentum, et ad uisitandum eum non omnes quidem simul, diuersis tamen temporibus omnes abeunt, portantes unusquisque secum, si quid apud se est, quod aegro possit gratum uideri. aliam uero ob causam nullus audet proximi sui obturbare silentium, nisi forte quis possit in uerbo in- struere, et uelut athletas in agone positos sermonis consolatione perungere.

multi ipsorum a tribus et quatuor milibus ad ecclesiam coeunt: ita longo a semetipsis spatio habitationis eorum cellulae dirimuntur: sed

SOZOMEN, VI. 31.   GREEK, c. 23 (Preuschen).

                                       τὴν πρακτικὴν ἠσχολοῦντο. ἰδόντες γὰρ ἡμᾶς τινες ἐξ αὐτῶν πόρρωθεν ἐρχομένους διὰ τῆς ἐρήμου, οἱ μὲν μετὰ ὕδατος ἡμῖν προυπήντησαν, οἱ δὲ τοὺς πόδας ἡμῶν ἔνιπτον, οἱ δὲ τὰ ἱμάτια ἔπλυνον. οἱ δὲ ἐπὶ τροφὴν παρεκάλουν, ἄλλοι δὲ ἐπὶ τὴν ἀρετῶν μάθησιν, ἄλλοι δὲ ἐπὶ τὴν θεωρίαν καὶ τὴν τοῦ θεοῦ γνῶσιν. καὶ ὅπερ αὐτῶν ἕκαστος ἠδύνατο, τοῦτο ἔσπευδεν ἡμᾶς ὠφελεῖν.

                                         καὶ τί ἄν τις εἴποι πάσας αὐτῶν τὰς ἀρετάς, μηδὲν ἐπαξίως λέγειν δυνάμενος;

 Ἐντεῦθεν δὲ ὡς ἐπὶ τὴν ἔνδον ἔρημον ἡκόντων ἕτερός ἐστι τόπος, σχεδὸν ἑβδομήκοντα σταδίοις διεστώς, ὄνομα Κελλία· ἐν τούτῳ δὲ σποράδην ἐστὶ μοναχικὰ οἰκήματα πολλά, καθὸ καὶ τοιαύτης ἔλαχε προσηγορίας. κεχώρισται δὲ τοσοῦτον ἀλλήλων, ὡς τοὺς αὐτόθι κατοικοῦντας σφᾶς αὐτοὺς μὴ καθορᾶν ἢ ἐπαίειν.

συνίασι δὲ πάντες εἰς ταὐτὸν ἅμα καὶ ἐκκλησιάζουσι τῇ πρώτῃ καὶ τελευταίᾳ ἡμέρᾳ τῆς ἑβδομάδος. ἢν δέ τις μὴ παραγένηται, δῆλός ἐστιν ἄκων ἀπολειφθεὶς, ἢ πάθει τινὶ ἢ νόσῳ πεπεδημένος, καὶ ἐπὶ θέαν αὐτοῦ καὶ θεραπείαν οὐκ εὐθὺς πάντες ἀπίασιν, ἀλλ' ἐν διαφόροις καιροῖς ἕκαστος, ἐπιφερόμενος ὅπερ ἔχει πρὸς νόσον ἁρμόδιον. ἐκτὸς δὲ τοιαύτης αἰτίας οὐχ ὁμιλοῦσιν ἀλλήλοις, εἰ μὴ λόγων ἕνεκεν εἰς γνῶσιν θεοῦ τεινόντων ἢ ὠφέλειαν ψυχῆς ἔλθοι τις μαθησόμενος παρὰ τὸν φράσαι δυνάμενον. οἰκοῦσι δὲ ἐν τοῖς Κελλίοις, ὅσοι τῆς

 Ἔρημον οὖν οἰκοῦσι [τὸν] τόπον, καὶ τὰ κελλία ἐκ διαστήματος ἔχουσιν, ὡς μηδένα γνωρίζεσθαι πόρρωθεν ὑφ' ἑτέρου, μηδὲ ὁρᾶσθαι ταχέως, μηδὲ φωνῆς ἐπακούειν, ἀλλ' ἐν ἡσυχίᾳ πολλῇ διάγουσιν ἕκαστος καθ' ἑαυτὸν καθειργμένος.

μόνον δὲ ἐν σαββάτῳ καὶ κυριακῇ ἐν ταῖς ἐκκλησίαις συνάγονται, καὶ ἀλλήλους ἀπολαμβάνουσιν.

πολλοὶ δὲ αὐτῶν πολλάκις καὶ τεταρταῖοι τεθνεῶτες ἐν τοῖς κελλίοις αὐτῶν εὑρίσκονται ἐκ τοῦ μὴ ὁρᾶν ἀλλήλους πλὴν ἐν ταῖς συνάξεσιν.

καὶ οἱ μὲν αὐτῶν ἀπὸ τριῶν σημείων καὶ τεσσάρων εἰς τὴν σύναξιν

B. P.   18

caritas in eis tanta est, et tanto inter semetipsos et erga omnes fratres constringuntur affectu, ut in admiratione et exemplo sint omnibus. unde et si quis forte uoluerit habitare cum eis, ubi intellexerint, unusquisque cellulam offert suam.

---

(8)   This passage makes it evident that Sozomen's Greek MS. in this place contained the longer form of the text found in the Latin.   It has already been indicated that there are in the Latin towards the end of the book a number of passages not found at all in the Greek—*e.g.* half the Latin account of Ammonius the Tall (*lat.* 23, *gr.* 24) and half that of Evagrius (*lat.* 27, *gr.* 27) are wanting in the Greek and Syriac (both I. and II.); and the short account of Origen (*lat.* 26) is wholly omitted. But in Soz. (VI. 30) this Origen is mentioned along with Didymus and Chronion (*lat.* Chronius, *gr.* Kronides), with whom he is connected in the Latin.   This additional fact makes it probable that in all this Nitrian portion of the book Sozomen's copy agreed closely with that used by Rufinus. On the other hand, there are places where Sozomen agrees with the Greek against the Latin: the most remarkable instance is the account of John of Diolcos :

GREEK, 33.	SOZOMEN, VI. 29.	RUFINUS, 33.
Εἴδομεν δὲ καὶ ἄλλον Ἰωάννην ἐν Διόλκῳ, πατέρα μοναστηρίων καὶ αὐτὸν πολλὴν χάριν ἔχοντα τό τε Ἀβραμαῖον σχῆμα καὶ τὸν πώγωνα Ἀαρών, δυνάμεις τε καὶ ἰάσεις ἐπιτελέσαντα καὶ πολλοὺς παραλυτικοὺς καὶ ποδαλγοὺς θεραπεύσαντα.	Ἰωάννῃ δὲ τοσαύτην ἐδωρήσατο δύναμιν ὁ θεὸς κατὰ παθῶν καὶ νοσημάτων, ὡς πολλοὺς ἰάσασθαι ποδαλγοὺς καὶ τὰ ἄθρα διαλελυμένους.	Erat in ipsis locis uir sanctus ac totius gratiae dono repletus, Ioannes nomine, in quo tanta erat consolationis gratia, ut quacumque moestitia, quocumque taedio oppressa fuisset anima, paucis ejus sermonibus alacritate et laetitia repleretur. sed et sanitatum gratia plurima ei a Domino donata est.

Dr Preuschen has collected a few other examples (*op. cit.* 183 ff.).

(9)   These are the main textual phenomena that have to be accounted for.   The solution of the problem offered in the Diagram (p. 268) is as follows: the *Hist. Mon.* was first written in Greek, and Rufinus and Sozomen used MSS. that preserved the primitive form of the book: at

SOZOMEN, VI. 31.

φιλοσοφίας εἰς ἄκρον ἐληλύθασι, καὶ σφᾶς ἄγειν δύνανται καὶ μόνοι διατρίβειν δι᾽ ἡσυχίαν χωρισθέντες τῶν ἄλλων.

GREEK, c. 23 (Preuschen).

ἔρχονται· τοσοῦτον μακρὰν ἀπ᾽ ἀλλήλων διεστήκασιν. ἀγάπην δὲ τοσαύτην ἔχουσι πρὸς ἀλλήλους καὶ περὶ τὴν λοιπὴν ἀδελφότητα, ὡς πολλοῖς βουληθεῖσι σὺν αὐτοῖς σωθῆναι ἕκαστον τὸ ἑαυτοῦ κελλίον σπεύδειν αὐτοῖς εἰς ἀνάπαυσιν δοῦναι.

---

the point marked R in the diagram a Revision of the Greek text was made, and the latter portion of the work was abridged: from this Revision have come the Syriac versions, and all known Greek MSS. which are all descended from a single archetype Γ. Thus the points wherein the Greek text differs from the combined authority of Ruf. and Soz. are to be attributed to the Revision; those wherein the Latin stands against Soz. and the Greek MSS. together are to be attributed to Rufinus' translation or to the Latin copyists[1].

(10) Two indications lend support to the Revision-theory here enunciated:

(a) Sozomen says of Helles ὡς καὶ πῦρ ἐν τῷ κόλπῳ κομίζειν καὶ μὴ καίειν τὴν ἐσθῆτα (VI. 28).

Rufinus has: ardentes prunas uestimento ferebat illaeso (c. 11).

Greek text: πῦρ ἐν κόλπῳ ἐβάσταζεν (c. 13, cf. A 59).

Here the Greek and Latin together make up Sozomen's text, and it is clear that all three texts are derived from a primitive text more faithfully preserved in this passage by Sozomen than by the other two[2].

(β) Syr. II. agrees with Soz. and Ruf. in placing Elias in a later position (c. 12) than that in which he stands in syr. I. and the Greek (c. 7). This shows that originally the shorter form of the Greek agreed

---

[1] Dr Preuschen, holding that the Latin is the original, has to devise a different theory. He believes that Sozomen had two Greek translations of the book, which he used simultaneously, (1) a copy of our abridged Greek text, and (2) the work of Timotheus, which was not the *Hist. Mon.* but a (lost) historical work containing copious extracts from it translated directly from the Latin (but cf. Sozomen's words, *supra*, p. 57). He offers some conjectures, which he himself acknowledges to be of a very shadowy nature, towards the identification of this Timotheus (p. 190).

[2] Except in the single point indicated, Soz. and the Greek text agree, while Ruf. presents a paraphrase. The Paris MS. 1627 (P⁵) reads καὶ μὴ κατακαίεσθαι. As however the clause is omitted in syr I. and syr II. it can hardly have stood in Γ. It would be so natural a gloss that it may safely be set down as one, especially as the word ἐσθῆτα is not found in it. In some extracts in the Brit. Mus. *Burney* MS. 50 a similar gloss is added at this point: καὶ ἀκατάφλεκτον διαμένειν.

with the longer form in a matter wherein they now differ, and points
to a lost Greek link between the two extant forms of the work.

(11) Many may regard such a Revision-theory as a mere *deus ex
machina*. But that a revision should have been made, and that it should
have so completely supplanted the original form of the work that this
latter survives only in a version and in a few stray citations, are
phenomena by no means unique in the history of texts. Indeed, the
brief investigation here made seems to offer illustrations of textual
problems that are found in far more important cases[1].

It is worth pointing out that the Syriac versions, especially No. III.,
show that the history of the text had fully worked itself out, and that all
the great families of MSS. had been formed, and leading variants and corruptions introduced, within a century of the writing of the book: since
about the year 500 there has been no further development.

(v) *The Authorship.*

In conclusion I offer a conjecture as to a possible author of the
Historia Monachorum. All that we learn about the author from the
book itself is that he was a monk in Jerusalem, and belonged to the
Monastery on Mount Olivet founded by Rufinus; that in 394 he went
to Egypt along with six companions to visit the solitaries; that at that
date he may have been a deacon, but was not a priest; and that he
returned to his monastery on Mount Olivet and wrote his book at the
request of the brotherhood there[2]. From the evident sympathy and
admiration manifested throughout his narrative for Ammonius the Tall,
Evagrius, and many others, it is clear that he belonged to that party in
ecclesiastical politics which was opposed to Theophilus of Alexandria and
St Jerome, and which found a leader in St John Chrysostom. When we

---

[1] Were the Nitrian passage the only one to be considered, it might be a
natural hypothesis that Rufinus, who had been to Nitria, enlarged the Greek
from his own recollections, and that Sozomen had both the short Greek text
and also Rufinus' Latin translation: there is reason for supposing that
Sozomen used Rufinus' *Hist. Eccl.* (cf. Gwatkin, *Studies of Arianism*, 98); and
a case might perhaps be made out in support of the view that Sozomen's first
account of Apollonius or Apollos (III. 14; cf. *supra*, p. 57, note) was based
upon the Latin of the *Hist. Mon.* But as a solution of the general textual
problem this theory fails, (1) because it cannot account for the additional
matter in the Latin Lives of Evagrius and Ammonius the Tall; (2) because
many of the points of agreement between Soz. and Ruf. are found in
Soz. VI. 28, which is certainly derived from the Greek book he attributes to
Timotheus (cf. *supra*, p. 57; and for such instances cf. (7) and (10) in the text
above).

[2] These facts are gleaned from the *Prologue* and c. I. on St John of
Lycopolis.

pass to the external evidence, there is but a single item forthcoming. It is established in § 8 beyond all reasonable doubt that Sozomen had before him this Greek work, that he abridged its contents, referring his readers to the original for fuller information, and stated that it was written by Timotheus bishop of Alexandria[1]. In this he is certainly wrong; for Timotheus died in 385, and a number of the facts recorded in the *Historia Monachorum* show it was written at a later date[2]. Lucius surmises with much plausibility that the author may have been some other Timotheus, wrongly identified by Sozomen with the bishop of Alexandria[3]. I venture to advance a suggestion which seems to cover the facts and likelihoods of the case. We learn from Socrates that the archdeacon of Alexandria at the end of the episcopate of Theophilus was named Timotheus, and that on the death of Theophilus in 412 he was put forward as a candidate for the see against St Cyril, Theophilus' nephew[4]. Now St Cyril had been a strong adherent of his uncle's ecclesiastical policy; it is therefore evident that the archdeacon Timotheus was the representative of the opposite party, and consequently a sympathiser with the Tall Brothers and the other solitaries persecuted by Theophilus; and this, as has just been seen, agrees with what is known of the author of the *Historia Monachorum*. The dates also would tally perfectly. And if the author was Timotheus archdeacon of Alexandria we have the best possible explanation of Sozomen's error in attributing it to Timotheus bishop of Alexandria. Nothing whatever is known of this Timotheus, except that he was archdeacon in 412; there is no reason why he may not have been a monk at Jerusalem between 390 and 400, before becoming one of the clergy of Alexandria. All things considered, I do not think there is any rashness in the view that this Timotheus may have been the author of the *Historia Monachorum*. But I offer the suggestion only for what it may be worth, and as the merest conjecture, to which I attach no importance.

[1] *Hist. Eccl.* vi. 29. I disregard altogether as worthless the various attributions made by the manuscripts. The larger number, Greek, Latin, Syriac, name St Jerome as the author; but the terms in which he speaks of the work, quoted in § 3, prove this attribution to be false. Cassian is named in one manuscript; but this is absurd.

[2] *E.g.* Theodosius' victory over Eugenius, the deaths of the two Macarii, the episcopate of Dioscurus the Tall, all which happened after 385.

[3] *Die Quellen*, etc., p. 188.

[4] *Hist. Eccl.* vii. 7.

APPENDIX II.

Detailed examination of Lucius' theory on the sources of early Egyptian Monastic History (supra, p. 52).

As explained in §8, the main purpose of Dr Lucius' article *Die Quellen der älteren Geschichte des ägyptischen Mönchtums*[1] was to establish the thesis that Sozomen did not derive his account of the Egyptian Monks (*Hist. Eccl.* I. 13, 14, III. 14, VI. 28—31) from the *Historia Monachorum* and the *Historia Lausiaca*; but that all three works were derived independently from a common source no longer extant; and that consequently the two Histories just mentioned are not, as they claim to be, the personal memoirs of their writers. The theory is discussed in its general bearings in the section referred to; but it is necessary here to examine the alleged minute discrepancies and the other points of detail on which Lucius relied to make good his position[2]. It must be remembered that he knew the *Historia Monachorum* only in the Latin translation of Rufinus, and the Greek text of the *Historia Lausiaca* only in the Long (interpolated) Recension. Dr Lucius' arguments will now be dealt with one by one[3].

(1) Palladius places Or in Nitria, Rufinus and Sozomen place him in the Thebaid.

Answer. There were two men called Or (*supra*, p. 40). Sozomen speaks only of the one mentioned in C, who did live in the Thebaid.

(2) Sozomen says that Apelles lived at Akoris; this he cannot have derived from A or C.

Ans. Akoris is the true reading of the Greek of C (*supra*, p. 14).

(3) In Sozomen's account of Benjamin is not found a remark "which by its absurdity betrays itself as an invention of Palladius" (cf. *supra*, p. 189).

Ans. Sozomen abbreviates throughout; it is surely more reasonable to suppose that the serious ecclesiastical historian thought it proper to omit from his work a grotesque and hardly credible statement which he found in Palladius, rather than to assume that Palladius introduced it on his own account into the matter he is supposed to have been plagiarising.

(4) In the account of the monks of Scete, Pior is the last of those mentioned in Sozomen, but he is one of the first in Palladius.

---

[1] Brieger's *Zeitschrift für Kirchengeschichte*, VII. 1885, pp. 163—198.
[2] *Loc. cit.* pp. 175—184.
[3] The signs A, B, C will be used as explained on p. 15.

Ans. There are two accounts of Pior in Palladius: the first is a mere appendage to that of Pambo, and in several manuscripts does not form a separate chapter; the substantive account of Pior, the one reproduced by Sozomen, comes later, in close connection with Moses the Libyan, exactly as in Sozomen (cf. *supra*, p. 53).

(5) A comparison of the order and grouping of the lives in Rufinus, Palladius, and Sozomen, shows that the latter cannot have relied on the two former.

Ans. It shows clearly that he cannot have relied upon A; but when B is taken as the *Lausiac History* the difficulty disappears. It is shown in § 8 that the order and grouping afford strong evidence that Sozomen relied on B and C.

(6) In that case it would have to be supposed that he used first one source and then the other, and even at times interwove his two sources; and also that he had other sources in addition to B and C, for the monastic portions of his History.

Ans. A historian in making use of two or more sources would naturally interweave according to the needs of his narrative, and the point of view in which he places himself. As to the use by Sozomen of other authorities besides B and C, it is difficult to see the point of the objection. The following Table will show that Sozomen in the monastic portions of his History used various sources, first one and then another, interweaving them according to his discretion[1].

SOZOMEN.	SOURCE.
Bk. I. 12 (end) on Philo's Therapeutae	Eusebius, *Hist. Eccl.* II. 17.
13 St Anthony	*Vita Antonii*[2].
Paul the Simple	*Hist. Laus.* (cf. A 28; *P. G.* xxxiv.— omitting interpolations).
14 Amoun of Nitria	
a. down to retreat to Nitria	*Hist. Laus.* (A 8, to σύμβιον αὐτοῦ).
b. remarks by Sozomen	
c. miraculous passage of the Lycus	*Vita Antonii* § 60.
d. cure of boy bitten by dog	*Hist. Mon.* c. 29 (Preuschen, p. 90).
e. Anthony's vision of Amoun's soul	*Vita Antonii* § 60.
Eutychian of Bithynia	Socrates, *Hist. Eccl.* I. 13.

[1] The Table was prepared before the appearance of Dr Preuschen's book: he also seems to find some difficulty in supposing that Sozomen should have used two sources alternately (p. 230).

[2] Montfaucon *In Antonii Vitam Monitum*, III. 13 (apud *Opera S. Athanasii*): "non modo res sed etiam integrae sententiae depromuntur" by Sozomen; Montfaucon says he has in places supplemented the *Vita* from sources unknown to us.

Sozomen.	Source.
Bk. III. 14 The two Macarii	*Hist. Laus.* (A 19 and 20).
Pachomius	*Hist. Laus.* (A 38)[1].
Apollonius	*Hist. Mon.* c. 8.
Anuph	*Hist. Mon.* c. 12.
Hilarion (cf. v. 10)	*Vita* by St Jerome[2].
Julian of Edessa	*Hist. Laus.* (A 1C2).
Monks in Asia and Europe	(?)
15 Didymus the Blind	Socrates, *Hist. Eccl.* IV. 25.
(VI 2 an anecdote about Didymus	*Hist. Laus.* (A 4).)
16 St Ephrem Syrus (body of the life)	
(end)	*Hist. Laus.* (A 101).
Bk. VI. 28—31 Egyptian monks	*Hist. Mon.* and *Hist. Laus.* (cf. *supra*, p. 53 ff.).
32—34 Asiatic monks	No clue to sources.

(7)   But if Sozomen had before him the *Historia Lausiaca* why did he not use it for Asia Minor, Palestine, Syria etc. ?

Ans. No doubt because for this part of his History he had access to fuller and better information ; the portion of the *Lausiac History* which deals with these regions is very meagre as compared with the Egyptian part, and Sozomen mentions many monks who are not to be found in Palladius.

(8)   Sozomen names Timotheus of Alexandria, not Rufinus or Palladius, as author of the work he is using.

Ans. The work he had just been using, when he introduces his mention of Timotheus, was the *Historia Monachorum* (cf. *supra*, p. 57), and neither Rufinus nor Palladius was the author of that book.

(9)   In the account of Macarius Junior (the Homicide) Sozomen introduces a saying as addressed to some monks whose names are not given; Palladius (A 17) records the same saying, and states that it was addressed to himself.

Ans. It is true that Palladius quotes the saying as having been addressed

---

[1] Sozomen first makes some general remarks of his own about the Tabennesiote monks, and then gives a mystical interpretation of their various garments, either his own or derived from some other source. Then he follows Palladius, changing the order, and adding a few comments of his own : the only piece of additional information is that the tablet Pachomius received from the angel was still preserved at Tabennisi: ἦν ἔτι φυλάττουσιν. Dr Preuschen entirely agrees with me that in this part Sozomen had no other source than the *Hist. Laus.* (*op. cit.* 182 and 228). He says : "Sachlich enthält er gar nichts über das von Palladius überlieferte hinaus."

[2] In his article on St Hilarion (*Neue Jahrb. f. deut. Theol.* 1894, pp. 157 ff.) Zöckler shows that Soz. used not only the *Vita*, but also local and family traditions.

to himself: Sozomen says: "Those who heard him relate that he used to say," etc. And therefore Sozomen is not using Palladius!

(10) Sozomen has a notice of Pachon which is in complete contradiction to the narrative of Palladius.

Ans. Lucius does not explain wherein the contradiction consists. What Sozomen says of Pachon is this: "Pachon also at that time was famous in Scete; and albeit he lived as a monk from youth to old age, neither vigour of body nor passion of mind nor demon ever caught him failing in regard of those things over which an ascetic should have mastery." There is nothing in this which contradicts Palladius' account of Pachon (A 29); on the contrary, it is evident that what Sozomen says of Pachon's life and conversation is suggested by the discourse on temptations which he delivered to Palladius, wherein he lays down that temptations come from three causes,— too great health of body, vain thoughts, and the demon. Here again it is merely a case of Sozomen's modifying in an impersonal sense the personal narrative of Palladius.

(11) Palladius quotes as addressed to himself an aphorism of Dorotheus (A 2); Sozomen quotes it as having been addressed to the demon or to Sleep personified. And in a note on this passage Valois, Sozomen's editor, says "it may hence be gathered that Sozomen had not before him the *Lausiac History* but derived his information from some other work."

Ans. Here, as in the two preceding cases, we are in the presence of a literary device on the part of Sozomen in order to eliminate the personal element of Palladius' narrative. The accounts of Dorotheus in Palladius and Sozomen tally perfectly except in this one detail. Valois' usual balance of judgment seems here to have failed him[1].

(12) The story of St Athanasius' concealment from the Arians in the house of a young virgin of Alexandria as given by Palladius is so different from that of Sozomen, that the latter cannot be supposed to have been derived from the former.

Ans. I can only ask the reader to compare for himself the two Greek texts (A 136, *P. G.* xxxiv. 1235; and Sozomen, v. 6). Naturally Sozomen did not transcribe the passage from Palladius word for word, and he adds some remarks of his own; but the two accounts are substantially the same.

(13) Lucius appeals to the threefold readings in the account of Anuph, already cited in Appendix I. iv. 7 (*supra*, p. 271) as proof that the texts are collateral derivatives from a common original.

Ans. From the discussions carried out in Appendix I. it is seen that this point is no more than a question of the textual criticism of the *Hist. Mon.*

This exhausts the reasons given by Dr Lucius in support of his theory that Sozomen used not the *Hist. Mon.* and *Hist. Laus.*, but a lost work from

---

[1] Similarly in the account of Eutychian (Soz. i. 12, Soc. i. 13) Sozomen eliminates all the personal details given by Socrates on his sources of information— *e.g.* νεωτέρῳ μοι σφόδρα τυγχάνοντι τὰ περὶ Εὐ. διηγήσατο.

which the writers of the other two books also borrowed. Tillemont, however, points out a discrepancy not noticed by Lucius, viz. that Sozomen couples together Be and Theonas and says that they were leaders of numbers of monks; whereas the *Hist. Mon.* makes this statement of Be only, and says that Theonas lived a solitary life, never speaking (*Mémoires*, x. 59). Here we have a real discrepancy: but such a lapse in the process of abridgment, whereby Sozomen reduces his source to less than a twentieth of its bulk, cannot be regarded as of any significance.

This examination of Dr Lucius' position amply justifies, I conceive, the statement made on p. 52, that, in the light of our present knowledge on the nature of the documents, his arguments do not raise even a presumption in favour of his theory.

Dr Preuschen holds with me that Sozomen's matter is derived from the *Hist. Mon.* and *Hist. Laus.* (*op. cit.* 180 ff. and 226 ff.). He raises however a question as to whether Sozomen used these two works directly, or in the form of extracts contained in some historical work now lost. He strongly inclines to this latter view, and thinks that the work of Timotheus referred to by Sozomen was not the *Hist. Mon.*, but such a collection as he postulates (*op. cit.* 189 and 230). In support of this view he points out that in Sozomen the monks are grouped on chronological and geographical principles (p. 230): but surely it is not too much to credit Sozomen with the first rudiments of the historical sense. Dr Preuschen's theory is due, I think, to the exigencies of his general position, that the Latin *Hist. Mon.* is the original, a question dealt with in Appendix I. For my part, I can see no reason whatever for hesitating to believe that Sozomen had before him not any set of extracts, but the books themselves.

APPENDIX III.

Amélineau's Theory of Coptic Originals (supra, p. 108).

The question whether portions of the Lausiac History were written in Coptic and translated into Greek by Palladius is discussed at considerable length in §§ 12 and 13 of this Study, and reasons that seem quite convincing are there pointed out in favour of the view that in each case hitherto brought forward the Greek is the original. M. Amélineau in many parts of his writings puts forward the theory that most of the Greek and Latin works dealing with Egyptian monachism are in a great measure translations from the Coptic: it seems proper, therefore, briefly to examine two or three of the more prominent cases, both on account of the important bearing the question has on the nature of our sources for Egyptian monastic history, and also because the acceptance or rejection of the general theory must exercise a strong influence on the particular case of the Lausiac History.

Apophthegmata Patrum.

The origin, nature and redactions of the *Apophthegmata* have been sufficiently explained in § 16 (p. 208 ff.). There exist in Coptic some of the lesser collections and one of the great collections there described.

(a) M. Amélineau has printed three of the lesser groups, one relating to St Anthony and two relating to Macarius of Egypt[1]. The majority of these apophthegmata exist in Greek also, and the translation, on whichever side it lies, is usually very literal. In his *Introduction* M. Amélineau brings forward two reasons in support of his view, both derived from that set of apophthegmata of Macarius of Egypt which substantially corresponds to the Greek set printed by Cotelier in his great alphabetical collection (cf. *P. G.* LXV. 257 ff. and XXXIV. 236 ff.)[2]. These reasons are:

(1) The Greek apophthegma 2. In the Coptic is found, instead of a mere "yes," the expression "by the grace of God and your prayers,"—a regular Coptic idiom.

[1] *Monastères de la Basse-Égypte (Musée Guimet* XXV) 15 ff., 118 ff., 203 ff.
[2] The Greek collection contains 41 apophthegmata, the Coptic 28: 22 are common to both collections.

(2) The Greek apophthegma 39. More accurate geographical details are found in the Coptic: thus where the Greek has vaguely "the mountain of Nitria," the Coptic has "the mountain of Pernouj"; and where the Greek mentions "a priest of the Greeks," the Coptic reads "a Greek, a priest of Padalas," naming the village to which he belonged[1].

Of these reasons only the latter, the presence of the name Padalas, deserves consideration. That a Coptic idiom should be found in a Coptic translation from the Greek can have no significance. As to the more accurate geographical details and the insertion of Padalas, it has been seen that not only Coptic scribes but also Syrian used to make improvements of this kind in the texts they were copying (cf. *supra*, pp. 126—7, 151).

On the other hand, the Greek origin of these sets of Coptic apophthegmata is demonstrated by the fact that some of them are attributed to Evagrius, who cannot be supposed to have written in Coptic[2]: and one is beyond controversy translated from the Greek, for it is a literal rendering of a passage in Evagrius' work entitled Μοναχός, and occurs in the long extract from that work preserved by Socrates[3].

(β) With regard to the great Coptic collection printed by Zoega[4], it may I think be demonstrated that it too was originally a Greek work. It is the redaction that is numbered ii on p. 209 *supra*, and is the same as the Latin one contained in Books V. and VI. of Rosweyd. An entire Greek copy is not known to exist, but Photius had one; and in the portion of § 16 which deals with the *Apophthegmata* it is shown that the three great Greek collections are for the most part made up of the same apophthegmata, being but different redactions of the same materials. Among the apophthegmata is one concerning abba Or which is taken verbally from the Lausiac History:

Apophthegmata.	*Historia Lausiaca* (*P. G.* xxxiv. 1028).
Ἔλεγον περὶ τοῦ ἀββᾶ Ὤρ, ὅτι οὔτε ἐψεύσατό ποτε, οὔτε ὤμοσεν, οὔτε κατηράσατο ἄνθρωπον, οὔτε ἐκτὸς ἀνάγκης ἐλάλησεν.	Ταῦτα δὲ ἔλεγεν ἐν τοῖς διηγήμασιν ἀνδραγαθήματα τοῦ ἀνδρὸς, ὅτι οὔτε ἐψεύσατό ποτε, οὔτε ὤμοσεν, οὔτε κατηράσατό τινα, οὔτε ἐκτὸς χρείας ἐλάλησέν τί ποτε.

The Greek apophthegma is from the alphabetical collection printed by Cotelier (*P. G.* LXV. 437); but that it stood in Collection ii, described by Photius, is proved by the fact that it is found in the Coptic and the Latin copies of that collection[5]. Now in his abstract of the contents of the latter Zoega sets down under abba Or: "nunquam mentitus est, nec nisi necessitate

---

[1] *Op. cit. Introduction* xlii—xlviii.

[2] *Op. cit.* pp. 157, 160, 195, 200.

[3] *Op. cit.* p. 195, and *Hist. Eccl.* IV. 23 Παρέβαλλον κατ' αὐτὴν τὴν σταθηρὰν μεσημβρίαν......ἀφήρπαζον.

[4] *Catalogus* 287 ff.

[5] Zoega 292; Rosweyd 653.

urgente locutus[1]." Supposing the Coptic to be the original, and Palladius to have translated the above passage and to have put it into his Lausiac History, what is to be said when we find the same translation in the Greek apophthegmata also? The similarity is such as excludes the possibility of their being independent translations; nor, if the Greek apophthegmata were translated from the Coptic, can the above passage be a later addition from the Lausiac History, for it occurs in the Coptic, as in the other versions, as part of the collection. We should be driven to the hypothesis that the Greek translator of the apophthegmata kept before him a copy of the Lausiac History, that he looked out and identified the various passages already occurring in it, and availed himself of Palladius' translation—an hypothesis so cumbrous and unlikely that it cannot be seriously put forward. M. Amélineau says that there are a number of passages in the Coptic apophthegmata and the Lausiac History which correspond[2]; if they are found also in the Greek apophthegmata verbally the same as in the Lausiac History, the case against M. Amélineau's theory will be overwhelming; even as it is, the single instance of abba Or will be enough, I believe, to satisfy us that the Lausiac History was the original source of such passages; thence they found their way into the Greek apophthegmata, and were in turn translated into Coptic.

The fact that a large number of the apophthegmata were verbally the same in the two great Greek redactions, and that both these redactions are known, from their surviving fragments, to have existed in Coptic, is an absolute demonstration that, although from the nature of the case the remote materials were probably for the most part derived from Coptic sources, still the actual *Apophthegmata* as known to us are an essentially Greek work.

Vita Pauli Eremitae.

In the same volume M. Amélineau prints a Coptic *Vita Pauli* which is shorter and simpler in style than the Latin. He maintains that it is the original and that St Jerome translated it[3]. An initial difficulty to this theory presents itself in the fact that St Jerome did not know Coptic: moreover at the end of the Life St Jerome's reference to himself as the writer stands in the Coptic just as in the Latin. To meet this latter difficulty Amélineau can only suggest that some Coptic copyist had before him the Latin also, and inserted from it the piece containing St Jerome's claim to the authorship. This again seems a cumbrous and unlikely hypothesis; and it is negatived by two facts of which Amélineau was unaware:

(1) there is a Syriac version which exhibits the same peculiarities as the Coptic, and has at the end the same mention of St Jerome as author[4]:

---

[1] *Op. cit.* 358.
[2] *De Hist. Laus.* 28.
[3] *Op. cit. Introduction* iv—xvii.
[4] Bedjan, *Acta* v.

(2) this redaction of the *Vita* exists in Greek also, and has been printed by the Bollandists, incomplete in Greek (*Analecta Boll.* II. 561), complete in a Latin version (*Acta SS.* die 10 Jan. I. 603). In the passage at the end St Jerome's name does not occur: but as it occurs both in the Coptic and Syriac versions of the redaction, it is inconceivable that it should have been added independently in the two cases.

Thus the shorter redaction is shown to be derived from St Jerome's Latin, probably by a process of abridgment, and the theory of the Coptic being the original of the Life of Paul is quite excluded[1].

Historia Monachorum in Aegypto.

M. Amélineau brings forward a Coptic idiom from the chapter on Amoun of Nitria in the Long Recension of the Lausiac History (A 8) as a proof that that work was in part derived from Coptic documents: but as the passage in question is one of the interpolations from the *Historia Monachorum*, this is the proper place to deal with it. After citing the passage: "Nolo occidere camelum neque ei dolium imponere ut moriatur," Amélineau comments thus: "Nunquam eo modo locutus esset graecus auctor; coptici vero semper scriptores quum actus actui succedit posteriorem in priore loco enuntiant nec dicunt: Iter feci ut viderem; sed: Vidi et iter feci; nec: Cubitum ivi; sed: Cubui et ivi[2]." The alleged Copticism lies in the "*ut* moriatur"; but *ne* is the word required by the Greek, ἵνα μὴ ἀποθάνῃ: and so it is in Hervet's translation, which M. Amélineau uses till he comes to this word[3]. Thus the passage means: "I won't kill my camel, nor will I put the jar on her lest she should die," and the Copticism vanishes.

Amélineau first put forward the theory that the *Hist. Mon.* was a translation of a Coptic document, in order to account for the presence of the same material in the Long Recension of the Lausiac History, but he had no positive argument to allege (cf. *supra*, p. 20). The problem has now been definitively solved on quite different lines, and there is no more any room for M. Amélineau's hypothesis.

Lately, however, he has printed two or three short fragments of the *Hist. Mon.* in Coptic, and he considers that they are from the original

---

[1] The Bollandists both in the *Acta* and in the *Analecta* express the belief that the Greek of the short redaction is the original, and that St Jerome only translated the work: but this was before the Coptic and Syriac versions were published. No Latin original of this redaction is known: but it may be worth while to record Erasmus' opinion that St Jerome must have written more than one redaction, so great were the divergences of the mss. that he had seen (cf. Rosweyd 21). Several copies exist of a Greek translation of the *Vita* as found in St Jerome's works.

[2] *De Hist. Laus.* 29.

[3] *P. G.* xxxiv. 1024 (Hervet's Latin), 1026 (Greek).

of the work[1]. It is, however, possible to demonstrate that the Coptic is a translation from the Greek. In Appendix I. (*supra*, p. 269) it has been shown that the words in the account of John of Lycopolis: ὅτι οἰκείῳ θανάτῳ ὁ χριστιανικώτατος βασιλεὺς Θεοδόσιος τελευτήσει occur twice in the Greek MSS., and that in the first place of their occurrence, early in the chapter, they are an interpolation which originated among the Greek MSS. But in one of the Coptic fragments this same corruption is found : " Thou wilt take them, and wilt be lord over them, and they shall obey thee, and thou shalt have honour with the kings. Now all things which he spake came to pass and were fulfilled. Afterwards he prophesied that the king Theodosius would not die with a different death, but that the Lord would visit him on his bed[2]." The passage is paraphrased and indeed quite altered in meaning; but its presence in this context shows that the Coptic is derived from a Greek text already vitiated by a corruption of Greek origin.

Thus the theory that the Greek and Latin works on Egyptian monachism were to a great extent translations of Coptic documents, has broken down in every case that has come under review: in every case it has been shown that it is the Coptic that is the translation.

---

[1] *L'Égypte chrétienne*, Tom. I. Fasc. ii. 498 (*Mémoires de la Mission*, etc.).
[2] *Op. cit.* 650 ; cf. *supra*, pp. 26 col. A and 27 col. C.

APPENDIX IV.

Redactions of the 'Vita Pachomii' (supra, p. 159).

As those who have written on St Pachomius have not furnished comparative Tables of the various redactions of the *Vita*, I think it may be of service to print those which I drew up as a preliminary study for § 13.

I do not consider it necessary to include in the Table the two Latin redactions: M. Ladeuze (*Muséon*, Avril 1897) has amply demonstrated that they are closely related to one another, and that they are derived from the Greek *Vita* (*gr*) and *Asceticon* by a process of combining and abridging the two works. It should, however, be observed that a few passages common to *lat*[1] and *lat*[2] are not found in *gr* (of course I do not refer to the Palladian passages in *lat*[2]). These additional passages are easily recognisable in the Latin translation of *gr* supplied by the Bollandists in the body of their third May volume (May 14th), where they are inserted in italics. These passages may be genuine, and may be an indication that our *gr* and the Greek original of *lat*[1] were both derived from an earlier Greek archetype. The question can be solved only by an examination of the Greek of *lat*[1], which is stated to exist at Paris[1].

All the references in the bohairic, sahidic and arabic columns are to the pages of M. Amélineau's volume of the Coptic Lives of Pachomius (*Musée Guimet* XVII), except those sahidic fragments marked with an asterisk, which are contained in Fasc. ii. of his volume of *Mémoires de la Mission archéol. du Caire* (cf. *supra*, p. 107). In the *gr* column the numbers refer to the chapters of the *Vita*.

gr	boh	sah	ar
1	1 (*init* vac)		337
2	2	314	340
3	7[2]		344

[1] *Catal. Cod. hagiogr. graec. Paris.* (compiled by the Bollandists and Omont), p. 47 no. 881. At the period of my last visit to Paris I had not yet entered upon the Pachomian question; I hope, however, soon to have an opportunity of examining this MS.

[2] When only single numbers are given it is to be understood that the text runs on continuously; *e.g.* that c. 2 of *gr* occupies pp. 2—7 of *boh* and 340—344 of *ar*. In *boh* and *sah* there are frequently considerable modifications and additions as compared with *gr*, and similarly in *ar* as compared with *boh-sah* (cf. *supra*, p. 169).

gr	boh	sah	ar
4	10	*537 (boh 13, 14	346
5	18	ar 350)	353
6	22—3		356—7
7	25		358—60
8	23—·5		357—8
9	⎫		360
10	⎬ lacuna in MS.		361
11	⎭		362
	26		363
12	27		364
13	29	*538	364
14			
15	30		366
			366—9 (Pall. cf. supra, p. 164)
16			
17	30	*543	369
18	32		371
19	34—6		372
			374
			376—8 (Pall.)
			378—80
20	39—40	295	384—5
21			599—600
22	36—9		380
			382—4 (Pall.)
	41—2		386
23	46—8		387
24	42		388
	43		390
25	44—6		391—3
	52—3		394
			395—402
	49		402
	50—2		404
	53		
26	53—6		405
	48—9		406—7
27½[1]	56	*521—537	553—5
28	58		557—8
29	61		555—7
30	64—5		558
31		(sah agrees closely with boh)	
32			
			560
	66		565—6
33½	67		552—3
34	69		566
35	70—2 and 79		567—8 and 575
	lacuna in MS.		568—9
36			

[1] 27½ signifies that only the later portion of gr 27 has a parallel in the Coptic Lives: (similarly the sign ½).

gr	boh	sah	ar
37			
38⅔	80		576
39½	81		577—8
40½	82		398—400
41	83		409—10
42	85	*545	407—9, 410—11
43	88		420—4
44	91	317—28	411
			412
45	92		413
			414
46	93		416—20
47⅔	95		424
			426
48	96		427
			429
49	99		430
			432
50	101—2, 75—7		434, 573—4
51	72—5		569—72
52	77—9, 102		574—5, 639
53			
			434
54			439—40
55½	102—3		441—2
56½	104		440
			442
57	109—10, 114—16		446—8
58	110		450—8
	112—4		
	116		448—50
	119	*547 (=boh 119)	458
59½	129		468
	130		468
60	141—151	*553 (=boh 141—2)	473
		*555	477—80
61⅔	103—4	*552	
62			
63			
64⅔	172		481
			482
	175		486
64½	178—80, 151		495, —
	180		497
65½	181		498
	185		502—518
	207—214		
	(*Vita* ends imperfect)		
65⅔	151		
66	⎱ *lacuna*	*557 (=ar 520)	518
67	⎰		529
			533—52
68	152		578, 491—5
69	157		580

(*sah* agrees closely with *boh* 91—103; cf. *supra*, p. 167)

gr	boh	sah	ar
70	165		582
	167		589—90
71			640—1
72			591
			595—9
73	168		590—1, 642
	169		484—5
	171—2		480—4
	173—4		485—6
			595
[Asceticon (cf. supra,			
p. 165 note)			605—39]
			640
74	⎫		643
75	⎮		643
	⎮	*561, *605	650
76	⎮	*571—7	652
77	⎮	297; *562—71	656
78	⎮	*577—84	659
79	⎮	313—4	661
80	⎬ lacuna	309	663
81	⎮		666
82	⎮	*586	667
83	⎮	*588	669
84	⎮		671
85	⎮		673
86	⎮		676
87	⎭		676
	Vita Theodori		
	214—23		
88	223	*604	679
89	235, 229		682
90	230		687
91	232		688
92	267		693
93	259, 276		697
94	278	*559 (= boh 283—5)	700
95	285		702
96	293	310	704

Towards the end (gr 74 to the end) ar adheres closely to gr; boh and sah, while agreeing together, depart widely from gr. In boh and sah the end of the Vita was enlarged into a separate Vita Theodori, the order being changed, and a great deal of new matter being inserted: in the Table only the parts are indicated which correspond roughly to the matter of gr and ar. There are parallels in sah to some of these additional passages on Theodore found in boh:

e.g.	sah	302	306-7	308	*584
	= boh	256	241-4	277	239

I have not found in boh parallels to some of the fragments of sah:
e.g. 299, 303, 328; *539, *560, *580, *590, *592.

I have not examined the *sah* fragments printed by Mingarelli.

As I am not dealing *ex professo* with the life of St Pachomius I have not felt called upon to undertake the laborious task of verifying these Tables, so as to be able to guarantee their accuracy and completeness. But yet it appeared to me that students would be glad to have them in the form in which I made them for my own purposes.

APPENDIX V.

Preuschen's Chronology of Palladius' Life (supra, p. 182).

In the chronological scheme of Palladius' life worked out in § 15 the year 388 is given as the date of his first arrival at Alexandria, and 400 as the date of his departure from Egypt. Dr Preuschen places his first sojourn in Egypt some five or six years earlier, c. 384—394 (*op. cit.* 233—246).

The substantive reason for the alteration is the following passage from the Epistle of St Epiphanius to John bishop of Jerusalem : "Palladium uero Galatam, qui quondam nobis carus fuit et nunc misericordia Dei indiget, caue, quia Origenis haeresim praedicat et docet, ne forte aliquos de populo tibi credito ad peruersitatem sui inducat erroris[1]." This letter was written at the latest in 394[2]; it seems clear that the person referred to was in the neighbourhood of Jerusalem at the time ; and I agree with Dr Preuschen that the Palladius here spoken of, Galatian and so-called Origenist, can hardly have been anyone else than Palladius, the author of the Lausiac History.

I feel that this is a serious difficulty in the way of the accepted chronology of Palladius' life ; and yet I have said in the note on p. 182 that I think Dr Preuschen's "system is encompassed by difficulties of a higher order." For:

(1) His system involves the rejection of the Life of Evagrius, not only as a part of the Lausiac History, but as in any way a work of Palladius. For the writer of the Life lived with Evagrius in Cellia at a date later than 394, and evidently was with him at his death there on the Epiphany, 400. This holds whether the short or the long form of the Life be taken as the original (cf. § 12, p. 131 ff.). Dr Preuschen is disposed to believe that the longer Life really was written by Palladius (*op. cit.* 258). I have shown (*supra*, 139—141) that "the evidence of the manuscripts tells as strongly as such evidence can tell in favour of the Life of Evagrius having stood, in its present form and

---

[1] Ep. LI. inter Epp. S. Hieronymi (*Vall.* I. 254; *P. L.* XXII. 527).

[2] Cf. Rauschen, *Jahrbuch der Christl. Kirche unter dem Kaiser Theodosius dem Grossen* (Freiburg, 1897), p. 553 : he maintains that the Letter of Epiphanius was written in 393 ; if so, Dr Preuschen would have to throw his chronology still earlier.

position, in the original Lausiac History." Dr Preuschen's chronology has, therefore, against it this whole body of manuscript evidence[1].

(2)　It is necessary, in order to make room for Dr Preuschen's theory, to get rid of the statement found at the beginning of the Lausiac History (A 1), that Palladius first came to Alexandria in the second consulship of Theodosius the Great, *i.e.* in 388.　Dr Preuschen holds this clause to be an interpolation, as it is not found in the Paris Greek MS. 1628 nor in the Latin Version II.　It stands, however, in all the other Greek MSS. and in *lat* I, *syr* I and *syr* II. This raises the difficult question, which cannot be discussed here, of the nature and authority of the Paris MS. 1628.　I only observe :

(a)　That though I regard this MS. as an important authority for the text, I cannot attach to it the same importance that Dr Preuschen does, at least in his critical discussions ;—when he comes to the actual construction of the text of two portions of the Lausiac History (John of Lycopolis and Pambo, *op. cit.* 98 and 119) he by no means follows the MS. so closely as his language would lead us to expect.　Especially in regard to clauses omitted in 1628 does he often refuse to follow its authority ; and on p. 238 he pronounces one such clause to be certainly genuine[2].　In thus holding himself free to depart from 1628, Dr Preuschen is, in my judgment, well-advised.　I have pointed out (*supra*, p. 139) that a section of the *Coislin* MS. 282 contains the same text as 1628 ; and the reader may see from the critical apparatus attached to cols. B on pp. 24—28, that some of the bits omitted by 1628 are found in *Coisl.* 282. Moreover there are wanting in 1628 some whole sections which certainly belong to the work,—*e.g.* the two passages hostile to St Jerome (*cf. supra*, p. 176), also A 109, 112, and in particular 102 (on Julian) which is witnessed to by Sozomen (*supra*, p. 260).　In short, this copy shows signs of abridgment ; and I therefore hold that its unattested omissions are not to be accepted.

(β)　In this position I think Dr Preuschen practically agrees with me ; but he maintains that the omission under discussion is attested by *lat* II.

---

[1] I do not understand how Dr Zöckler, in a review of Preuschen's work, can accept his chronology, and at the same time maintain the Palladian authorship of the Life of Evagrius as found in the Lausiac History (*Theologisches Literaturblatt*, 1898, No. 10).

[2] In this Dr Preuschen acts on a definite principle, viz. that in the one case (A 13) no explanation is forthcoming to account for the insertion, while in the other (A 1) he thinks that such an explanation may be found, as follows : Palladius says that when he came to Alexandria he met there Isidore the Xenodochus.　Now from Socr. VI. 2, or Soz. VIII. 2, it may be gathered that this Isidore returned to Alexandria, after an absence of a few months, about the time of Theodosius' victory over Maximus, *i.e.* in 388, the year of Theodosius' second consulate.　Preuschen supposes that some reader of the Lausiac History, familiar with Socrates' History, connected [quite inconsequently] this return of Isidore to Alexandria with Palladius' meeting him there, and added the year in a marginal gloss : "in the second consulate of Theodosius" etc. which found its way into the text (*op. cit.* 236).　I confess this explanation does not seem to me satisfactory : it is too ingenious.

The question arises, Is this a case of mere coincidence in error, or is it real attestation? To establish the latter alternative, it would be necessary to show that there is a definite relationship between MS. 1628 and *lat* II. Dr Preuschen states that a close relationship does exist; but certainly what he brings forward (*op. cit.* 222) in support of his statement by no means proves it[1]. For my part, I believe that MS. 1628 and *lat* II, as well as *lat* I, *syr* I and *syr* II, represent earlier strata of the text than that found in the great body of Greek MSS.: but I see no evidence of any special connection between 1628 and *lat* II; and on the point noted *supra*, p. 113, in regard to the sets of proper names in the Life of Pambo, they take opposite sides[2]. In such omissions, more than in any other corruptions, are coincidences in error easy; and *lat* II itself is so corrupt that, though it may have considerable weight in attesting the readings of other authorities for the text, it can claim but little for its own.

(γ) The text which really is akin to 1628 is not *lat* II but *syr* I. I might give a number of facts in proof of this; but I confine myself to one that seems decisive. As observed *supra*, p. 86, these two differ from all other known copies of the Lausiac History in that the short Introduction on the holy women ushers in the story of the Alexandrian virgin who harboured St Athanasius (A 136). Dr Preuschen holds that this is the primitive arrangement (*op. cit.* 253); but I am unable to accept his theory on the original structure of the work, and for this reason: Dr Preuschen accepts as genuine the section A 125—134 on Paula, Eustochium and others, omitted in MS. 1628, *syr* I and some other copies, and he (rightly, I think) attributes the omission to the desire to eliminate the attack on St Jerome with which it opens (*op. cit.* 218, 252, 253). But if this section be genuine, and I do not think there can be any doubt of it, then the very grammar shows (as demonstrated *supra*, p. 41) that the opening words of A 125, ἐν αἷς καὶ Παύλῃ τῇ Ῥωμαίᾳ, must have formed one context with συντετύχηκα παρθένοις τε καὶ χήραις. The rearrangement of the text found in 1628 and *syr* I is of a kind that can hardly be attributed to chance coincidence, and it therefore establishes a real relationship between the two texts. Accordingly any passage of the received text,

---

[1] Besides the omission of the passage under debate, he only instances a tendency to eliminate references to unorthodox persons; but the process is carried out in quite different ways in the two texts. The fact that Evagrius' name (A 29) is turned into Eulogius in 1628 and simply omitted in *lat.* II; and that "Origenes, Didymus, Pierius and Stephanus" (A 12) are in 1628 turned into "Athanasius and Basilius," and in *lat* II into "sancti antiqui patres orthodoxi sacerdotes Domini" (cf. *supra*, p. 67), is surely a proof of anything else rather than of textual relationship.

[2] I have pointed out (*supra*, p. 87) that the Brit. Mus. copy of *syr* II also omits the clause under debate, while the Vat. copy retains it. The Brit. Mus. text has further corruptions, and it is evident that the omission is a mere accident: it lends no support to Dr Preuschen's position.

omitted in 1628 but found in *syr* I, must be retained as genuine. The passage under debate stands in *syr* I (cf. Bedjan 19)[1].

I think I have justified my statement that the difficulties in the way of Dr Preuschen's dates for Palladius' first sojourn in Egypt are of a higher order than the difficulty which his chronology is intended to obviate. Of course this difficulty remains, and we have to face St Epiphanius' statement that Palladius was in Palestine in the year 393 (or 394). That he should have paid a visit to Palestine during the nine years he tells us he spent in Cellia,

---

[1] Dr Preuschen puts forward as a support of his theory the consideration that it renders possible the identification, made by Gamurrini, of the Pilgrim to the Holy Places with Silvia the sister of Rufinus the Prefect. Palladius tells us (A 142) that he travelled from Jerusalem to Egypt with this Silvia, and Gamurrini understands this of Palladius' first journey in 388. But Rauschen (*Jahrb. der Christl. Kirche*, 544) shows that there is a grave difficulty in the way of supposing that the Pilgrim's journey to Egypt should have taken place after 386. Dr Preuschen's scheme of chronology removes this difficulty. As the point is of some literary interest I will enter upon it. This Pilgrimage has come to be called on all hands the *Peregrinatio Silviae*, and it is not sufficiently kept in mind that the identification of the Pilgrim (whose name nowhere occurs in her work) with the Silvia referred to by Palladius is nothing more than a plausible conjecture of Gamurrini's: any one who reads his Preface will perceive this. I believe that the identification is quite wrong, and for the following reason: there can be no doubt that the section of the Lausiac History containing the passage about Silvia should come immediately after the reference to the Sack of Rome by Alaric (A 118) :— this is its place in Meursius' text and the allied mss. (group β, *supra*, p. 139), in 1628 and *syr* I, and in *lat* I (*syr* II and *lat* II vac). Moreover the section opens with the words κατ' ἐκεῖνο καιροῦ in all the Greek mss. except 1628; they are attested by *syr* I (ܟܒܗ, Bedjan 137), and, *pace* Preuschen, by *lat* I (*postea*, which stands in the Cassinese mss. as well as in the *Paradisus Heraclidis*). Thus the connection of Palladius' journey with the Sack of Rome in 410 is established on the best textual evidence, and the identification of the Pilgrim with Silvia is shown to be erroneous. The journey referred to by Palladius was probably on the occasion of his banishment to Syene. In his edition of the *Peregrinatio* ("Palestine Pilgrims' Text Society," 1891) Dr Bernard of Trinity College, Dublin, challenged, on grounds entirely different from mine, the currently received identification of the Pilgrim with Silvia.

Dr Preuschen's proposed chronology may appear to receive some support from yet another identification that he suggests—that of the Alypius, whom Palladius met when he was with John of Lycopolis, and whom he calls ὁ ἄρχων τῆς χώρας (*P. G.* xxxiv. 1113), with Faltonius Probus Alypius, who in 378 was uicarius Africae, and in 391 prefect of Rome (Rauschen, *op. cit.* 27 and 337). But the identification of the ἄρχων with the uicarius is impossible. Alypius had ceased to be vicar of Africa in July 380 (Rauschen, *op. cit.* 67), and Palladius' visit to John cannot be placed as early as 380; for he was at the time of his visit already a disciple of Evagrius in Nitria, and Evagrius did not come to Egypt till after the Council of Constantinople, 381 (cf. *supra*, p. 181).

though nowhere suggested by his language, and in apparent contradiction to its obvious meaning, cannot be said to be absolutely excluded. His statement that he lived nine years in Cellia is a mere passing allusion, and would remain substantially and sufficiently true, even though he had been absent for some months. Such a supposition does not do any real violence to the text : when a man says in passing that he lived so many years at a place, this is never taken so literally as to preclude even prolonged absences. Palladius says similarly of Evagrius that he dwelt for sixteen years in Cellia ; and yet there is some evidence that he left it for a time (cf. *supra*, p. 147). If this suggestion be not considered admissible, the matter must be left in the category of outstanding difficulties. But the years 388 and 400 must be maintained as the limits of Palladius' first stay in Egypt.

I am sorry that my book should thus close with a point of disagreement from Dr Preuschen. It is in the nature of things that I should have had throughout to emphasise points of disagreement rather than points of agreement. But no one, probably, is able to appreciate more fully than I do the amount of patient labour and of good work that his book contains, and its sterling worth as a contribution to the study of monastic origins.

Printed in the United States
150783LV00010B/74/A

9 781417 970919